GOING GLOBAL

WELLESLEY STUDIES IN CRITICAL THEORY, LITERARY HISTORY, AND CULTURE
VOLUME 27
GARLAND REFERENCE LIBRARY OF THE HUMANITIES
VOLUME 2194

Wellesley Studies in Critical Theory, Literary History, and Culture

William E. Cain, *General Editor*

GOING GLOBAL:
THE TRANSNATIONAL RECEPTION OF THIRD WORLD WOMEN WRITERS

Edited by
AMAL AMIREH AND LISA SUHAIR MAJAJ

GARLAND PUBLISHING, INC.
A MEMBER OF THE TAYLOR & FRANCIS GROUP
NEW YORK & LONDON
2000

Published in 2000 by
Garland Publishing, Inc.
A Member of the Taylor & Francis Group
29 West 35th Street
New York, NY 10001

10 9 8 7 6 5 4 3 2 1

Library of Congress Cataloging-in-Publication Data is available from
the Library of Congress

Printed on acid-free, 250-year-life paper
Manufactured in the United States of America

For John

*In memory of Jean Caroline Stoltenberg Majaj (1934–1986)
and for Nadia*

Contents

Acknowledgments

First and foremost, the editors would like to thank all the contributors to this volume: Eva Paulino Bueno, Patricia Geesey, Bishnupriya Ghosh, Mohja Kahf, Jeanne Kattan, Alpana Sharma Knippling, Marnia Lazreg, Sally McWilliams, Therese Saliba, Ella Shohat and Jennifer Wenzel. We value and appreciate both their intellectual contributions to the collection and their cooperation and patience throughout this lengthy process. We hope we will have a chance to work with them again on future projects.

We would also like to extend special thanks to Mona Fayad for her role in helping to initiate the project and for her work on it during its early stages. Her enthusiasm was essential to the conception of the collection, and her contributions were significant. We hope to work with her in future on the feminist issues that concern all of us.

Lisa Suhair Majaj is grateful to family and friends for their continued encouragement. Most of all I thank Andreas N. Alexandrou: without his unwavering support this project would never have reached completion. Much gratitude to the friends who sustained and inspired me throughout, especially Souad Dajani. I thank the Women's Studies Program of Northeastern University for providing library resources, office space, and intellectual exchange during my 1998–1999 stay as a visiting scholar.

Amal Amireh would like to thank family members for their love and support. I am especially grateful for Amalia Saar's friendship. All thanks go to my husband John Dixon. His intellectual and emotional support made my participation in this project possible.

List of Contributors

EDITORS

Amal Amireh is Assistant Professor in the Department of English at Al-Najah University, West Bank (Palestine). Her articles and reviews have appeared in *Interventions: Feminist Dialogues on Third World Women's Literature and Film* (Garland Publishing, 1996), *The Women's Review of Books, World Literature Today, Middle East Studies Association Bulletin, Edebeyat: A Journal of Middle East Literatures, Al Jadid Magazine, Against the Current,* and *Sotour.* Other work is forthcoming in *Signs: Journal of Women and Culture* and in *Intersections: Gender, Nation and Community in Arab Women's Texts.* She is coeditor, with Lisa Suhair Majaj, of a collection titled *Etel Adnan: Essays on her Work and Life* (McFarland, 2000). Her book on representations of working-class women in nineteenth-century American culture is forthcoming from Garland.

Lisa Suhair Majaj writes on Arab-American, Arab and postcolonial literature. Her essays have appeared in various collections and journals, including *Memory and Cultural Politics: New Essays in American Ethnic Literatures* (Northeastern University Press, 1995), *Arabs in America: Building a New Future* (Temple University Press, 1999) and *U.S. Ethnicities and Postcolonial Theory* (University of Mississippi Press, 2000). She is coeditor, with Amal Amireh, of a collection titled *Etel Adnan: Essays on her Work and Life* (McFarland, 2000) and is coeditor, with Paula Sunderman and Therese Saliba, of *Intersections: Gender, Nation and Community in Arab Women's Texts.* Her creative writing has appeared in various journals and has been anthologized in collections such as *Food for Our Grandmothers: Writings by Arab-American and Arab-Canadian Feminists* (South End Press, 1994), *Worlds in Our Words: Contemporary American Women Writers* (Prentice Hall, 1996) and *The Space between Our Footsteps: Poems and Paintings from the Middle East* (Simon and Schuster, 1998). She has been a USIS visiting writer and lecturer in the West Bank (Palestine) and Jordan, and in 1998–1999 was a visiting scholar in Women's Studies at Northeastern University.

CONTRIBUTORS

Eva Paulino Bueno teaches Spanish at Mukogawa Women's University, in Nishinomiya, Japan. She has published *Resisting Boundaries: The Subject of Brazilian Naturalism* (Garland, 1995), and *Mazzaropi, O Artista Do Povo* (EDUEM, 1999). She has co-edited *Imagination Beyond Nation: Latin American Popular Culture* (University of Pittsburgh Press, 1999), and *Naming the Father* (Lexington, 1999). Her articles and essays have appeared in *Chasqui, Criticism, Revista de Sociocritica, MLN,* and others. She is currently writing a book about the representation of AIDS in several countries, and is co-editing the *Feminist Encyclopedia of Latin American Literature*.

Patricia Geesey is Associate Professor of French at the University of North Florida. Her articles on Maghrebian literature and on North African immigration in France have appeared in *The French Review, Substance, Dalhouisie French Studies,* and *World Literature Today*. She is currently preparing a monograph on Algerian women's writing from France and Algeria.

Bishnupriya Ghosh is Associate Professor in the Department of English, Utah State University, where she teaches postcolonial literature and theory, cultural studies and film, and functions as the vice-chair of the Women's Studies program. She has published several essays on Indian writing in English, Indian film, and the South Asian diaspora, and is coeditor of the anthology *Interventions: Feminist Dialogues on Third World Women's Literature and Film* (New York: Garland Publishing, 1997). In 1999 she received a Rockefeller Resident Fellowship at the Institute for Research on Women at Rutgers University, to launch a project on gender, sexuality, and religious fundamentalisms in the context of globalization. She is currently working on a manuscript on postmodernity and the Indian novel in English.

Mohja Kahf is Assistant Professor in the English Department, University of Arkansas, Fayetteville, where she teaches comparative and Arabic literature. She also serves on the faculty of the Middle East Studies Program at the university. Her book, *Western Representations of the Muslim Woman: From Termagant to Odalisque,* was published by the University of Texas Press in spring 1999. Her articles include "Braiding the Stories: Women's Eloquence in the Early Islamic Era," in *Windows of Faith: Muslim Women's Scholarship Activism in the United States,* edited by Gisela Webb (Syracuse University Press, 2000).

Jeanne Kattan is Associate Professor of English in the English Department at Bethlehem University, West Bank (Palestine). She has published several articles on English language testing and on Palestinian women's activism.

Alpana Sharma Knippling is Associate Professor of English and Women's Studies at the University of Nebraska-Lincoln. She is the editor of *New Immigrant Literatures in the United States: A Sourcebook to Our Multicultural Literary Heritage* (Greenwood Press, 1996). She has also published on postcolonial literature, film, and theory in edited volumes and in such journals as *Modern Fiction Studies* and *Semiotics.* She is currently at work on a book on Indian women's literature in English; her essay on Mira Nair is forthcoming in a collection of essays on the films of Mira Nair.

Marnia Lazreg is an Algerian-born professor of Sociology and Women's Studies at the graduate school and University Center at Hunter College, City University of New York. She is a former fellow of the Bunting Institute, Radcliffe-Harvard, and the Pembroke Center for Research and Teaching on Women, Brown University. She has taught at a number of colleges including the Graduate Center of the New School for Social Research, Sarah Lawrence College, and Hampshire College. She has published on social theory, social class, cultural movements, human rights, and gender, and is the author of *The Emergence of Classes in Algeria* and of *The Eloquence of Silence: Algerian Women in Question.* She has organized and led training workshops on gender and development in Asia and the Middle East and is the founder and director of the Association for Research on Algerian Women and Cultural Change (ARAWOC).

Sally McWilliams is Assistant Professor in the English Department at Montclair State University, New Jersey, where she teaches graduate and undergraduate courses in international women's fiction, literary theory, and women's studies. Her publications focus on the complexities of gender, culture, sexuality, and postcolonialism, especially in contemporary writings by women from Africa. She is currently working on the pedagogical and social implications of teaching international lesbian literature in the United States undergraduate classroom.

Therese Saliba is on the faculty of Third World Feminist Studies at the Evergreen State College and is currently associate editor of *Signs: Journal of Women in Culture and Society*. Her essays on postcolonial literature, media representations, and feminist issues have appeared in various journals and collections, including *College Literature* (1995), *Seeing Through the Media: The Persian Gulf War* (Rutgers University Press, 1994), and *Arabs in America: Building A New Future* (Temple University Press, 1999). From 1995 to 1996, she was Senior Fulbright Scholar at Bethlehem University, West Bank (Palestine). She is producer of the video-documentary, "Checkpoint: The Palestinians after Oslo" (1997).

Ella Shohat is Professor of Women's Studies and Cultural Studies at the City University of New York Graduate Center. She is the author of *Israeli Cinema: East/West and the Politics of Representation* (University of Texas Press, 1989), coauthor (with R. Stam) of the award-winning *Unthinking Eurocentrism: Multiculturalism and the Media* (Routledge, 1994), and coeditor of *Dangerous Liaisons: Gender, Nation, and Postcolonial Perspectives* (University of Minnesota Press, 1997). Most recently, she is the editor of *Talking Visions: Multicultural Feminism in a Transnational Age* (MIT Press, 1998).

Jennifer Wenzel recently completed her dissertation, "Promised Lands: J. M. Coetzee, Mahasweta Devi, and the Contested Geographies of South Africa and India." She has also published articles in *Alif: Journal of Comparative Poetics, Southern African Review of Books,* and *Tulsa Studies in Women's Literature.* She taught literature and composition at the University of Texas at Austin from 1993–1998, and in 1998–1999, she taught literature at the University of Montana in Missoula.

Going Global

Introduction

AMAL AMIREH AND LISA SUHAIR MAJAJ

The idea for this book originated one spring out of a growing sense of frustration. At the time we were both graduate students in the United States, working on our dissertations, teaching, and doing the obligatory conference rounds. In some ways it was an opportune time to be an Arab or Arab-American woman in the American academy. The burgeoning academic fields of postcolonialism, multiculturalism and ethnic studies had sparked increased interest in Third World[1] women and their literature. The efforts of feminist scholars inside the academy to correct the limitations of a Eurocentric feminist movement and to make space for Third World women to speak of their own experiences instead of being represented as the "Other" seemed to be coming to fruition. We found ourselves, along with colleagues with similar backgrounds, increasingly included on conference panels, at literary events, and in anthologies and journals.

However, we quickly discovered that this gesture of inclusion was not innocent, but instead often functioned to contain our voices within a predefined space. Discursive, institutional, and ideological structures preempted our discourse and determined both what we could say and whether we would be heard when we spoke. If we critiqued our home cultures or spoke of issues confronting Arab women, our words seemed merely to confirm what our audiences already "knew"—that is, the patriarchal, oppressive nature of Third World societies. If we challenged this ready-made knowledge, we were accused of defensiveness, and our feminism was questioned and second-guessed. We found ourselves occupying a predefined role, positioned as what Mary E. John calls "native

1

informants from 'elsewhere' " (23). Our very identities were constituted
for us: although neither of us sees herself as a Third World woman, we
were often viewed as only that, denied an identity in the plural. Events
such as the Gulf War in 1991 complicated matters yet further. As Arab
women in the United States during a time of political tension, our status
as "mediators" between East and West, the United States and the Middle
East, was highlighted. Yet our identities also served to silence us at a time
when we most felt the need to speak.

Our experiences teaching in American classrooms and conversing
with colleagues made clear to us that what we felt was not unique.
Rather, similar tensions functioned to define and confine the discourse
about Third World women more generally, compromising both the liberatory promise of feminism and the possibility of transnational communication. Although Third World women and their writings had begun to be
granted more and more space within First World contexts, this gesture of
inclusion did not challenge the already-defined discursive landscape that
continued to assign to Third World women and their works what Uma
Narayan aptly terms " 'Preoccupations' in the dual sense of 'concerns'
and 'pregiven locations' " (123). As Chandra Talpade Mohanty reminds
us, "The existence of Third World women's narratives in itself is not evidence of decentering hegemonic histories and subjectivities. It is the way
in which they are read, understood, and located institutionally which is
of paramount importance" ("Feminist Encounters," 34). Nor did current
discourse pay sufficient attention to the processes of translation, editing,
publishing, and marketing that had brought Third World women's texts
into First World marketplaces and pedagogical contexts in the first place,
or to the impact of these processes on how such texts were received and
read. What was lacking, we felt, was a historicization of the construction
of Third World women and their texts in Western contexts as both mediators and mediated, and an analysis of the role of the reception process in
this construction. Instead of viewing Third World women as markers of
"cultural authenticity" whose texts provided "windows" into the presumed alterity of other cultures,[2] we wanted instead to focus on the context of reception and to analyze the processes set in place when these
voices traveled to other contexts.

This project is situated at a historical moment of increasing globalization. It is, by now, a critical commonplace to note the accelerated
movement of capital, populations, and cultural artifacts across national
borders. For the most part, this has been a movement from center to pe-
riphery, as material and cultural products from the First World flood the

markets of the Third World. But, as many recent studies have shown, this flow is not unidirectional. Third World populations—workers, students, immigrants, and postcolonial intellectuals—constitute a significant portion of most First World metropolitan centers, creating a "Third World" *within* the First World. Whereas Hollywood productions often seem to hold a position of cultural dominance across the globe, other cultural artifacts do travel to the center from the peripheries: Brazilian *telenovelas,* Mexican soap operas, Indian cinema, "world music," and of course postcolonial literature such as the texts discussed in this collection (see, for instance, Featherstone, 65; Grewal and Kaplan, 13–17). As Ella Shohat and Robert Stam argue, "It is simplistic to imagine an active First World unilaterally forcing its products on a passive Third World . . . [moreover] there are powerful reverse currents as a number of Third World countries (Mexico, Brazil, India, Egypt) dominate their own markets and even become cultural exporters" (Shohat and Stam, *Unthinking Eurocentrism,* 31).

However, this cultural flow from the peripheries to the center is still governed by the balance in power relations governing First World–Third World interactions. In general, as Barbara Harlow notes, the Third World "is seen to provide the raw materials for the 'First World's' critical apparatus that will transform that material into consumable commodities for its properly schooled readership" (190; see also Mitchell, 475). Moreover, as Mary E. John reminds us, "Just what arrives in other places is itself a product of the relations of power and marginality that structure the circulation of knowledge within nations" (69–70). Contexts of reception significantly influence not only how specific works are read, but also which texts are translated, marketed, reviewed, and taught, and which issues are prioritized. We need, therefore, to keep in view the "difficult negotiation between insistence on multidirectional flows of power in global context and continued vigilance about specifically western forms of domination" (Friedman, 6).

Moreover, as Edward Said has argued in his essay "Traveling Theory," a theory or idea that travels to different contexts gets partly or fully accommodated or incorporated and is "to some extent transformed by its new uses, its new position in a new time and place" (227). Said's argument can be extended to all cultural products, including Third World women's texts, which, in the process of moving across national/cultural boundaries, are transformed by the reception context, their meanings reproduced and reshaped to fit local agendas. The essays in this collection focus on these traveling texts within their old and new contexts. In tracing the production and transformation of textual meanings within shifting contexts of reception, these essays examine how the publishing, circulation, and teaching of texts in both First and Third Worlds reproduce, alter, or challenge the asymmetries of power among different groups of people; how Third World women are themselves constructed in the process of transnational mediation to meet First World expectations; and how the politics of inclusion and exclusion shape the formation of multicultural, feminist, and postcolonial canons. In so doing, the essays probe both the possibilities and the limitations of feminist and multiculturalist projects in a global age.

In order to even begin to examine the reception of Third World women writers and their texts, we must first acknowledge the material apparatuses that make possible this "migration" or cultural flow. Obviously, Third World women's texts do not "travel" by accident. Unless originally written in English, they must be translated and then published; they must be distributed; and they must be brought to the attention of readers through critical apparatuses such as reviewing and through institutional forums such as inclusion in university courses. Market forces play a significant role in such processes: decisions about translating, editing, publishing, distributing, and course adoption are all made with economic as well as literary factors in mind. Third World women's texts are thus commodified, as literary decisions come together with marketing strategies and assessments of audience appeal (ranging from interest in the "exotic" to feminist solidarity) to foreground certain texts and repackage or silence others.

For instance, which books are chosen for translation in the first place? Those that uphold assumptions about Third World women as victims of religion, patriarchy, tradition, and poverty, and that play upon the fascination with "difference"? Or those that challenge expectations of "Third World" experience, presenting women as active agents within their own cultures? The answer often depends on a publisher's assessment of marketability, which is itself based on predictions of a range of factors, including popular appeal, classroom utility, and the like. Thus, books deemed capable of crossing categories, such as novels whose "realism" makes them usable not only in literature classes but also in sociology, political science, or history classes, are often chosen for translation over books of poetry or *avant garde* fiction, which are typically viewed as commanding a narrower literary market. Similarly, the issues that come into play during the translation process itself—for instance, decisions to shorten or reshape a text—are addressed with a target audience and sales figures in mind.

The overall relationship between Third World women writers and their texts on the one hand and First World readers and mediators on the other hand is shaped by these market forces. The translators, editors, publishers, and critics who make Third World women's texts available and known in First World contexts function not simply as disinterested literary specialists, but also as what Mike Featherstone calls "design professionals," filling a role similar to that of the "cultural specialists and intermediaries working in the film, television, music, advertising, fashion, and consumer culture industries" (61). As "design professionals," these literary intermediaries not only determine the availability and physical appearance of a book, but also shape textual meanings. They thus participate in what André Lefevere, in his discussion of English patronage of African literature written in English, calls "patronage by stipulation." As Lefevere observes, "Patronage selects the themes that can be treated, emphasizes certain techniques and rejects others, according to the changing appreciation of elements of the poetics" (467).

Given the key role of literary intermediaries in shaping the content as well as form of the canon of "Third World literature" available in the West, it is clear that the view of Third World women's texts as providing unmediated glimpses into "Other" cultures is not only naive, but also highly problematic. The entire range of processes by which a text "travels" from a Third World to a First World context, including translation, packaging, advertising, and distributing, is carried out within the context of intricately intertwined economic, literary, and discursive forces. The extent to which market forces come together with, and exploit, the prevailing discourse about "Third World women" may be illustrated through the example of the novel *Nisanit,* by the Jordanian author Fadia Faqir. This highly political novel, originally written in English, depicts Arab–Israeli and intra-Arab conflicts through the viewpoint, in part, of a female protagonist. The cover illustration of the 1987 American King Penguin edition reflects none of the political themes of the novel, however, but taps instead into audience assumptions about Arab women. The cover features the image of a woman completely draped in black, set against an expanse of geometric tile. The image has a curious familiarity—that of the veiled, faceless Arab woman, her body completely shrouded, moving across an already-marked-out space. But it bears virtually no relationship to the actual novel, in which women and men live their lives within a complex weave of political, social, and economic pressures that are not reducible to a unidimensional "Islamic" or "patriarchal" oppression. Within the space of this book cover, assumptions about the "oppression" suffered by Third World women come together with interest in the "exotic veiled Third World woman" to create an eye-catching image, one designed not to reflect the actual content of the book but rather to attract readers and generate sales. This example, one among many, suggests the extent to which marketing pressures exploit what Mohanty calls the "Third World difference" separating First World and Third World women (see "Under Western Eyes"), emphasizing Third World women's "exoticism" and "difference" in the interest not of transcultural communication, but of profit. Although First World feminists may buy and read such books out of a sense of feminist solidarity, their readings are shaped by this interplay of market forces and discursive pressures. The result, all too often, is that the sense of an essential difference between First and Third World women not only remains unchallenged, but is, in fact, reinforced.

This issue of the relationship between First and Third World women is of paramount importance to the study of reception. Indeed, one can say that the history of the reception of Third World women's texts in the West reflects in miniature the history of the relations between First and Third World women. The slogan "Sisterhood Is Global" was central to the second wave of Western feminism and formed a cornerstone of the "global feminism" of the 1970s and 1980s. The philosophical basis of this feminist discourse, humanism, emphasized the universal nature of women's oppression. The United Nations' International Women's Decade (1975–1985) gave further impetus to the feminist project during this period. U.N. international conferences, such as the ones in Mexico City in 1975, Copenhagen in 1980, and Nairobi in 1985, brought First and Third World women together to discuss issues believed to be of concern to all. Third World women's writings appeared in anthologies side by side with writings by Western feminists, as in the landmark but by no means lone anthology edited by Robin Morgan, *Sisterhood Is Global: The International Women's Movement Anthology* (1984).[3] African, Latin American, Indian, and Middle Eastern texts became increasingly available to both academic and popular audiences, thanks to publishers such as Heinemann, Zed Books, and Three Continents Press.[4] Certain Third World women writers—the Egyptian Nawal El-Saadawi, the Chilean Isabel Allende, and the Guatemalan Rigoberta Menchú, to name a few—became celebrities in the First World, welcomed on conference panels and book tours and at universities.

The contributions and significance of this phase of feminism should not be underestimated. Global feminism brought First and Third World women together within the project of feminism: it encouraged cultural exchange, shed light on some important Third World women's issues, and cleared a space for Third World women in the First World. From the beginning, however, global feminism had its limitations. Its assumption of universalism resulted in an insensitivity to differences among women—differences that have been increasingly brought to light in the 1980s and 1990s. Although global feminism cleared some space for Third World women, at the same time it limited this space. The same international conferences that brought women together were also the sites of much tension and division among these women, as differences surfaced over which issues should be given priority, how agendas should be set, and, ultimately, how First World–Third World power relations should be addressed.[5] Moreover, it became increasingly apparent that certain paradigms determined the relationship between First and Third World women within feminist discourse: in particular, the "saving brown women from brown men" model, the "victims of culture" model, and the "feminist by exposure to the West" model. In all of these paradigms, the asymmetry of power between First and Third World women was maintained and never questioned.

Not only did Third World feminists find their issues delineated and predetermined by these models, Third World women authors found their texts read in accordance with these paradigms. This affected both how texts were interpreted in the West and how authors were read and received in their home countries. An example is the Egyptian writer Nawal El Saadawi, whose "celebrity" in the West over the last two decades served to delegitimize her with her Egyptian and Arab readers. Local critics and readers felt that El Saadawi was writing for a Western audience, not for them. The warm First World reception of her as the lone Arab woman's voice in the West was seen as proof that she was saying what the West wanted to hear. Her feminist critique of her culture, many argued, simply reinforced existing stereotypes about Arab culture in the West, with the result that Arab women were harmed more than helped.[6]

Moreover, instead of being received and read as literature, and assessed on literary grounds, Third World women's literary texts have been viewed primarily as sociological treatises granting Western readers a glimpse into the "oppression" of Third World women. Once again, the reception of Arab women writers is a case in point. Their work has been hailed as "lift[ing] the veil" from what one reviewer called the "unimaginable world of Arab women" (Harrington). The blurb on the cover of the Lebanese writer Hanan Al-Shaykh's *Women of Sand and Myrrh* declares that "little is known of what life is like for contemporary Arab women living in the Middle East," and promises the reader that Al-Shaykh's novel will provide a glimpse into this "still-closed society." Similarly, the blurb on the back cover of the Egyptian writer Alifa Rifaat's *Distant View of a Minaret* states that the stories in this book "admit the reader into a hidden private world." The knowledge acquired by the Western reader as a result of this transcultural encounter does not forge a bond between First and Third World women, however, but merely emphasizes the Western reader's superiority to these "Other" women. Indeed, most reviewers of Arab women's texts seem to conclude that Arab-Muslim culture "is vastly different from the West," especially regarding its treatment of women (Terry). Even when similarities are acknowledged, these merely accentuate the hierarchical relation between First and Third World women. Thus, for one American feminist reviewer, reading a book by El Saadawi was a reminder of where Western women "have come from" (Gornick).[7]

Given this assumption of an intrinsic difference between First and Third World women, it is perhaps not surprising that the issues highlighted by Western feminists at conferences, in book reviews, and in scholarship have not always been a priority for Third World women. Whereas First World feminists have tended to focus on sexual oppression and on the cultural dimensions of "patriarchy," Third World feminists often seek to address political and economic oppression.[7] Frequently, however, they find their issues sidelined within feminist contexts. As Cheryl Johnson-Odim has noted, "Many Third World women feel that their self-defined needs are not addressed as priority items in the international feminist agenda, which does not address imperialism. . . . Third World women resident in Euro-America also feel neglected in the agenda-setting process" (322). The result of this Western domination of global feminism is not only the prioritizing of certain issues and the obscuring of others, but also the colonization and homogenization of Third World women's experiences. As Mohanty argues, global feminism "discursively colonize[s] the material and historical heterogeneity of the lives of women in the third world, thereby producing/re-presenting a composite, singular 'third world woman'—an image which appears arbitrarily constructed, but nevertheless carries with it the authorizing signature of Western humanist discourse" ("Under Western Eyes," 53).

In response to the homogenization of women's oppression within feminism, a new theoretical model evolved, one that challenged the universalizing tendencies of global feminism with a "politics of location" emphasizing specificity and locality. This new model is reflected in the title of Amrita Basu's anthology *The Challenges of Local Feminisms*, a book that was conceived as a corrective to Morgan's *Sisterhood Is Global* (see Basu, 1–21). The term *politics of location* was first used in the early 1980s by the American feminist Adrienne Rich following a trip she took to attend a conference in Nicaragua. Her travel across borders led Rich to reassess her perception of her own location in North America. Though marginalized as a woman, a feminist, and a Jew, Rich realized, she nevertheless had more power than many other women and men who did not share her White privilege. She realized, moreover, that White and nonwhite women may have different priorities, and that White women should relinquish their "missionary" stance *vis à vis* other women and should instead acknowledge these different priorities. In the process of working through these issues, Rich coined the term *politics of location* as a way to examine the implications of one's standpoint in shaping political perspectives and knowledge, and to explore alternatives to the homogenizing tendencies of global feminism.

This evolving focus on the politics of location, with its emphasis on the local and cultural specificity of other women's lives, helped to deconstruct the hegemonic use of gender as a universal category and to encourage interest in and receptivity to other cultures. Third World women's texts became welcomed for their "authenticity," and Third World women were admitted into Western feminist circles because they were "authentic insiders" who could speak for or criticize their cultures from a knowing position. Such inclusion had its positive aspects: it sometimes worked to correct misrepresentations of other cultures that were based on stereotypes and ignorance. But the focus on authenticity has not been unproblematical. Not only were Third World women construed as representatives of their culture, they were often viewed as if they *were* their cultures. Narayan describes the perils of authenticity well: "The 'Authentic Insider' position sets up a 'proprietary relationship' between Third World individuals and the 'culture' of their nation or community, in ways that have the potential to function as a set-up" (143). The inclusion of a single Third World woman on a conference panel, for instance, or of a Third World woman's text on a curriculum, was invested with expanded significance: what was represented, it seemed, was not just one woman's ideas, but an entire nation or culture. The result has been that Western perspectives appear multifaceted and diverse, rich with difference and tension, while "the Third World perspective appears seamless and monolithic" (Narayan, 143).

One example of the ways in which politics of location have functioned in relation to the reception of Third World women's texts may be seen in the case of the *testimonio*. This narrative genre was popularized in the American academy in the 1980s as a vehicle through which Third World individuals could speak out with directness and immediacy on behalf of themselves and their communities. Several *testimonios* by Latin American women became extremely popular in the American academy, to the extent that some have become virtually canonized. Indeed, one of these, *I . . . Rigoberta Menchú, an Indian Woman in Guatemala,* won its author the Nobel Peace Prize in 1992.

Through the genre of the *testimonio,* Third World women's voices were heard in the First World and their plight both as women and as members of an oppressed group was publicized. At the same time, however, as many critics of this genre have shown, the reception of testimonial writing often ignored the highly mediated nature of these "authentic" narratives (Beverly; Carr; Franco). The recent controversy surrounding perhaps the most respected *testimonio, I . . . Rigoberta Menchú,* is a striking illustration of the overdetermined and tension-ridden position occupied by Third World women and their traveling texts. As Eva Bueno demonstrates in her article in this collection, Menchú's book is enshrined in the American canon of *testimonio* for its poignant and supposedly faithful reflection of the difficult life of an indigenous Guatemalan woman and her community during the civil war. But a recent book written by David Stoll, *Rigoberta Menchú and the Story of All Poor Guatemalans* (Westview, 1998), challenges the authenticity of this account, claiming that Menchú's life story is closer to a political truth than to a real truth. Stoll produces witnesses who contradict Menchú's account of herself and some of the events she talks about in her book. Among the most important of these disputed "facts" is Menchú's subaltern status—a matter of particular significance given the tendency to link Third World women's authenticity with their victimhood. In calling into question the view that a *testimonio* is of necessity a literal version of reality—the embodiment of an "authentic voice" on both an individual and a cultural level (Moore; Omang)—Stoll's argument highlights the tendency of the reception context to conflate Third World women's texts with Third World women's lives. In construing *testimonios* as the literal embodiment of Third World women and their communities, what is obscured is the fact that *testimonios* are constructed narratives that are often highly mediated—not just by the usual array of translators, editors, and publishers but also by anthropologists or others who record and shape the oral testimony. This conflation of Third World women, their texts, and their cultural or national identities leads to a sense of betrayal when gaps are discovered between the facts of a life and the facts of a text. At the same time, it obscures the array of processes that determine which *testimonios* are given attention in First World contexts and in what form they reach First World audiences. The controversy surrounding Menchú's authenticity illustrates the limitations of the "authentic insider" position "conferred" on Third World women by Westerners. As Narayan points out, "The power to confer 'authenticity' is also the power to call it into question" (Narayan, 145). Indeed, the West that at one point gave Menchú the Nobel Peace Prize is now questioning the veracity of her story.

The problematic reception of the *testimonio* illustrates Caren Kaplan's warning that "Recourse to a politics of location . . . does not always result in a transformative feminist critical practice" (*Scattered Hegemonies,* 144). A politics of location may serve to encourage a celebration of difference and cultural relativism that mystifies rather than sheds light on power relations. As Kaplan observes, "A politics of location is not useful when it is construed to be the reflection of authentic, primordial identities that are to be reestablished and reaffirmed. We should be suspicious of any use of the term to naturalize boundaries and margins under the guise of celebration, nostalgia, or inappropriate assumptions of intimacy" (*Questions,* 187). Arif Dirlik issues a similar warning: "The celebration of the premodern pasts . . . in the name of resistance to the modern and the rationalist homogenization of the world, results in a localism or a 'Third-Worldism' that is willing to overlook past oppressions out of a preoccupation with capitalist or Eurocentric oppression and that in the name of the recovery of spirituality affirms past religiosities that were themselves excuses for class and patriarchal inequalities" (37).

The politics of location can also lead to a superficial inclusion that masks appropriation. Thus, for instance, through a process that Dirlik calls the "appropriation of the local for the global," different cultures are admitted "into the realm of capital only to break them down and to remake them in accordance with the requirements of production and consumption, and even to reconstitute subjectivities across national boundaries to create producers and consumers more responsive to the operations of capital" (32). This kind of appropriation is increasingly evident in the ethnic-foods aisle of grocery stores, the "world music" section of chain music stores, and the reshaping of specific cultural objects to fit a homogenized view of "global culture." (Consider, for instance, the renaming of the traditional Arab *dirbakeh* as, simply, a "world drum.") An unquestioning emphasis on the politics of location may thus have unintended consequences: it may lead to a conservative nostalgia that ultimately reinforces oppression; to an exploitation of localism to serve the interests of global capitalism; or to a focus on the individual at the expense of the larger historical context.

Feminist theorists such as Lata Mani, Chandra Talpade Mohanty, Elspeth Probyn, and Gayatri Chakravorty Spivak, among others, have recognized the limits of a politics of location and have called for a modification and extension of the concept. Location, they suggest, should be seen as a question of both "where we speak from and which voices are sanctioned"; it should allow us to acknowledge boundaries, not as mythic "differences" that cannot be "known" or "theorized," but as the sites of historicized struggles" (Kaplan, 149). Despite the problematics of a politics of location, they argue, feminists should not abandon the local, but should "work in and against it" (Probyn). Kaplan's reconception of the politics of location in order to achieve a transnational feminist practice is worth quoting at some length:

> Only when we utilize the notion of location to destabilize unexamined or stereotypical images that are vestiges of colonial discourse and other manifestations of modernity's structural inequalities can we recognize and work through the complex relationships between women in different parts of the world. A transnational feminist politics of location in the best sense of these terms refers us to the model of coalition or . . . affiliation. As a practice of affiliation, a politics of location identifies the grounds for historically specific differences and similarities between women in diverse and asymmetrical relations, creating alternative histories, identities, and possibilities of alliances. (139)

Kaplan's reconfiguration of the politics of location brings to the foreground the context of reception within which the possibilities of affiliation and coalition are of necessity situated. In their eagerness to make space for "difference" and to establish rapport and intimacy with Third World women, Kaplan argues, Western feminists have too often failed to historicize "the relations of exchange" governing the entry of Third World women and their texts into First World spaces. For instance, they have failed to analyze the economic, historical, political, discursive, and ideological factors governing "literacy, the production and marketing of texts, the politics of editing and distribution, and so on." In contrast, an examination of the politics of location in relation to both the production and the reception of theory and texts "can turn the terms of inquiry from desiring, inviting, and granting space to others to becoming accountable for one's own investments in cultural metaphors and values." This accountability is of crucial importance, for it is this that can "begin to shift the ground for feminist practice from magisterial relativism (as if diversified cultural production simply occurs in a social vacuum) to the complex interpretive practices that acknowledge the historical roles of mediation, betrayal, and alliance in the relationships between women in diverse locations" (Kaplan, *Questions,* 169).

In focusing on the reception of Third World women's texts, rather than on an unexamined celebration of "voice," we seek to accentuate Kaplan's call for feminist accountability. Similarly, we seek to highlight the role of both accountability and the reception process in fostering a transnational feminist practice able to avoid the pitfalls of global feminism as well as of a limited politics of location. Focusing on the processes of reception provides a way of moving beyond the local/global binary that so often traps Third World women between the impress of "local" agendas and an equally limiting "universalism." Reception theory requires that we pay attention to the connection between the global and the local—without, however, requiring that we choose between them. Given the interrelation of global and local forces, this is crucial. It should be emphasized, for instance, that we are *not* arguing that "correct" readings of necessity occur in the home culture. Rather, in any context both the reading of a text and its reception are constructed according to local agendas (whether First World or Third World), which are themselves intimately informed by global forces. Although historicization of the relations of production and reception requires a focus on the local context, this must always be viewed in relation to the global dimension. Reception analysis draws our attention not simply to the ways in which local responses may resist globalizing tendencies, but also to the ways in which local responses are themselves shaped by the global discourse.

As the previous discussion shows, this collection has benefited greatly from the recent work of postcolonial feminist scholars such as Spivak, Mohanty, Grewal, Shohat, and Kaplan, all of whom have raised issues relating to the reading of Third World women's texts in the West. Treatment of the issue of reception, however, has so far taken the form of individual essays appearing in various collections, or of mention within books on other topics. This is the first book to focus entirely on the politics of reception of Third World women writers and their texts. In a sense this collection thus seeks to answer the call of the editors of *The Post-Colonial Studies Reader* for more studies to be done in this area. As they put it: "the processes of patronage and control by which the colonial and neo-colonial powers continue to exercise a dominant role in selecting, licensing, publishing and distributing the texts of the post-colonial world, and the degree to which the inscriptive practices, choice of form, subject matter, genre, etc. is also subject to such control, have received far less attention than they deserve" (Ashcroft et al., 463). We hope our collection will contribute to filling this gap in postcolonial studies.

In focusing largely on literary texts, we seek to acknowledge and highlight the importance of literary works in global transcommunication and in the production of cultural representations. At the same time, however, it should be noted that this focus also reflects the limits imposed on transcultural exchange by the imbalance in power relations between the First and Third Worlds: the latter produces creative texts that travel to the former to be studied and theorized. We are also aware that the majority of the contributors to this anthology are located in the First World U.S. academy. Nonetheless their identities defy easy categorization: Although they cannot be said to be "Third World" women, many of them will not fit the category of "First World" women either. Like the texts they study, all have traveled across borders, and their work, like their identities, reflects the traces of this travel.

The essays in this collection do not focus solely on the U.S. locale but consider different contexts of reception: North and South American, European, South Asian, and Middle Eastern. The book is divided into three sections. Section I, "Women's Texts, Global Scripts," focuses on the problematics of reading Third World women's writing within a transnational context in which global and local discourses intersect and collide, producing overdetermined contexts of reception. Section II, "The Writer as Text," examines the conflation of text and author in the reception of Third World women's writing, and the implications of this conflation/reconstruction for Third World women's self-narrations. Section III, "Resistant Readings," explores strategies for moving beyond the local/global binary, positing ways of reading Third World women's writing in a global context.

In the collection's opening essay, "The Triumphant Discourse of Global Feminism: Should Other Women Be Known?" Marnia Lazreg explores the implications of the academic feminist idea of the "Other" woman for Third World women and the project of feminism more generally. Despite Western feminism's liberatory impulse and objectives, Lazreg argues, the construction of Third World women as "Other" functions to reinscribe relations of power between women, empowering First World feminists at the expense of Third World women. The structural relation of Western feminism to Third World women affects the reception context in three ways. It casts Third World women authors as players in a "theater of the indigenous"; it enables Western feminists "to distance themselves from Other women at the same time as they appear to be closing the gap between them"; and it serves to vindicate First World women in their prejudices—"because now the natives themselves are speaking the way some of 'us' did in the olden days when we were branded prejudiced." Given this reception context, Lazreg concludes, "it is crucial to ask whether 'western' audiences, feminist or otherwise, should insist on the knowability of these women"—for the feminist discourse is "but a discourse with global ambitions."

In her essay "An Affair to Remember: Scripted Performances in the 'Nasreen Affair'," Bishnupriya Ghosh explores the "scripts" that situate not only Third World women's writing but Third World women themselves. Ghosh traces the ways in which Taslima Nasreen, the Bangladeshi author who "escaped" to the West after the publication of her controversial novel *Lajja* resulted in a death threat against her, became a "text produced and deployed for various strategic reasons in Bangladesh, India and the West." Whether demonized or portrayed as a victim, Nasreen was "deployed as a signifier for material, political, and historical anxieties and concerns." The reactions she elicited in both Eastern and Western contexts, Ghosh argues, were *predetermined* by scripts produced by the First and Third Worlds about each other. But while Nasreen's reception reflects the overdetermination and the commodification of these scripts, Ghosh suggests, it also points toward the ways in which the process of transnationalism and globalization "opens these scripts up to debate."

An essay by Therese Saliba and Jeanne Kattan on the reception of Palestinian women's texts in the West Bank continues the focus on what Ghosh describes as the "sites of . . . consumption," where the responses to texts are scripted by "social and material practices, political transactions and ideologies." However, this essay shifts discussion away from the Western reception context, in which the roles of power, economics, literacy, and the marketing of so-called Third World women in the global economy are often obscured, to the context of origin: in this case, the Palestinian homeland. In the transnational context of reception, argue

Saliba and Kattan, what gets left out of the exchange between Palestinian writers and Western readers are the Palestinian women readers who are often (in the words of novelist Liana Badr, whom they interview) "the aim, source and origin" of Palestinian women writers. As a result, they point out, "the texts that become representative of Palestinian and Arab women's lives for metropolitan readers, ironically, may not even be available to or read by the very women they purportedly represent." Basing their discussion on interviews they conducted with Palestinian women writers and with the editor of a feminist magazine, as well as on the results of a study they carried out analyzing the reception of Palestinian and Arab women's literature at several Palestinian universities, Saliba and Kattan examine the predicament of cultural production and reception within the context of continuing Israeli occupation and nationalist struggle. This context, they argue, determines and delimits both the perceived social role of Palestinian women's writing and its reception.

As Ghosh shows in the case of Nasreen, through the process of reception a Third World woman can herself become a text. This collapsing of writer and text, we argued above, is particularly encouraged by the fact that Third World women's writing in general is valued for its "authenticity." The reception process often complicates the authority of Third World women autobiographies and autobiographers as they give voice to their own experiences. The controversy about Menchú's *testimonio* discussed earlier is a good illustration of this complex relationship between author, text, and the context of reception. In her essay for this collection, "Race, Gender, and the Politics of Reception of Latin American *Testimonios,*" Bueno investigates the reception of Latin American *testimonios* within United States academic contexts, questioning why texts that meet certain expectations about who can "speak" for a community are popularized, while texts that do not meet the political agenda of readers in the United States are ignored, regardless of the power of their narratives. Bueno focuses her discussion on the canonical text *I . . . Rigoberta Menchú;* on *Let Me Speak,* a *testimonio* by Domitila Barrios de Chungara and Moema Viezzer that is well known to Latin American specialists; and on *Child of the Dark,* a text by Carolina Maria de Jesus that is hardly known any more. Bueno blames the invisibility of *Child of the Dark* on the fact that its author, a Black woman of Brazil, has been viewed not as a community spokesperson, as were the authors of the other two texts, but as a "sexual female being," and on the racial hierarchies that allot Blacks and Indians "certain spaces within the political and cultural spectrum," even within the realm of *testimonios.* She concludes her essay by pointing toward the tension between *testimonios* and testimonial beings as agents of expression and as subject matter "to be written about"—a tension that mutes the voices of Third World women.

The essays by Mohja Kahf and Patricia Geesey continue this examination of the ways in which autobiographical narratives by women are both limited and transformed by the "horizon of expectations" (see Kahf's essay) that readers bring to a text. The tension between a speaking subject's narrative and the institutional processes through which this narrative is transmitted and received is the subject of Kahf's essay "Packaging 'Huda': Sha'rawi's Memoirs in the United States Reception Environment." This essay analyses the extent to which the processes of translation within a context of stereotypes of Arab women transform and limit the "range of meanings" in the Arabic text of Egyptian feminist Huda Sha'rawi's memoirs. Kahf identifies three main conventions through which an Arab woman is typically construed: as "a victim of gender oppression . . . as an escapee of her intrinsically oppressive culture . . . [and] as the pawn of Arab male power." This set of expectations, Kahf argues, shapes the translation of Sha'rawi's memoirs in significant ways. For instance, in the English text, in contrast to the Arabic, the author's "engagement with Arab men in [satisfying] relationships . . . is minimized; her orientation toward Europe is exaggerated; . . . her command of class privilege is camouflaged . . . [and] her story, which in [the Arabic text] is the story of a public figure, is recentered . . . around private life and the 'harem.' " Such packaging not only changes the subject of these memoirs, but situates her within a "harem of Third World difference." In contrast, Kahf argues, the significance of Sha'rawi's feminist legacy extends beyond this limited sphere and must be assessed within a global context of relevance.

Geesey's essay, "Identity and Community in Autobiographies of Algerian Women in France," likewise examines the effect that dominant discourses about Arab-Muslim women have on the way in which North African women's autobiographical texts are constructed and read. In this essay, Geesey explores the framing and marketing of three Algerian women's narratives in France, analyzing the effect of the reception context on "whether or not these works are read as challenging, or as insidiously reaffirming the dominant discourse about North African women in France." While the autobiographies function as testimonials, she notes, the narratives "may be read on several levels as texts that seek to reformulate the debates on assimilation, integration, cultural and identity politics within a new discursive territory." In particular, they point toward the possibility of "narrative strategies that might resist appropriation and (re)inscription into the dominant discourse on North African Muslim women," and hence, toward an "in-between" space between assimilation and alterity.

Geesey's point about this "in-between" space that Third World women's narratives may create or claim is elaborated upon by the essays in the last section of the book, which all suggest ways of reading Third World women's texts that resist overdetermined reactions. The first essay in this section, " 'Sharp contrasts of all colours': The Legacy of Toru Dutt," by Alpana Sharma Knippling, deals with the reception of a nineteenth-century Indian writer, reminding us that transnational reception and interaction is not restricted to the modern and postmodern periods. Rather, such cultural interactions occurred in earlier periods as well, especially in colonial societies such as India under British rule. As Shohat and Stam put it, "globalization is not a new development . . . it must be seen as part of the much larger history of colonialism" (151). In her essay, Knippling makes clear the extent to which Third World women in the transnational era occupy a space fraught with tension. Despite their efforts to set forth their own aims and agendas, the "material production and dissemination" of their texts is paradoxically "sustained by the institutional mechanisms of that mainstream culture." Knippling examines the impact of these institutional mechanisms on the late nineteenth-century Indian poet and translator Toru Dutt, a writer whose critical reception has tended to veer between a glorification of her as a "true Indian daughter" and a dismissal of her as "imitative of Western poetic trends." For Knippling, Dutt's life and work constitute "an overdetermined site upon which both colonial and anti-colonial imperatives competed to weave a complicated pattern indeed." However, Dutt was nonetheless able to negotiate the "risk-ridden, in-between, yet productive space in the international arena of textual production and reception." Her refusal to "settle neatly into only one side of any number of binary relations: female/male, colonized/colonizer, Indian/Western, original/imitative, young/old, sheltered/'free,' and so on," provides evidence for the argument "that Third World feminists should not find it necessary to consolidate their politics in binary terms." Rather, as Knippling shows, resistance takes shape at interstitial locations, where literary and material practice are "rooted in the struggle for social justice."

Such productive negotiation of tensions requires attention to what Jennifer Wenzel, in her essay "Grim Fairy Tales: Taking a Risk: Reading *Imaginary Maps*," calls the "difficulty, and necessity, of teaching oneself and allowing oneself to be taught to read." Wenzel focuses her essay on the role that attention to the *process* of reading can play in negotiating, and perhaps avoiding, scripted responses to Third World women. She discusses the difficulty of reading a text such as *Imaginary Maps,* Gayatri Spivak's translation from Bengali of three stories by Mahasweta Devi, from "a space on the map far removed" from the realities of Mahasweta's texts. Seeking to find a way to read this text without appropriating it into already scripted responses, Wenzel shows how *Imaginary Maps,* through its narrative collaboration between Mahasweta and Spivak, "problematizes the transformation of reading into writing and thus, in some ways, teaches a reader to read it." Much of her essay traces the process of learning how to read the text. This process, as Wenzel makes clear, requires engagement with ambivalence as well as with historical specificity. Moreover, it requires an acknowledgment of the role of the reader in constructing meaning. Indeed, Wenzel concludes, "one potential lesson of *Imaginary Maps* is that the responses we construct are always fairy tales that we want and need to hear"—fairy tales that "are never innocent."

It is clear, as Wenzel's essay among others suggests, that the "sites of consumption" at which Third World women's texts are constructed include college campuses. Sally McWilliams's essay explicitly focuses on the undergraduate classroom as a site of reception, exploring the dynamics of the engagement between American undergraduate students and Third World women's texts. The typical paradigms of reading employed by students, McWilliams says, include one of two colonizing approaches: either they "try to interpret the texts according to criteria they have used for everything they have ever read . . . the 'we are one' point of view," or they take the text as "a representation of the 'exotic other.' " By examining the effect of the politics of location on the politics of reception, however, students are able to engage in "a multifaceted discussion about interpretive approaches, hierarchies of authority surrounding types of texts . . . and the role of authenticity . . . in the production of knowledge in the classroom." Such discussion shifts classroom dynamics away from "neo-colonial reading strategies" toward polyvocal, historically situated sites of knowledge and interpretation.

The final essay, by Ella Shohat, "travels" not only between different continents but also between different genres of writing. The essay explores the role played by reception contexts in several disparate geographies in legitimizing certain categories of identification and delegitimizing others. Shohat examines how the United States constructs dislocated subjects who have already been displaced in other Eurocentric contexts (as seen, for instance, in her own experience of growing up as an Iraqi in Israel), and whose United States experience then confronts them with "the border patrols of new world naming." By placing her own journey (Iraq, Israel, United States) *vis-à-vis* that of the artist Lynne Yamamoto (Japan, Hawaii, United States), Shohat creates a kind of a dialogue between geographies and histories that are usually kept separate. This strategy illustrates the theoretical arguments she has put forward elsewhere, as in her co-authored *Unthinking Eurocentrism,* which argues for discussing cultures "in-relation" rather than as "neatly fenced-off areas of expertise."[9] Shohat particularly challenges the "predicament of the single hyphen" in the master narrative of immigration to the United States. In this master narrative, the hegemonic discourses of the reception context, fixed within the rigid boundaries of the nation-state and its often concomitant nationalist ideology, dictate which identities in multiply-hyphenated identities are granted credence, and which are made invisible or even censored. Shohat makes her argument largely through the case of Arab-Jews, a community that has already been displaced within the context of Asia and Africa (e.g., from Morocco to Israel) prior to its arrival in the United States. Reading Shohat's partially autobiographical essay against the backdrop of her scholarly work, which has challenged the academic reception of the term "postcolonialism"[10] as well as critiqued the hegemonic narrative of "feminism,"[11] facilitates a reexamination of the relationship between the institutional reception of critical ideas and that of the critics voicing them. Her essay brings into focus the issues explored throughout the collection, making clear the impact of reception contexts in determining not only how texts are received but also how writers and others are constructed as subjects.

It is our hope that this collection will contribute to a transnational feminist practice bringing women together through real cross-cultural dialogue. By exploring the reception contexts of Third World women's writing, and by drawing attention to the power relations governing the production and reception of both writers and texts, we hope to bring new insight to the relationship between First and Third World women. Our focus on the reception context is part of a larger project being enacted within feminist discourse at the present time, that of historicizing Third World women's cultural production as a way of counteracting the homogenizing tendencies of both global feminism and postcolonialism. We believe in the value and significance of transnational exchange: we want cultural and national borders to remain open, and we want travel across these borders to continue. However, at the same time we believe that women in particular, in both the First and the Third worlds, need to remember that the journey is neither easy nor straightforward. To borrow a phrase from Annette Kolodny, we still need to "dance through the minefields" of global and transcultural travel.

NOTES

[1]We have decided to use the term "Third World" in our discussion and in the title of this book despite its many limitations. The division of the world into First, Second, and Third Worlds has increasingly been called into question. At the same time, however, relations between margin and center have not been leveled by the forces of globalization. As the essays in this book make clear, although the currents of globalization and transnationalism have disseminated cultural products across national and cultural boundaries, hierarchies of power persist. The term "postcolonial" challenges the hierarchy between "First" and "Third" worlds, but also runs the risk of obscuring the historical contexts from which these hierarchies of power arise. We agree with Ella Shohat's assessment that "The concept of 'Third World' is schematically productive if it is placed under erasure, as it were, seen as provisional and ultimately inadequate" ("Notes on the 'Post-Colonial'"). In this book, we use the term "Third World" advisedly, with an awareness of its limitations but also with a recognition of its usefulness in keeping relations of power at the foreground.

[2]Uma Narayan suggests that Third World women in the West are assigned three major roles: they can be "Emissaries," "Mirrors," or "Authentic Insiders" (121–157). We believe this last role has been the most common in recent years and also the most pernicious. This is the reason we focus on it here.

[3]Other books with a similar approach include Chilla Bulbeck, *One World Women's Movement* (London: Pluto Press, 1988); Charlotte Bunch, *Feminism in the 80s: Bringing the Global Home* (Denver: Antelope, 1985); Jill M. Bystydzienski, *Women Transforming Politics: Worldwide Strategies for Empowerment* (Bloomington: Indiana UP, 1992).

[4]For instance, Zed Books issued their Women in the Third World series. For a discussion of the significance of this series see Mohanty, "Under Western Eyes," 75. Heinemann publishes series on African and Caribbean writers and has published works by Nadine Gordimer, Bessie Head, and Buchi Emecheta.

[5]As an example of this tension, see Nawal El Saadawi, Fatima Mernissi, and Mallica Vajarathon, "Organizer's Dialogue: A Critical Look at the Wellesley Conference" *Quest* 9.2 (1978): 101–108. Participants criticized the conference for not being international enough and for being American planned and controlled in both content and form. Third World participants, they protested, were

reduced to a passive audience listening to papers read in English by Western women about Third World cultures.

[6]For a detailed study of El Saadawi's reception in the West, see Amal Amireh's "Framing Nawal El Saadawi: Arab Feminists in a Transnational Context," *Signs,* forthcoming, Autumn 2000.

[7]For a more detailed account of the relationship between Arab women authors and Western publishers, see Amal Amireh's "Arab Women Writers Today," *Against the Current* (March/April 1997): 21–23.

[8]See Indrani Mitra and Madhu Mitra, "The Discourse of Liberal Feminism and Third World Women's Texts: Some Issues of Pedagogy," *College Literature* 18 (1991): 55–63.

[9]Ella Shohat and Robert Stam, *Unthinking Eurocentrism: Multiculturalism and the Media* (London and New York: Routledge, 1994), 6.

[10]Shohat, "Notes on the 'Post-Colonial,' " *Social Text* 31/32 (Spring 1992): 99–113.

[11]Shohat, ed., *Talking Visions: Multicultural Feminism in a Transnational Age* (Cambridge, MA: M.I.T. Press and the New Museum, 1998).

WORKS CITED

Amireh, Amal. "Problems and Prospects for Publishing in the West: Arab Women Writers Today." *Against the Current* (Mar/Apr 1997): 21–23.
———. "Framing Nawal El Saadawi: Arab Feminism in a Transnational Context." *Signs: Journal of Women in Culture and Society* (forthcoming, Autumn 2000).
Aschcroft, Bill, Gareth Griffiths, and Helen Tiffin, eds. *The Post-Colonial Studies Reader*. London: Routledge, 1995.
Basu, Amrita, ed. *The Challenges of Local Feminisms: Women's Movements in Global Perspectives*. Boulder: Westview, 1995.
Beverly, John. "Through All Things Modern: Second Thoughts on *Testimonio*." *Boundary 2* 18, 2 (1992): 1–21.
———. "The Margin at the Center: On *Testimonio*." In *De/Colonizing the Subject: The Politics of Gender in Women's Autobiography*. Sidonie Smith and Julia Watson, eds. Minneapolis: U of Minnesota P, 1992. 91–114.
Bulbeck, Chilla. *One World Women's Movement*. London: Pluto Press, 1988.
Bunch, Charlotte. *Feminism in the 80s: Bringing the Global Home*. Denver: Antelope, 1985.
Bystydzienski, Jill M. *Women Transforming Politics: Worldwide Strategies for Empowerment*. Bloomington: Indiana UP, 1992.

Carr, Robert. "Crossing the First World/Third World Divides: Testimonial, Transnational Feminisms, and the Postmodern Condition." In *Scattered Hegemonies: Postmodernity and Transnational Feminist Practices*. Inderpal Grewal and Caren Kaplan, eds. Minneapolis: U of Minnesota P, 1994. 153–172.

Dirlik, Arif. "The Global in the Local." In *Global/Local: Cultural Production and the Transnational Imaginary*. Rob Wilson and Wimal Dissanayake, eds. Durham: Duke UP, 1996. 21–45.

Featherstone, Mike. "Localism, Globalism, and Cultural Identity." In *Global/Local: Cultural Production and the Transnational Imaginary*. Rob Wilson and Wimal Dissanayake, eds. Durham and London: Duke UP, 1996. 46–77.

Franco, Jean. "Going Public: Reinhabiting the Private." In *On Edge: The Crisis in Contemporary Latin American Culture*. George Yudice, Jean Franco, and Juan Flores, eds. Minneapolis: U of Minnesota P, 1992. 65–84.

Friedman, Susan Stanford. *Mappings: Feminism and the Cultural Geographies of Encounter*. Princeton: Princeton UP, 1998.

Ghosh, Bishnupriya and Brinda Bose. *Interventions: Feminist Dialogues on Third World Women's Literature and Film*. New York and London: Garland, 1997.

Gornick, Vivian. "About the Mutilated Half." *New York Times,* 14 March 1982, 3.

Grewal, Inderpal and Caren Kaplan, eds. *Scattered Hegemonies: Postmodernity and Transnational Feminist Practices*. Minneapolis: U of Minnesota P, 1994.

Harlow, Barbara. "Memory and Historical Record: The Literature and Literary Criticism of Beirut, 1982. In *Left Politics and the Literary Profession*. Lennard J. Davis and M. Bella Mirabella, eds. New York: Columbia UP, 1990. 186–208.

Harrington, Maureen. "Veil Lifted to Reveal Unimaginable World of Arab Women." *Denver Post,* 13 February 1994, G–80.

John, Mary E. *Discrepant Dislocations: Feminism, Theory, and Postcolonial Histories*. Berkeley, Los Angeles, and London: U of California P, 1996.

Johnson-Odim, Cheryl. "Common Themes, Different Contexts: Third World Women and Feminism." In *Third World Women and the Politics of Feminism*. Chandra Talpade Mohanty, Ann Russo, and Lourdes Torres, eds. Bloomington and Indianapolis: Indiana UP, 1991. 314–327.

Kaplan, Caren. "The Politics of Location as Transnational Feminist Practice." In *Scattered Hegemonies: Postmodernity and Transnational Feminist Practices*. Inderpal Grewal and Caren Kaplan, eds. Minneapolis: U of Minnesota P, 1994. 137–152.

———. *Questions of Travel: Postmodern Discourses of Displacement*. Durham: Duke UP, 1996.

Lefevere, André. "The Historiography of African Literature Written in English." In *The Post-Colonial Studies Reader*. Ashcroft et al., eds. London: Routledge, 1995. 465–470.

Mitchell, W. J. T. "Postcolonial Culture, Postimperial Criticism." In *The Post-Colonial Studies Reader*. Aschcroft et al., eds. London: Routledge, 1995. 475–479.

Mitra, Indrani and Madhu Mitra. "The Discourse of Liberal Feminism and Third World Women's Texts: Some Issues of Pedagogy." *College Literature* 18 (1991): 55–63.

Mohanty, Chandra Talpade. "Feminist Encounters: Locating the Politics of Experience." *Copyright* 1 (Fall 1987): 30–44.

———. "Under Western Eyes: Feminist Scholarship and Colonialist Discourse." In *Third World Women and the Politics of Feminism*. Chandra Talpade Mohanty, Ann Russo, and Lourdes Torres, eds. Bloomington and Indianapolis: Indiana UP, 1991. 51–80.

Mohanty, Chandra Talpade, Ann Russo, and Lourdes Torres, eds. *Third World Women and the Politics of Feminism*. Bloomington and Indianapolis: Indiana UP, 1991.

Moore, Molly. "Nobel Winner's Work Disputed; Scholar Claims Guatemalan Exaggerated her Horrifying Story." *Washington Post* 21 January 1999, C01.

Narayan, Uma. *Dislocating Cultures: Identities, Traditions, and Third World Feminism*. New York: Routledge, 1997.

Omang, Joanne. "When the Facts Stood in the Way of the Crusade." *Washington Post* 25 January 1999, C02.

Probyn, Elspeth. "Travels in the Postmodern: Making Sense of the Local." In *Feminism/Postmodernism*. Linda J. Nicholson, ed. New York: Routledge, 1990. 176–189.

Rich, Adrienne. *Blood, Bread, and Poetry: Selected Prose, 1979–1985*. New York: Norton, 1986.

Rifaat, Alifa. *Distant View of a Minaret*. London: Heinemann, 1989.

El Saadawi, Nawal, Fatima Mernissi, and Mallica Vajarathon. "Organizers' Dialogue: A Critical Look at the Wellesley Conference." *Quest* 9, 2 (1978): 101–108.

Said, Edward W. "Traveling Theory." In *The World, the Text, and the Critic*. Cambridge, MA: Harvard UP, 1983. 226–247.

Al-Shaykh, Hanan, *Women of Sand and Myrrh*. Trans. Catherine Cobham. New York: Doubleday, 1989.

Shohat, Ella. "Notes on the 'Post-Colonial.' " *Social Text* 31/32 (Spring 1992): 99–113.

————, ed. *Talking Visions: Multicultural Feminism in a Transnational Age.* Cambridge, MA: M.I.T. Press and the New Museum, 1998.

Shohat, Ella and Robert Stam. *Unthinking Eurocentrism: Multiculturalism and the Media.* New York: Routledge, 1994.

————. "From the Imperial Family to the Transnational Imaginary: Media Spectatorship in the Age of Globalization." In *Global/Local: Cultural Production and the Transnational Imaginary.* Rob Wilson and Wimal Dissanayake, eds. Durham: Duke UP, 1996. 145–170.

Spivak, Gayatri Chakravorty. "Can the Subaltern Speak?" In *Colonial Discourse and Postcolonial Theory: A Reader.* Patrick Williams and Laura Chrisman, eds. New York: Columbia UP, 1994. 66–111.

Stoll, David. *Rigoberta Menchú and the Story of All Poor Guatemalans.* Boulder: Westview, 1998.

Terry, Sara. "Journey into the Heart of a Radical Woman." *Christian Science Monitor,* 5 September 1986, B5.

Wilson, Rob and Wimal Dissanayake, eds. *Global/Local: Cultural Production and the Transnational Imaginary.* Durham: Duke UP, 1996.

SECTION I
Women's Texts, Global Scripts

The Triumphant Discourse
of Global Feminism:
Should Other Women Be Known?

MARNIA LAZREG

This is a reflection on the ups and downs, twists and turns, permutations and mutations of the academic feminist idea of the "Other" woman, sometimes called Third World, Muslim (if not improperly "Islamic"), Black, Oriental or Asian, African, in a word, the world's woman. But this world is "worlded" by others who do not include themselves in it as a subject of study. Theirs is a geographically small world but one politically, economically, and intellectually large. It has made what Max Weber called "universal history," the kind of history that speaks of the "West's" presence in one way or another, on the market place, in government palaces, and at home, around the television set. It is this kind of history that gathered thousands of women together in Beijing and Houairu, China, in 1995. Though some women from remote villages had their trips paid for by international organizations who sent them to commune in a sisterhood made to order, they were all but ignored by their well-educated "Western Universal" sisters when they sat to dinner with them in their hotels. In my youth I objected to the Weberian cultural arrogance. But I am not so sure now that he was wrong after all. No matter how well he understood the scope of the economic might of the West, he had not anticipated the rise of feminism as an intellectual and social movement that expanded the "universal" function of the "West." Had he done so, he would have further substantiated his claim. Hiding behind the lofty and unimpeachable calls for equality, choice, human rights, etc., Western feminists have promoted conceptions of individual and institutional change modeled after their own societies. Although they sometimes espouse a relativistic stance by denouncing universalism in the social sciences, they paradoxically present their constructions of change for Other women in a decontextualized fashion that assumes a universal order of values. They fail to appreciate that their own cultures and societies form the implicit context for the changes they hold up for Other women to emulate. Presumably there are universal issues with which human societies grapple, and which they resolve in different ways. However, what the triumphant feminist discourse addresses is not diversity as such, in-itself, but difference from-itself; it seeks to obliterate that which is different from itself as if this act were a necessary condition of its own reproduction.

As a formerly colonized person, I initially reacted to academic feminism with spontaneity (a drawback Frantz Fanon denounced in his work), that kind of immediate elation you feel at thoughts and movements that seem to deconstruct the well-ordered system of ideas that rules the world. As I started teaching about women in a program about women, with women who wore their feminism on their sleeves but not in their hearts, I soon realized that a good idea is not necessarily a different idea. I also learned, more than ever before, that there are limits to the discourse of liberation from without, just as there are limits to freedom from above. Oftentimes, the without and the above are one and the same. These limits, situational, personal/psychological, and institutional, define the terms of the reception of Other women's intellectual production and translatability.

LIMITS OF THE FEMINIST DISCOURSE

Situational

Feminism, as an organized reflection on equality between women and men, originated in countries referred to as "Western," a fact that should neither disqualify it as a good idea nor serve as an excuse for nationalism and Western bashing. It goes without saying that practices that reflected a similar end existed in many societies. But it is precisely this Western originary source of the feminist discourse that is so important to contemporary academic feminists who have done much to expand the idea of feminism but who have also misappropriated it for personal and institutional reasons.

A major consequence for Other women of the origins of the feminist discourse is its presumed normalcy in the context of Western societies. English, American, French women can make demands, reasonable or outrageous, and present them as part of an evolving history of perfecting their political and economic institutions. They can appeal to the Bill of Rights, the Declaration of the Rights of Man (sic) and the Citizen, the heritage of the Enlightenment, the suffragette movement, etc. to ground their demands. Without seeking to belittle it, I suggest their struggle is business as usual in their societies, which may explain why, no matter how spectacular their accusations or revelations of abuses against women, these do not have the shock value of similar events originating in "Third World" societies. Underlying the struggle of Western feminists is the assumption that they belong to perfectible societies, whereas Other women's societies are by definition "traditional," impervious to change from within, and unknowing of what is good for women. This seldom recognized fact allows Western feminists to perceive themselves as fundamentally different from Other women whom they tend to define as "oppressed" and in need of liberation. The cultural roots of Western feminism result in two related outcomes. On the one hand, they empower Western feminists when the latter encounter women from other societies, especially those from the "Muslim" world, whom they understand only through the reductive (and misunderstood) categories of religion, which dissolve their individuality, if not humanity. Consequently, the discourse of liberation reinscribes relations of power between women. On the other hand, they compel women from non-Western societies to speak from "Western women's perspectives," which means that they must speak about their cultures while fleeing from them instead of perfecting them from within. Thus, empowerment for Western feminists is a condition of the alienation of Other women. When some of these Other women rebel, they are incorporated into the normal academic feminist discourse as dissenters, or as typifying reactions informed by ethnicity or "diversity." Their incorporation is meant to shore up the capacity of the discourse to embrace others, when in reality it marginalizes them further. It does little to transform the discourse itself.

Personal/Psychological

It is difficult to determine the impact on one's psyche of living in powerful countries unabashedly defined as "advanced" or "developed." The discourse of development that permeates European and North American societies creates a mind-set that prevails not only among women from these countries but also among those who come as students to Western countries, and who begin to reproduce the same discourse as they apply it to the people back home. It is a mind-set which, before the advent of academic feminism, was kept in check by Left political commitments or critiques. However, with the demise or decline of the Left, feminism has provided less of a critique and more of a license to document, in word and image, the multiple ways in which women are victimized by the vestiges of traditions in the "developing" societies. The comfort derived from situational power and grounding in a different history creates among many academic feminists a sense of entitlement, a will to know and change the world. Feminism has provided them with an ideology of liberation, a tool (through programs of study), and sources of funding (from international organizations) they could never dream of prior to the women's liberation movement. The study of Other women has opened up a new horizon, a new frontier for academic feminists. The *world* is now open to their ideas of liberation, their concepts and programs, their training in gender analysis. They have achieved the Universal, they are universal. This universalism is, however, predicated on Other women's localism—a process that is now fashionably and problematically called globalism. The wider the frontier is pushed back, the more local Other women become. In return for providing contacts and allowing academic feminists forays into their countries, Other women, among them the elite, are courted, invited to guest-teach, given a forum in American and European universities. They are also used as teaching tools, native sources of immediate information compiled through interviews and discussions with students and faculty. This sometimes takes on a grotesque characteristic. For instance, an undergraduate student from Columbia University once sought me out for a long interview to illustrate the method of reading culture in the (re)construction of a Muslim native's biography. I declined the honor, arguing that my life was private, not a public event for classroom discussion unless I chose so. This student was stunned by my refusal and did not seem to understand that I would wish to exist for myself and not for others. The triumphant feminist discourse as disseminated in universities had already turned me into a datum to fill a space in theorizing about Other women.

Institutional

The establishment of women's studies programs throughout North America and Europe resulted in the professionalization of gender. This means that no matter what the benefits of such programs are for students (and there are many) the subject of women, now subsumed under the less threatening concept of gender, has become a professional pursuit. Students interested in classes about women, about themselves, must be graded, and some fail their courses. When taught about Other women, students must take tests that gauge how much they know about sensational beliefs and customs, even though they are sometimes taught by women whose knowledge of these subjects is shaky. Textbooks compound the professionalization of the study of women by delineating its specialness. They display blown-up pictures of tattooed, teary-eyed, lined faces of women of different colors that would make National Geographic green with envy. The process of getting funding for starting a project somewhere in the vast Third World, or encouraging students to write dissertations on the newly discovered women, has become part and parcel of women's studies programs, reinforcing the need for more professionalization. This increases distanciation and fosters an instrumental attitude towards Other women whose lives are seen merely as providing the opportunity to be mined for documentary evidence of "diversity," "oppression," or in Gloria Steinem's words, "outrageous" tales.

RECEPTION AND ITS PERMUTATIONS

This rapid review of the limits to the feminist discourse and enterprise indicates that Other women are necessary to it for at least three main reasons. First, the feminist discourse cannot maintain itself by focusing on the Western experience alone. For its theorizing, it needs to study and confront Other women's experiences to gauge its explanatory power. Second, its institutionalization as a normal discourse (in Thomas Kuhn's sense) requires information about Other women by Other women themselves in order to sustain students' and funders' interests. Documenting, studying gender practices that are sensational, or simply different, is often at the heart of funding proposals. Third, the field of research for students and professors needs to be kept large and varied to permit an ever-increasing production of books. How do these factors impact on the reception of Other women's writings? Reception is in effect an encounter between a purveyor of facts/ideas and a listener/receiver. A number of processes enter into play in the politics of reception: theatrical indigenization, distanciation, and cleansing/vindication.

Theatrical Indigenization

This is the process whereby a woman from the "Third World" speaks to a "Western" audience as an expert, although her expertise takes a secondary role and her native outlook and origins are emphasized. In this situation, the Other woman is invited to speak "on" a subject; her role is defined as that of filling in gaps or adding information about her society or culture. The transaction appears fair. She is flown in and given a forum. In return, students, faculty, and the public at large learn from a woman from a far-away place. However, a whole range of unspoken assumptions and factors is concealed in this apparently fair transaction. To begin with, the speaker (even when she prefaces her speech with a caveat) is a "loaded" subject; she carries with her historical/cultural baggage. She is seen as representing her culture. She speaks her culture. Whatever she says must be true, and if a member of the audience who may know better dares to disagree, she/he is seen as anti-feminist. The point is not for the speaker to speak the truth but simply to speak. Her speech is not meant to be debated; it is implicitly impeached as a debatable speech. Questions typically are in the nature of "can you say something more about . . . ?" Everybody knows the name of the game, with the exception perhaps of the occasional speaker who may (if she is the naïve sort who has not yet hit the international circuit) truly believe that she has made a contribution to women in her country by speaking. Speakers tend to be the same because conferences must feature women who are already *known*. They are supposed to be colorful, exciting speakers. Yet their stage presence is also derided. Often the audience comes to be entertained and seems to forego information. In fact, it may have no expectation of content at all. When a speaker wishes to avoid falling into the cliché of the cultural critique of gender in her society, she is often quickly asked, out of context, about customs that were not the focus of her talk. The audience insists on information about "oppression," not analysis of the institutional context within which "oppression" becomes meaningful. Thus, a chasm exists between the speaker and the audience, a chasm created by the academic climate of women's studies programs and reinforced by the popular culture's shallow understanding of Other women and places. The more indigenous a speaker appears, the better; the more "exciting" a speaker is, the better. Sometimes, too, native speakers fulfill the additional function of validating academic feminists who can then claim that their critiques of other cultures are substantiated by those made by indigenous women themselves. This theater of the indigenous trivializes Other women's speech. In doing so, it shores up the correctness, validity, if not "truth" of the "Western" academic feminist discourse. In other words, the much touted openness of academic feminists to "Third World" women is predicated upon these women's indigenization—that is upon their trivialization as native speakers whose role is to provide the occasional piece of up-to-date information, but more importantly to entertain, in one way or another, audiences hungry for tales about women.

Distanciation

This mechanism enables "Western" feminists, rooted as they are in their historical and political systems, to distance themselves from Other women at the same time that they appear to be closing the gap between them. The requirement of "diversity," the need to be inclusive, and the hunger for knowledge of different women's life circumstances combine to compel academic feminists to read and welcome literature from Other women. However, many do so as professionals of gender studies who gather facts, good and bad, oftentimes without bothering about accuracy, which they impart to their students and harness as evidence of what is wrong with other cultures and religions. The separation of the self from the object of its study (a hallmark of the scientific enterprise) happens to occur in a field—women—that has been much abused both in the West and the "Third World." The conviction that the women out there are in bad straights whereas we, here, are more equal than not, lies behind the phenomenon of distanciation. The late anthropologist Michele Rosaldo noted that many American women do not wish to identify with Other women whose cultural practices they deem repulsive. In fact, distanciation is not grounded in the rejection of these practices; it is a form of resistance to equality, to acceptance of Other women. Distanciation permits one to be sexless, to be the measure of others, to forget that womanhood everywhere, including the "West," has been the subject of contention, mishandling, and inequality. Distanciation insists on specialness, on entitlement, on belonging to the group that worlds the world.

An unintended consequence of distanciation is the degree to which texts written by Other women, even when they seem to be made part of the canon and are taught with care, reinforce prejudices about Other women. For instance, an undergraduate student in a class I taught once wrote a paper filled with unexamined conceptions of women in the Middle East. When asked to explain what she wrote, she mentioned that she thought she was being a good feminist by indicting Middle Eastern cultures (taken as a monolith). Besides, she added, "This is what we learned in my feminist class last semester." No matter what modes are devised for reading texts authored by Other women for an American undergraduate classroom, the outcome appears to be the same: "We are better off than they are." As another student in a Women and Development course put it: "I am so glad I am an American." This reaction is commonplace among students from new immigrant families, as well as natives. Perhaps what is at the heart of this surplus of prejudice is a shaky sense of self. To be able to embrace others, to learn from them, and see our humanity in theirs, requires a profound knowledge of ourselves and our culture. Books from Other women, about their lives or their cultures, may not enlighten "us" here if we are not secure enough in our understanding of ourselves and unless we have a perspective on our own history instead of accepting it as a given.

Books by Other women are expected to tell us something about *their* cultures, their lives. In societies where there is a market for women's books, the market influences the reception of the book. First of all, and depending on the culture "represented," the same women tend to be published: Assia Djebbar for Algeria, Fatima Mernissi for Morocco, Nawal El Saadawi for Egypt. Occasionally, a new name is added to the list, but the outcome remains the same: a few individuals are made to represent the countries they come from. Their manufactured notoriety gives their speech greater authority and meaning. Their books are thus received as convenient sources of "truthful" information for a public in need of native support for its own prejudices. Other women are complicitous in this process. They value large audiences, feel that they are better appreciated here than back home, and affirm their roles as the indigenized purveyors of legitimacy. Their books often appear simultaneously in English and in their mother tongue, and their audience is here and not there. Their reputation was made here and not there. Western audiences experience them vicariously as the symbolic daggers in the hearts of native men these readers essentially despise, and as the only beings who could undo a religion they perceive as beyond the pale. Is it any wonder that local women, many of whom are illiterate, have never heard of them or do not feel they have much in common with them?

Cleansing and Vindication

This process of vicariously partaking in the indictment of a culture may also be accompanied by a form of cleansing of the self through vindication. After all, many books authored by "Third World " women have appeared since the advent of feminism in the West. Many of those that are translated are written with "us" in mind, thus helping "us" to cleanse "ourselves" of any prejudices we thought we might have—because now the natives themselves are speaking the way some of "us" did in the olden days when we were branded prejudiced. "We" are vindicated. A feminist once announced at a post-Beijing conference that "August 1995 (the date of the conference) is a landmark because it showed that feminism is a global movement." She was not thinking of "global" women. Instead, she had in mind, "her" conception of what feminism is.

This does not mean that "Third World" women should not write. Many do, often unbeknownst to the translators busy translating the "Third World" canon in the West. It does mean that writing about women for Western audiences is a perilous journey, for such writing does not consider the layers of inter-mediations, or the geopolitical contexts that frame their audiences' tastes. Moreover, women are not the only ones to be complicitous in making the feminist discourse triumphant; men have their part in it, too. For example, Malek Alloula, author of *The Colonial Harem,* dug into the colonial archives to reproduce postcards sent by French soldiers at the turn of the century to their friends back home, displaying nude bodies of Algerian women. In apparently getting even with his former colonizers, he managed to dehumanize women one more time, as man to man. His audience enjoyed the pictures. The reception of this work was mediated by the pictorial representation of women, which foregrounded women's bodies while erasing the colonial producers. Those of us who are keenly aware of the politics of reception may devise ways of teaching texts written by Other women in ways that preclude their being used as so much fodder in the mill of prejudice. I remain convinced that only a de-centering of the self will make it possible for foreign audiences to "receive" Other women's work as reflecting another modality of being human. This requires educating not only students but also educators in redefining their purpose in life, acquiring a genuinely critical perspective on their culture, and relinquishing the intoxicating tendency to world the worlds of others. Perhaps, women from the "Third World" who write about women have been taken in by the notion that as women they are a context unto themselves. Hence, their willingness to write ex-nihilo so to speak, outside of a grounded position, which, although critical, might still express faith that change will take place from within as it is presumed it does in "Western" societies. Could these women be an unrecognized vanguard? They might if they had evolved their own views for their own audiences back home, and if they had transformed the terms of the academic feminist discourse.

Given the politics of reception of Other women's work and speech, it is crucial to ask whether "Western" audiences, feminist or otherwise, should insist on the knowability of these women. The many conferences, seminars, and courses devoted to these Other women have not yielded a deep understanding of them. Generalizations and stereotypes still flourish, and for some societies (such as the Middle East) these stereotypes seem to hold greater sway than they did *before* the advent of academic feminism. At first glance, a shift seems to have occurred, from portraying Other women as victims to portraying them as individuals endowed with agency. However, the emphasis is still on what customs, traditions, religions *do* to women. Women's achievements are couched as struggles "against" not "for." There is resistance from the faceless and nameless women who do not write about themselves to reveal their innermost. The triumphant discourse is but a discourse with global ambitions. What we need is the expression of reality by those who live it and on their terms.

An Affair to Remember: Scripted Performances in the "Nasreen Affair"

BISHNUPRIYA GHOSH

Even in the postmodern era, with its alleged short circuits in memory, some affairs die hard. What became known as the "Rushdie affair" snowballed into a set of narratives that seem to have set the stage for any writer "persecuted" by orthodox (conservative and fundamentalist) Muslims. Such was the fate of Taslima Nasreen, an author whose "escape" to the West became an international incident in Europe and a national embarrassment for Bangladesh. Early in the "Nasreen affair," she was nicknamed "the female Rushdie" on the NPR show "All Things Considered" (14 June 1994). Soon after her flight from Bangladesh (August 1994), Rushdie wrote an open letter, carried by twenty European newspapers, in sympathy with Nasreen and against "lynch justice and terrorism"; in the letter, he apologized to her for having to wear his name around her neck. But the name and its baggage stuck.

In cultural criticism and postcolonial studies, the dominant effect of the Rushdie affair has been to turn our attention to the geopolitics of transnational reception-contexts—in other words, not just sites of production but also of *consumption*. What are the responses to controversial texts? In what ways are these responses "scripted" in differing and politically-divided Third and First World reception-contexts? What kinds of social and material practices, political transactions and ideologies engender these processes of "decoding"[1]? In this essay, I look at the Nasreen affair by focusing on three different geopolitical reception contexts, Bangladesh, India, and Europe, and by analyzing the "scripted" responses to Nasreen in those contexts.

Nasreen's case is especially interesting for an exploration of the politics of reception because the English translation of her controversial novel *Lajja* (for which she had a death threat issued against her) was not readily available; so *she* and not her novel became the text produced and deployed for various strategic reasons in Bangladesh, India, and the West. In an address to a conference, "Writing and Thinking at the End of an Epoch," Elke Schmitter draws our attention to the lessons of the Rushdie and Nasreen affairs: in the postmodern global production of literary publicity, authors are stripped of their intended audiences and become free-floating signifiers for local agendas; thus the worlds that those authors mediate become less relevant to readers than the authors-as-text as commodified signifiers.[2] Very few of the commentaries in the Western press refer to *Lajja;* the drama of Nasreen's escape and her status as a victim of Islamic religious intolerance become the dominant foci. While in the West she was only text governed by the Rushdie subtext, the majority of the Bangladeshi and Bengali Indian scriptors had read *Lajja* in the Bengali vernacular. Yet the initial discussions of the novel in the Bangladeshi and Indian presses soon disappeared in favor of scripted responses to Western allegations. The Bangladeshi reaction to these responses reveals a predictable set of anti-Western ideas that mirrors the Western act of demonization. The reports on Nasreen from Calcutta, located in West Bengal (India) where Bengali is also spoken, discuss both the novel and her politics, but even here Nasreen appears as a subaltern Bangladeshi Muslim Bengali who is read into another set of South Asian hegemonic narratives. In our era of global cultural hegemonies disseminated through a global media and the logics of transnational capital, the Western responses in many ways engendered the Third World ones. In other words, given the perceived present (and historical) economic and political imbalances, the Third World defensively responded to the West's denunciation of an "unfree" world.

I will argue that in both Third and First World reception contexts, Nasreen is deployed as a signifier for material, political, and historical anxieties and concerns. Nasreen is either demonized or victimized in the presses of Europe, India, and Bangladesh. (These will be my primary foci, but I will also draw on some newspaper articles in the United States and some responses from the Middle East.)[3] The authors of the various responses I examine here *use* certain historical and contemporary narratives—of the "subaltern" woman writer, of Western "imperial intervention," of "rabid Muslim fundamentalists," and so forth—to craft their pieces; in this sense, these writers *perform* ideologically "scripted" responses, masking and closing over the real geopolitical and national conflicts.

Thus I am interested, here, in perusing not only the scripts that define the various interpretations of Nasreen's views and work, but also the historical, material, and political relationships that shape their discursive context. But before moving to these particularities, and in awareness of the postcolonial critical outpouring on subalterneity and transnational reception-contexts in which "Third World women writers" are produced and consumed, I must register a cautionary note: I use the idea of the subaltern in Spivak's sense of a *differential* position of oppression, one which engenders the subaltern's speech/silence within dominant discourses, not the easy pop generalization of the term through which subaltern equals victim. For many Bangladeshi orthodox Muslims, Nasreen is the aggressor, not a victim; for reasons I will explore later, they opt not to "hear" her pro-Bangladeshi commitments, choosing to brand her as a traitor. Nasreen becomes a "subaltern" figure in both Western and Third World discourses, and even in feminist attempts to champion her cause. I will look at the ways in which Nasreen is produced in the news, not the subalterns that *she* produces in her work[4]; I am less invested in exploring her "voice" and her *production* of knowledge than in examining the way she has been "decoded" or *consumed* as subaltern.

I will briefly outline my conceptualization of the responses in the Nasreen affair as simulacric, overdetermined scripts before moving to a short discussion on the theorization of transnational reception-contexts. The bulk of the paper will be an exploration and analysis of these responses in terms of enscripting and performance. The responses are arranged according to geopolitical locations: Bangladesh, India (as one aspect of the "subcontinent"), and the West (Europe and the United States). The diasporic responses will obviously confuse these geopolitical boundaries and this, as I will make clear, will be an important intervention into the hegemony of those national and international divides. The last set of responses will be grouped under an ideological position— that of feminist readings—since this position cuts across geopolitical boundaries.

SCRIPTED RESPONSES AND THEIR IMPLICATIONS

In the postcolonial era, certain narratives and acts of signification—"the free world," "Third World women" as victims, "regressive Muslim fundamentalists" who pose a challenge to democracy—exist as epistemological effects of the colonial past. As the Rushdie affair has shown, in pitched encounters between the First and Third worlds (roughly corresponding to the ex-colonial powers and the colonies, respectively) these narratives are dislocated and used as "scripts" to explain contemporary First World–Third World. The act of enscripting and performing a political position and response must be understood in terms of a burgeoning global economy and media, and the corresponding postmodern discursive and material contexts.

On the one hand, mobile populations crossing and recrossing various nation-state or other geopolitical boundaries have created new and complex community alliances and antagonisms, linkages that can no longer be understood within the dominant ideologies of (modern) nation-states. Several theorists of transnational contexts have analyzed how multilocational diaspora, for example, complicate and challenge the internal consistencies of discourses set up in the colonial, early postcolonial, and cold war periods.[5] On the other hand, theorists such as Arjun Appadurai (1990) have noted the effect of increasing global commodification on identities and texts within transnational capitalist structures of exchange; this global economy creates certain cultural flows that enter and are stored in collective memory banks ("cultural warehouses").[6] Telecommunications, more access to and control of technology, and an emergent visual *lingua franca* have resulted in a spectrum of shared and dislocated "signs" familiar to all those who have access to reading/viewing/ listening apparatuses. By "dislocated" I mean "signs" that are plucked from their historical material context of exchange, and exist as free-floating signifiers that are then used for other purposes: for instance, the notion of worship by dancing and singing in certain sects of Hinduism is now subsumed into the Hare Krishna sign, which is used in Western popular culture and film to connote several dimensions of the East-West exchange—the threat of Eastern evangelism, comic Otherness (the "dancing" as a sign of undignified practices of worship), the residual memory of the hippie spiritual cornucopia, etc. These signs therefore exist in the postmodern simulacra of transnational exchange: "the real is produced from miniaturized units, from matrices, memory banks, and command models—and with these it can be reproduced an infinite number of times."[7] When we take into account narratives constructed around a sign, in cases where there is a long history of narratives (such as in the relationship between the East and West), we can call them *scripts*.

I use the term *scripts* to connote several features of the cultural exchange within which the idea of the "subaltern" takes shape. A "subaltern" Other is exchanged as a sign between, say, the Third World and First World reading public or between the upper and middle classes within a nation-state; this sign (operating at the metonymic level) *enters* and *becomes* the heart of a narrativization of the hegemonic relations between the two exchangers of meaning. For example: a narrative or *script* of the West as being the realm of progress, freedom, and the guaranteed expression of individuality assumes a subaltern Other who desires residence in similar circumstances. Then a historical moment arrives when a person or group from the "East" or "Third World" appears to be in need of the West's free and progressive support. My contention is that often this "moment" is already scripted or anticipated; the *performance* or a (predetermined) demonstration of need is always about to begin. Thus the perceived subaltern figure or group fits easily into the screenplay, *filling* the absent center. The reading/decoding of an event resurrects a script by *condensing* the subaltern into a certain feature (a personality trait, action, remark) and then *amplifying* that feature to fill the whole narrative space.

I deliberately use the idea of "scripting" to establish the predetermined nature of the narratives that the First and Third Worlds produce about each other. The Nasreen case is one in which the geopolitical investments in acts of narrativization become exposed without effort. One simply has to put together news releases from a particular nation—the immensely complicated French reception is the best example here—to see how granting Nasreen "political asylum" had more to do with European, Western, and national identities than with her plight. Nasreen as signifier (a textualized point of reference) *enters into* and *fills* these French scripts. In such cases of political manipulation, simulacric prescripted notions of progress, freedom of speech, and so forth become useful in shaping public perceptions. This brings us to another point of analysis, one that moves beyond the post-structuralist comforts of simply identifying occurrences at the level of signification.

The production of scripts must be placed in their material and political contexts of exchange. As the French example will show, the dislocated reproduction of a script has a contextual force-field that gives it re-visibility. These force-fields may incorporate many, sometimes conflicting, relationships: in this instance, the French reading of their "liberal" history (via Voltaire) engages with the French discomfort and recuperation of their "liberal" anti-fundamentalist take on Algeria. These political and material relationships create an overdetermined script of French liberalism, which is then taken out of those contexts and mapped onto the scripts of the Nasreen affair (scripts constructed around Nasreen as a sign—the syndrome of the Third World woman/writer in distress). The performance of given scripts—some of which entail deliberate misreadings or major exclusions—as a signifying practice for current tensions *masks* those present conflicts, often deflecting attention or closing over the gaps and contradictions of the historical moment.

As any project of demystification will show, an exploration of such overdeterminations reveals the various alliances and antagonisms that create them, and prevents any binary mode of reading transnational texts. The scripts turn out to be unstable, produced and then dismantled, the excess in the overdetermined symbolic exposing the dynamic force-field of power relations behind each script.

Such exploration is made possible because, in an era of transnational cultural exchange, these scripts are constantly under contestation and critique by mobile populations who do not occupy stable locations in the world. Westernized liberals in Bangladesh with ties to their Bengali counterparts in India, as well as the Bangladeshi diaspora in Europe and the United States, address the Nasreen affair in ways that complicate easy First World/Third World, Islamic/Christian or Islamic/secular, male/female dichotomies; their responses reveal the new, complex, and unstable linkages that are emerging in this transnational era. By marking the series of shifting political positionalities that emerge from the Nasreen affair, positionalities that implode binary hegemonic relations, I hope to add to the recent analyses of transnational political and discursive relationships.

CONVERSATIONS ON TRANSNATIONAL CULTURAL EXCHANGES

There has been a surge of critical commentary on the politics of location in the 1990s, as critics scramble to theorize an era of diaspora and displacement. As Caren Kaplan (1994) notes, linear history has failed to account for the complex linkages of self, culture, and politics that emerge under transnational capitalism; hence the recent emphasis on space, place, and position within the globalizing processes of transnational capitalism.[8] While bell hooks, Michelle Wallace, and Adrienne Rich have all approached the problem from the question of production, Kaplan has asserted the need to also historicize the processes of "editing," "distributing," and "consuming" (139). Elspeth Probyn brings the two sites together in her evocation of the sites from "where we speak and [from] which voices are sanctioned."[9] Others, such as Robert Carr and Jennifer Browdy de Hernandez, analyze conventions historically emerging as a result of these relations of production and consumption: they both enter into a conversation on the "testimonial" as a reinscription of the subaltern "testifier" into the liberal voice of the "scribe."[10]

In another set of conversations, First World feminism has come under attack from several third wave feminists who critique the humanist stress on producing "voices" from the third world. Caren Kaplan and Amarpal Dhaliwal, in two separate essays, interrogate the anthology *Our Feet Walk the Sky* for its attempt to "include" and failure to then account for heterogeneous differences within South Asian women's experiences.[11] To whom, asks Dhaliwal, does this anthology speak? Perhaps the model consumer of corporate publishing in sync with the liberal discourses of multiculturalism and absorbed by the neocolonial passion for difference. Liberal feminism reproduces the image of the female individualist by eliciting self-expression and self-disclosure from the subaltern. If the subaltern is invisible, to *whom* is this invisibility visible? The arguments of Kaplan and Dhaliwal build on Chandra Mohanty's (1991) warning that there are epistemological problems in First World feminist productions of knowledge about the Third World.

I place my reading of Nasreen in the context of recent conversations on the use of certain South Asian women writers analyzed by postcolonial scholars. Particularly of interest to my project is work by Inderpal Grewal, Amarpal Dhaliwal, Anuradha Dingwaney Needham, and others on the Indian diaspora, included in a special issue of the *Socialist Review* (1994).[12] The writers in that issue variously critique the homogenizing and overdetermined production of "South Asia" as a label for a multi-locational and heterogeneous diaspora, the modernist privileging of nation-states as defining locations even in conversations about migrancy and displacement, and the need in First World reception-contexts that makes such hegemonic gestures possible, even required.

Grewal's sharp and sensitive argument about Bharati Mukherjee's representation within the academy and the press in the United States is an excellent illustration of the arguments presented in this volume. Grewal argues that the contemporary consumer passion for difference, with all the humanist residues implicit in cultural studies and multiculturalism, unproblematically authenticates the subaltern "voice" and "text," often leading to other exclusions in the subaltern's context of production.[13] A writer who presents Indian women protagonists from an upper middle-class, urban perspective, Mukherjee is used repeatedly in ethnic studies or women's studies courses as *the* diasporic South Asian voice. In her critique of Mukherjee's novel *Jasmine,* which features the escape of a South Asian (Punjabi) woman to the United States, following communal violence in her home state, Grewal points out Mukherjee's "conservative and positivist view of South Asian women and communal relations in South Asia." Such a view, she argues, excludes the agency of Indian peasant women who deal with communal violence in their daily existence, and participates in the discourses of freedom which see America-the-good as the place where the simple Indian girl becomes a "woman who thinks for herself" in the classic spirit of Euro-American feminism.[14]

To critique Mukherjee's voicing of certain subaltern concerns is to focus on the site of production and the politics of the encoder. But as theorists of locational politics have emphasized, the site of consumption is equally integral to restoring full signification—*who* uses this text and for *what* purpose. The academic divvying up of the minority pie creates an institutional situation where some works, such as *Jasmine,* assume an overdetermined significance: this text can be taught in courses that can be cross-listed, and therefore considered available, for ethnic studies, cultural studies, the multicultural or diversity requirement, women's studies, postcolonial studies, and every other necessary but underfunded knowledge base that polishes the images of universities as bastions of liberal inclusion. Thus, as Grewal suggests, the antiracist and liberatory rhetorics in *Jasmine* must be understood as replicating the exclusionism of progressive modernist gestures: differences in class, religion, location, and so forth are elided by both encoder and the decoder.[15]

I have gone to some lengths to present these analyses because they bring some important issues into focus. First, the case of Mukherjee illustrates the way in which the "voice" in a text is still read as the "expression" of its "author"—the originator of meaning—especially in the case of ethnic or gendered others. Mukherjee herself is scripted through the humanist rhetorics of liberal feminism and multiculturalism. Thus the question of receiving subaltern texts almost always brings into play a politics of identity. Second, it is equally clear that this politics of identity can come into play because of certain material and cultural practices that govern (cross)cultural exchanges; here, the academy and corporate publishing are the institutions/practices that enforce the conditions of a capitalist economy on textual practices. My analysis of Taslima Nasreen will take both these assumptions into account, but the institution I will focus on is the press in India, Europe, and the United States. My extrapolation of voices from the press will, of course, in its turn, subalternize (not record) the non-literate publics in all these spheres since their reactions to the event are represented by the educated, middle-class journalists, writers, and intellectuals. But again, my intention is not to "include," in classic humanist style, every voice, only to trace the differential subalternity in each rhetorical gesture to which I have access from a First World location. The politics of my own location should be the lens through which this essay is read. As Kaplan (1994) notes:

> Most important, feminists with socioeconomic power need to investigate the grounds of their strong desire for rapport and intimacy with the "other." Examining the politics of location in the production and reception of theory can turn the terms of inquiry from desiring, inviting, and granting space to others to becoming accountable for one's own investments in cultural metaphors and values. Such accountability can begin to shift the ground of feminist practice from magisterial relativism (as if diversified cultural production simply occurs in a cultural vacuum) to the complex interpretive practices that acknowledge the historical roles of mediation, betrayal, and alliance in the relationships between women in diverse locations. (139)

With Kaplan's warning in mind, perhaps it is best to frame my own position in reading the Nasreen affair, for I do write this partly in solidarity with her. Since the essay attempts to juxtapose various scripts in order to expose their constructedness, it is necessary to point to my own (overdetermined) response to the use of Nasreen as a signifier.

First, the question of access: as an academic working in a First World location, I have more access to the Western press releases than I do to those from Bangladesh and India. I am, however, a native speaker of Bengali and have depended on news items collected from Calcutta and Bangladesh that also address this affair. But my spatial dislocation limits the depth of my research into those subcontinental presses. I am also limited by my lack of knowledge about other Indian languages, and so I have focused on news in English and Bengali. These parameters have produced only certain kinds of scripts for the reader's consumption here. Second, the issue of cultural identity. I was brought up in a liberal Hindu tradition, which probably implies I may initially start with a harsher view of Islamic fundamentalism than a Muslim believer might have. I have tried, as much as is logically possible, to confront my internalized prejudices against fundamentalist Islam by recognizing that these new religious militancies comprise some of the dominant anti-imperialist movements of our time. I do find some biographical affinity with Nasreen in that she is a liberal atheist who has lived in an urban cultural milieu that privileges Bengali literature and language over folk traditions and other Indian languages and literatures. These considerations create an uneven level of knowledge in the essay: for instance, I am capable of presenting a sustained analysis of Bengali (Dhaka and Calcutta) liberal traditions in tolerance, but offer only fragmented glimpses into Bengali and Bangladeshi rural folklore. The West Bengali/East Bengali divide (East Bengali referring to those who live in India but were originally from Bangladesh) gives me less access to Bangladeshi culture than someone from an East Bengali family in Calcutta would have. As a diasporic nonresident in the United States, having lived in several cities, I also present a more urban middle-class perspective on this affair.

THE "NASREEN AFFAIR"

The National Moment

The "Nasreen affair," repeatedly claimed as an internal problem by the Bangladeshi government, had its beginnings outside of Bangladesh, in India, 1992, with the destruction of the Babri Masjid, an event to be understood in context of India's history of Hindu-Muslim violence. It was argued that Babar, the Muslim ruler and conqueror, had desecrated the temple constructed to mark Ram's birthplace (Ram, the hero of the Hindu epic *Ramayana,* is worshipped as a god throughout India); Babar had built the Babri Masjid on the ruins of that Hindu temple. Under renewed Hindu militant fervor, fueled by religious sectarianism, Babar's mosque was torn down in a riot in December, 1992. Almost immediately, communal violence swept over India as Muslims took revenge by destroying Hindu temples, and Hindus retaliated in turn; when the death toll had risen to a thousand, violence spread to Bangladesh and Pakistan, both of which have an Islamic majority.

In February 1993, Taslima Nasreen, a practicing gynecologist and writer in Bangladesh, known for her outspoken feminist tracts against Islamic laws pertaining to women, published *Lajja*—a novel that effects a strong critique of Muslim violence against Hindus in Bangladesh. Perhaps little would have happened if the moment had not proved ripe for Muslim fundamentalist groups to strengthen their political position by attempting to destabilize Begum Khaleda Zia's government. Moreover, national prestige became the issue, since *Lajja* was picked up by Ananda publishers in Calcutta (where the same language, Bengali, is spoken), and Nasreen was misquoted by a Calcutta newspaper for criticizing the *Qur'an.* Even though none of the scripts I analyze later in this paper really address *Lajja*—except as "sign" of an existent problem—I digress here to present a short reading of the novel and why it, and not simply Nasreen's alleged critique of the *Qur'an,* might have offended the Islamic fundamentalists in Bangladesh.

"Lajja" translates as shame. Nasreen indicts all Muslims in Bangladesh of "shameful" complicity with, participation in, or acquiescence to the violence against Hindus following the Babri Masjid riots in India.[16] The novel's title reverberates: by the end of the national debacle, Nasreen is produced as the image of Bangladesh's shame when confronted with transnational approbation.

Even before she wrote this particular piece, Nasreen was well known for her anti-communal and feminist writings. Born 25 August 1962 in Mymensingh, Nasreen came from a liberal background—her father too was vociferously anti-communal—and was quite outspoken about the effect of Islamic fundamentalism on women. Women have been the focus of much of her writing; she published several feminist tracts in newspapers, and her novel *Nirbachito Kolom* is a polemic against the increasing commodification of women in Bangladesh. When interviewed in May 1994, she outlined her plans for a new book—*Qur'aner Nari* (the woman in the *Qur'an*). Clearly she was a target, a sign of everything that was wrong with "liberal" Bangladesh, in the eyes of Bangladeshi Muslim fundamentalists. But I would argue that, even though the final straw seemed to be Nasreen's alleged criticism of the *Qur'an, Lajja* contained something that deeply offended these fundamentalists.

The novel is written in a journalistic documentary style with the fate of one Hindu family at the center of the narrative. Suranjan Dutta, a disaffected, unemployed Hindu youth, is the central character; he is a generation apart from his father, Sudhamoy, who had participated in Bangladesh's struggle against Pakistan from 1964 to 1971. Bangladesh, partitioned off from India along religious lines in 1947 when the British left (and known then as East Pakistan), ceded from Pakistan in 1971. The liberation war with Pakistan was based on perceptions of shared linguistic, cultural, and geographic commonalities within East Pakistan, ties that set off that imagined community from West Pakistan. Sudhamoy, the father in *Lajja,* thus has a secular vision of Bangladesh as a nation bound by ties of language, geography, culture, and a shared vision of civic peace. The arguments between father and son foreground different perceptions of Bangladesh as a nation: the patriotic father still believes in the magical promises of a newborn, secular nation, but the son, bitter and disillusioned, foresees an all-Muslim state where Hindus have very few civil rights and therefore argues for emigration to India.

Through this personal frame of a family story, Nasreen weaves the history of Hindus in Bangladesh (citizens who have remained in Bangladesh because they believe in national, rather than religious, allegiances): their dreams, fears, anxieties, and beliefs; their friends and neighbors, both Hindu and Muslim; their family and relatives, most of whom have fled to Hindu-dominant India. Large sections of the novel detail specific violent acts against Hindus taking place at the time, as well as similar past acts encouraged by the rising Islamic fundamentalist control over the state and the people. There are pages and pages listing temples burnt, businesses looted, and families violated. These lists break the rules of narrative realism—especially when they are mentioned in conversations between friends and neighbors—and make *Lajja* a historical document. Nasreen painstakingly, and in a journalistic manner, details places, streets, different localities, and families in such a way that the reader loses the sense of inhabiting a novelistic world and begins to treat those details as facts. Along with these lists, Nasreen intersperses Bangladeshi legal and political tracts pertaining to religion and nationhood: she mentions acts and statutes that discriminate on grounds of religion, even as she quotes and paraphrases several political thinkers who had called for a secular nation.[17] Nasreen offers fragments of the official history of Hindus in Bangladesh. Through her personal frame of one family and their network of relatives, friends, and neighbors, however, she also includes feelings, viewpoints and/or knowledges that remain in the popular memory of heterogeneous communities within the nation.

While *Lajja* works through several conflicts that the main protagonists have to negotiate, the central conflict is that of civic nationhood versus religious nationhood. In this case, Nasreen plays the omniscient narrator who makes critical comments that reiterate her views expressed elsewhere. In various interviews she has claimed that "culture" (the Bengali language and literature) is *the* definitive force in nation building. She indicts the *mullahs* who exercise political power in Bangladesh by arguing that these same fundamentalists were traitors to the Bangladeshi cause during the liberation war; they had sided with Pakistan and the idea of a Pan-Islamic culture (thus the use of religion as the nation-building tie). Here, I use the term fundamentalist to denote the scriptural activists in Islamic public spheres who want to translate the sacred texts directly "into thought and action."[18] Since *Lajja* rewrites history and questions religious politics, it is no surprise it was banned in Bangladesh. A journalist, Suhas Chakma, points to the fact that the current Bangladeshi government has a history of repressing alternative cultural documents: it had banned *Ekattorer Jishu* and *Smriti Ekkator,* controversial films that raised the specter of local collaborators (with West Pakistan) during the 1971 liberation war.[19]

Nasreen uses gender to effect her critique of Bangladeshi politics and individual political responsibility. She presents gender as the overdetermined symbol of all other unequal relations. For instance, the marginal position of Hindu *men,* their lack of civic rights, political power, and economic privilege within the Islamic state, is represented by the father's symbolic loss of sexual potency. This emasculation takes place in 1971, and so the new nation generates an impotent Hindu subject. Moreover, the two climactic events of violence and revenge are figured through two rapes: the abduction and possible rape of Maya, the Hindu daughter, which marks the moral destitution of the Dutta family; and the rape of a Muslim prostitute by Suranjan, the son, as revenge for Maya's abduction. (The latter scene is graphic in its violence and sympathetic to the plight of the economically deprived Muslim woman who submits to the rape for money).

What is poignant here is the passion for Bangladesh that resounds through *Lajja.* Even as she is marginalized, Nasreen seems to perceive herself as constructed by the Bangladeshi nationalist and gendered discourses. In being a part of that nation, she asserts her Islamic right of *ijtehad* (the right to debate), which, critics argue, disappears under fundamentalist controls over interpretations of the *Qur'an.* In *Lajja,* Nasreen takes on the Bangladeshi state, religion, and citizens, indicting all Muslims for participating in—or at least condoning and acquiescing to—the violence against the Hindu minority. She uses her position as a woman as an entry point into nationalist and religious politics, thereby transgressing many kinds of boundaries (speech, gender, citizenship) as she interrogates the various inequalities. By the same token, gender is not a unified category for her, but one redefined by the kind of nationalism one believes in as well as one's religion.

For the sake of analysis, the reception to the Nasreen affair within the Bangladeshi nation can be categorized into three kinds of reactions: Muslim fundamentalist political opposition to the Zia government, that is later articulated as *jihad* against the West (and India); the Bangladeshi liberal opposition to Muslim fundamentalists; and finally, the liberal re-actions of the Bangladeshi diaspora in Europe and the United States. Each of these reactions reveal a set of positionings in relation to the Bangladeshi body-politic, positionings that implode any internal consis-tency of a national response to the Nasreen affair.

Bangladesh, a nation of 116 million people with a Muslim majority, is not an Islamic state—in that not all national laws are based on the reli-gion. In fact, it boasts a democratically elected woman leader whose government has brought economic liberalization and social reform in the past few years. The Jamaat-i-Islami, which is the largest Muslim funda-mentalist party in the opposition, holds only eighteen out of three hun-dred seats in the parliament. This is also the organization that was banned in 1971 for collaborating with West Pakistan and *against* Bangladeshi independence. Certainly, *Lajja* lashes out against such anti-Bangladeshi stances by posing a central question: why, since Hindus and Muslims had fought shoulder to shoulder on grounds of *geographic* and *cultural* integrity in 1971, are Muslims now killing Hindus on the basis of religious divisions inflamed by those very people who had traitorously stalled Bangladeshi independence? Perhaps this question was too accu-rate to be tolerated. But perhaps, also, Nasreen's history of being an out-spoken feminist and Westernized liberal made her an easy scapegoat for the Jamaat-i-Islami's anti-Khaleda/anti-liberal agendas.

With Nasreen as target, a thirteen-party coalition of Muslim funda-mentalist political groups, headed by the Jamaat-i-Islami, became possi-ble. After Nasreen's book appeared in Calcutta, she visited that city in May 1994. At this time, a Calcutta newspaper misquoted Nasreen: she was said to have criticized the *Qur'an* in an interview. In reality, she had criticized the *Shariat* laws governing the marriage and divorce of women and men. However, this was a cue that the Bangladeshi fundalmentalists could not give up; they created a furor, ransacking newspaper offices and holding demonstrations demanding governmental action against Nas-reen. The Khaleda government, bowing to pressure, ordered Nasreen's arrest on 4 June 1994 under the penal code 295, which stipulates that cit-izens can be arrested for violating the religious feelings of their fellow citizens; if found guilty, Nasreen would be imprisoned and subjected to two years hard labor. Reportedly her passport was also seized, although the government denied this, and in panic, Nasreen appealed to the Women's Writer's Committee in New York (a branch of the international writer's organization P.E.N. [Poets, Essayists and Novelists]). Fleeing ar-rest, Nasreen disappeared from public view.

On 10 June Syed Nazrul Islam, a member of the Islamic Preachers Party, offered a *fatwa—takka one lakh* ($2500)—for Nasreen's life. Immediately, on 11 June Dhaka progressives and intellectuals rallied to protest the death threat and demanded a governmental investigation. Caught between the devil and the deep sea, on 15 June the Zia government ordered an inquiry into the *fatwa*. But the fundamentalist uprising was not to be checked. On 26 June another politician, Muhammed Alam, backed up the *fatwa* with another *takka* fifty thousand in a public rally, and this was followed the next day by a general strike protesting Nasreen's absence. The Committee for Resistance against Nonbelievers was set up, which called for Nasreen's public execution. In an attempt to quell further violence, the government seized explosives from the offices of the Jamaat on 30 June 1994.

Aftershocks rippled through the subcontinent. While the Indian government was conspicuous in its silence (fearing offence to its Muslim minorities), Nepal condemned Bangladesh's antidemocratic activities. Sri Lanka banned *Lajja* on 19 July 1994. A ripple effect: what seemed to be an internal fracas among pro-Islamic groups, the Bangladeshi government, and Dhaka's artists, intellectuals, and students acquired a new dimension in July when the West entered the conversation. So far, India was the only other nation involved in this affair. But on 3 July violence erupted in Dhaka following reports that Nasreen was being sheltered by a Western "ambassador." This occurred on the same day that the educational body of the UNESCO, Washington, and Norway appealed to the government for clemency on Nasreen's behalf. On 14 July President Clinton's appeal was protested in Dhaka by pro-Islamic groups who dissociated themselves from the death threats, and the United States rebuked Bangladesh sharply for anti-U.S. threats against the embassy at Dhaka. Bangladesh–West relations became strained in the weeks that followed: on 16 July Amnesty International charged the Bangladeshi government for "endorsing" the death threats; on 19 July the European Union instructed their diplomatic envoy to offer Nasreen asylum; this was backed by a similar offer made by Klaus Kinkel, Foreign Minister of Germany. The fury of the fundamentalists now turned against the West and India: the Islamic United Action Committee was set up specifically to decide on this affair, and they declared *jihad* against all enemies of Islam. Pakistan joined in the protest against Western interference in an Islamic country.

In the middle of all this, Nasreen made a court appearance on 3 August. On 9 August there were rumors of her meeting with the Norwegian

governmental representative and the possibility of her receiving a Norwegian passport. On 10 August, Nasreen fled the country. Almost immediately, the Jamaat accused the government of concocting a plot to aid
her escape; pro-Islamic supporters harassed Nasreen's parents in their
home on 15 August. With the onset of renewed violence, the Commonwealth decided to send a representative, Sir Ninian Stephen, former
governor-general of Australia, to act as a mediator between the government and the opposition parties. Black Thursday was observed to protest
Sir Stephen's arrival and there was an outcry from all quarters about renewed colonial interference. On 13 October the United Action Council
(including several thousand fundamentalists headed by the thirteen-party
alliance) besieged the Secretariat, freezing all government business.
They presented an eleven-point charter of demands, including an anti-
blasphemy law, the restriction of all NGO activities, and the establishment of the Islamic code for all spheres of life in Bangladesh.

   The pro-Islamic reaction against Nasreen is in many ways a reaction
to history; certainly Sir Stephen's visit was decried as a colonialist gesture. But it is also the *use* of history in a certain way. In anticolonial
movements in most parts of the world, (male) nationalist forces often
used women as signifiers of surviving/indigenous cultural authenticities.
As Deniz Kandiyoti (1991) shows in her analysis of the position of
women in the nineteenth- and twentieth-century modernist movements
in the Middle East (and as Yuval-Davis and Anthias have argued elsewhere), postcolonial national prestige often combines Western (modern)
notions of national sovereignty with antimodernist emphasis on traditional values: the dignity and reclusivity of Muslim women are juxtaposed to the demonization and sexual commodification of their Other,
the Western woman. As I read it, a similar move is made by the Muslim
fundamentalists in Bangladesh, who point to increasing Westernization
as the collapse of Bangladeshi identity: Nasreen is criticized for her
"moral laxity," as evidenced not only in her feminist tracts but also in her
two failed marriages and one love affair.[20] The fundamentalist critics of
Nasreen perform this script—one of moral laxity as sign of Bangladesh's
weakened cultural sovereignty—in order to mask their political opportunism. They use Nasreen as a signifier to undermine the growing feminist movement in Bangladesh that challenges the fundamentalists'
prescription of gender roles, and to mobilize their political opposition to
Begum Zia's liberal reforms. In other words, the historical anticolonialist
nationalist script is revitalized for new purposes; it is organized around a
newly signified "traitor"—the Westernized feminist Nasreen.

Such an antiliberalization, anti-Zia script is overdetermined by Bangladeshi perceptions of economic disparities between the First and Third Worlds. As Partha Chatterjee (1993) explains, the narrative of the modern nation incorporates a narrative of capital, in which social progress depends on the rational and egalitarian distribution of wealth.[21] In the Bangladeshi postcolonial economic experience, however, and that of other countries, the movement of transnational capital has led to an increased polarization of the wealthy and the indigent within nations. The Bangladeshi fundamentalists censured Nasreen for her luxurious lifestyle; ironically, as if to reinforce the disparity of wealth in the Third and First worlds, her tastes were depicted as "Spartan" by the French press.[22] The luxury to reflect on one's sexual needs dovetails into this script as a sign of decadence. Issues pertaining to wealth became even more focused when the Nasreen case became a source of anxiety for Bangladeshis who wondered if the West would "punish" their country and withhold crucial financial help and foreign investment. When Bangladesh received $1.9 billion from international donors in April 1995, in a two-day World Bank meeting, the Bangladeshi government had to pledge that they would step up investments in women's programs. A Bangladeshi nonresident, writing in the *Financial Times* on 25 March 1995, worried about the demonization of Bangladesh at a time when the country had undergone economic liberalization and was opening up to Western investment.[23] Clearly, Bangladesh's financial dependence on the West fueled the anti-Western script regarding economic disparity so well utilized by the fundamentalist forces.

The national fundamentalists thus enter into a larger Islamic discourse against Western capitalism. These Bangladeshi Muslim fundamentalists ally themselves with the poor of the world: they envision another global revolution with the scriptural activists (and not the proletariat) acting as the champions of the exploited—taking over after the collapse of the Soviet bloc. Edward Said, writing in the Egyptian paper *Al Ahram,* reiterates the economic link: he argues that Islamic militancy is born of the continued economic imperialism of the West and is a symptom of increasing poverty in "developing" countries with large Muslim populations. Islamic militants often react to the Western (and Israeli) demonization of the Islamic world by viewing the West as an "ahistorical world of pure despotism. Pure rage, pure violence, all of it in some way targeting 'us', a group of innocent victims who happen to ride buses or go about some harmless daily business, unconnected with decades of suffering imposed on an entire people."[24] Nasreen, despite her loyalty to Bangladesh, became a pawn in the performance of certain anti-Western militancies; she was branded as a traitor to the Islamic new world order. Following her reception in Europe, an Islamic conference was held in Casablanca, Morocco, on 9 December 1994 where the fifty member states criticized Nasreen for tarnishing "the image of Islam" around the world. The Sudanese minister of state argued that the Islamic renaissance has been resisted by the West through manipulation of icons such as Rushdie and Nasreen.[25] Such formulations echo the Bangladeshi fundamentalist identification with a world Islamic bloc; their eleven-point charter, for instance, sought to bring Bangladesh more in line with laws based on Islam that were already in place in Pakistan.

Of course, the anti-imperialist rationale promoted by the Islamic bloc becomes a little muddied when Bangladeshi fundamentalists lump Hindu-dominant India together with the Europe and America: they declare *jihad* against all hegemonists, in the subcontinent and the West. A Bangladeshi writer in China's *Mainichi Daily News* writes of the Hindu fundamentalists' fabrication of the seized passport story—invented to embarrass Bangladesh.[26] In such renditions, political, economic, and cultural dominance is overdetermined as Western (proto-colonial) and Indian (subcontinental Hindu). Such a conflation, given India's own experience of colonialism, exemplifies the kind of unstable political positionings that emerge from such events.

The Bangladeshi fundamentalists' performance of championing poorer militant Muslims offended by the feminist Nasreen and her Western supporters masks their anti-Zia political agendas. Such scripting—and they claim to speak for the entire nation—also *excludes* liberal Bangladeshi voices, responses that are also ignored by the Western press. Bangladesh boasts a heritage of Western-style liberalism that has its roots in the Bengal Renaissance (in colonial undivided India) of the mid-nineteenth century. This liberal impetus, channeled into the modernist discourses of secular nationhood, is exemplified by Sudhamoy (the father in *Lajja*), who supports egalitarian civic, linguistic, and cultural ties within nations, rather than religious ones. As the subaltern studies scholars tell us, this Western secularist tendency constructed communalism (affiliations to communities based on class, religion, or ethnic differences) against nationalism (the insistence on a horizontal brotherhood).[27] Partha Chatterjee argues that after decades of failed Western-style democracy in India and Bangladesh, these older affiliations to/narratives of community have surfaced to challenge the liberal inclusion model of a national imagined community.[28]

The Nasreen affair can be read against the backdrop of this reemergent conflict between secularism and communalism. Certainly, Dhaka liberals and intellectuals waged their own war against fundamentalism: on 7 July Bangladeshi artists staged a demonstration supporting Nasreen. Also in July, in sympathy with their Bangladeshi/Bengali counterparts, a corresponding two-hundred-strong rally of Maoists, students, writers, and poets marched against the Bangladeshi diplomatic commission in Calcutta. On 30 July, in the Chittagong incident, the Jamaat clashed with the All-party Students Society (an anticommunal group that called Golam Azam, the head of the Jamaat, a "war criminal" for his role in the 1971 war). On 8 August Bangladeshi secularists, in a meeting of the Committee against Butchers and Collaborators of 1971, accused the Jamaat chief of trying to turn Bangladesh into a fascist state. Using Enlightenment rhetoric, they complained that the Jamaat would undo the religion-state demarcation and return Bangladesh to the "Dark Ages."[29] These sentiments were echoed in Nasreen's own rhetoric: on one occasion, she indicated that Bangladesh needed someone like Kemal Ataturk (the Turkish liberal reformer *par exemplar*) at the helm of affairs and, on another, she referred to Martin Luther King's civil rights "I Have a Dream" speech.[30]

These Bangladeshi liberal formulations evoke several (Western) historical scripts: of the American Civil Rights movement (perceived of as internal critique within the West, but in the best liberal tradition); of fascism and war criminals; of "enlightened" rulers like Ataturk; of progress as best exemplified in democratic institutions. Borrowing from the West's liberal heritage is an easy step for a tradition that has its historical roots in the Westernized nineteenth-century Indian middle-class intelligentsia. Bengali liberal social reformers styled themselves as nation-builders; these were urban modern men whose successors are the secular upper-middle-class city-dwellers in Bangladesh and India—a section from which Rushdie and Nasreen hail. Thus, the liberal/intellectual forces in Bangladesh are aligned with other urban centers—in this case, Calcutta—against the "ignorance" of rural villagers. In one of the rallies noted above, the liberals flaunted cut-outs of snakes parodying the fundamentalist's threat that they had mobilized the villages and, if Nasreen was not captured, snake-charmers would let their snakes loose all over the country. This mockery of the threat of the snake marks a divide in urban and rural myths. The snake—particularly, the cobra *(keootay shap)*—represents an indigenous hidden power (read "the people"). One manifestation of this myth can be traced to an anti-British folk rhyme prevalent in Bengal that exemplified grassroots anticolonialism during World War II:

> *Sara Re Ga Ma Pa Dha Ni*
> *Bom phelechche Japani*
> *Bomer modhdhye keootay shap*
> *British bole baap re baap*
>
> [Do Re Me So Fa La Ti Do
> The Japanese have dropped a bomb
> There is a cobra in the Bomb
> The British cry out in fear] (translation mine)

What the British find in the bomb then, is not Japanese but Indian aggression, coiled and deadly as the growing anticolonialism; here, the connotation of the *keootay,* symbolizing a masked betrayer in the home, is fully exploited. In the Bangladeshi context I have been examining, far from symbolizing superstition (as the liberals saw it), the cobra symbolizes popular resistance. The liberal urban scripting of rural Bangladesh masks a class anxiety: the middle-class fear of being overrun by the militant poor who, in the urban middle-class view, would not be able to govern a nation. The liberal posturing reveals this middle-class intelligentsia's memory of and investment in their historical role of nation-building. This is not to say that the Dhaka liberals were intentionally pro-West; they too had problems with the West's projection of Bangladesh as a poor and ignorant nation. But their scripted response shows that the divisions in perceptions of the Nasreen affair cannot be read as a simple West/non-West dichotomy. These liberals are cultural hybrids, and their multilocationality marks one of the complex transnational relationships I have alluded to earlier.

One also needs to note that, ironically enough, Bangladeshi liberal secularism is also tied up with the Bangladeshi Left. An eight-party Left democratic conglomerate called a meeting on 27 July 1994 to protest the Jamaat-headed demonstrations against Nasreen. The Left claims to have the real pulse of Bangladesh, and so the Nasreen affair is portrayed as a struggle between the Left and the fundamentalists over "the [real Bangladeshi] people"; they emphasize class affiliations over religious ties, declaring Nasreen to be the champion of women and those oppressed by religious dogma. The Left has further been joined by other "progressives," such as the Rights Protection Committee, who espouse ties with West-based agencies (such as Amnesty International).

The Bangladeshi diasporic response to the Nasreen affair deserves attention since many of these reactions were articulated by those who saw themselves as culturally and politically marginalized in their Western nations of residence. Their comments are, thus, addressed as correctives to the dominant Western readings of the event. While some pro-Islamic comments seemingly align the nonresident speakers with Islamic fundamentalists, others target Western liberal hypocrisy for excluding Muslims from their definitions of progress. Such comments are articulated by those who obviously believe in liberalism and, often, count themselves as citizens of the West.

Dilip Hiro, the author of *Islamic Fundamentalism,* exposes the Western hypocrisy of singling out certain kinds of anti-democracy. For instance, he argues in the *Observer,* Bangladesh's poverty, lack of technological development, and violation of human rights receive more attention than the injustices (and even the acceptance of monarchy) that occur in the oil-rich gulf countries such as Saudi Arabia. "Don't tar all of Islam with the same brush," warns Hiro,[31] implying the covert racism in the West's look at Bangladesh. Shahid Mahmud, writing in the *Baltimore Sun,* argues that Rushdie and Nasreen are icons of the West's "vulgar liberalism," which has chosen to ignore the plight of poor Muslims in India[32]; others compare the hue and cry raised over a single woman's plight to the West's silence over the persecution of thousands of Muslims in Bosnia. Another writer, in the *Mainichi Daily,* pleads for a clearer understanding of the different branches of Islam. This writer argues that Sunni Islam, as practiced in Bangladesh, is very "unstructured" and that the Jamaat *mullahs* do not represent Islamic fundamentalism in the villages to any extent.[33]

Others seek to restore the sense of Bangladesh as a functioning national body politic with its own safeguards against religious intolerance. In an official capacity, A.F.M. Yusuf, from the Bangladesh High Commission in London, writes in the *Times* that the West's "Islamophobia" and fundamentalist "scaremongering" has produced a series of unsupported rumors; he refutes the fact that Nasreen's passport was ever seized, and proceeds to outline the legal options that would been available to her if she had not fled the country.[34] Still others point to Bangladesh's "quiet revolution," her progress as a nation that had gone unnoticed in the West,[35] and the fact that, now, Bangladesh is forever demonized as the realm of underdevelopment, superstition, and darkness. These nonresidents clearly accept the Western scripts of progress and capitalism, but claim allegiance to Bangladesh by placing her squarely among the civilized nations of the world. As bicultural emigrants to the West, they take responsibility for acting within a critical (Western) democracy, and for imagining the Bangladeshi nation along with their liberal compatriots/nation-builders in Bangladesh. By creating horizontal alliances across nation-state boundaries, their presence in the West and links to the East confuse neat geopolitical divides.

The three kinds of scripts I have demarcated in this section on Bangladesh reveal precisely the collapse of older discursive limits and differences, which had formulated the Third/First World or East/West distinctions. I now turn to similar categorizations of South Asian and Western scriptings of this event to show how clear subject positionings based on structural borders (men/women, liberal/fundamentalist and so forth) can be further dismantled.

The Subcontinental Debacle

In my earlier presentation of events, I briefly alluded to the fact that the Nasreen affair began in India and was further aggravated by the publication of her book and her interview in Calcutta. I now focus on Calcutta's reaction to Nasreen, because I have access to those press releases and also because Bengal shares a cultural affiliation with Bangladesh.[36]

India's response to the Nasreen affair can be mapped into four categories: issues of Indian hegemony in the subcontinent; religious sentiments (and the status of Islam) versus the rational/ secular argument; feminist responses (which will be dealt with in a later section); and questions of *Lajja*'s literary merit. The reaction against Nasreen in Bangladesh was obviously pitched as much against the Indian Hindu valorization of her work as it was against the Khaleda Zia government. When the novel was published in predominantly Hindu Calcutta, Nasreen was championed as a brave crusader. These reactions were picked up by Muslim fundamentalists in India; for example, Syed Shahabuddin, the Janata Dal leader, called for a ban on *Lajja* in India. After her escape to the West, India—notorious for banning any work that might offend its many religious minorities (e.g., *Satanic Verses* and *The Last Temptation of Christ*)—would not grant Nasreen a visitor's visa, finding the issue too sensitive for India's own fragile communal harmony.

At one level, many of these responses foreground India's perception of her relationship to Bangladesh as a member of the subcontinent; they are overdetermined by scripts governing the fifty-year-old India–Bangladesh relationship. Bangladesh is perceived of as a splinter community of the

Indian nation: this is especially so in the state of West Bengal, which is now home to the East Bengalis who immigrated to India following the 1947 partition and the 1971 war. Bangladesh is also the nation that was "saved" by India acting as big brother in her intervention into the 1971 East Pakistan–West Pakistan war. In other subcontinental political transactions, such as the nonaligned summits, India has also performed the role of the leader. In this context of Indian subcontinental political hegemony, if Nasreen had to be "saved," India would take the lead—not the West.

In the Indian press, anti-West sentiments, similar to those expounded by the Bangladeshi traditionalists fearing renewed colonialism, are expressed on grounds of criticizing Western postimperial relationships to the ex-colonies. An Indian journalist criticizes the West for intruding in a national affair, given that Nasreen, unlike Rushdie, was not a "citizen" of the West and should, therefore, play by the rules of her own milieu.[37] The West is further taken to task for imposing its "liberal standards" of conduct upon an emotional issue and a form of geopolitical militancy that it could not possibly understand.[38] Nasreen may be either valorized or criticized for her role in the shape of things, but the West is always the wolf at the door that the subcontinent must face together. In another attack, Bhagirath Misra rather pompously challenges Nasreen's sensational depiction of Islamic oppression of women; he argues that if she were an adept student of history, she would know that women are oppressed everywhere, and that Islamic repression is simply delicious consumption for the West in a climate of anti-Islamic feelings. In flowery rhetoric he attempts to show how the West makes a "luminous star" out of a "firefly" (Nasreen).[39] A third entry strenuously criticizes the South Asian countries for not offering Nasreen asylum first, thereby letting the West demonize Bangladesh; subcontinental fears of escalating communal violence are taken to task as being soft on religion.[40] These scripts present a notion of subcontinental responsibility for religious intolerance, a notion that, when seen from the Bangladeshi perspective, clearly reveals India's hegemonic role in the subcontinent—India's attempt at creating subcontinental standards and situations that ignore the national sovereignty of nations within that geopolitical space. Such fear of Indian hegemony has to be understood in the context of India's various takeovers of the princely states following Independence in 1947, her tense relationship to Nepal, and Bangladesh's memory of dependence on India for liberation from (West) Pakistan.

Besides India's performance of political hegemony, there is the Hindu-Muslim script in which Nasreen appears, once again, as a victim.

This script has its own history in the late nineteenth- and early twentieth-century Hindu nationalist perceptions that construed Hinduism as the more liberal of the two religions. These perceptions were fueled by a communally oriented political imaginary, which was itself the effect of precolonial Hindu–Muslim tensions and the colonial Divide and Rule policies. Thus, conceptions of Indian superiority determine the analyses of Islam that appear in the Indian press. One entry supports Nasreen but defends Islam by saying that her plight was not the result of a rigidity inherent in Islam itself, but of an ossified version of Islam found in particularly backward, poor, and illiterate societies where the checks and balances modulating power are not fully in place.[41] Here, Bangladesh is cordoned off from the rest of the Islamic world. The author argues that Nasreen should have taken refuge in another Islamic country.[42] Such critiques of religion come from India's (particularly Bengal's) long history of rational secularism (referred to before in my discussion of the Dhaka liberals). The Bengali diaspora writing in the West add to the complaint that Bangladeshi fundamentalism runs counter to Bengal's liberal traditions of religious tolerance propounded by Ram Mohan Roy and other luminaries in the nineteenth century.[43] This parochial Bengali variety of liberalism is reinforced by other Indian rationalists, who banded together in the Indian Rationalist Association to critique the rise of religious fundamentalism in South Asia. On 27 December, the IRA harangued the Indian government for refusing Nasreen a visa. Although the IRA located their own tradition in nineteenth-century anticolonial nationalism, they echoed Western [Enlightenment] rhetorics, viewing Indian secularism as presently under the "shackles of superstition."[44] Instead of recognizing communal intolerance to be the resurfacing of narratives of community that were submerged under imagining nation (Chatterjee 1993), these rationalists lumped all fundamentalisms together as superstition. They called for a horizontal alliance across nations in the subcontinent for those who oppose religious fundamentalism of any sort.

In their scripting of Nasreen and Islamic fundamentalism, these "rationalists" masked their real target: the rising *Hindu* fundamentalism in India. The IRA's call for an International Alliance against Fundamentalism was fueled by the event known as the "milk drinking miracle." In 1995, thousands of devotees flocked to a Hindu temple to witness a miracle: the sight of the elephant-headed god, Ganesh, drinking milk. The Indian rationalists accused the country of being in the "grip of mass hysteria" and offered a "scientific explanation" for the event.[45] Nasreen simply became the occasion for speaking out against communal tensions sparked by competing fundamentalisms in India.

Finally, an Indian script unique to the Calcutta press can be found in those responses that reproduce the cultural imperialism of West Bengalis toward their Bangladeshi counterparts. Calcuttans boast of Bengali literary luminaries and see themselves as the arbiters of Bengali language. Thus, eighty percent of the responses from the Calcutta press, unlike responses in Bangladesh and the West, discuss the literary quality of *Lajja* as a novel. Nasreen is depicted as an inferior, less literary, and overly journalistic writer: one writer comments on the fact that she writes a "document" and not a "novel," and that her "harangue style" in *Lajja* is more suited to the "podium" than the "pen."[46] Of course, numerous unfavorable comparisons are made between her direct style and Rushdie's highly acclaimed satirical and metaphorical one.[47] Never mind the fact that Nasreen's will to history is somewhat different from Rushdie's more Western, postmodern take on the subcontinent, and never mind the fact that Nasreen's testament to inequality is addressed to a nonelite public! Fellow writers vacillate between criticizing her literary style and supporting her as a writer-in-exile. For instance, in contrast to those who criticize her style, Annadashankar Ray places Nasreen in a distinguished canon, comparing her to Thomas Mann and Alexander Solzhenitsyn, other writers who wrote under repressive circumstances.[48] They claim to follow Nasreen's own self-styling as a literary figure: in interviews, she had evaluated Bengali literature with reference to West Bengali writers (Rabindranath Tagore and Buddhadev Guha), and traced her literary influences to Soviet (Maxim Gorky, Leo Tolstoy) and Western (Virginia Woolf) giants.[49] But then, these were interviews conducted while she visited Calcutta, where she was *asked* about her literary affiliations and evaluations.

A world alliance of writers seems to emerge from across the borders of Bangladesh, the subcontinent, and the West (see next section). A Bengali literary reference that appears in a news item on Nasreen—*Ore nabin, ore amar kachcha/Adhmoradher ghgha mere tui bachcha* [O young ones, O my fervent ones/ Awaken the half-dead with a blow;] (translation mine)—represents Nasreen as the emergent eternally young intellect who will shake up the half-dead world of tradition with a jolt of ire and fire. The Bengali *litterateurs'* discussions of literary merit reinstate Calcutta as the cultural center for the Bengalis, glossing over the East Bengal–West Bengal (Calcutta-Dhaka) tensions among present day Calcuttans.

As these different types of subcontinental responses suggest, the debate about Nasreen situates the subaltern as a differential position in the force-fields generated by geopolitical power exchanges. That is, Nasreen, India, and Bangladesh assume the dominated/silenced subject-position in particular hegemonic relations: for instance, Bangladesh is produced as economically, politically, and culturally lacking in the Indian press, even as India assumes a subaltern position to the West. When Nasreen is exchanged as a signifier in the Indian context, she is championed; in Bangladesh she is seen as the dominant aggressor affiliated with the West. Thus the signification of the subaltern figure (the person or the national community) changes drastically given different loci of power.

Woman in International Frame

Now we move to the outermost geopolitical limit—the "First" world. Of course, the diasporic responses have already propelled us into that sphere, but the West's questions of identity and responsibility deserve separate categorization.

The European responses to Nasreen's plight can be categorized into three parts: the furor over writers' freedom and the role of "free speech" in neocolonial humanism; the celebration and scrutiny of democratic spheres, including questions of "human" rights under nonegalitarian political regimes; and Western feminist readings of the plight of Third World women (dealt with separately in the last section).

One set of Western responses can be characterized by their commitment to intellectual freedom. As early as 31 July 1994 forty-three German writers rallied behind Nasreen, and she was invited to the German Booksellers Fair. On 17 August one hundred French-speaking intellectuals called on the Bangladeshi government to offer Nasreen protection in her own country. On 18 August she was awarded the Kurt Tucholsky prize of 150,000 crown ($19, 500) by the Swedish chapter of P.E.N.; the Turkish chapter of P.E.N. made Nasreen an honorary member on 3 August, dissociating Turkey from any links with Islamic repressive regimes. Gunter Grass appealed to Khaleda Zia (in an open letter, July 1994), in her roles as "premier" and as "woman." On 28 September the International Writers Parliament was created to combat the religious and political persecution of authors, and fifty top international authors met in Lisbon; they drafted a proposal for "refugee cities" using Nasreen's case and her difficulty in getting a French visa as an example of the precarious position of the outspoken intellectual. On 24 November when Nasreen did visit France, she appeared on the National Network, Channel Three, with renowned writers such as Wole Soyinka, Vargas Llosa, and William Boyd. All this is very different from the sharp criticism of Nasreen's literary merit that we saw in the Calcutta press. Nasreen becomes a sign of one more writer whose silence is a "loss to the whole world" (Mary Blume's reference to Stephen Spender's article, "With Concern for Those Not Free," when she adds Nasreen's *Lajja* to the list of "Books that Won't Burn" cataloged in the Index on Censorship).[50]

The script of the writer who pays the price for eternal vigilance, the new crusader, is an overdetermined one in that it reproduces the classic paradigm of the writer and modern/intellectual's inevitable alienation from the world and the concomitant act of "forging" the "conscience of [his] race," and the iconographic value of liberals fighting religious intolerance. The Voltaire reference discussed below exemplifies the latter, as do the constant references to the "Rushdie affair." In fact, on 14 June 1994, even before Nasreen fled to the West, the NPR show, "All Things Considered," staged the Nasreen dilemma. The show began with the sound bite of the Islamic call to prayer and ended, inevitably, with the voices in prayer degenerating into a babble of angry voices; Nasreen was fictionalized in the show, offering her point of view, and became nicknamed "the female Rushdie."[51] This staging provides the best example of the idea of *performing* a script that I have tried to establish in this paper. Other evidence of this script of writer-crusader appeared in the countless letters to the editor that were exchanged in the Western presses regarding this event: one man begins his entry in *Newsday Inc.* with the sentence, "I feel privileged to live in a country where speaking one's mind requires only a rebuke"; others bewail the "self-appointed thought police" and express relief over the fact that Europe is no longer suffering from "the religious disease."[52] Here, of course, the prescribed implications of the Dark Ages clouded by religious "disease" still rampant in the "developing" world are evident.

An article in the *Guardian* reinforces the humanist value of voice by applauding Nasreen's "giving voice to a silent revolution."[53] Within these concerns over intellectual freedom, we can identify a cluster of meanings constructed around the issue of free speech/voice in a critical democracy, a cluster that obviously overlaps with Western perceptions of selfhood, particularly public selfhood and its relation to speech and action. Nasreen is congratulated as the "humanist" subject who speaks out against oppression, and Europe as the agent that acts on her behalf. (Note all the letters sent on her behalf to the Bangladeshi government officials who were willing to give her protection if she would return to her country and face the charges brought against her.) Nasreen is both to be saved, and to be the savior of the sanctity of human freedom. The honor of saviorship, perfected as ideal by European colonialism, is bestowed on her through a round of human rights awards.

As Baudrillard cautions us, these discursive simulacric formulations have their reality-effects. Nasreen is cited as a "rebel" in the United States Department of State 1994 Human Rights Report (March 1995); this document often governs United States policy toward the countries cited as human rights violators. The French Edict of Nantes Prize for people who promote "tolerance and freedom of conscience" was awarded to Nasreen on 4 November 1994. To make up for her French visa problem, on 30 November 1994, Alain Juppe, the foreign minister of the Balladur government, presented her the French human rights award of $10,000; the award goes to those who fight for "freedom of opinion and opposition to all forms of religious intolerance."[54] The crowning moment came, on 15 December 1994 at Strasbourg, when Nasreen was awarded the Sakharov prize for human rights, a prize previously awarded to Nelson Mandela and the Bosnian newspaper *Oslobojenje*. At least at this point, some French intellectuals protested the excessive media exploitation of her case and complained of the "Nasreen mystification." By 1996, Nasreen had become one of the Oxford Amnesty lecturers on political dissent. As is evident here, the writer/free speech/human rights cycle of scripts overflows into the next category of scripts: the celebration of the Western democratic ideal. It is this ideal that maintains the other rights elucidated in this section.

A 1993 song by the group Pet Shop Boys images the "free" Soviet union metaphorically moving West: "there where the air is free, you'll be what you want to be." It is a pop reference to be taken seriously, and the Nasreen debacle demonstrates the West's renewed sense of righteousness after the fall of the USSR. Much of the rhetoric analyzed in this category focuses on Islamic fundamentalist states as the new centers of repression that would soon fall to the Western democratic ideal. In the German rendition of this script of (another) new world order, Nasreen was falsely reported to have said that Helmut Kohl was the man to deal with the fundamentalists; this "recommendation" from the victim, said to have taken place in an interview with the *Focus* magazine, was soundly denied by Nasreen. The Islamic fundamentalist "persecution" of Nasreen spiraled into an outcry against the German Orientalist, Professor Annemarie Schimmel, who won the German Book Trade prize. The reason for the outcry? Professor Schimmel had tried to elucidate the background to the death threats against Rushdie, attempting to explain Arab anti-West sentiments. While the German government, priding itself as one of the few European nations to build effective bridges with Arab nations, granted Schimmel this peace award, the public reacted with violent outrage. In the meantime, the Swedish conservative Prime minister, Carl Bildt, used Nasreen's arrival in Sweden on 9 August to further the image of his government as liberal, merciful, and the protector of democratic rights all over the world. Once again, Nasreen-as-signifier filled an already existent script of democratic toleration, a script that was harnessed by various political interests for specific (masked) agendas.

Perhaps the most interesting, here, is the French example, given France's strained relationship to Algerian fundamentalism. The use of Nasreen in this case reveals the West's uncertainty and confusion in the postcolonial era; attempts to forge new ties with the ex-colonies are constantly aborted by colonial hangovers of political and economic superiority. As early as 3 July the Paris-based Women's Alliance for Democracy called for daily rallies outside the Bangladeshi diplomatic commission. But when Nasreen arrived in Europe, France offered her a twenty-four-hour visa on the grounds that her presence would jeopardize national security. (France had also denied Rushdie a visa earlier that year.) This created a furor in the French press over the fact that France had "bowed down" to political terrorism. This was a "slap in the face" for France. French television host Bernard Pivot, on whose program Nasreen was supposed to appear on 13 October 1994, asserted that France welcomes dissidents, even though the spineless Balladur government does not; he cited Voltaire as an example of the French spirit, referring to the latter's famous critique of the "monster of intolerance."[55] On Voltaire's tricentennary, 22 November 1994, the Arte Channel aired a three-hour special on Voltaire deliberately dubbed "The Voltaire Affair." The French premier, M. Balladur, who had earlier responded with irritation to his government's decision on the Nasreen visit by asserting that France was a "civilization of uniformity" and did not follow the Anglo-Saxon model of diversity, now entered a debate with the foreign ministry on how to restore credibility to his tarnished image. (It is speculated that this comment targeted young unemployed xenophobic French youth sullen about losing jobs to immigrants.) Further, it is important to note here that Balladur was also being careful about offending Islamic fundamentalists in France, given a recent case where a French court upheld the decision to expel two girls from school for wearing headgear. This outraged Islamic fundamentalist groups in France; the possibility that the European court might uphold the girls' side of the case created much tension between liberals and Islamic groups in France. Moreover, the French government had denounced the Algerian fundamentalist party that had won the elections from the secular revolutionary government (in power since Algerian independence from France, 1962). French sensitivity on the issue of fundamentalism was further exacerbated by a prime time television show, *La Marche du Siecle,* which "doctored" (by adding beards) the pictures of three French Muslim citizens to make them look more like stereotypical "Islamic fundamentalists." (The three men in the photograph were supposed to represent the response of French Muslims to Algerian fundamentalism.)[56] Amid this French crisis over its liberal and democratic identity, dependent on a demonized repressive Other (read Islamic fundamentalists), the government finally welcomed Nasreen on 16 October 1994. At first, she refused to appear in France, but finally did arrive there on 24 November 1994. She was then given as much security as a head of state and was feted by the Paris literary world.

Clearly there are several determinants of the responses that allude to Western democracy. A Hobbesian reference to life before the social contract is made in the *Christian Science Monitor* where the Nasreen case is seen as a "challenge to the freedom of thought posed in the most *brutish* terms" (emphasis added).[57] *Brutish,* in context of Hobbes's work, implies a developmental trajectory in which Bangladesh has not quite figured out the civilized operation of the social contract. Rushdie's status as a British citizen protected by his rights in the democratic sphere is mapped onto Nasreen—she, too, becomes a protégée of the West. An entry in the *Times,* 7 September 1994, describes Nasreen's entry into the West as her "steps to freedom beyond ideology," suggesting, of course, that the West has few narrow worldviews that limit and repress its citizens.[58] Freedom of speech and action are certainly the key ingredients of the Western democratic recipe, but these items are highly priced in the world's moral bazaars—usually by "Othering" (and conflating) developing countries as not having quite made it. The conflation of the logic of freedom and the technological/material development presents the irony of this ideal: freedom is a commodity with a price tag available to countries that can afford certain organized checks and balances. Demystifying such ideological scripts becomes crucial when we see their reality-effects—for instance, the structural adjustment policies of the International Monetary Fund (IMF) that lay out a developmental trajectory for many Third World economies.

Other literary and cultural references creep into the discursive ma-
trix constructed around Nasreen in the West. Descriptions of Nasreen's
"escape" present symbolic codings of the West as coolly rational (with
Sweden as a prime example) and the Third World as a chaotic tropical
realm: an article in the *Financial Times,* titled "Safe from Screams of Intolerance," tells of Nasreen's escape from the "steamy streets" of Dhaka
to her new hideout in the "cool Swedish forests."[59] One does not necessarily have to quibble with adjectives, but the hot/cold analogy, with reason and elected government versus chaos and confusion, has a resonance
in British colonial texts that found India simply climatically unsuited to
reason: "Most of the inhabitants of India do not mind how India is governed. Nor are the lower animals in England concerned about England,
but in the tropics the indifference is more prominent . . . ," an observation
that E. M. Forster then links up to the sweat that "pressed the flesh,"
"pricked" the eyes, "scalded" the trousers, and made "domes of hotwa-
ter" accumulate under Indian headgear (*A Passage to India*).[60] In other
news items from the Western press, some blame for such Third World de-
bacles follows another orientalist cluster: the weak and despotic East.
For instance, an editorial in the *Christian Science Monitor,* 29 July 1994
reads Nasreen as a pawn for hard-liners against the government, a situation the government was wrong to "appease"—a reference to the historical calamities brought about by appeasement policies of the past.
Another item in the *Times* harnesses Anglo-American conservative
rhetoric, criticizing the Bangladeshi government for being too "soft" on
the militants.[61] While freedom is espoused as a rational ideal that grants
one respite from ideology, ideology is here construed as religion in particular (after the collapse of Communism) with Islam as the most pernicious example. Another article in the *Times,* following the one cited
above, strikes a Christian note in its title, "Martyred by the Mullahs."[62]
The connection between Western humanism and Christian tolerance is
refuted by liberal Islamists: a writer in the *Saudi Gazette* argues that Europe has a long history of religious persecution—why, asks the writer,
are Americans, with their persecuted Puritan ancestors, not savvy to
this?[63] Other diasporic Muslims living in the West take a liberal stance:
for example, Swedish Muslims welcome Nasreen as Swedes, applauding
Lajja but warning her against some minor factions that cannot be controlled even in Sweden. Most striking is an error that appears in a description of *Lajja* reported by the Angence France Presse on 3 August
1994.[64] The news release notes that the novel features a graphic scene involving the rape of a "Hindu" girl, while in actuality the rape of Maya

(the Hindu sister) is only surmised and the actual rape described is the revenge taken on a poor Muslim prostitute by Suranjan, the disaffected
Hindu protagonist of the story.[65] Where Islam can be slammed it is done,
and this error shows how Nasreen's own complicated arguments about
the relationship of women to Islam are streamlined by the Western press
to suit the script of a liberal West versus an intolerant East.

Feminist Circuits

While the Rushdie affair overdetermines all the scripts we have looked at
so far, the feminist scriptings of Nasreen in Bangladesh, India, and the
West mostly address the problems and implications of solidarity. I have
chosen to categorize them in a separate section because feminists all over
the world align themselves with horizontal alliances stretching across
national and geopolitical boundaries. Of course, as I have already noted
in the earlier section on transnational cultural exchanges, the problems
inherent to such acts of solidarity have been addressed by several postcolonial and feminist critics. The feminist responses to the Nasreen affair
are categorized according to geopolitical location, in keeping with wide
differences in local and national feminist struggles.

    Of the press clippings I gathered for this project, there were few
Bangladeshi feminist responses; most of what I could piece together
came from Calcutta and European presses quoting Bangladeshi women
on the Nasreen affair.[66] What is interesting in these references is the
ambivalence toward Nasreen that is evident in their comments. While
Nasreen is celebrated as a feminist hero in Western circles, some Bangladeshi feminists see her predilection for controversy as deleterious to the
painstaking work done by women's groups in Bangladesh. In a discussion organized under the aegis of the Bangladeshi daily, *Bhorer Kagoj*
(*The Morning Paper*), a group of feminists representing various elements
of the women's movement in Bangladesh (ranging from a well-known
woman poet, to a television personality, a professor at the Dhaka University, and the head of the Women's Rights group) expressed their resentment against Nasreen. Begum Suphia Kamal notes that she had urged
Nasreen to join in the struggle for women's rights, especially in her capacity as a gynecologist, but that Nasreen chose instead to embark on a
path of individual struggle; others, too, noted Nasreen's lack of interest
in collective enterprise. While Nasreen seemed readily available for interviews by the Western press following her notoriety, Bangladeshi femi-

nists felt she had little time to profile Bangladeshi feminism or even join in Bangladeshi women's demonstrations.

The views of these women reveal their construction of a collective mode of feminism where lone crusaders are regarded as traitors to the cause. Carolyn Wright, a Fulbright research fellow in Bangladesh who made Nasreen's acquaintance between 1989–1991, reiterates their perception of Nasreen as hungry for the spotlight. Wright notes that Nasreen was known for "pushing people's buttons" and for devaluing the work of her "fellow women writers and activists."[67] The Bangladeshi feminists' responses to Nasreen express their resentment at the victim-figure significations extended to all Bangladeshi women in the Western press; here, local feminist responses are scripted in reaction to anticipated international (Western) ones. Perhaps the Bangladeshi feminists' script also masks their fear of a fundamentalist backlash against the hard-won gains they have made under the Zia government. Nasreen responded to these feminist comments by acknowledging her distance from the women's movement in Bangladesh in an interview with Dipankar Ray of *Jugantor,* a Calcutta daily.[68] Thus, it is ironic that she became the figure whom Bangladeshi feminists were later forced to discuss in many international women's forums: the Bangladeshi representative at the Beijing women's conference received the spotlight because of the Nasreen affair and used the attention to explain how Bangladeshi fundamentalists use and control women for electoral purposes.[69]

For feminists in Bangladesh, Nasreen also transgresses class and religious borders of behavior and discourse. Some of these (more genteel) middle-class women, are offended by what they see as Nasreen's stridency and vulgarity. Others point to better, more brilliant Bangladeshi feminist writers, such as Begum Sakawat, who address the problems of women from an Islamic (but not fundamentalist point of view). These feminists argue that Nasreen, a self-acknowledged atheist, derives most of her thinking from the Hindu epics, *Ramayana* and *Mahabharata*. In view of such allegations, the fact that a Calcutta male intellectual, Annadashankar Ray, likened the metaphoric "fall" of Bangladesh to Lanka's destruction on account of Sita (the heroine of the *Ramayana*) only added fuel to fire.[70]

The reference to Sita, in an essay that also features Helen of Troy and the fall of that empire, points to the overlap of religious and gendered imagery. The depiction is a resoundingly male characterization of a historic conflict now waged in Bangladesh, with Nasreen (as Helen) now filling the center of that struggle. (Of course, there is little reference to the fact that the political confrontations occur between two *women* leaders—Khaleda Zia, the head of government, and Sheikh Hasina, the leader of the Jammat opposition.) Unlike in the case of Rushdie, whose genius was touted in press releases, descriptions of Nasreen are far more personal and often allude to her femininity; they relate to her size, shape, dress, and looks. We are told that she is "diminutive," "unwavering" and "tiny"; that she appears, on one occasion, wearing a resplendent orange-and-gold sari; that she has "steady eyes" and "soft skin."[71] I can't remember anyone describing Rushdie in quite the same way. Thus, even accounts that portray Nasreen as lone feminist crusader still inscribe her within a gendered system of cultural signs.

Women journalists and feminists in the Indian press are more unambiguously on Nasreen's side than are the Bangladeshi feminists. An Indian woman journalist points to the fact that while Rushdie's private life was never the index by which his literary output was measured, Nasreen faces closer scrutiny because she is a woman—her three marriages are often cited as signs of her "moral laxity," which, in turn (according to fundamentalist conservatives), accounts for her critiques of the Shariat laws.[72]

Indian men, too, offer sympathy, though sometimes through various mythifications. I have already pointed to the "Helen of Troy" metaphor. The sensationalist journalist Khuswant Singh talks mostly about himself in an article that begins, "I wish the girl had written a better book."[73] Interestingly enough, some of the most misogynist depictions of Nasreen come from the young male Indian diaspora. In a discussion of Nasreen on the Internet, one Indian immigrant to the United States accused her of "promoting sexual anarchism in the name of feminism"; of grabbing the spotlight—allegedly, when her sexual anarchism did not get enough attention, Nasreen started to criticize Islam ("Islam bash"); and of changing men like clothes. This gendered response can be explained by critical examinations of the conservatism of diasporic Indian men whose sense of emasculation in the West and fear of cultural attrition leads them to enforce far more rigorous gender standards (on South Asian women in the West) than their liberal counterparts do in South Asia (a recent example of this argument is made by Gurinder Chaddha in *Bhaji on the Beach*).[74]

"We came, we saw, we were horrified, we intervened." Lata Mani's (1989) classic formulation of the Western feminists' horrified response to the trials of Third World women presents the terms of this third cycle of scripts. In this final category, I place the Nasreen affair in context of the debates within feminism that have challenged the Western feminist paradigm of producing Third World women as "passive victims."[75] The paradigm is coherently outlined by Rebecca Santos, writing in the *South China Morning Post,* who represents Nasreen as "the Gloria Steinem of the East"; the article is in response to an article by Gloria Steinem in the *London Times,* and Santos argues that that piece comes as a "great irony" at a time when the oppression of women is escalating in Muslim countries.[76] The Western feminist response, then, is determined by both the feminists' imperial reading of the Third World and of fundamentalism as a particular threat to women's rights at this historical juncture. This kind of response is precisely what was anticipated by the Bangladeshi feminists in their withdrawal of support from Nasreen.

The Western feminist response, of course, makes the classic empathetic gesture of transcending lines of class, nation, and religion in celebration of a true global sisterhood.[77] Women's organizations in India, China, Paris, Turkey, Sweden, and other nations rallied to the Nasreen cause even before her entry into the West. An article in the *Washington Post,* 12 April 1995 criticizes the brand of academic feminism that insists on recognizing differences within the global sisterhood, pointing to the fact that women's struggles in the Third World can gain much from First World aid. The author also draws our attention to the difficulty of policy-making in a context where First World interventions are constantly regarded with hostility.[78] Some of these feminist writers extend their criticism to their own Western male counterparts: an article in the *Scotsman* points out that "even western commentators, view her [Nasreen] as an unruly, threatening woman"; the author cites the *Times Educational Supplement*'s descriptions of Nasreen as "haughty" and a "man-eater," and the *Financial Times*' comment that her chain-smoking "seems deliberately designed to offend."[79] But then, sighs this feminist writer: how did such a worldly spirit develop in such a conservative society?

On the edges of Western feminism, in March 1996, a year and a half after her great escape, Nasreen still found it difficult to celebrate International Women's Day. Speaking in Paris, she reaffirms her marginal status within Western feminism:

> *I suspect it is precisely because we still see women as weak and without defence . . . that we have judged it so well to institute a day for women. Has anyone ever had the idea of a day for men?*[80]

TO CONCLUDE: THE LOGICS
OF TRANSNATIONAL SCRIPTS

In my perusal of the scripts emerging from the Nasreen affair, I have tried to show how Nasreen is produced as a sign within a preexistent script that is best understood as a product of overdetermination. The French brouhaha over Nasreen's visa and the Bangladeshi fundamentalists' use of Nasreen as a sign are the most extreme examples, and so I take them up here to make a few concluding remarks.

The Bangladeshi fundamentalist script on Nasreen runs something like this: Nasreen's criticism of Islam violates the beliefs of the majority of Bangladeshis, who would prefer a state based on Islamic laws, and she exemplifies the evils of Western liberalization promoted by the present Zia government. Such a script has many causes/sources: the link between sexual expression, luxury, and the West; the view that liberal and antitraditional views are signs of decadent modernity; the belief that failed civic structures should be replaced by religious values, if Bangladesh is to survive as a nation; the growing distance between a liberal, urban, educated elite and the "real" Bangladesh. Within this script, snakes become signifiers of people's power based on faith; seized passports imply both the erosion of civil rights and the birth of a new moral order. These simulacric signifiers and the narratives that are constructed around them all appear in the overdetermined fundamentalist response to the Nasreen affair.

But the fundamentalist scripting is opened up to debate by the liberal progressive forces in Bangladesh. The liberals' parody of the snake myth, for instance, uses Western enlightened rhetoric that critiques popular "superstitions" as products of irrationality and ignorance. What the differences *between* scripts in a particular milieu reveal is the overdetermined ideological constructedness of each narrative that masks political opportunisms and agendas in the name of (social and religious) ideals and principles. The differences between the Bangladeshi liberal and fundamentalist scripts precisely expose the contradictions that those ideologies attempt to close over: for instance, both the left and the fundamentalist right claim to speak for "the people," but the very debate itself is proof that all of Bangladesh does not speak in one voice at all. Moreover, drawing horizontal relationships between communities living in widely different geopolitical spaces furthers my argument about these "scripts" as free-floating signifiers, which can be locationally and contextually adapted for use. The Bangladeshi liberal forces, with their affiliations with cosmopolitan urban centers, explode the national appropriation of Nasreen. They exemplify the mobile multilocational populations I alluded to in my introductory remarks; populations whose allegiances implode stable antagonisms between East and West or, in this case, Bangladesh and the world.

A similar argument may be made about the French case. Arguably, there are two major material and political relationships that shaped the French response to the Nasreen affair: First, the French liberal reaction to the Balladur government, a government that did not do justice to France's long liberal tradition (consider issues raised in "The Voltaire Affair"), and second, France's relationship to its colonial past, her postimperial responsibility to Algeria and accountability to new ethnic immigrants (consider the French ethnic crisis over the two schoolgirls' headgear and the television program row over the "false" beards). These mutually conflictual relationships both enter into the French scripting of the Nasreen matter, a script that can be articulated in the following way: France has a time-honored tradition of liberal resistance against religious intolerance, and we must live up to such a reputation by offering Nasreen asylum. Such attention to Third World distress might make reparations for France's colonial history in Algeria.

This overdetermined liberal script (with its simulacric signifiers in "Voltaire" and "fundamentalists' beards") might have stood on its own, despite its overdetermined symbolic excess, had it not been for France's Islamic diaspora. The discussions of Nasreen bring to the fore the row over the video editor who doctored the pictures of the three French citizens from the northern town of Lille; the men point to the falseness of the "beards" that have clear iconographic value as markers of Islamic fundamentalism for the French viewing public. Identifying as French citizens, and not Muslims, the three men protest their lack of belief in religious fundamentalism. The beards exist at the level of simulacra, and the incident exposes the contradictions inherent in the French liberal script. The Nasreen issue presented a way for France to voice opposition to Islamic fundamentalism without appearing to bear overt political hostility toward the Algerian Islamic Salvation Front as an enemy *par exemplar:* French liberalism could take the grand stance against the suffocation of free speech, without seeming to promote French civil values over Algerian lived ones. French immigrants, then, even when they act as citizens, implode the internal consistency of scripted national histories and traditions (of the modern era).

As these examples show, Nasreen becomes the signifier whose absence and displacement onto other signifiers (Rushdie, Voltaire, headgears, beards . . .) resounds in the scripts that are produced about her. Her case exemplifies the logic of exchange in our transnational material and symbolic contexts. While scripts are increasingly commodified and dislocated from their place in the real, the presence of mobile and multilocational populations opens these scripts up to debate.

In light of my arguments, perhaps it is necessary to end with my own overdetermination in representing the Nasreen affair. I have earlier explained my locational politics, and here I attempt to clarify the agendas implicit in this essay. Politically, I find myself in empathy with Nasreen. But keeping Caren Kaplan's call to distrust of such empathy, I have tried to distance my own feminist reading in this essay. As a feminist reacting with dismay to *Hindu* fundamentalist controls over women's sexuality and reproduction in the contemporary Indian context, I find myself applauding Nasreen's feminism. By the same token, as a postcolonialist, I find myself wary of the Westernized demonization of religious fundamentalism—especially keeping in mind the various analyses that pose religious militancy as the force that now fills the anti-West vacuum.

NOTES

[1]Stuart Hall, "Encoding, Decoding," *The Cultural Studies Reader,* Simon During, ed. (New York: Routledge, 1993): 100–1.

[2]Elke Schmitter, "Boycott Lufthansa: literature and publicity today—a few ruminations and a suggestion," Trans. Wilhem Werthern, *TriQuarterly* 94 (Fall 1995): 155–60.

[3]I extend my thanks to Radharani Ray for collecting news items from Calcutta for this project.

[4]Gayatri Chakravarty Spivak, "Can the Subaltern Speak?" in *Marxism and the Interpretation of Culture,* Lawrence Grossberg and Cary Nelson, eds. (Urbana and Chicago: U of Illinois P, 1988) 271–313. For a critique and retheorization of subalternity, see Sara Suleri, "Woman Skin Deep: Feminism and the Postcolonial Condition," *Critical Inquiry* 18 (Summer 1992): 271–313.

[5]See, for example: Stuart Hall, "Cultural Identity and Diaspora," in *Identity: Community, Culture, Difference,* John Rutherford, ed. (London: Lawrence and Wishart, 1990); Rey Chow, *Writing Diaspora: Tactics of Intervention in Contemporary Cultural Studies* (Bloomington: Indiana UP, 1993).

[6]Arjun Appadurai, "Disjuncture and Difference in the Global Economy," *Public Culture* 2,2 (Spring 1990): 1–24.

[7]Jean Baudriallard, "The Precession of Simulacra," in *A Postmodern Reader,* Joseph Natoli and Linda Hutcheon, eds. (Albany: State U of New York P, 1993), 342–375.

[8]Caren Kaplan, "The Politics of Location as Transnational Feminist Critical Practice," in *Scattered Hegemonies: Postmodernity and Transnational Feminist Practices,* Caren Kaplan and Inderpal Grewal, eds. (Minneapolis: U of Minnesota P, 1994), 138.

[9]Elspeth Probyn, "Travels in the Postmodern: Making Sense of the Local," in *Feminism/Postmodernism,* Linda Nicholson, ed. (New York: Routledge, 1990), 176–189.

[10]See Robert Carr, "Resisting Autobiography: Outlaw Genres and Transnational Feminist Subjects," in *De/Colonizing the Subject: Politics and Gender in Women's Autobiographical Practice,* Julia Watson and Sidonie Smith, eds. (Minneapolis: U of Minnesota P, 1992), 115–138; Jennifer Browdy de Hernandez, "Of Tortillas and Texts," in *Interventions: Feminist Dialogues on Third World Women's Literature and Film,* Bishnupriya Ghosh and Brinda Bose, eds. (New York: Garland, 1996), 163–184.

[11]Kaplan (1994); Amarpal Dhaliwal, "Reading Diaspora: Self-Representational Practices and the Politics of Reception," *Socialist Review* 24, 4 (1994): 13–44.

[12]This special issue (*Socialist Review* 24, 4, 1994) is an excellent resource for essays on South Asian identity, especially the following essays: Inderpal Grewal, "The Postcolonial, Ethnic Studies and the Diaspora"; Jasbir Puar, "Writing My Way 'Home' "; Anradha Dingwaney Needham, "Fictions of National Belonging"; and Amarpal Dhaliwal, "Reading Diaspora."

[13]Grewal (1994); Gayatri Spivak and Sneja Gnew, in "Questions of Multiculturalism" (*The Cultural Studies Reader*) talk of a politics of location where identity is produced at the site of reception by those who hear the subaltern speak.

[14]See analyses of similar problematics in R. Radhakrishnan, "Ethnicity in the Age of Diaspora," *Transition* 54, 104–115; Chandra Talpade Mohanty, "Cartographies of Struggle: Third World Women and the Politics of Feminism," in *Third World Women and the Politics of Feminism,* Mohanty et al., eds. (Bloomington: Indiana UP, 1991), 51–80; Lata Mani, "Multiple Mediations: Feminist Scholarship in the Age of Multinational Reception," *Inscriptions* 5 (1989), 1–23.

[15]The kinds of differences present within the "South Asian diaspora" are examined closely by other critics in this volume. For example, Amarpal Dhaliwal explains how the term "South Asian" is used to represent subjects from Bangladesh, Bhutan, India, Maldives, Nepal, Pakistan, and Sri Lanka, but is overdetermined by an Indian identity and, more specifically, a Brahmanical, middle-class

identity that overdetermines the term *Indian*. Even the idea of *diaspora* may exclude generational, regional and locational differences *within* the Indian diaspora: Punjabi communities in the United States constitute their cultural identity differently from those in the United Kingdom; Bengali communities in the United States profess regional cultural differences from the Gujarati diaspora; and even within one region-and-not-nation community in the United States, the change in the immigration laws in 1965 created different waves within generations of immigrants, waves demarcated by literacy, class, and labor skills.

[16]I am aware that Taslima Nasreen's *Lajja* has been translated into English, but I have not seen that version yet. My readings are from the Bengali text published in Calcutta, 1993.

[17]For instance, a list of past offenses against Hindus that Suranjan recollects continues for six pages. See Taslima Nasreen, *Lajja* (Calcutta: Ananda Publishers, 1993), 36–40. For an example of what I characterize as political tracts, see page 13.

[18]I am following Barbara Stowasser's differentiation between Islamic modernists, conservatives, and fundamentalists as a basic map. Stowasser argues that conservatives and fundamentalists are often lumped together in the pop generalization "Islamic fundamentalism"; in reality, the overlap between the two groups is relatively small. The conservatives believe in the scriptures and use them to legislate what custom, in turn, has long established—they base legislation on their interpretation of the scriptures; they also reject the "historicized *ijtihad*" and the admissibility of concepts such as "public interest" (14). Fundamentalists (traditions in Islamic fundamentalisms reach back into the Middle Ages) emphasize the *literal* application of the scriptures to everyday situations and locations (20–23). See Stowasser, "Women's Issues in Modern Islamic Thought," *Arab Women: Old Boundaries, New Frontiers,* Judith Tucker, ed. (Bloomington: Indiana UP, 1993), 3–28.

[19]Suhas Chakma, "In Sympathy with Devils," the *Telegraph,* 8 May 1994.

[20]Sonali Chatterjee, "Gritty Woman," the *Telegraph,* 18 June 1994. The Deniz Kandiyoti piece, "Identity and Its Discontents: Women and the Nation," first appeared in *Millenium: Journal of International Studies* 20, 3 (1991): 429–443.

[21]Partha Chatterjee, *Nation and Its Fragments* (Princeton: Princeton UP, 1993).

[22]French press quoted in a feature in the *Guardian,* 1 August 1994, T11.

[23]Letter to the Editor in the *Financial Times,* 25 March 1995.

[24]Edward Said, "War on 'Islamic Terror'," *Al Ahram,* 27 March 1996.

[25]From the BBC report from the Voice of the Islamic Republic of Iran on 10 July 1995, which quotes Ghazi Salah-al-Din, Minister of State in the Sudanese Foreign Ministry, in Khartoum (in an interview with Isam Hasan in Teheran, broadcast by the Iranian radio, 8 July 1995).

[26]From the *Mainichi Daily News,* 16 July 1994.

[27]See Gyanendra Pandey's analysis of nationalism and communalism in *Communalism in Colonial Northern India* (New Delhi: Oxford University Press, 1990).

[28]In fact, Chatterjee (1993) challenges Benedict Andersen's modernist conception of nation, which does not work quite as well in postcolonial contexts.

[29]Reported in the Agence France Presse, 9 August 1994. The news reports collected here are all from a Lexis search conducted by me at Utah State University, March 1996.

[30]Reported in the *Guardian,* 19 August 1990.

[31]The *Observer,* 7 August 1994.

[32]Shahid Mahmud, President of the Pakistan Forum, writing in the *Baltimore Sun,* 14 January 1995.

[33]*Mainichi Daily News,* 16 July 1994.

[34]The *Times,* 28 June 1995.

[35]Letters to the Editor, *South China Morning Post,* 18 August 1994.

[36]My rendition of Pakistani, Sri Lankan, and Nepalese reaction is brief because I have no access to material from there, nor am I familiar with the languages.

[37]N. J. Nanporia, "Through an Occident of Faith," the *Telegraph,* 9 August 1994.

[38]Ibid.

[39]Paraphrased from a Bengali newspaper, "Taslima, Try to Go to the Source" [my translation], Bhagirath Misra, *Amrita Bazaar Patrika* (27 August 1993); his denunciation of Nasreen meets opposition by Anuradha Dutt, "Thank God for Taslima," *Amrita Bazaar Patrika* (5 June 1994), with the argument that firsthand experiences count best toward cataloging oppressions. Other accounts of Nasreen's singling out of Islam (e.g. Parvez Hafeez, "The Sacred and the Profane," the *Telegraph* [19 July 1994]) point to the fact that there was no hue and cry over Sikh intolerance in a similar case where ten million rupees were offered for the death of the Pakistani author Sadiq Hussain.

[40]The *Times,* 2 July 1994.

[41]Danial Latifi, "Where Mullahs Rule the Roost," *Amrita Bazaar Patrika,* 29 June 1994; see also Nazreen Hussain, "Writes and Wrongs about the *Qur'an,*" the *Telegraph,* 22 July 1994.

[42]Ibid.

[43]*Financial Times,* 13 August 1994.

[44]Agence France Presse byline, 28 December 1995.

[45]Ibid. For a critical documentary on Hindu fundamentalism from a Leftist perspective, see Anand Patwardhan's *Father, Son and Holy War,* in which he makes similar observations on the mass hysteria following the 1987 Roop Kanwar sati.

[46]"Low Art, Moral High," the *Telegraph,* (17 June 1994).

[47]"Gritty Woman," the *Telegraph,* 18 June 1994.

[48]Annadashankar Ray, "Troy Destroyed for One Woman," *Amrita Bazaar Patrika,* 24 June 1994.

[49]See *Jugantor* interview (22 May 1994).

[50]Feature by Mary Blume, "Censorship Watch: Books That Won't Burn," the *International Herald Tribune,* 30 September 1995.

[51]NPR show, "All Things Considered," 4 June 1994, Transcript # 1503–7.

[52]Letter in *Newsday Inc.,* 23 June 1994; also from an Inter Press Service report, 19 July 1994.

[53]Feature in the *Guardian,* 1 August 1994, T11.

[54]Reported by the Deutsche Presse-Agentur, 30 November 1994.

[55]Reports from the Agence France Presse between 14 October 1994 and 24 October 1994.

[56]Report from the Agence France Presse, 23 November 1994.

[57]Article in the *Christian Science Monitor,* titled "The Islamic Thought Police," 21 July 1994.

[58]Reported by the Times Newspapers Limited, 7 September 1994.

[59]Reported by The McCatchy Newspapers Inc., 12 August 1994; article titled "Woman in the News: Safe from Screams of Intolerance."

[60]E. M. Forster's *A Passage to India* (London: Harcourt Brace and Company, 1924), 123.

[61]The *Times,* 2 July 1994.

[62]The *Times,* 9 September 1994.

[63]The *Saudi Gazette,* 1 January 1995.

[64]Reported by the Agence France Presse, 3 August 1994.

[65]*Lajja,* 139.

[66]Feature in *Amrita Bazaar Patrika,* 19 September 1994.

[67]Caroline Wright writing in the *Christian Science Monitor,* 18 August 1994.

[68]*Jugantor,* 22 May 1994.

[69]Agence France Presse byline, 1 September 1995.

[70]Annadashankar Ray, "Troy Destroyed for One Woman," *Amrita Bazaar Patrika,* 24 June 1994.

[71] Reported in the *Scotsman,* 11 April 1995; byline for Agence France Press, 3 August 1994.

[72] Anuradha Dutt, "Thank God for Taslima," *Amrita Bazaar Patrika,* 5 June 1994. Nasreen later clarified her comments on the *Shariat* laws (making things even worse, according to the *mullahs*) by asserting that she had suggested, "We need to move beyond these ancient laws, if we want progress." Quoted in the *San Francisco Examiner*, 29 May 1994.

[73] Khushwant Singh, "God save us from the godmen: with malice towards one and all," the *Telegraph,* 20 June 1994.

[74] From an online discussion, newsgroups: soc.religion.islam; moderator Ahmad Hashem. 2 March 1996.

[75] For an elaboration on how I read these debates and place myself within them, see my introduction to *Interventions: Feminist Dialogues on Third World Women's Literature and Film.*

[76] Rebecca Santos, writing in the *South China Morning Post,* 22 June 1994.

[77] For the seminal critique of the idea of "global sisterhood," see Chandra Talpade Mohanty's "Under Western Eyes: Feminist Scholarship and Colonial Discourses," in *Third World Women and the Politics of Feminism* (Bloomington: Indiana UP), 51–80.

[78] The *Washington Post,* 12 April 1995.

[79] The *Financial Times,* 11 August 1995.

[80] Reported by the Agence France Presse, 8 March 1996.

WORKS CITED

Appadurai, Arjun. "Disjuncture and Difference in the Global Economy." *Public Culture* 2, 2 (Spring 1990): 1–24.

Baudriallard, Jean. "The Precession of Simulacra." *A Postmodern Reader.* Joseph Natoli and Linda Hutcheon, eds. Albany: State U of New York P, 1993. 342–375.

Carr, Robert. "Resisting Autobiography: Outlaw Genres and Transnational Feminist Subjects." In *De/Colonizing the Subject: Politics and Gender in Women's Autobiographical Practice.* Julia Watson and Sidonie Smith, eds. Minneapolis: U of Minnesota P, 1992. 115–138.

Chatterjee, Partha. *Nation and Its Fragments.* Princeton: Princeton UP, 1993.

Chow, Rey. *Writing Diaspora: Tactics of Intervention in Contemporary Cultural Studies.* Bloomington: Indiana UP, 1993.

Dhaliwal, Amarpal. "Reading Diaspora: Self-Representational Practices and the Politics of Reception." *Socialist Review* 24, 4 (1994): 13–44.

Forster, E. M. *A Passage to India*. London: Harcourt Brace and Company, 1924.

Ghosh, Bishnupriya. "Introduction." *Interventions: Feminist Dialogues on Third World Women's Literature and Film*. New York: Garland, 1996. xv–xxxiii.

Hall, Stuart. "Cultural Identity and Diaspora." In *Identity, Community, Culture, Difference*. Jonathan Rutherford, ed. London: Lawrence and Wishart, 1990. 222–237.

———. "Encoding, Decoding." *The Cultural Studies Reader*. Simon During, ed. New York: Routledge, 1993. 100–1.

de Hernandez, Jennifer Browdy. "Of Tortillas and Texts." In *Interventions: Feminist Dialogues on Third World Women's Literature and Film*. Bishnupriya Ghosh and Brinda Bose, eds. New York: Garland, 1996. 163–184.

Hiro, Dilip. *Holy Wars: The Rise of Islamic Fundamentalism*. New York: Routledge, 1989.

Kandiyoti, Deniz. "Identity and Its Discontents: Women and the Nation." *Millenium: Journal of International Studies* 20, 3 (1991): 429–43.

Kaplan, Caren. "The Politics of Location as Transnational Feminist Critical Practice." In *Scattered Hegemonies: Postmodernity and Transnational Feminist Practices*. Inderpal Grewal and Caren Kaplan, eds. Minneapolis: U of Minnesota P, 1994. 137–152.

Mani, Lata. "Multiple Mediations: Feminist Scholarship in the Age of Multinational Reception." *Inscriptions* 5 (1989): 1–23.

Mohanty, Chandra Talpade. "Cartographies of Struggle: Third World Women and the Politics of Feminism." In *Third World Women and the Politics of Feminism*. Chandra Talpade Mohanty, Ann Russo, and Lourdes Torres, eds. Bloomington and Indianapolis: Indiana UP, 1991. 1–47.

———. "Under Western Eyes: Feminist Scholarship and Colonial Discourses." In *Third World Women and the Politics of Feminism*. Chandra Talpade Mohanty, Ann Russo, and Lourdes Torres, eds. Bloomington and Indianapolis: Indiana UP, 1991. 51–80.

Mukherjee, Bharati. *Jasmine*. New York: Grove Weidenfeld, 1989.

Pandey, Gyanendra. *Communalism in Colonial Northern India*. New Delhi: Oxford University Press, 1990.

Patwardhan, Anand. *Father, Son and Holy War*. 1990 (Film).

Probyn, Elspeth. "Travels in the Postmodern: Making Sense of the Local." In *Feminism/Postmodernism*. Linda Nicholson, ed. New York: Routledge, 1990. 176–189.

Nasreen, Taslima. *Lajja*. Calcutta: Ananda Publishers, 1993.

Radhakrishnan, R. "Ethnicity in the Age of Diaspora." *Transition* 54 (November 1991): 104–115.

Schmitter, Elke. "Boycott Lufthansa: Literature and Publicity Today—A Few Ruminations and a Suggestion." Trans. Wilhem Werthern. *Triquarterly* 94 (Fall 1995): 155–60.

Spivak, Gayatri Chakravorty. "Can the Subaltern Speak?" In *Marxism and the Interpretation of Culture*. Lawrence Grossberg and Cary Nelson, eds. Urbana and Chicago: U of Illinois P, 1988. 271–313.

——— and Sneja Gnew. "Questions of Multiculturalism." In *The Cultural Studies Reader*. Simon During, ed. New York: Routledge, 1993. 193–202.

Stowasser, Barbara. "Women's Issues in Modern Islamic Thought." In *Arab Women: Old Boundaries, New Frontiers*. Judith Tucker, ed. Bloomington and Indianapolis: Indiana UP, 1993. 3–28.

Suleri, Sara. "Woman Skin Deep: Feminism and the Postcolonial Condition." *Critical Inquiry* 18 (Summer 1992): 271–313.

Yuval-Davis, Nira and Floya Anthias, eds. *Woman, Nation, State*. Houndmills, Basingstoke, Hampshire: Macmillan, 1989.

NEWSPAPERS AND NEWS SERVICES

Agence France Presse, 2 August 1994–8 March 1996.

Amrita Bazaar Patrika (Bengal), 27 August 1993–19 September 1994.

Al Ahram (Cairo), 27 March 1996.

Baltimore Sun, 14 January 1995.

Christian Science Monitor, 21 July–18 August 1994.

Deutsche Press–Agentur, 30 November 1994.

Financial Times (London), 13 August 1994–11 August 1995.

Guardian (London), 19 August 1990–1 August 1994.

International Herald Tribune, 30 September 1995.

Jugantor (Calcutta), 22 May 1994.

Mainichi Daily News (China), 16 July 1994.

McCatchy Newspapers Inc., 12 August 1994.

Newsday Inc. (New York), 23 June 1994.

Observer (London), 7 August 1990.

San Francisco Examiner, 29 May 1994.

Saudi Gazette, 11 January 1995.

Scotsman (Edinburgh), 11 April 1995.

South China Morning Post (Hong Kong), 22 June–18 August 1994.

Telegraph (Calcutta), 17 June–22 July 1994.

Times (New Delhi), 2 July 1994–28 June 1995.

Times Newspaper Ltd., 7 September 1994.

Washington Post, 12 April 1995.

Palestinian Women
and the Politics of Reception

THERESE SALIBA AND JEANNE KATTAN

Recently, considerable attention has been given to the West's construction of a "Third World literature" and its reception in the First World context, particularly in the metropolitan university. However, claims to the transnationalism of "Third World literature," or the fluid movement of texts across national borders, tend to overlook the reception of these texts within their own countries, thereby obscuring the roles of power, economics, literacy, and the marketing of so-called Third World authors, particularly women, in the global economy. Transnational feminists argue that feminists need to understand the material conditions that shape women's lives in diverse locations, particularly in a world "structured by transnational economic links and cultural assymetries" (Grewal and Kaplan, 3). Literary reception is intricately bound by these global economic structures, as well as by what Aijaz Ahmad calls the "complex set of metropolitan mediations"—involving selection, translation, publication, etc.—that determine how "Third World" texts are received in the West (45). These mediations, and the cultural and economic assymetries that determine the circulation of "Third World women's literature" in the global marketplace, may be at least partially laid bare by analyzing the reception of these texts in their "homeland." In this study, we examine the reception of writings by Palestinian women, which enjoy global recognition as a result of the *Intifada,* within the context of a state of continuing occupation and limited autonomy, where there is little access to publishing houses and the circulation of literary texts is severely limited. Literary reception is thus conditioned by the material conditions of military occupation, as well as by a social/political context bound by the imperatives of nationalist struggle.

Through both qualitative and quantitative research, we set out to explore two major issues: on a theoretical level, how can the reception of Palestinian women's literature in the West Bank and Gaza illuminate the relationship between national and women's liberation in the context of (post)nationalist struggle; and on a practical level, how accessibile is women's literature in the college curriculum to educated young women on college campuses, and how integrated into the curriculum is it? In surveys, female literature students at several Palestinian colleges and universities were asked to identify Arab and Palestinian women writers they had read, and how and if these writings had influenced their understanding of gender relations or women's issues. The survey also examined the often contested relationship between feminism and nationalism; students were asked to classify these writers as nationalist, social, and/or literary writers, choosing one to two of these classifications. In addition, they were asked to explain how these women writers affected them personally and Palestinian society more generally. In analyzing the attitudes of female literature students towards women's writing, we seek to understand how Israeli military occupation, Palestinian nationalism, and social attitudes have affected Palestinian women's literary production, dissemination, and reception among Palestinian women.

We also interviewed Palestinian writers Liana Badr and Sahar Khalifeh, as well as Fedwa Labadi, editor of the Palestinian feminist magazine *Kul al-Nisa'*, to analyze how their writings were influenced by their contexts of both production and reception. In particular, we asked how they characterize "feminist" writing in the context of nationalist struggle, and how the marketing of women's writing has influenced their methods of production and their conception of audience. While literature has often been one of the modes of raising feminist consciousness, particularly among educated women, this potential has been reduced for Palestinian women by a number of factors, including the cultural strangulation of occupation and the imperatives of the nationalist struggle. Indeed, our survey reveals very limited circulation of women's literature within the Palestinian territories and its limited use within the university curriculum.

Before we proceed, it is necessary to qualify our use of the term *feminism* above and its translation across cultural contexts. *Feminism* as a term does not exist in the Arabic language, yet *tahrir al-ma'rah* (women's liberation) has a long history—as some have suggested, over a century of struggle.[1] Regarding the use of the word *feminism,* Palestinian women's health scholar, Rita Giacaman clearly explains the limits of this term in women's organizing:

> . . . we are against the use of the word 'feminist' precisely because of the western connotations it harbours. Look we are trying to build a movement which all Palestinian women feel is habitable . . . If we are going to frighten off a single woman because of a word, then it is better to ditch the word. So instead of calling our programme a feminist agenda, we'll call it an agenda for women . . . It is how we agree and define the agenda that is important, not which label we pin to it. (37)

In our survey, then, we identify this women's agenda broadly in literary terms as *katibaat ijtimaa'iya nisuwiya,* or women's social writings. However, we also agree with Giacaman's definition of feminism as "an ideology that calls for the social integration of women" as "part of a wider ideology calling for equality across all spheres and for all sectors of political and civil society." Giacaman calls this an "internationalist aspiration," not merely a Western one, as the term often implies (36). In this article, we use the term "feminist," as did some of our interviewees, to designate this women's agenda and the ideology behind texts as well as approaches to women's literature. Certainly women's literature may be written, taught, or interpreted from a nonfeminist standpoint, with little attention to women's social issues. This distinction, at the level of acquiring information and interpreting it, is an important one in analyzing the ways in which literary texts and their dissemination may promote gender consciousness among women.

As teachers of English language and literature ourselves, we are particularly interested in literature as a site of women's resistance, and we believe that the teaching of literature should "negotiate a discursive reality with the world outside the classroom" (Pathak et al., 193). In the context of a Palestinian society in transition, yet still engaged in a struggle for national independence, we believe that a reading context receptive to literature that treats issues of feminism and nationalism would offer women more resources in their struggle for equality on the joined national and feminist fronts. Nevertheless, it is important to recognize that literary production and dissemination is only one site of resistance for Palestinian women, especially for most of our students who came of age during the *Intifada* years. While the gains and setbacks for women resulting from their involvement in the national resistance have been the subject of much academic and activist writings, most analysts agree that initial assessments overestimated the social advances for women during this period (Dajani, Giacaman). Yet Giacaman describes women's participation in the *Intifada* and the ensuing process of self-criticism and self-correction as empowering: "What we have, in effect, is a revolution of rising expectations amongst Palestinian women; precisely a consciousness change" (40). This changing consciousness, then, is likely to affect the society at several levels, and to include women's rising expectations for more gender equity in cultural production and in the educational curriculum.

The reception of women's writing in the Palestinian "homeland" is also intricately linked to the general educational and literacy opportunities for women in Palestinian society. According to a 1995 report, *Requirements for Gender Development in Palestinian Society* (al-Rawi), on average, the illiteracy rate among females in Palestinian society is twice that of males; however, literacy among younger women has increased so rapidly as to exceed male literacy rates. Indeed, "the rising educational levels of Palestinian women in the West Bank and Gaza in the past two decades is an important indicator of social transformation" (Abu Nahleh, i). Statistics from a 1993 report show that females ages sixteen to nineteen enjoy a higher literacy rate than males the same age: approximately 88 percent of women in that age group can write, while an additional 10 percent can write with difficulty; in contrast, among their male counterparts, approximately 80 percent can write and another 16 percent write with difficulty. If we compare these rates with earlier generations of women, the increased educational opportunities for women are astounding. For women ages forty to forty-nine, the literacy rate is approximately 48 percent, and for those sixty years or older, the rate is approximately 10 percent.[2] These increased rates of literacy among young women, however, do not necessarily translate into increased job opportunities for women. In relation to our research, we also found that rising female literacy rates did not translate into a marked increase in reading behavior, nor into significant changes in the curriculum to address the needs of female students. Recently, however, the Curricula Unification Project, headed by Dr. Fathiya Nasru, has been formed to prepare students for "an active life in building a society where both sexes participate equally and without prejudice" (al-Rawi, 44). Furthermore, the project calls for a revision in teaching methods, which rely on memorization, exam preparation, and concern only with the report card. Such

methods "are highly unpopular with female students and affect their feelings about education" (45). Thus, despite the findings of our study,
which suggest minimal attention to women writers and to feminist interpretations of texts in the content of literature courses, Palestinian teachers and researchers, including many women, are actively involved in
transforming the educational system in what they hope to be a new era of
gender and national equality in Palestine.

GLOBALIZING TEXTS, LOCALIZING RECEPTION

With the globalization of publishing and the rise of "Third World Literature" in metropolitan universities, such texts have experienced their own
diasporas and have met with varying responses, from the lucrative reception of Nobel Prize winner Naguib Mahfouz (Colla) to the manipulative
reframing and (mis)interpretations of Egyptian feminist Nawal El Saadawi
(Amireh, "Framing"). Much of what "First World" readers know of these
writers is conditioned by the "metropolitan mediations" that first brought
them public attention, as well as by the interpretive frameworks that lent
them "currency" within the global market (Ahmad).

    Ahmad argues that in cultural theory, as it developed in metropolitan
or Western countries, "exclusive emphasis on the nation, and on nationalism as the necessary ideology emanating from the national situation,
has been a *logical* feature of Third-Worldist perspectives" (92). As a result, interpretive practices of cultural theorists tend to overlook class and
gender formations, as "Third World" literary texts become determined
solely by "the colonial encounter" (92). Ahmad's theory, however, cannot account for the growing popularity in metropolitan countries of Arab
women's writings, an interest that some critics link to the West's growing
hostility to Islam (Amireh "Problems," 22). Arab women's texts are more
often interpreted not within the anticolonialist/nationalist framework,
but rather within one that ascribes the worst forms of sexism to Arab-
Islamic culture. More often, these interpretations discard the entire
political-historical context of women's literary production, rendering
Arab society as a timeless, unchanging world of "traditions" hopelessly
oppressive to women.

    In other words, regardless of what women actually write about, in-
terpretation within the Western context tends to focus primarily, though
not exclusively, on gender oppression. In this sense, Ahmad's theory of
nation-centered criticism applies more aptly to the interpretive frame-

work that has often ensnared Arab, and more specifically Palestinian, women within their own countries, trapping them between the competing ideologies of nationalism and feminism. In the words of an Algerian feminist, Arab women find themselves "caught between two legitimacies: belonging to our people or identifying with other oppressed women" (Helie-Lucas, 113). Many feminists have argued that nationalist ideology is inherently masculinist, imposing the burden of cultural transmission and the role of national signifier upon women while reinforcing "a definable [generally oppressive] gender regime" (Kandiyoti, 376, 378). Cultural formations, such as literature, may provide descriptive negotiations of the apparent theoretical contradictions of feminism and nationalism, thereby defining alternatives to the "double bind" theory. In the case of Palestinian women writers, for whom Zionist colonization, nationalist struggle, and the imperialist designs of "peace" are not things of the past but very much a present daily reality, the competing and intersecting interpretive frameworks of nationalism, women's social agenda, and the need to prove their literary merit within their own society as well as within the global market are all determining factors of reception.

Writing from within the national struggle, Palestinian women writers have had to contend with the often conflicting currents of nationalism and feminism, not only within their writing, but also in terms of how their writing will be received in the territories, in the Arab world, and internationally. As in the metropolitan centers, where women writers have had to prove their literary merit as equals of men, so, too, Arab women writers have come under scrutiny for writings that have been characterized as "too personal" by male critics, and hence not literary enough (see Allen). In the case of many Palestinian women novelists, however, the nationalistic impulse tended to win out over more personal prose; as critic Joseph Zeidan argues: "the search for personal identity became absorbed in the search for national identity, even to the extent of sacrificing the former for the sake of the latter" (170). Feminist theorists have made similar observations of the Palestinian women's movement in general, which has only as recently as 1990 set out a definable feminist agenda (Dajani, 47). For women writers, then, the challenge was to write "an artistically sound novel and to get [their] political message across" (Abu al-Shabab, quoted in Zeidan, 173). Emphasis on the homeland and nation, rather than on the struggle for women's freedom in a conservative society, was one criterion of literary merit. This aptly describes Sahar Khalifeh's early beginnings as a writer bent on proving her equality with male writers:

When I started writing, I started imitating men. I just wanted to be successful as a writer like men. And when I wrote *Wild Thorns* (1976), the [male] Egyptian publisher who rejected it said, "One of the main reasons that I don't like this novel and I'm not going to publish it is that it does not have a woman's identity."

I said, "What do you mean?"

"If I put my finger over the name, nobody would know that this is a novel written by a woman."

That was true to a certain extent; to a *big extent* that was true. I wanted to be successful in portraying the suffering of my people like a man, because women usually have portrayed their own suffering as women, and I wanted to prove that as a woman, I can do better than men.[3] In fact, *Wild Thorns* was the first novel that came out under occupation. . . . This novel brought me my reputation as a writer, maybe because nobody could guess that it was written by a woman, or maybe because this was something astonishing or exciting or exotic that a woman, especially an Arab Muslim woman, is writing like men. (Personal Interview)

Although there exists much debate in feminist theory about gendered notions of writing (a debate we are not interested in engaging here), Khalifeh's comments do support the "common knowledge" of women's literature being about women's suffering, as well as the need for women to earn their literary merit by writing nationalistic literature. In contrast, when Khalifeh wrote what she calls her "first feminist novel," *Sunflower* (1980), it was met with hostile reviews[4]:

Between 1976 and 1980 was a period of experimentation for me . . . So I started reading more and more and more until I became a real feminist. When I wrote *Sunflower,* leftist men were really angry at me and many critics wrote very biased and negative reviews, saying that I'm a male-hater, I try to convince all women to divorce their husbands the way I divorced my husband, that I'm a senseless, insensitive woman, that I tried to divide the national front—all these bad things that women everywhere in all women's movements, especially women pioneers usually face.

Khalifeh goes on to describe how a leftist magazine that regularly published her writing boycotted her work as "punishment for [her] becoming a feminist." It is significant to note that only her first novel, *Wild*

Thorns, has been translated into English, and that *Sunflower* remains un-translated, although this lapse cannot be attributed to the latter's lack of literary merit.[5] Khalifeh's case supports Ahmad's assertion that Third World literature in the metropolitan centers gains currency through its emphasis on "the colonial encounter." In contrast, in the homeland, Khalifeh is widely known for her pioneering work as a feminist writer. Yet in asserting a feminist perspective, Khalifeh initially faced criticism from all sectors of Palestinian society, including leftist men and women:

> I felt I was being sentenced for a crime, but why? Because I knew better . . . And to prove that I knew better, later on they *all* shifted and started talking like me, theorizing like me about women, mentioning the same issues we used to clash upon. And you find that my views are in fact mild in comparison with what the new generation of writers, younger women and leftist men are talking about. I'm considered mild, but since I've had the reputation of a "vehement feminist," this label still drags me down. (Personal Interview)

This generational shift in Palestinian gender politics within the past two decades is evidenced in the support that women's projects have received from male donors and sometimes participants. For example, the Women's Training and Resource Center in Nablus, which Khalifeh herself founded and directs, is maintained with the support of local businessmen and their assistance,[6] demonstrating increasing societal support for feminist issues.

This increasingly feminist agenda is also reflected in the writings of Liana Badr, a Palestinian refugee and recently returned exile now work-ing with the Ministry of Culture. Her works in translation include *A Compass for the Sunflower, Balcony over the Fakihani,* and *The Eye of the Mirror.* Although in 1991 Badr argued that Palestinians needed an in-dependent state from which to wage the battle against sexism (Shaaban, 157), in a 1995 interview she critiques this very position:

> Why go to war or engage in conflict to liberate Palestine if I will come here and be a slave again? When we were outside, I was working with women in the Palestinian organizations and many of them didn't ac-cept my point of view. They told me, "We have a battle men and women together, and after that we will liberate ourselves as women." But I think that unless we have the courage to confess that we don't want to be slaves and if we want to lie to ourselves and say "Oh, we are

very happy, we are in a very good situation." This is just a lie. And all of us today, Palestinian women know, that we have many restrictions and they don't accept us as equal persons in the society. So unless we face this conflict, we will lose everything. (Personal Interview)

While both Badr and Khalifeh tend to emphasize the interdependencies of nationalist and feminist agendas in their more recent writings, the persistent tensions between nationalism and feminism in Palestinian women's literature seem to elicit different interpretations in different contexts. In the metropolitan centers, readers have been conditioned to focus on themes of gender oppression within Arab women's texts (Amireh, "Problems," 22), whereas our research shows that in the Palestinian context, nationalistic themes prevail in the interpretation of women's writings.

FEMALE STUDENTS' RESPONSES

Our survey was distributed to female students at five major Palestinian colleges and universities, including Bethlehem University, Birzeit University, Islamic University (Gaza), An-Najah University (Nablus), and Al-Quds Teacher's College (Jerusalem). Closures during March–June 1996 made it particularly difficult to distribute surveys to students: attendance was low during this period as students faced roadblocks in trying to get to school, and two major institutions, Hebron University and Abu Dis College, were suddenly shut down by the Israeli authorities on claims that these schools were harboring "Islamic terrorists" in the wake of a series of suicide bombing attacks inside Israel. As a result, we had 475 respondents, fairly equally distributed from the five institutions listed above. These female students were all either sophomores (36 percent), juniors (32 percent), or seniors (32 percent) majoring in the fields of Arabic language and literature (46 percent) or English language and literature (52 percent). The vast majority were between the ages of eighteen to twenty-two (82 percent); 8 percent were between the ages of twenty-two to twenty-five, and only 2 percent were between twenty-six to thirty-five.[7]

In order to determine the "transnationalism" of Arab women writers, students were given the names of five authors whose works are fairly well distributed in the West in English translation, as well as in Arabic. These include the celebrated Palestinian poet Fedwa Tuqan, whose autobiography *Mountainous Journey* (1985, trans. 1990) is distributed by St.

Martins Press; Sahar Khalifeh, the Palestinian novelist mentioned above, whose novel *Wild Thorns* (1976, trans. 1985, al-Saqi) became popular in the United States during the *Intifada*[8]; Hanan Ashrawi, who was Palestinian Minister of Higher Education and is now (1999) a member of the Palestine Legislative Council, and who has written poetry in English as well as an autobiography chronicling her role in the Madrid Peace Conference entitled, *This Side of Peace: A Personal Account* (Simon & Schuster, 1995)[9]; Liana Badr, mentioned earlier, whose works have been published in England as part of Garnet's series on Arab women writers; and finally, one non-Palestinian author, the Egyptian feminist writer Nawal El Saadawi, whose writing has, in many ways, come to represent Arab women in the West, from her collection of essays, *The Hidden Face of Eve,* to her numerous novels and memoirs. (Thirteen of El Saadawi's books have been translated into English, and some are available in French, German, and Japanese as well; see Amireh, "Framing," 2).

Students were asked to identify each author through the following categories: "I have never heard of her"; "I have heard of her, but have never read her work"; "I have read some of her writing in class"; "I have read some of her writing outside of class." For Nawal El Saadawi, 69 percent said they had never heard of her, 20 percent had heard of her, 5 percent had read her work in class, and 6 percent had read her work on their own. For Liana Badr, 86 percent had never heard of her, 12 percent had heard of her, none had read her work in class, and only 1 percent had read her work on their own. For the prominent political figure, Hanan Ashrawi[10] only 3 percent said they had never heard of her, 83 percent recognized her name, 3 percent had read her work in class, and 12 percent had read her work outside of class. Sahar Khalifeh, labeled "one of the foremost Palestinian novelists" (Jayyusi, 589), was unknown to a surprising 76 percent of students, whereas 19 percent claimed to have heard of her. Only 1 percent had read her work in class and 3 percent had read her work on their own. Finally, acclaimed Palestinian poet Fedwa Tuqan was familiar to 98 percent of respondents; 47 percent had read her works in class, and 39 percent had read her works on their own.

When students were asked to identify titles from the above authors, far fewer responded. For Tuqan, 37 percent of students responded, most of them listing poetry; the collection *Wahdi Ma al-Ayyam* (*Alone with the Days* 1952) was most frequently mentioned, but her book *Mountainous Journey* was also cited by twenty respondents. For Khalifeh, only five respondents mentioned *Wild Thorns* and two mentioned *Sunflower*. For Ashrawi, most respondents (3.6 percent) said they had read newspaper articles by her, and only one listed *This Side of Peace*. *The Stars over Jericho* and *Balcony over the Fakihani* by Liana Badr were listed by 1 percent of respondents. And for Nawal El Saadawi, the respondents (6.7 percent) listed a variety of books, the two most frequently mentioned being *Woman and Sex* (*al Mara wal Jins*) and *The Hidden Face of Eve* (*al Wajh al Ari Lil Mara al Arabiyya*).[11]

Students were then asked to identify these writers by one or two of the following classifications: nationalistic *(wataniya)*, women's social writings *(kaatibat ijtimaa'iya nisuwiya)*, or literary *(adabiya)*. These categories are highly constructed, but are commonly used within Palestinian society to designate different literary forms; they also shape the way Palestinian women's literature has been read and interpreted, both inside and outside the society. From student responses, it appears that they interpreted "nationalistic" to mean supporting the Palestinian national struggle; "women's social writings" (which we use alternately with "feminist") as addressing women's rights and empowerment in society and family; and "literary" writings as having artistic merit, which in the Palestinian context, unlike the West, is not devoid of political content (see Jameson). For Nawal El Saadawi, no one listed her as a nationalist, perhaps because to them "nationalism" means Palestinian nationalism, rather than Arab nationalism more generally. Of the 147 responses, 93.9 percent said she was a feminist, whereas only 1.1 percent identified her as a literary writer. This finding reinforces the claims of some Arab critics that, although Saadawi has received literary acclaim in the West, in the Arab world she is seen more as a polemical writer and essayist than a literary talent (Amireh, "Framing," Zeidan). For Liana Badr, there were only twenty-two responses: 50 percent nationalist, 14 percent feminist, 36 percent literary. For Hanan Ashrawi, of the 283 responses, the overwhelming majority, 68 percent, classified her as nationalist, with 25 percent as feminist, and 6 percent as literary. For Sahar Khalifeh, of the fifty-one responses, 25.4 percent saw her as nationalist, 33.3 percent as feminist, and 41 percent as literary. Finally, for Fedwa Tuqan, we received 517 responses (remember students could pick two categories): 39 percent nationalist, 7 percent feminist, and 54 percent literary.

From these classifications, it is interesting to note that nationalistic writing is given precedence, along with concerns for literary style, whereas emphasis on women's social issues has been given minimal attention, if not by the writer, then certainly by the readers of these texts, as well as by the professors who teach them. Among the Palestinian writers, only Khalifeh was perceived as more concerned with women's social is-

sues than with nationalism; and overall, women's writings were categorized as "social" (or "feminist") only 14.6 percent of the time among
female readers familiar with these works, who, in turn, constituted approximately 26.5 percent of survey participants.[12] It is also significant
that the most popular woman writer, Fedwa Tuqan, is also seen as the
least concerned with women's issues. Of course, the predominance of
the "nationalist" and "literary" classifications can be as much a matter of
how texts are taught and how the student's interpretive consciousness is
shaped, as how they are written.

Tuqan, in fact, is such a case in point. Her canonization within Arabic letters may be attributed, in part, to a centuries-long Arabic poetic
tradition, which includes women's voices usually writing and reciting
elegies for male relatives in the tradition of al-Khansa, the pre-Islamic
poetess (Malti-Douglas, 161–2, 169). While Tuqan's early poetry is
often characterized as romantic and personal, after the 1967 war, perhaps
influenced by the rising women's involvement in the nationalist struggle,
her poetry became more reflective of the collective national struggle.
Nevertheless, her autobiography, *A Mountainous Journey* (read by 4.2
percent of respondents), exposes women's "imprisonment" within the
private house of Palestinian society, as "the political struggle is at once
present and occulted, superceded most often by the gender vision of the
narrator" (Malti-Douglas, 163). As critic Fedwa Malti-Douglas points
out, Tuqan is, herself, legitimated within the overlapping male discourses that frame her narrative: the introduction to her autobiography,
written by renowned Palestinian poet Samih al-Qasim; his comparison
of her to Taha Husayn (author of *Al-Ayam*); and her tutelage in poetry
under her brother Ibrahim, to whom her own poetic writings were often
attributed. So although her autobiographical narrative focuses on a gender critique of Palestinian society through her personal experience, such
a critique can be readily overlooked in the teaching of her poetry, which
has achieved the status of high culture in the elegiac *(ritha')* tradition.

Moreover, Palestinian women tend to read different writers than
those who have gained popularity in the West. For example, when students were asked to write in the names of other authors they had read
who had not been mentioned in the first section of the survey, the Arab
women writers who gained frequent mention—Mai Ziadeh (22.5 percent), Ghada Al-Samman (9.9 percent), Nazik Al-Mala'ika (8 percent),
Bint Al-Shati (7.6 percent), Samira Azzam (5 percent), Suad Al-Sabbah
(4.2 percent), Al-Khansa' (3.8 percent), and Salma Khadra Jayyusi (3.6
percent)—like Tuqan, all belong to an older generation of writers who

began publishing (in many cases, long) before the 1970s, many of whom have now become canonized in Arab letters. Significantly, these names appeared more frequently than those of most of the "transnational" writers, especially Badr and Khalifeh. These findings expose the metropolitan bias in the survey, and in Western constructions of "Third World Literature," which tend to focus on more globally marketable contemporary writers and on prose writers more often than poets. It is important to note that, apart from Tuqan, students wrote in these authors' names; therefore, the representation of Arab women writers in the college curriculum and in women's leisure reading would have most likely been higher had these authors' names been given in the survey, rather than those who receive wider circulation in the West. Clearly, students have more access to writings by established, modern writers than more contemporary ones. Mai Ziadeh (1886–1941), a Palestinian writer of poetry and prose, hosted a salon for Arab intellectuals in Cairo, where she lived most of her life; she earned the title "the martyr of Arab feminism" after she committed suicide after bouts of depression and mental breakdowns (see Ahmed, 187–88). Ghada Al-Samman (b. 1912) is a Syrian writer of short stories, novels, and poetry; and Nazik Al-Mala'ika (b. 1923) is a celebrated Iraqi poet who began to experiment with free verse in Arabic poetry. While many women writers of this earlier generation wrote across several literary genres, including novels, short stories, journalism, essays, and poetry, Tuqan and Al-Mala'ika, as well as many others, were best known for their poetry. As "the most sacred literary medium for the Arabs," poetry has allowed more space for female poetic voices (Malti-Douglas, 161–62). Furthermore, the oft-cited maxim of African American feminist poet Audre Lorde that "Poetry is not a luxury" also applies to Palestinian writers for whom poetry has become a "safe-house" (Lorde, 37), or, in the words of Mahmoud Darwish, "a country of words" (31) to counter the statelessness of Palestinian existence. And poetry is also economical, not just in language usage, but also in production and distribution—an important attribute given the lack of publishing houses in the Palestinian territories.[13] Poetry, then, a genre relatively marginal in "Third World literature," remains the dominant form of literary expression for Palestinians. In contrast, the English language writers students have read are mainly novelists and essayists. Jane Austen, George Elliot, and the Brontë sisters were the names mentioned most frequently; a few mentioned Virginia Woolf and Alice Walker. Several also mentioned Agatha Christie, Madame Curie, and Helen Keller.[14]

In order to determine the perceived social effects of reading women's literature, students were then asked what the effects of this literature had been on them personally and on Palestinian society as a whole. Although these were two separate questions, the responses were similar for both, and so we decided to combine them. This conflation of responses exposes another potential bias in the survey, which relies on Western constructions of the individual, or the personal/collective binary, an assumption that clearly was not shared by the students surveyed. It is also important to note that only 43.2 percent of the sample answered these open-ended questions. The responses, in order of frequency, were as follows:

1. They evoked feelings of nationalism and the Palestinian struggle (27.3 percent of comments given);
2. They made me aware of feminist issues, problems, equality, the right to an education, oppression by men. They made me feel strong in the fight for my rights (24.8 percent);
3. They moved my emotions and made me appreciate literature (14 percent);
4. I frankly did not read enough to enable me to pass judgment. Their books are not available, or we do not have the money to buy books (8.8 percent);
5. They did not affect me or the society at all. Men are better writers (6.8 percent);
6. I am proud of their literary achievement; I wish I could write like them (5.5 percent);
7. They helped me in shaping my personality (4.8 percent);
8. They have helped me shape my religious values (3.5 percent);
9. They made me think about our reality, our social, economic, and political problems (2.5 percent);
10. I wish we could be exposed to these women writers. I wish we could have seminars/workshops on their work (2 percent).

These student responses reflect a range of women's perspectives, with varying emphases on nationalist, feminist, literary, and religious interpretations of women's literature. For example, one respondent attacked Nawal El Saadawi because she was "against religious values," as well as Fedwa Tuqan because she "only represents her personal life." Other women felt inspired by these writings.

The results of our survey highlight two major points: first, as previously stated, Palestinian women tend to read different writers than those "transnational" writers who have gained cultural currency in the West. Second, the accessibility and distribution of women's literature in the college curriculum among educated young women is quite low. This neglect of women's literature may have negative social consequences, in that students may not learn to value women's lives and experiences or consider women's contributions to society and culture, as expressed by those students who wrote that women writers did not affect the society at all, and men are better writers.[15] While over half of the students had been exposed to some women's literature in class, most of these had read Tuqan (47 percent) and another large percentage, with considerable overlap (about 23 percent) had read Mai Ziadeh. All other women writers had been read by less than 10 percent of the female literature majors in their courses. The obvious solution to this problem is to include more women writers throughout the literature curriculum in both English and Arabic; however, our findings also show that when women's literature is taught (as with Tuqan), emphasis in interpretation is placed on nationalistic and literary elements of the writing, while attention to gender issues or analysis is marginal or nonexistent. One solution to this problem came from the students themselves, who requested workshops or seminars on women writers. While this proposal suggests initiative on the students' part, workshops and seminars remain marginal to the main curriculum and relegate women's issues to an extra-curricular activity. This marginalization and neglect of women's literature, moreover, accords women's literary production less "cultural currency" within the educational curriculum and, by extension, within Palestinian society. However, the responses of female literature students, which place women's social issues (24.8 percent) nearly on par with nationalist concerns (27.3 percent), support Giacaman's claim of "a consciousness change" among Palestinian women of the *Intifada* generation.

THE PREDICAMENT OF PALESTINIAN
CULTURAL PRODUCTION

If nationalist struggle and social attitudes have played a determining role in the reception of women's literature in Palestine, then the Occupation and Israel's assumed role as cultural arbiter have also contributed to "the predicament of Palestinian cultural production" (Tamari). In this sense, Palestinian writers, because of their history of displacement and occupation, face obstacles not shared by other Third World authors. Sociologist Salim Tamari asserts that "one of the major consequences of the war of 1967 was the dismemberment of Palestinian society from its 'natural' cultural terrain in the neighboring Arab countries." Palestinians were suddenly culturally isolated, as Arab "books, newspapers and journals were no longer available in the West Bank and Gaza" (98). Furthermore, Israeli restrictions on people's movement made their access to Arab festivals, theatres, universities, and cultural forums extremely limited, and Palestinians no longer had access to Arab films produced in the vibrant cultural centers of Cairo and Beirut. According to Tamari, only state-controlled radio and television programs continued to reach Palestinian audiences, but "their cultural fares [were] of dubious value." Tamari explains, however, that this cultural isolation was not decidedly a negative thing; it forced Palestinian writers, poets, musicians, and artists to recreate new forms of national culture, forms that emerged in local colleges and municipalities despite Israeli censorship on publications and performances. Thus, the dual predicaments of cultural isolation and Israeli censorship fed the production of new theatrical and literary events, beginning in the early 1970s. Yet another contradictory effect took hold in East Jerusalem, "where Israeli law was unilaterally extended in 1968, and the Arab sector was annexed in 1980, a measure of legal freedom allowed for the limited flourishing of a Palestinian press and theater . . . Clearly, cultural isolation became an incentive for creativity and independence." The Israeli military regime was "as hostile to the articulation of a Palestinian national sentiment, as it was keen at suppressing its manifestations—both political and cultural." Apart from banning public assemblies and closing universities and schools, the Israeli regime also censored texts and banned imported books, nearly three thousand titles in the 1980s, at the zenith of censorship policies. However, Israeli attempts to destroy Palestinian cultural and national expression tended to backfire, as artistic forms became increasingly nationalistic in content. This revival of national identity was most evident in folklorist dance and musical performances, which, by the late seventies, "forged into the direction of experimental, cosmopolitan, and—tentatively—internationalist currents; thus what began in theatre, later influenced painting and literary production" (Tamari, 99). The generation of writers, like Sahar Khalifeh, who produced works in the wake of this nationalist resurgence were most influenced by these movements.

Tamari argues that today Palestinian cultural production faces two major obstacles: lack of institutional support, funding, and infrastructure, and the predominance of amateurism, which he attributes to "the uncritical and 'heroic' image with which Palestinian art and literature are received in the Arab world and among local audiences," an attitude that reinforces "a spirit of false achievement and self-assurance." Given Tamari's assessment, it is all the more striking to realize that feminist writers, such as Sahar Khalifeh, Hanan Ashrawi, and Liana Badr, who have been actively engaged in questioning masculinist assumptions of nationalist heroism and identity for nearly two decades, have been largely ignored by male cultural critics and within the educational curriculum. Tamari argues that a separate set of standards have been used to judge Palestinian art that "elevate it beyond critical assessment,"[16] and predicts that this special status of Palestinian art will end as Palestinian society becomes "normalized" through the new political arrangements orchestrated by the "peace process." Tamari turns to "young artists" who will "have to define their vision within the needs and vision of a new and altered society" (100). Certainly, many feminist writers have already set forth an altered vision of society through their work.

One such writer is Liana Badr, whose writing of exile and refugee experience is better known outside Palestine. Much of her work has been translated into English. Even since her return to the West Bank in 1994, she remains relatively unknown inside the Palestinian territories (her name was only recognized by 12 percent of female literature students), although she has been fairly widely published in the Arab world and internationally. Despite her lack of recognition inside the territories, Badr feels that it is more difficult to have a good reputation in the Arab world and internationally than to reach the people who were "the aim, source and origin of [her] literature." The problem, she explains, lies in publishing and distribution; yet her exclusion from Palestinian letters may also exemplify the tensions between the outside (Palestinians in exile) and inside (Palestinians under occupation), as well as the reception of her persistent feminist message. According to Badr, the cultural suppression and strangulation experienced by those under occupation was not as great for those in exile, who enjoyed a climate of relative freedom of expression:

> As a Palestinian movement outside, we worked a lot in the cultural field to build the independent Palestinian characteristics in literature and arts. All of us encouraged each other to express our views and experiences, but here no one had the same opportunity because they were living in poverty and under occupation. So many of the best people ei-

ther went outside to work and to have opportunities, or they lost everything here. I knew several people who were very good writers or
painters and they are nothing now because they didn't have the ability
or chance to continue their professions here. (Personal Interview)

Although Badr experienced certain cultural advantages living "outside,"
free from the repressions of Israeli censorship and occupation, she also
faced the difficulty of finding a publisher because of her constant up-
rooting. As a result, her series of publishers—in Damascus, Lebanon,
Morocco, and Egypt —reflect her series of exiles, though she was not always published in the same country where she lived. Everytime she
moved into another exile, she had to "establish everything from zero"
(Personal Interview).

Badr, a former journalist and writer of historical fiction, blames the
lack of distribution and knowledge of her writing within Palestine on the
cultural isolation and censorship Palestinians faced under Israeli rule,
censorship that continued to be enforced even after the implementation
of the Oslo Peace Accords:

> In Palestine the people don't know me, not because my type of writing
> isn't read here, but because they were deprived of all the means of cul-
> ture during the occupation years. You know, they were not allowed to
> have a single book here. Even two years ago, at the beginning of the
> Oslo agreement, a friend of mine from Tunisia who likes *The Eye of
> The Mirror,* tried to bring this as the only book with him on his return,
> and the Israelis confiscated it at the border. So if you go to the libraries
> now, you don't find books for anybody, nothing intellectual or related
> to culture . . . But we have also another problem: first, that we don't
> have the means of cultural distribution; and second, the people lost the
> habit of reading because they were always burdened by getting bread
> and they weren't living in a healthy society. (Personal Interview)

Like Tamari, Badr faults the weak infrastructure and censorship for the
limits of cultural production and dissemination. Yet Tamari speaks as an
insider who has witnessed the fluctuations in Palestinian cultural production over time; whereas Badr speaks as an exile, returning after nearly
thirty years to find the cultural landscape radically transformed. Badr
also expresses concern for the audience and subjects of her literature,
who have "lost the habit of reading" under the burdens of the occupation.
Interestingly, she connects the need for cultural revival with the people's

survival and their need to "feel themselves again." For Badr her position in the ministry of culture allows her a space from which to wage this struggle to disseminate culture again among the people:

> I feel that we must wage a kind of battle to revive the arts, to renovate the cinemas and theatres, to revive the cultural vision of the people . . . I was astonished when I came back because there wasn't anything to see, nobody is showing videos or going to cinemas, all the cinemas are closed, there are no theatres, there are no clubs for writers, no debates, nothing. It wasn't the same place I left. (Personal Interview)

What happens, then, when reading (or other forms of cultural exchange) becomes a privilege in a society where poetry and cultural expression are a necessity for survival? Although Badr and Tamari offer somewhat differing diagnoses for the ailments of culture—isolation, strangulation, or amateurism—they both seek new forms of cultural revival to ensure Palestinian survival. In order to counter the effects of the occupation, and to move beyond forms of "heroic" nationalistic production, young artists will need to address the needs of "a new and altered society" (Tamari). However, the society must also establish the conditions for cultural revival and exchange among its citizens, such as access to literature, stronger reading habits, and cultural forums. As hope for a new society declines with the present crisis in the peace process, this battle will continue to depend on the Israeli government, which remains, to a large extent, the arbiter of Palestinian culture.

EVERY WOMAN: A FEMINIST MAGAZINE

The issues of distribution and audience for a new "feminist" magazine surfaced during the *Intifada* years, as women from the Democratic Front for the Liberation of Palestine began to discuss the idea of establishing a magazine for women. In February 1991 the magazine *Al-Ma'ra* (*Woman*) was first issued as a two to three page appendix to the Palestinian magazine *Al-Ousbou'a al-Jadid* (*The New Week*), which operated with a license from the Israeli government. The appendix was coordinated with the Jerusalem Women's Studies Center, under the editorship of Fedwa Labadi, who, after several issues, broke with the Palestinian weekly because the male editors tried to intervene too much in their work. According to Labadi, "We have to be independent so they don't interfere in our issues."[17] The new independent magazine established by the Jerusalem Women's Studies Center appeared monthly up till February 1996, when it became a quarterly magazine due to shortages of funding. First entitled *Al-Mar'a* (*Woman*), and later *Kul al-Nisa'* (*Every Woman*), the magazine has been operating without a license from the Israeli authority (which continues to hold jurisdiction over Jerusalem), except that they have obtained permission to print a single edition. As a result, the Women's Center must continually change the name of the magazine for each issue and print each time, "This is a one-time issue." As Labadi explains, "It's *Kul al-Nis'a,* but each time it's a little different. The last one was *Intakhibu: Kul al-Nisa'* (*Elections: Every Woman*) and the previous one was *Saut Kul an-Nisa'* (*The Voice of Every Woman*); the first one was *Sahat Kul al-Nisa'* (*The Health of Every Woman*). Each issue changes the first word of its title because they do not have a license and are forced to comply with arbitrary Israeli regulations. Furthermore, many taxi drivers refused to deliver the magazines because the center does not have the proper permit.

Kul al-Nisa' sets itself apart from other women's magazines available in the Palestinian territories in that it is primarily concerned with women's issues, not just fashion or politics. Labadi defines the purpose of the magazine as "Feminist . . . concerned with Palestinian women's issues first of all." The magazine addresses a range of topics including political, economic, social, and health issues facing women in Palestinian society, with some articles addressing international women's issues, especially in the Third World and Arab countries. The magazine remains true to its feminist commitment, despite the urgings of some would-be readers to include articles about fashion and beauty.[18] Yet the magazine also provides a democratic space for writers (mostly women, but also some men) to submit articles and have their work published. Readers are encouraged to submit topics of interest, for which the editor solicits writing from specialists, although none of the writers are paid, due to lack of funds.[19] "If a woman contacts us and wants to put an article in the magazine, we publish it for her. We try to promote new, unpublished writers."

Since splitting off from the more mainstream *al-Ousbou'a Al-Jadid,* the magazine has faced many obstacles to circulation: limitations on publishing and movement by occupation authorities, economic obstacles, both in the distribution of materials and among Palestinian women who do not have the money to buy the magazine, and a lack of feminist consciousness or interest among women. Indeed, the woman's magazine paid a high price for its independence, including the loss of official permits under Israeli authority, increase in cost of paying drivers to deliver the magazine, and a decline in circulation. Later, they were able to hire a driver with Jerusalem identity (and therefore the requisite yellow license plates) to distribute the magazine around the West Bank and Gaza Strip and also to the Arab villages inside Israel. Presently, their circulation is about one thousand and reaches mostly urban educated women and women connected to women's organization. One of the main problems with distribution is the limitation on movement enforced by Israeli checkpoints, which surround all of the Palestinian "autonomous zones," as well as the fact that villages and most camps remain under Israeli rule. Drivers cannot reach refugee camps and remote villages to deliver the magazine, and women in these places are unable to come to the city and towns and buy the magazine. The other problem for rural and refugee women is not so much illiteracy, which Labadi claims is not a big problem, but economic constraints. As Labadi explains, the magazine "was not expensive, only three shekels ($1) and now it costs ten shekels ($3.35). Two, three years ago it was only three shekels, but even three shekels was expensive for women because they don't have an independent income. If we send it to them free, they can read it, but they can't buy it." These findings resonate with the comments of some literature students who said they did not have the money to buy books by women.

Apart from economics, Labadi also attributes lack of interest in the magazine to social and political factors, which continue to limit women's awareness about feminist issues. Like Badr, she feels that a general lack of interest in reading has become endemic in the culture as a result of the hardships of the occupation, despite growing literacy rates among women. According to Labadi, the daily problems women face due to the occupation and their participation in the national struggle have had adverse effects on women's interest in reading, because they don't have time for reading or other leisure pursuits. "A woman is crying because one of her sons is arrested or another woman's house was demolished or another woman's son was killed. We have many problems, and I think these problems make our people less interested in reading and in building the culture. *The Israeli occupation, I think, is the manager of our culture*" (personal interview, emphasis mine).

Since the Oslo Peace Accords, Palestinians have faced new obstacles in the building of civil society and national culture, and a new form of isolation, this time from each other, as the agreement has divided up the Palestinian areas into what many now call "*bantustans*" and limited people's movement through a network of checkpoints. Not only does the magazine face difficulty contacting contributers, but these physical roadblocks also evoke a psychological response among writers. As Labadi says, "Now people are not in the best mind to write. Because they can't move, *they also have obstacles in their minds*" (Personal Interview, emphasis mine).

The general lack of interest in reading in Palestinian society also has socio-cultural components. One plausible explanation is that the society is an oral culture, as seen in the popularity of dramatic performances and poetry recitations, and academic research has often devalued oral literacy.[20] Furthermore, although the decline in reading as a leisure activity has been exacerbated by the occupation, this tendency is not exclusive to Palestinian society, but may be a side effect of the globalization of the mass media. For example, one reviewer attributes the popularity of Naguib Mahfouz in Egypt not to his writings, but to the many popular films that have been made from his novels (Colla). Interestingly, Labadi reiterated the fact that reading is not viewed as pleasurable within the society; those who frequent their library on women and gender come mainly to do research, not out of curiosity or for leisure reading. Similarly, the incidence of leisure reading was relatively low (below 40 percent) among female literature students in our survey. Another contributing factor may be that living and social arrangements do not allow for the kind of private space that is conducive to reading, although all the colleges and universities have libraries. In *A Room of One's Own,* Virginia Woolf asserts that one of the reasons women have not produced more literature is that they have been denied the "private space" necessary for literary production. This notion of "private space" is not a universal construction, nor is such space necessarily desirable across cultures and classes of societies. Yet one might also argue that private space is also necessary for reading or for finding pleasure in it, and in general, except among very elite classes of the society, such space is a luxury most Palestinians cannot afford.[21]

At present, most women who read *Kul al-Nisa'* are interested in both reading and gender issues, but, Labadi argues, even many educated women do not bother to read books or magazines. For example, the center donates several copies of the magazine to the Woman's College in Ramallah, but very few students pick them up and look at them. A few years ago, the staff discussed adding more popular appeal to the magazine by including articles on fashion, etc., in order to reach a broader audience, but opted to maintain its feminist commitment to educate women "and keep at the same level, not to be at the lowest level like other magazines." With proper funding, staff support, and a hoped-for loosening of restrictions by Israeli authorities, Labadi would like to increase distribution of *Kul al-Nisa* to all the universities and colleges, as well as to camps and villages. But clearly, distribution alone will not contribute to more widespread reception of the magazine; consciousness-raising about reading and feminist issues must accompany this push.[22]

CONCLUSION

Significantly, the disinterested response to women's writing among young, educated women is reconfirmed by some of the findings of our study. However, this response is tempered by a growing interest among female students in women's issues. We would argue that a feminist consciousness, or interest in gender issues, has not been widely fostered within the education system, and this neglect is reflected both in limited interest in the feminist magazine *Kul al-Nisa'* and the minimal exposure even literature students have had to women's literature and feminist theory. It is important to continue the momentum of women's "consciousness change" (Giacaman) from the years of occupation and the *Intifada;* thus consciousness-raising about the value of reading and feminist issues is urgent to prevent what Badr terms "the return to slavery," especially with the rising tide of conservatism within Palestinian society. The increased rates of literacy among young women, although striking, will not alone bring about social transformation. Young women have to be sensitized to the actual, as well as possible, contributions of women to society and culture. Given the conditions of Israeli occupation, it is understandable why Palestinian women writers have sacrificed their search for personal identity to the search for national identity (Zeidan, 170). The critique of gender relations remains present in their work, but is often suffused within the nationalistic content. The value placed upon nationalistic themes in literature has similarly filtered down to readers, and to women students, who need to be challenged to search for their personal identities while engaged in the every day struggles for freedom as a people.

On the Western front, the texts that become representative of Palestinian and Arab women's lives for metropolitan readers, ironically, may not even be available to or read by the very women they purportedly represent. This gap in literary reception exposes how market forces and "metropolitan mediations," including preferences for prose over poetry, contemporary texts over "classics," and feminist interpretations of Arab women's lives over nationalistic writings, determine which Arab women's texts will circulate in the global market. That is not to say that the women writers read by Palestinian women are more authentically representative of Arab women's lives, but that they are more widely received. And if one function of literary texts is to bridge the gap between cultures, then those texts that have more common "cultural currency" in the Arab world are the ones that can best translate Arab women's lives to Western readers. If the Palestinian curriculum can be criticized for its narrow focus on certain modern, nationalistic writers, then too, metropolitan teachers of "Third World" or Arab literatures often fall short of addressing the wealth of literature, some available in translation, that is widely read in the Arab world, as represented by writers like Tuqan, Ziadeh, and Al-Mala'ika. Some balance between "local" and "transnational" women's literature may be struck in both Western and Palestinian classrooms. Furthermore, as texts are produced and received within contexts, Western readers need to understand how occupation, economics, and social relations circumscribe and often delimit the cultural production of Palestinian women writers and their exchange with Palestinian women readers who are "the aim, source and origin of [their] literature" (Badr), but who are more often than not, left out of the global exchange.

ACKNOWLEDGMENTS

We are grateful to the Fulbright Association for a fellowship that allowed us to conduct this research. We would also like to thank Alice Nelson and Tom Wright for their insightful comments on this essay.

NOTES

[1]Here we are paraphrasing Nawal El Saadawi's discussion of the term *feminism* in *The Progressive Interview*. For a variety of Arab feminist arguments that have been translated into English, see *Opening the Gates: A Century of Arab Feminist Writings,* Miriam Cooke and Margot Badran, eds.

[2]See *Educational Network,* Nos. 12 and 13 (June–Sept. 1993), 7, cited in al-Rawi's *Requirements for Gender Development in Palestinian Society,* 11.

[3]It is important to note that although women play minor roles in the novel, the narrative provides a clear critique of conservative gender roles, arranged marriage, and the patriarchal authority embodied in the character Abu Adil al-Karmi, whose dictates are challenged by the younger generation.

[4]Although Khalifeh did not discuss it in her interview, she wrote an earlier novel *Lam Na'ud Jawari Lakum* (*We Are No Longer Your Slaves,* 1974) which, according to Zeidan, "dwells on the tragic clash between defiant female individu-

alists and rigid patriarchal social values on the West Bank in the 1960s." Zeidan describes the work as "a modest artistic achievement" (178).

[5]Zeidan argues that "Khalifeh's literary skills, especially language, reach maturity in *'Abbad al-Shams*" (185).

[6]As Khalifeh explains, "Females do not own a lot of money."

[7]In instances like this where the percentages do not add up, it means that several students did not answer this question.

[8]Khalifeh's other novels include *Abbad al-Shams* (1980) or *Sunflower,* mentioned above, *Bab al-Saha* (1990), and *Mudhakkirat Imara'a Gayr Waqi'iya* (1986) or *Memoirs of an Unrealistic Woman,* which has been translated into Italian and German. A short excerpt of this novel appears in *Anthology of Modern Palestinian Literature,* Salma Khadra Jayyusi, ed. (New York: Columbia University Press, 1992).

[9]Unlike in the Indian context of Ahmad's study, there has not been a significant move to English among the Palestinian "bourgeois intelligentsia." In fact, Hanan Ashrawi, who studied at the American University of Beirut and completed a Ph.D. in English at the University of Virginia, is the only woman writer in our study who writes primarily in English.

[10]At the time of the survey, Ashrawi had recently won a seat on the Legislative Council for the East Jerusalem area. She then accepted a position as Minister of Higher Education with the Palestinian Authority.

[11]For an insightful discussion of the refashioning of this title for a Western English-speaking audience, through which the literal translation, "The Naked Face of the Arab Woman," was changed to *The Hidden Face of Eve,* see Amal Amireh's essay "Reframing Nawal El Saadawi: Arab Feminism in a Transnational World," *Signs: Journal of Women in Culture and Society* (forthcoming, Autumn 2000).

[12]This number was obtained by adding the percentage of students who had read the four Palestinian women writers and dividing by four.

[13]Although there are no publishing houses in the West Bank and Gaza Strip, some organizations like PASSIA, The Arab Thought Forum, and Palestine Studies Center have their own publishing units.

[14]We speculate that these may be some of the few female names in English that students are familiar with.

[15]Although, for the sake of simplicity and focus, we did not interview male students for their responses, we believe there is also significant interest among male students in gender issues. In fact, in a 1995–96 Bethlehem University English literature course in "Feminism," one-third of registered students were male. Male students also benefit from reading women's literature.

[16]Like Tamari, Aijaz Ahmad argues that there is a missionary zeal behind the "overvalorizing" of what has already been designated as "Third World Literature" (85).

[17]It is interesting to note that in Sahar Khalifeh's novel *'Abbad al-Shams* (1980), or *Sunflower,* mentioned earlier, the protagonist Afaf is a magazine journalist engaged in a struggle with her editors about the existence of a special women's column: if it should exist at all or if it should get equal space, that is, half of the magazine (see Zeidan, 183).

[18]One recent issue included biographies of all the women candidates running for the Palestinian Legislative Council in January 1996. Two thousand issues of this edition were distributed free, especially to women who attended workshops held throughout the Territories on women and the first Palestinian elections. The workshops informed women of their voting rights and also encouraged them to support women candidates. A more recent issue included an interview with, and photography by, a Swedish photographer whose work was exhibited at the U.N. women's conference in Beijing; she photographs women in grassroots movements internationally, as well as homeless women. Other articles addressed the legal rights of working women, women working in the media field worldwide, the Islamist women's movement, teenage women's physical and psychological changes, as well as poetry, and even included a recipe for lasagna with spinach and cheese (an unusual dish for Palestinians). According to Labadi, "We try to represent different feminist perspectives, such as the Islamist feminist."

[19]The magazine is funded from outside, and each year the Women's Center looks for different sponsors to fund one or two issues. In 1996, for example, the Ford Foundation funded two issues. As a result, the center must be continually engaged in raising funds for the magazine. In general, to produce 1000 copies costs $3000.

[20]In *Unthinking Eurocentrism,* Ella Shohat and Robert Stam discuss how Eurocentric thinking "values literacy over orality and assigns the prerogative of interpreting history to the literate European. But one can appreciate literacy as a useful tool and still question the equation of the written with the lofty, the serious, the scientific, and the historical, and of the oral with the backward, the frivolous, and the irrational" (298).

[21]A recent study by the Birzeit University Community Health Unit found that 25 percent of the Palestinian population lives in dwellings of a density of three persons or more per room. See Penny Johnson, "Social Support: Gender and Social Policy in Palestine," Women's Studies Program, Birzeit University, 1997.

[22]Labadi and the Jerusalem Women's Studies Center have also recently been involved in video production to reach women through other media.

WORKS CITED

Abu Nahleh, Lamis. "Gender Planning and Vocational Education and Technical Training in Palestine: An Initial Framework." *Gender and Society,* Working Paper #4. Palestine: Women's Studies Program, Birzeit University, 1996.

Ahmad, Aijaz. *In Theory: Classes, Nations, Literatures.* New York: Verso, 1992.

Ahmed, Leila. *Women and Gender in Islam: Historical Roots of a Modern Debate.* New Haven, CT: Yale UP, 1994.

Amireh, Amal. "Problems and Prospects for Publishing in the West: Arab Women Writers Today." *Against the Current* Mar./Apr. (1997): 21–23.

———. "Framing Nawal El Saadawi: Arab Feminism in a Transnational World." *Signs: Journal of Women in Culture and Society,* forthcoming, Autumn 1998.

Allen, Roger. *The Arabic Novel: An Historical and Critical Introduction.* Syracuse, New York: Syracuse UP, 1982.

Ashrawi, Hanan. *This Side of Peace: A Personal Account.* New York: Simon & Schuster, 1995.

Badr, Liana. *A Balcony over the Fakihani.* Trans. Peter Clark and Christopher Tingley. New York: Interlink, 1993 (1983).

———. *A Compass for the Sunflower.* Trans. Catherine Cobham. London: Women's Press, 1989.

———. *The Eye of the Mirror.* Trans. Samira Kawar. Reading: Garnet, 1994 (1991).

———. *Najoum Ariha* (The Stars over Jericho) Cairo: Dar al-Hilal, 1993.

———. Personal interview. Bethlehem, 21 December 1995.

Colla, Elliott. "Multiplying Mahfouz." Rev. of *Naguib Mahfouz: The Pursuit of Meaning.* Rasheed el-Enany. *Stanford Humanities Review* 5 (1995): 182–188.

Cooke, Miriam and Margot Badran, eds. *Opening the Gates: A Century of Arab Feminist Writings.* Bloomington and Indianapolis: Indiana UP, 1990.

Dajani, Souad. "Between National and Social Liberation: The Palestinian women's movement in the Israeli occupied West Bank and Gaza Strip." *Women and the Israeli Occupation: The Politics of Change.* Tamar Mayer, ed. New York: Routledge, 1994. 33–61.

Darwish, Mahmoud. "We Travel Like Other People." In *Victims of a Map.* Trans. Abdullah al-Udhari. London: Al Saqi Books, 1984. 31.

Giacaman, Rita. "Palestinian women, the *intifada* and the state of independence: an interview." Interview by Graham Usher. *Race & Class* 34 (Jan./Mar. 1993): 31–43.

Grewal, Inderpal and Caren Kaplan, eds. *Scattered Hegemonies: Postmodernity and Transnational Feminist Practices.* Minneapolis: U of Minnesota P, 1994.

Helie-Lucas, Marie-Aimee. "Women, Nationalism and Religion in the Algerian Struggle." *Opening the Gates: A Century of Arab Feminist Writing*. Margot Badran and Miriam Cooke, eds. Bloomington: Indiana UP, 1990. 104–114.

Husayn, Taha. *Al-Ayyam*. Cairo: Dar al-Ma'arif, 1971.

Jameson, Fredric. "Third World Literature in the Era of Multinational Capital." *Social Text* (Fall 1986): 65–88.

Jayyusi, Salma Khadra. *Anthology of Modern Palestinian Literature*. New York: Columbia UP, 1992.

Johnson, Penny. "Social Support: Gender and Social Policy in Palestine." *Palestinian Women: A Status Report*. Birzeit University: Women's Studies Program, 1997.

Kandiyoti, Deniz. "Identity and Its Discontents: Women and the Nation." *Millennium: Journal of International Studies* 20, 3 (1991): 429-443.

Khalifeh, Sahar. *Lam Na'ud Jawari Lakum*. Cairo: Dar al-Ma'arif, 1974.

———. *Abbad Al-Shams* (*Sunflower*). Beirut: Munazzamat al-Tahrir al-Filastiniyyah, 1980.

———. *Mudhakkirat Imra'ah Ghayr Waqi'iya* (*Memoirs of an Unrealistic Woman*). Beirut: Dar al-Adab, 1986.

———. *Bab Al-Saha* (The Courtyard's Gate). Beirut: Dar al-Adab, 1990.

———. *Wild Thorns*. Trans. Trevor Le Gassick and Elizabeth Fernea. New York: Interlink, 1991.

———. Personal interview. Nablus, 21 August 1991.

Labadi, Fedwa. Personal interview. Jerusalem, 12 March 1996.

Lorde, Audrey. "Poetry Is Not a Luxury." *Sister Outsider*. Freedom, CA: The Crossing Feminist Press, 1984.

Malti-Douglas, Fedwa. *Woman's Body, Woman's Word: Gender and Discourse in Arabo-Islamic Writing*. New Jersey: Princeton UP, 1991.

Pathak, Zakia, Saswati Sengupta and Sharmila Purkayastha. "The Prisonhouse of Orientalism." *Textual Practice*, 5, 2 (Summer 1991): 195–217.

al-Rawi, Rosina-Fawzia. *Requirements for Gender Development in Palestinian Society*. East Jerusalem: Jerusalem Media & Communication Center, 1995.

El-Saadawi, Nawal. *The Hidden Face of Eve: Women in the Arab World*. Trans. Sherif Hetata. Boston: Beacon Press, 1982 (1980).

———. *Al Maru Wal Jins*. Cairo: Maktabat Madbuli, 1983.

———. *Al Wajh Al-'Ari Lil Mara Al-'Arabiyya*. Beirut: al-Mu'assasa al-'Arabiyya lil-Dirasat wal-Nashr, 1977.

———. "The Progressive Interview: Nawal El Saadawi." *The Progressive*, April 1992, 32–35.

Shaaban, Bouthaina. *Both Right and Left Handed: Arab Women Talk About Their Lives*. London: The Women's Press, 1988.

Shohat, Ella and Robert Stam. *Unthinking Eurocentrism: Multiculturalism and the Media*. London and New York: Routledge, 1994.

Tamari, Salim. "The Predicament of Palestinian Cultural Production." *Palestine-Israel Journal* 2 (1995): 98–100.

Tuqan, Fedwa. *Wahdi Ma Al-Ayyam*. Beirut: Dar al-'Awda, 1974.

———. *A Mountainous Journey*. Trans. Olive Kenny. Minnesota: Greywolf Press, 1990.

Zeidan, Joseph. *Arab Women Novelists: The Formative Years and Beyond*. Albany: State U of New York P, 1995.

SECTION II
The Writer as Text

Race, Gender, and the Politics of Reception of Latin American *Testimonios*

EVA PAULINO BUENO

The phenomenon called *testimonio*—testimonials—has gained considerable attention in the study of Latin American texts in the United States in the last ten years, even though the practice of giving testimony is an old one, and texts about testimonials exist in abundance. In this century alone, the testimonials of the survivors of concentration camps, as well as those given by people fleeing their countries in dictatorship-ridden Latin America, constitute moving monuments to human endurance and courage under the most extreme repression, torture, and suffering. In this essay, I want to discuss the peculiarities of the reception of some testimonial texts in the North American university. In the process, I hope to clarify some questions about the almost total concentration on the study of women's testimonials,[1] and to explore the reasons why the vast majority of texts studied in the United States come from people of Indian origin.[2] ("Indian," here, does not encompass the peoples called Native Americans who live in the United States. Indeed, as far as the study of testimonials in North American academia goes, Indians always live outside this country.) The exclusionary nature of the practice of *testimonio* and its political reverberations have so far gone not just untheorized, but mostly unquestioned In this essay, I want to ask why this has been so, and whose interests have been served in the maintenance of this situation.

For this study, I will use three main texts: *I . . . Rigoberta Menchú; An Indian Woman in Guatemala,* by Rigoberta Menchú and Elisabeth Burgos-Debray, *Let Me Speak!,* by Domitila Barrios de Chungara and Moema Viezzer, and *Child of the Dark,* by Carolina Maria de Jesus. The first of these texts is very well known in the North American academic circuit; the second one is known by people who specialize in Latin American texts; and the third one, after a period of relative "success" with students of political science and Latin American history, has almost totally disappeared from shelves and college syllabi. In the two first cases, the women giving their testimonials appear as representatives of their group—in Menchú's case the Quiché speaking Indians of Guatemala, and in Domitila de Chungara's case the miners of Bolivia. In general, both have been considered as representatives of the wider segment of peasants and political victims of the terrorist governments of their respective countries. And, as if inexorably, both Menchú and de Chungara become *the* representatives of most of the people of Guatemala and Bolivia, respectively.[3]

In great contrast, no intellectual group or political movement ever claimed that Carolina Maria de Jesus's text represents a segment of Brazilians, or that she herself is a voice for a community. Even when *Child of the Dark* was constantly in the syllabi of university courses, Carolina de Jesus was never taken to be speaking for the Blacks of Brazil, or for the women of Brazil, or for the peasants of Brazil. At most, she was considered a voice speaking against the evils of *favelas* (shantytowns) and on behalf of *favelados* (the people who live in *favelas*).[4]

Two of the reviews quoted on the covers of the book demonstrate how Carolina de Jesus stands out as an individual speaking *from* (or even *against*) her background. The review in the *New York Herald Tribune* says that *Child of the Dark* is "the raw, primitive journal of a street scavenger . . . who fought daily for survival for herself and her three illegitimate children." In the piece quoted from the *New York Times Book Review,* de Jesus is referred to as "a witness to the vicious fights, the knifings, the sordid sex life of the *favelados*—prisoners of poverty, prey of the unscrupulous, breeders of revolution."[5] On the other hand, the covers of the books by de Chungara and Menchú immediately present these women as leaders of their societies. *Let Me Speak!* refers to de Chungara as "a leader of a Housewives' Committee, dedicated to improving miners' and peasants' conditions." This book, the *Library Journal* writes, is "an important document from a usually silent group." *Two Thirds,* also quoted in the back cover, refers to *Let Me Speak!* as "the story of a people as much as . . . the story of an individual."[6] The excerpt from the review in the *London Times* on *I . . . Rigoberta Menchú* summarizes other commentaries: "This is a fascinating and moving description of the culture of an entire people."

Two questions preoccupy me at this point: first, what kind of community can produce an individual who can express, in her personal history, the history of the whole community? And, second, what historical circumstances give some women the power to speak from inside their communities and represent them to the outside world? Adrianne Aron, writing about testimonies as "a therapeutic tool in the treatment of people who have suffered psychological trauma under state terrorism," states the following:

> In many areas of Latin American people with little preparation for public expression—most notably, women—have come forward with their testimony to challenge oppressive power structures and to reappropriate for themselves and their communities the moral standards and social order taken away by the repression. (175)

Among these women Aron mentions the Mothers and Grandmothers of the Plaza de Mayo in Argentina, the Co-Madres (Committee of the Mothers and Relatives of the Disappeared, Political Prisoners, and Assassinated) of El Salvador, and the GAM (Grupo de Apoyo Mutuo—Mutual Support Group) of Guatemala. But the existence of these groups in the countries mentioned still does not explain why their members are mostly women. Could it be because women have traditionally been seen as nurturing, as deeply embedded in the dynamics of the group, rather than as separate individuals? Or could the reason be more simply that, precisely because of their gender, they expect more respect (or less violence) from the political powers of their countries? Whether we accept all or none of these possibilities, another question still remains in relation to all testimonial texts in general: to what extent have these women been able to speak *as* women, and to what extent have they had to totally ignore their gender and become, instead, *communal beings*? And, if they have become communal beings, why are some communities seen as worthier of telling their stories than others? *Child of the Dark, Let me Speak!*, and *I . . . Rigoberta Menchú* together provide an excellent occasion for the discussion of these matters. I will use them not so much as antagonistic examples of testimonial texts, but as complementary ones.

Since the conditions that the three women portray in their texts have many similarities, it is strange that in this latest surge of interest in testimonial texts by Latin American women, Carolina de Jesus's text is never mentioned. Here we have, on one side, two texts produced by two oppressed Latin American women of Indian heritage, and their enthusiastic reception by North American academics; and on the other side, a text produced by an oppressed Black woman, and its non-reception by North American academics. It surely cannot be either the subject matter or the formats of the books themselves (de Jesus's diary format, as opposed to Domitila de Chungara's and Rigoberta Menchú's more traditional oral testimonial accounts) that determine this difference. Books, as cultural artifacts, do not exist in a vacuum. Rather, as I hope to demonstrate, Carolina de Jesus's race, as well as her self-depiction as a *sexual* female being, contributed to the fact that her work was not hailed even as a precursor when the study of *testimonios* became fashionable in the United States. And it is the political energies existing within the North American academic world that determined the different reception of these testimonials.

Of course these energies are a world onto themselves, but any discussion of *testimonios* needs to acknowledge their existence. Consider, for instance, George Yúdice's opening paragraph in "Testimonio and Postmodernism" where he says that "[m]ore than any other form of writing in Latin America, the *testimonio* has contributed to the demise of the traditional role of the intellectual/artist as spokesperson for the 'voiceless' " (15). That is, because of *testimonio,* the formerly silent people can now have a direct, unmediated access to the public. The problem with Yúdice's statement is that it ignores the fact that, if it were not for the heavy sponsorship of testimonial texts in the North American university, these texts would have never achieved such a high degree of political and intellectual provocation in the country. It is true that Rigoberta Menchú's book reached the North American classrooms in numbers never before seen for a book of this kind. However, because of the high volume of scholarship generated about *testimonios,* and *I . . . Rigoberta Menchú* especially, the most measurable result has been that the people whose voices have been heard most are those who work in North American academic institutions. In other words, the study of *testimonio* has been transformed into a game of mirrors in which North American academics who write, speak, and publish on the subject assume the position of spokespersons for the rest of American academics, determining which book is worthy of study and why.

Of course, it is quite encouraging that this subject, the *testimonio,* has attracted the attention of so many scholars in the country. The problem that needs to be addressed is that the scholarship generated around the testimonial narrative from Latin America has created a very rigid canon. This canon, dictated from top to bottom, follows an oppressive pattern and ends up creating a given set of "oppressed" who are Indians, live "far away," and conduct very strict, if any, sex lives. As it is pre-

scribed now, in the United States, the study of *testimonios* has become
the construction of a form that, on the one hand, effaces the individuality
and the gender of its authors and, on the other, promotes their identity exclusively as representatives of their communities. Moreover, it has become entangled in rigid formulas that detract from the testimonials'
initial liberating and democratic impulses.

At this point, I must emphasize that I believe that the plight of the people represented by the three women is equally important: the poor of
Brazil, the miners in Bolivia, and the Guatemalan Indians all deserve respect and liberty to pursue their lives with dignity. Moreover, the lives of
Carolina de Jesus, Domitila de Chungara, and Rigoberta Menchú offer
examples of extraordinary courage and resistance during moments of extreme suffering. Any people should be proud to have among their members
such individuals who can persevere in duress, fight against their oppressors, and yet keep a generous attitude towards their fellow human beings.

This essay does not intend to assess these texts, or their authors,
much less to compare the suffering that each portrays. Rather, it intends
to be a reflection on the factors—race, sex, place of origin—that determine that some books become part of a "canon" of testimonials, whereas
others either attract little attention or become "out of fashion" even when
the conditions that gave rise to them have not disappeared. The study of
testimonios has become prominent in the United States since the last
years of the 1980s, especially in departments of Latin American Languages and in departments of Languages and of Humanities. As I see
them, however, the factors leading to this interest in the *testimonio* are
extremely complex, extrapolating merely academic concerns, and becoming the vehicle of ideological and political practices. What I want to
suggest is an "opening" of the canon, so that more texts, from different
places, can be fully incorporated into the study of testimonial texts. And,
although it might be clear by now, I will stress that I do not agree with intellectuals of Dinesh D'Souza's persuasion, whose claims that Menchú's
text is not good literature are fraught with political intentions. I believe
that D'Souza's statement that the study of this book is a "romanticizing
of (the) suffering" of the oppressed only serves a political agenda whose
intent is, ultimately, *not* to hear the oppressed at all, but to ignore their
appeals to justice, or to silence them completely.[7] In what follows, I will
review the existing scholarship on the *form* of the *testimonio* and propose
the reasons why, I believe, Carolina Maria de Jesus's book, *Child of the
Dark,* has never been considered part of the *testimonio* canon.

I

Carolina Maria de Jesus's account, unknown in the disciplinary context of the studies of *testimonios,* has many differences from both Domitila de Chungara's and Rigoberta Menchú's books. In April 1958 Audálio Dantas, then a young reporter working with a local newspaper, met Carolina Maria de Jesus in a ceremony for the opening of a playground near Canindé, in the state of São Paulo, Brazil. She was one of the residents in a slum nearby. What called Dantas's attention to Carolina de Jesus was the fact that, in an argument with some adults who were taking the children's place on the playground toys, she threatened to put their names in her book. Curious about this "book," Dantas approached de Jesus and asked to see it. It took him some time to gain her confidence, but she finally showed him a number of notebooks in which she had two kinds of text. In one, she wrote stories; in the other, she wrote her diaries. After looking at the material, Dantas simply discarded the fictional stories as "childish fantasies" and took the diaries to his newspaper office. These diaries speak in very exacting detail about her life as a single mother who picks paper and scrap metal from the street and sells it in order to feed herself and her children. Excerpts from de Jesus's diaries appeared in the newspaper and attracted considerable attention. In two years, a somewhat edited version of the whole text of the diaries appeared in print with the name of *Quarto de despejo* (literally "room where garbage is dumped").

When the book appeared, ten thousand copies were sold in three days and, "in less than six months ninety thousand copies were sold in Brazil and today it is still on the best-seller list, having sold more than any other Brazilian book in history" (translator's preface, 13). Carolina, we are told in the preface, used the profits from the book to buy a brick house, but finally died in abject poverty.[8]

Domitila Barrios de Chungara's book originated in a much more prestigious circumstance: her participation in an international event in 1975. On this occasion, Domitila, a woman of the Bolivian Andes, wife of a miner and mother of seven children, began to give her testimony to Moema Viezzer, who later edited and published it. The book, which in English has the forceful title, *Let Me Speak!,* in Spanish has the more tentative, almost plaintive title, *Si me permiten hablar . . .* (*If you allow me to speak . . .*). "The idea for this testimony," Viezzer writes in her introduction, "arose out of the presence of Domitila Barrios de Chungara at the International Women's Year Tribunal, organized by the United Nations and held in Mexico in 1975" (9). The material for the book was collected during Viezzer's interviews with Domitila in Mexico and Bolivia, Domitila's speeches at the Tribunal, and other conversations, dialogues, and discussions Viezzer had with several groups of people, including Latin American exiles living in Mexico and representatives of the press, radio, and television.

Like Domitila de Chungara's, the last of the three books also had its beginnings far away from the author's native country, in an even more rarefied political as well as geographical context. This book resulted from a conversation-interview between a woman from a different class and educational background, Elisabeth Burgos-Debray, and the person who gave testimony, the Quiché Mayan Indian, Rigoberta Menchú. The interviews took place in Paris, during a week Rigoberta Menchú spent at Burgos-Debray's house. Menchú was in Paris under the sponsorship of a number of solidarity groups as a representative of the "31 of January Popular Front." In 1983 the Editorial Argos Vergara of Barcelona published, in Spanish, *Me llamo Rigoberta Menchú y así me nació la conciencia* (*My name is Rigoberta Menchú and thus my conscience was born*). The book was quickly translated into English as *I . . . Rigoberta Menchú; An Indian Woman in Guatemala.*[9]

This book has become, ever since it appeared in print in English, a gospel of testimonial narratives. Innumerable classes have been taught, books written, papers published, and conferences held on it. In the 1995 MLA convention, for instance, a very well-attended session was dedicated solely to the discussion of ways to teach this text. In the Twentieth Century Literature Conference in Louisville, in February 1996, there was also a whole session dedicated to *I . . . Rigoberta Menchú*. It seems clear that *I . . . Rigoberta Menchú* has not only become canonical, but that the very canon has been formed on the basis of it.[10] Far more crucial is that the exclusion of other *testimonios,* in turn, raises the question of the depth of the North American academics' political framework and the conditions in which they operate. That is, the political and ideological agendas espoused by the academics who have been discussing the testimonial narratives reflect primarily the disciplinary conditions and academic imperatives of the United States, and not necessarily the interests of the people *testimonios* represent.

Some problems inevitably derive from this situation. One of the first is that, because *I . . . Rigoberta Menchú* was originally published in Spanish, the word *testimonio* has taken on a totally *Spanish* American coloration. Roberto Carr remarks on this fact in his comparison between Menchú's book and *Lionheart Gal,* by Honor Ford-Smith, a Jamaican woman: whereas Menchú's book has had successive re-editions, Ford-Smith's has had only few and occasional reprintings. Carr attributes this difference to "the growing interest in Central and Latin America," as opposed to the considerably less interest in the Caribbean (*"Representando el testimonio,"* 82). The overwhelming number of essays and conference papers on the testimonial of Rigoberta Menchú show that, indeed, the North American academics' interest in testimonial narratives is anything but inclusionary. But the Caribbean texts are not the only ones left out of the study of *testimonio*. Clearly, North American academics are *not* interested in *all* Latin American texts; if that were the case, they would study a wide range of testimonials, from all countries that produce them.

And why are academics interested in sponsoring these two testimonial narratives, de Chungara's and Menchú's, almost exclusively when, if given a space, North American Indigenous peoples, Black people, or battered women, to mention only a few of the oppressed in this country, would also offer their testimonies? Could it be that these people are too close to us, and therefore not exotic enough to merit the attention? Or is it that human suffering sprawled on our sidewalks and shelters and factories and farms lacks the distance that would transform it into an aesthetic object? To judge from the massive interest especially in *I . . . Rigoberta Menchú, testimonios* are only about Indians of Central America preferably those whose own political convictions do not disturb those of the sponsoring North American academics.[11] Any testimonial narrative has to measure up against this standard, otherwise it will not qualify.[12]

One of the reasons for the sponsorship of these testimonials is, undoubtedly, the larger political question of the genocide that the United States has recently financed in Central America. (United States interventions in the Americas have been constant for more than a century, but the most recent scandalous examples happened in Central America, especially El Salvador, Nicaragua, and Guatemala.) North American academics, in their effort to sponsor the testimonials of some individuals from some of these affected areas, hope to make reparations for what their country has been responsible for. But even this guilt is not so simple.

At this point, Gayatri Spivak's now famous question, "Can the subaltern speak?" and her not so equally famous answer—"No"—will help us understand why even the best intentioned North American academics might be contributing to the continuation of a system of privilege for some and oppression for the majority. As Spivak writes, even the most committed ethnographer or solidarity worker carries with her, embedded in the very core of her intellectual project, the traces of a colonial construction of the Other. In the process of "contacting" the subaltern Other, the ethnographer, or solidarity worker, neutralizes the sheer *reality* of the difference which the Other represents. This *flattening out* of the Other— subaltern—enables the ethnographer/solidarity worker to become oblivious to her relatively privileged position both in comparison with the Other and in relation to a global system of power relations. As a result, the subaltern does *not* speak. It is the representative of an intellectual/ academic project who speaks in the subaltern's place. In the specific case of the North American academics' interest in the *testimonio,* the project will advance first and foremost the cause of the intellectuals, and only tangentially will it affect the cause of the subalterns.

This absence of self-consciousness on the part of North American academics is, it seems, pervasive. Recalling George Yúdice's words about how the *testimonio* has enabled the voiceless to have a voice without the need of intellectuals as their spokespersons, it is interesting to observe what another critic, Doris Sommer, has to say about the elite writers in Latin America. She writes the following:

> The [Latin American] elite wrapped itself in lyrical ponchos (as Josephina Ludmer showed for Argentina) or stepped to tropical rhythms (as in Gilberto Freire's idyllic anthropology of Brazil, *The Masters and the Slaves* [1946]), not only to speak *for* one's people but also to speak *to* powerful outside competitors for markets and territories. ("The Places of History: Regionalism Revisited in Latin America," 120)

In another, earlier, essay, when discussing what she calls "the illusion of immediacy" in Rigoberta Menchú's text, Sommer writes that "Some of us are . . . reluctant to doubt a writer's sincerity or the possibility that a text can offer inviolable truth, even though we are aware that this is textual construct" ("Rigoberta's Secrets," 32). So, for Sommer, other people's texts are "textual constructs," in the same way that only readers of less reputable (less canonical) *testimonios* are greedy. Yúdice's and Sommer's statements seem to suggest a position of almost divine neutrality for the *elite North American academics.* It is as if, now, for Yúdice, with the demise of the traditional role of the academic "as a spokesperson for the 'voiceless,' " we will finally hear the oppressed peoples's voice, totally unmediated. And, for Sommer, wrapping oneself in lyrical ponchos and presenting an "idyllic" version of one's country are faults that befall only the Latin American elite; the North American intellectual elite is free from such follies. After all, as Sommer says, even though reluctant, we do doubt a writer's sincerity—in this case she is referring to Elisabeth Burgos-Debray's interventions in Rigoberta Menchú's oral testimonial to transform it into a book. What both Yúdice and Sommer ignore is that they, as members of the North American academic elite, have been in the position to receive these literary/sociological/testimonial productions from Latin America, and that they, more than anybody else, constitute "the powerful outside" that will determine how a book, or an idea, or a cause from Latin America fares in the United States. In other words, North American intellectuals/academics are anything but "neutral" with respect to their actual role in the instantiation of the study of any Latin American text.

Conversely, due to the extreme power North American elite intellectuals exert on the reception of Latin American texts and subjects in this country, these intellectuals can also dictate, or at least strongly influence, their demise. Sommer has a very interesting passage about how, when reading Menchú's text, some readers "deriving perhaps from certain (autobiographical?) habits of reading . . . project onto the persona we are hearing a present and knowable self, despite being told that the voice is second or third hand." And Sommer wraps up the paragraph with a statement which, I believe, can function both for the anonymous reader and for the well-known North American academic: "I suggest that these projections of presence and truth *are hardly generous*" ("Rigoberta's Secrets," 32; emphasis mine).

Consider John Beverley, who has been one of the champions of the study of *testimonios* in general and of Rigoberta Menchú's book in particular in the United States. In his last publication on Menchú, "The Real Thing (Our Rigoberta)," Beverley announces an epitaph for the *testimonio* as a viable field of study. He writes that even Menchú "also senses that returning to *testimonio* is now beside the point; there are other things that she has, or wants, to do" (139). This claim sounds very strange, especially because Beverley also quotes from a passage in which Menchú, referring to *I . . . Rigoberta Menchú, An Indian Woman in Guatemala,* clearly says that "what the book has are fragments, and I hope one day *we could republish it* with new materials" (137, emphasis mine). If Menchú says that she would like to republish the book with yet more materials, how can Beverley say that for Menchú, returning to *testimonio* is "beside the point"? It seems to me that, at least according to the passage Beverley quotes, Menchú still believes in the *testimonio* as an important medium, whereas Beverley is the one who is ready to move on to new, more fashionable subjects.

In other words, it is impossible to believe that *testimonio* has won its (little) space in the canon of texts in the United States based on its own humanitarian, moral, or literary merits. The *testimonio* has acquired importance because it has been sponsored by a group of intellectuals at elite institutions who have placed Rigoberta Menchú's book on their syllabi and begun to generate a somewhat voluminous scholarship about it. In fact, as we can see from the examples of the numerous conferences, essays, and books on Rigoberta Menchú's work, the *testimonio*—or, rather, *I, . . . Rigoberta Menchú's testimonio*—has become *the* primary tool that gives voice to many intellectuals in the United States. To deny such an evident fact is naive, or, worse still, disingenuous.

To try to correct the record, it is necessary to remember that people other than Rigoberta Menchú (and Domitila Barrios de Chungara) have given their testimonies and have had these testimonies transformed into books which are (usually) available for study. It is important that we, teachers in the United States, make available to our students a wider range of *testimonios,* from different places of the world. And yet, even taking into consideration the factors related to the dynamics specific to the North American academic, there still remains the question of why some ethnic groups among Indigenous peoples have gained more prominence than others in the recent study of testimonial practice.

What seems to be clear is that, at some point in the history of Western Culture, Blacks and Indians were allotted certain spaces within the political and cultural spectrum, and their roles were established. Sociologist Darcy Ribeiro's simple explanation about the classification of people is, perhaps, a good way to start looking at how the discourse on race can be constituted. According to Ribeiro's classification, there are the "Witness People," who are "survivors of *high autonomous civilizations that suffered the impact of European expansion.* They are modern survivors of the traumatizing action of that expansion and of their effort at ethnic reconstitution as modern national societies" (*The Americas and Civilization,* 80; my emphasis).[13] The Witness People are located in India, China, Japan, Korea, Indochina, the Islamic countries, and, in the Americas, "they are represented by Mexico, Guatemala, and the peoples of the Andean highlands, the two former being survivors of the Aztec and Maya civilizations, the latter of the Inca" (81). Both de Chungara and Menchú would, therefore, be in this category.

What stands out in this explanation is both the choice of the adjective "high" used to qualify civilizations, and also Ribeiro's exclusion of Black Africans from the list of Witness peoples. They are, as we see later in Ribeiro's classification, lumped in the category of "New Peoples" who "emerg[ed] from the conjunction, deculturation, and amalgamation of African, European, and indigenous ethnic stocks" (83). I believe it is not necessary to stress the difference between the adjective "high" used for the "Witness People," and the sense of confusion expressed by the accumulation of the words "conjunction," "deculturation," and "amalgamation," chosen to describe the "New People." If the "Witness People" are "high" precisely because they remained "pure," then it follows that the "New People," mixed up, are "low."

Suppose we ask why Ribeiro does not place the descendants of African Blacks among the testimonial peoples of the Americas. After all, they are also the "modern survivors of the traumatizing actions of European expansion," since it was Europe's need to colonize and make the Americas profitable that caused the greatest commerce in African slaves. Besides, even a superficial look at the American racial and cultural panorama reveals that, except for those countries Ribeiro names as inhabited by the "Witness People," or by the "Transplanted People," the Black heritage is strong and important as a basis for the very definition of the other countries' identities.[14] Ribeiro's classification demonstrates a conscious choice to keep the two types of culture apart for the reason of color. The significance of such classifications can be fully comprehended when we remember that, historically, Blacks in America suffered the longest continuous slavery and, once freed, have been made to occupy the lowest positions in society and suffer continuous discrimination.

One other way of looking at the different situation between Blacks and Indigenous peoples is offered by Carlos Rangel in his discussion of the European construction of the myth of the Native American "noble savages." In a footnote in *The Latin Americans: Their Love-Hate Relationship with the United States,* Rangel asks why Europeans did not encounter the noble savage in Africa. His own answer is this:

> Quite certainly because the African savages had been known since antiquity and were not, therefore, truly exotic. *Europe found no noble savages in Africa because it was not seeking them there.* And this is why the blacks were perceived by Western consciousness simply as savages—without qualification, in the exact, pejorative meaning of the word. (93, my emphasis)

Quite naturally, the "noble savages" were found where the Europeans sought them—in the Americas. Christopher Columbus's descriptions of the inhabitants of the land he discovered on October 12, 1492 can be seen as a foundational moment in the creation of a utopian discourse about the Americas and its original peoples.[15] However, the need to conquer and obtain gold at any cost soon dispelled the notion of the uncooperative Indian's "natural goodness," and inaugurated the massacres that constituted "the greatest genocide in human history" (Todorov, 5).[16] Later, when the struggles for liberation from the mother countries began in Latin America, the local political elites recuperated the myth for their purposes and started using their real or invented Indian heritage as a means to differentiate themselves from the European model. "Honorary Indians" sprang up from every elite group in Latin America, while these elites remained oblivious to the actual living conditions of the real Indians among them. Moreover, even in those countries where Blacks constituted a large part of the population—such as Brazil—no one ever claimed identity as an "honorary Black." The stain of slavery was, by then, deeply rooted and associated with Blacks, precisely because they had been taken as slaves for such a long time before America was "discovered."

The "natural goodness" or "nobility" of the Indian, and the—as it were—"natural propensity" of Blacks for being enslaved was basically ingrained by the time Europe started its expansion in the mid-sixteenth century. Because they had been routinely enslaved, the Blacks of Africa could not claim what Ribeiro calls "high autonomous *civilization*"; even the mere acknowledgment that Blacks had *any* civilization would have at least hindered their enslavement in the first place. The need to deny a Black culture and civilization led to their being placed in a category other than human, and to their routine brutal enslavement, against which not even the Christian church lifted its voice. Like the primitive inhabitants of the Americas, African Blacks were denied their native language and forced to learn their captors' language, their religion, their culture. In the Americas, thrown together with others who were sometimes from completely different cultural and linguistic backgrounds, Black Africans had to re-create their cultures in extremely adverse conditions, always under the threat of brutality, torture, and death at the hands of their White owners.[17]

I believe that the almost exclusive interest in testimonials by people of Indian origin derives from the dismissal, or the denial, of a specific Black culture in the Americas. It seems that Black culture and the struggle to maintain it in every possible form is "discounted" and read under the guise of, in Darcy Ribeiro's words, "amalgamation," "acculturation," or "impurity." Blacks in Latin America in general, and in Brazil specifically, are not accorded a degree of independent culture; in most cases, Black cultural manifestations are merely lumped together under the rubric of "folklore." The denial of a Black culture leads to the denial of the work of Black artists and intellectuals as representative of a culture. In this sense, the form of *testimonio,* as it has been commonly understood, cannot accommodate the Black experience. A Black person will always be seen as speaking only for himself/herself.[18] The community, which gives its members a sense of belonging, is impossible in the absence of a society that accepts and cherishes the cultural contribution of its members. Domitila de Chungara and Rigoberta Menchú speak and give their testimony in the name of their people from the very core of this sense of belonging, of togetherness with their kin. Carolina de Jesus, who grew up without a family, did not attend social or educational institutions that could have given her a sense of community; never married, she had no other society but the one represented by her young, dependent children. Her testimony, written as a diary, cannot picture her poverty as exemplary; as Carlos Vogt writes, poverty in *Child of the Dark* "is not a symbolic construction with pedagogical goals, but a social state of real need against which the only possible struggle is dictated by the means this state makes possible" (208).

And thus, with the example of Carolina de Jesus's exclusion from the studies of *testimonio,* we can ask again what *testimonio* is, after all. If it is presumed to be the form that opens a space—or that *is* the space— for those who bear testimony to a condition of stress, oppression, and suffering of a people, it should be available to whoever needs to represent the stress, oppression, and suffering of this people. It should be available to all. And all nonfictional account of a people's struggle should be considered testimonials, even in formal terms. But, as the study of testimonio in the United States shows, that is not the case.

II

The study of *testimonio* in the United States has been informed by the writings of academics such as Margaret Randall, who distinguishes *testimonio* from other genres by its use of direct sources. Randall writes that *testimonio* implies

> the delivery of a history not through generalizations which characterize the conventional texts, but through particularities of the voice or voices of the protagonist people; the immediacy (an informer relates

an episode he/she has lived, a survivor passes on to us an experience
that nobody else can offer, etc.); the use of secondary material (an introduction, other interviews, documents, graphic material, chronologies
and additional materials which help make up a living picture); and a
high aesthetic quality. ("Qué es, y cómo se hace un testimonio?" 22-
23, my translation)

Elsewhere in the essay, Randall enters her instructions for anybody who
wants to work with *testimonio,* saying that he/she has to have a profound
knowledge of the ideology of the proletariat, to prepare a detailed ques-
tionnaire with meaningful questions, to take a notebook where things related to the interview will be written down, to know how to operate
apparatuses such as a tape recorder, and to be able to transcribe the oral
testimony in two copies. An imperative point, according to Randall, is to
have the assistance of somebody who speaks the language of the informer, in order to avoid wrong interpretations. Randall's admonition is
triggered by the bad example given by Oscar Lewis, who wrote *Los hijos
de Sanchez, Pedro Martinez, and Cuatro hombres y cuatro mujeres.* According to Randall, even though Lewis was a good writer, used detailed
techniques, and had access to funds that enabled him to use a great number of technical apparatuses, his books do not reflect *la verdadera histo-
ria* because he started his project by choosing his informer according to
preconceived ideas about what he believed worthy of study (25).

There are, I believe, several problems with Randall's instructions.
The first one is that she seems only fitfully aware of the problematic nature of the process of representing anybody, especially a person from a
different culture who speaks a different language. Even though the "author" has become a much more vexed entity in the testimonial narrative,
in which the text is the result of interviews and conversations between
the witness and the compiler, there still exists at least an "author effect."
That is, the compiler has to make the final decisions as to which repetitions to keep and which to discard, which verb tenses to correct in order
to avoid unnecessary interference and which to keep in order to maintain
enough of the witness's own pattern of speech. Randall simply infers that
any group or person about whom a testimony is written will have their
interests best served by somebody who has a deep knowledge of the history of the *proletariat* struggle. As a whole, the project will consist, then,
in the attempt to right the wrongs done to the proletariat as a group. The
person who speaks, the witness, even if she speaks from her own personal experience, will have her individual history elided for the ultimate

good of the proletariat. No other way is possible for the testimony, which will scorn mere personal histories, or histories that do not advance the cause of the "proletariat." And, lastly, Randall seems to be suggesting that a person who has a deep knowledge of the history of the proletariat will never conduct interviews, take notes, or do the final editing with any bias or prejudice.

What Randall seems to take for granted, in her study of the *testimonio* is, first and foremost, that there exists a group of people—those schooled in the history of the proletariat—who can be divinely impartial towards their subject. Second, Randall presumes the existence of an ideal witness who, for her part, is also divinely impartial, never at odds with her society, and able to speak in the name of all other people from her community. The witness is one with the community, and neither gender, class, nor age will interfere with this person's testimony, because it is the community's testimony and the person's voice is the voice of the community. It is as if the witness becomes totally disembodied, transparent, a mere agent for the entity called "the community." Yet, Domitila, Rigoberta, and Carolina are women, and the fact of their gender and of how it is constituted in their respective cultures is of utmost importance, both as an underlying reality to the experiences they narrate and as an explanation for the reception of their testimonials. Whether their testimonials are viewed as demonstrating what Lynda Marín calls a "mediated selfhood" (62), or viewed as a way of exploring "the alterity of [a] collective and therefore problematic 'we' " (Marín, 63), these women speak out not simply as political beings, but as female beings from a specific culture.

When, for instance, Domitila de Chungara describes her imprisonment and her torture, it is clear that the specific types of suffering she is subjected to at the hands of her captors are meant to attack her *female* self, especially because she is pregnant. During the torture, she tries to stop her contractions, because the leader of the torturing soldiers is waiting for the child to come out for him to decapitate it (147). After the child is stillborn, due to the excruciating torture Domitila endures, she has to suffer the humiliation of having a gynecologist examine her in front of the soldiers, who laugh and make fun of her (151–3). Rigoberta Menchú herself, even though she does not suffer this kind of physical torture, suffers the psychological torture of knowing that her beloved mother is being repeatedly tortured and raped by soldiers. And later, when she decides to renounce marriage (220–6), she does so with the complete knowledge that a single woman, in her culture, is at best an anomaly. Finally, for Carolina Maria de Jesus, her predicaments are connected to the fact that, because she is an adult woman who has sex, she can get pregnant, and once she gives birth, she will be the only person responsible for the child's welfare. Neither the state, nor a family, nor the neighbors will care for those born of her body: as a woman, she is automatically a mother, and as a single mother, she is the sole recourse for her children. When John Beverley, in an authoritative, formal account—"The Margin at the Center: On *Testimonio*"—mentions that the older literary forms, such as the novel and the short story, originated in a time of transition from a feudalist to a capitalist mode of production, he does not discuss the fact that these forms depicted a specific kind of social arrangement in which the binary opposition of *male/female* was rigidly set. In the time frame he presents, the public-domestic realms existed in a symbolic economy where the woman was assigned a role outside the means of production and was either "elevated" to the role of nurturer, keeper of the domestic fire and or morality, or placed in the category of "whore." Beverley stresses the *testimonio* as a cultural phenomenon linked basically to matters of national identity and to the preservation of a culture oppressed by capitalist forces. The result is that, as Randall suggests, the ideal witness is a "communal being" who cannot set herself apart in terms of her individuality, much less her gender.

For both Beverley and Randall, the welfare of the group is foremost in the roots of the *testimonio*. No wonder Randall excludes the biography and the autobiography from the *testimonio* form: if the individual, private life does not speak directly of the community life, it is looked upon suspiciously, because individuality is, itself, a bourgeois construct. The *testimonio* is, and can only be, for Randall, the history of a group, in which the individual can only function as a mouth to transmit the truth her eyes have seen. Other parts of the body are not involved, as long as the witness comes from the correct group. One of the consequences of ideologizing the form of *testimonio* has been the overwhelming disdain of gender.

Indeed, both *Let Me Speak!* and *I . . . Rigoberta Menchú,* start with memorable statements of the authors' commitment to the cause of their communities. In the opening page of *Let Me Speak!* Domitila de Chungara says:

> I don't want anyone at any moment to interpret the story I'm about to
> tell as something that is only personal. Because I think that my life is
> related to my people. What happened to me could have happened to
> hundreds of people in my country. I want to make this clear, because I

recognize that there have been people who have done much more than
I for the people, but who have died or who haven't had the opportunity
to be known. (15)

In the opening page of *I . . . Rigoberta Menchú,* we see exactly the same
sentiment, when Menchú says:

I'd like to stress that it's not only my life, it's also the testimony of my
people . . . what has happened to me has happened to many other people too: my story is the story of all poor Guatemalans. My personal experience is the reality of a whole people. (1)

On the other hand, the narrating mode of Carolina de Jesus's book is
very different: she starts by recording a perfectly domestic affair, her
daughter's birthday. The problem, she immediately states, is that she is
not able to buy her child a pair of shoes because "we are slaves to the cost
of living" (17). Her struggle, which can be seen as a constant struggle to
obtain money, at first sight seems devoid of a larger political context.
However, the "cost of living," as de Jesus points out throughout her text,
is the product of economic factors, which are, in their turn, the result of
political events upon which the poor have no influence. There are yet
other differences in the very form of de Jesus's text. One of them is the
fact that de Jesus's account is taken from the diary she wrote. Her text,
because she is reporting a daily struggle, has the immediacy of the local
daily news: she reports on the place where she lives, a slum around São
Paulo, at the same time as she makes pointed commentaries on the political and economical situation of Brazil. At no moment in her text does de
Jesus say that she is speaking for her people, or for any people. Hers is a
voice that does not claim for itself a polyphony. Her narration is made
without either the physical or the temporal distance both Rigoberta
Menchú and Domitila de Chungara have when they give their testimonies away from their countries, some time after the events they describe took place.
    Carolina de Jesus's text, even though it is the narrative of the oppres-
sion and suffering of an individual whose life can be seen as exemplary
of the lives of others of her race and class, has never been called a *testimony*. Indeed, it seems that this self-taught woman who barely went to
school is speaking outside a culture, as a member of no race, as a representative of only herself. Carolina Maria de Jesus is a Black woman in a
country where Blacks, even more than a century after the official free-

dom of the slaves (signed into law by Princess Isabel in 1888), are still considered second-rate citizens and are routinely denied jobs and other opportunities on the basis of their race. Moreover, as a woman alone, Carolina de Jesus is also speaking from outside a familial, social, and economic tradition: she has no parents, no brothers or sisters, no husband, no stable job, and, unlike Domitila de Chungara and Rigoberta Menchú, she has no community—the miners for de Chungara and the Quiché for Menchú—to go back to and about which to speak.[19] And yet, she is a woman and she does not renounce the possibility of having sex. As a result, at least as far as the prescriptions for the study of *testimonios* go, a book like *Child of the Dark* is excluded from the list of possible titles.

III

The question, at this point, is not just how we can explain Carolina Maria de Jesus's work, or how we can understand her differences from and similarities both to Domitila Barrios de Chungara and Rigoberta Menchú. Rather, I believe, we should question why the work of this Black woman is not ever mentioned in the studies of *testimonios*. The mentioning of a family affair, or a child's birthday, followed by the mentioning of the family's slavery to the cost of living in a country plagued by inflation and corruption, at once implicate Carolina de Jesus and her small family within an economy *that goes beyond her and the slum*. This wider world, however, can only appear in de Jesus's text as a reflection of her own thoughts. De Jesus does not participate in any formal public activity engaged in the welfare either of women or of the slum dwellers in Brazil; in the most immediate sense, she represents nobody but herself and her fatherless children.

Like Rigoberta's mother, Rigoberta herself, and Domitila, Carolina is also the citizen of a country in which it is possible for a mother not to be able to buy food and clothes for her children. The difference is that Carolina is a single mother. Each one of her children has a different father.[20] Carolina does not have any help, either from a public welfare system or from the children's fathers. Because she has young children who need to be cared for, she cannot hold a job that would require regular hours. In addition, she is Black and has no school diploma. The solution, for her, is to make a living picking paper and scrap metal from the garbage bins on the street, while her children are left locked in her shack. Carolina de Jesus, besides the fact of the historical configuration of her race, also has to deal with the specificity of her gender and of her class. Because she has no family, she is the sole provider for her children and the sole arbiter of her decisions. She is therefore the "head" of the household, and she knows, for instance, that drinking would denigrate her and put her children in danger. In spite of the appalling suffering and humiliation she is subjected to, she does not give in to despair. However, hers are "individual" choices, since she is accountable to no one. She cannot claim any affiliation to a group, family, or community, except the one represented by her three children who depend on her for everything. And yet, at a certain point in her diary, she writes: "Here in the favela almost everyone has a difficult fight to live. But I am the only one who writes of what suffering is. I do this for the good of the others" (37–8).

For Carolina de Jesus, the struggle for survival is made even more difficult because she has to safeguard her shack against the attacks of neighbors—men, women, and children—who can easily transform her and her family into scapegoats. Even in the slum, she is an outsider because she has no husband. Her struggle against the neighbors is recorded in her diary and documents the increasing deterioration of her situation: "the terrible neighbors I have won't leave my children alone" (18); "maybe Dona Rosa or . . . Mary Angel fought with my children" (18); "Dona Rosa, as soon as she saw my boy José Carlos, started to fight with him" (20); "Dona Cecília appeared. She came to punish my children" (20). Carolina's days are long and hard; she has to carry as much as forty pounds of paper and scrap metal so that she can make a few *cruzeiros,* buy the basic necessities—rice and beans, usually—and feed the children. When she is at work, she still worries about the children, because she is afraid that "those human beasts are capable of invading my shack and mistreating my children . . . they wait for me to leave so they can come to my shack and hurt my children . . . When the children are alone they can't defend themselves" (24). Very clearly, Carolina cannot lean on any kind of communal feeling, neither a real nor a fantasy one.

Yet, there is another world besides the slum. There is, after all, the wider society, which has institutions and which should (but does not) provide for persons like Carolina and her children. Carolina has nowhere to turn for help. One episode in her diary dramatizes this situation: one day, a neighbor accuses Carolina's ten-year-old son of raping her daughter. The boy denies it. Carolina considers interning him in a state-run children's correctional facility, because at least there the boy would be out of trouble. When she asks a judge to arrange for the boy's admittance to the facility, he tells her that if he goes there he will really become a criminal. The justice system, she later discovers and records in her diary, keeps these correctional facilities as a kind of school where abandoned children learn how to become thieves and prostitutes. The streets of São Paulo, she says, are infested by these illiterate, venereal disease-ridden children whom nobody cares about.

If we compare the immediate communities both Domitila de Chungara and Rigoberta Menchú come from to the community—the slum—where Carolina de Jesus lives, the contrast could not be sharper. De Chungara and Menchú both belong to established families, where each member has a position and is accorded the dignity of that position. De Chungara is a mother and a wife; Menchú is a daughter and she has her *Nahual,* a protective spirit, which will go through life with her (18). Both assert that they learned their ways in the tradition of their communities, while both find consolation and strength in this tradition. For them, the national societies surrounding their communities carry the meaning of evil, of impending destruction; therefore, they cling to their inner communal identity at the same time as they bypass their national societies and speak through their testimonies, in a language other than their maternal one, to "Europe," or the "First World," or an international audience.

In contrast, the community where Carolina lives is shot through by fights between people from the different Brazilian regions. There, poverty, disease, and drunkenness conjugate to make most people almost totally oblivious to the possibility of solidarity: Bahianos fight with Pernambucanos, Italians steal from Brazilians, Portuguese cannot be trusted. Once Carolina states, "The only thing that does not exist in the favela is friendship" (21). However, in spite of the endless hostility, Carolina is charitable: she lends money and gives food to those who are in a more difficult situation; she gives shelter to a group of boys running away from the state correctional facility, and other times she shares "her streets" with a man who needs to collect the scraps just as badly as she does. In other words, at this point, Carolina de Jesus, just as Rigoberta Menchú and Domitila de Chungara, is not just a victim: she becomes an *agent* who can act out of her situation in order to act upon the world. But she has nobody—academic or solidarity worker—interested to hear her story. Therefore, she writes it herself.

What makes Carolina de Jesus's account even more compelling is the fact that, even though she only went to school for two years, she reads the newspapers in the newsstands and is aware of the political complexities of the wider society beyond her slum and her immediate daily life. Her subjectivity, formed and shaped almost in total isolation from a sympathetic community, comes out in the text, where she comments on the situation of Blacks in Brazil, on the lot of women, and on the political successes of the country. The comments are sharp and highly sophisticated, and reveal that Carolina de Jesus is not just writing about her own life, but about the life of the poor and dispossessed of Brazil. Once, for instance, after relating the ordeal of the poor waiting in line to get some broken crackers from a factory owner, she comments that when they got the crackers, the poor were as happy as "Queen Elizabeth of England when she received the 13 million jewels that [Brazilian] President Kubitschek sent her as a birthday present" (59). Later on the same day, upon noticing how a mailman whom she knows looks shabby and hungry, she says that President Kubitscheck, "who likes pomp, should give his mailmen other uniforms" (72). Carolina makes connections, relates her immediate life to the country's political life, and draws conclusions about both international politics (for instance, the relationship between a subservient, gift-bearing Brazil and Imperial England) and the hypocrisy this government has with respect to the life of its subjects. The Brazilian mailman dresses in rags so that the Brazilian president can send jewels to the Queen of England, in the same way that the ladino farm owner is fat (to the point of scaring the girl Rigoberta), while the *campesinos* are all thin and sickly.

Two points however, seem to register an unsurpassable difference between Carolina de Jesus's text, and de Chungara's and Menchú's. First, Carolina *wrote* her life, daily, in her house, whereas Rigoberta Menchú and Domitila de Chungara *spoke* their lives in a different country, to two women, Elisabeth Burgos-Debray and Moema Viezzer, respectively, who could be said to have developed a "bond of commitment" towards them.[21] But Carolina interacted with a male reporter, Audálio Dantas, who, presumably, just like Elisabeth Burgos-Debray and Moema Viezzer, "cleaned" the original text from repetitions, wrong verb tenses, and misspelled words. Dantas's work with de Jesus's text should not be considered any more problematic than Burgos-Debray's and Viezzer's editing of Menchú's and Chungara's testimonials.

Second, for Carolina de Jesus, her slum is not, to borrow Benedict Anderson's formulation, an "*imagined* community"; rather, it is a very concrete community with its daily troubles and its accumulations of grievances and humiliations. Unlike Domitila and Rigoberta, Carolina does not have any distance from the events she records in her diary; her descriptions are almost simultaneous with the events. In *Child of the Dark,* "poverty is presented with the materiality and concreteness of a physical object, and not as a mortification of the flesh for the redemption of the spirit" (Vogt, 208). In other words, de Jesus never looks at her circumstances with nostalgia, because she does not have any distance from that which she describes. The community, as well as the hunger she describes, is right there, knocking at her door, threatening her children, asking for food.

It is not that Carolina de Jesus is not conscious of the problems she shares with some of her neighbors, all as miserable as she is. The problem, here, is that, because she does not have the cushioning of a strong community tradition, she tends to write as a self—herself—and not as a voice of the community. At the same time, the nation Brazil does not have a space for her—a poor, barely literate, Black single mother—to speak. If she ever asked whether she could speak, the answer would have been a simple "no." So she speaks without asking permission.[22]

Carolina Maria de Jesus's drama of writing, at once a liberating and an antagonizing device, sets her apart from her community and becomes even more poignant because she has to collect the material—the notebooks in which she writes—literally from the garbage of the larger society. Menchú and de Chungara go outside their country to speak a language not readily available to all their countrymen; de Jesus, for her part, even though she does not go out of Brazil, sets herself apart from her neighbors by using a device—writing—viewed with suspicion by them. The target audience for her diary is primarily herself; she writes in order not to go crazy. For Menchú and de Chungara, the target audience becomes, by default, an international community who can help correct, or at least address, the situation in their respective communities.

Even though the three women share a desire to help and protect their immediate communities (the miners, the Quiché, and the three children) their relationships with their oppressors are very different. For these reasons, evil in de Jesus's book has proper names—those of her neighbors'—whereas de Chungara refers to "a manager" or to "the company" as those who exploit the miners, and in Menchú's book, evil is embodied in "the ladinos," "the soldiers," or the "Military Commissioner." Because Carolina de Jesus gives proper names to those who oppress and afflict her, once the book was published, the neighbors revolted against her and stoned the truck that was taking her belongings to her new house (introduction, 5). For de Chungara, the consequences are persecution and torture, and for Menchú, the destruction of part of her family, persecution, and exile.

Child of the Dark is, therefore, a dramatization of Carolina Maria de Jesus's inability to re-create her immediate community and her country in utopian models. For her, at least during the process of writing the diaries, the immediate gratification resides not in a sense of bonding with a sympathetic listener, but in the conscious attempt to try to make sense, at least for herself, of her life and her struggle for survival. It does not mean, however, that her relationship with the world is only passive. She knows that the relationship the nation can have with the *favela* is not simply one of oppression and that, no matter how isolated she finds herself, she still belongs to a larger society. This explains why, even though she writes her diary primarily for herself, ultimately she writes, if not for Brazil, at least to a "Brazil" in her mind; a "Brazil" that understands her and that she, in turn, can understand.[23] In addition, she knows enough about the wider society to use some of the institutionalized forces of the country: she calls the police when neighbors' fights get out of hand; and she accepts the intervention of the journalist Audálio Dantas so that her diaries can be published.[24] In her refusal, or inability, to reimagine her immediate society as an idyllic one, Carolina de Jesus ends up having to deposit in the national institutions a degree of trust that neither Domitila de Chungara nor Rigoberta Menchú has for their respective countries, or, at least, for the ruling forces of their countries. And, as we have discussed, in this national entity her blackness, ironically, renders her, if not nonexistent as a citizen, at least almost totally invisible.

Ultimately, for Carolina de Jesus, the issue of her race is resolved as a will to endurance, not as a member of an ethnic group,[25] but as a woman —a Black woman—who has to survive so that her children can survive. As a member of a group or a race continuously threatened into silence through slavery, joblessness, and oppression, Carolina does not rely on an idealized concept of kinship, tradition, or community. Her body, a Black one, is all she owns; her voice, a woman's voice, is all she can use to represent her plight and that of her children. Carolina's text, as well as her life, cannot be taken as paradigmatic of all women of Brazil, much less of all women in Latin America. As the type of an organic intellectual, she speaks from the space of the people: not all the people, not even all the Black people, nor, as we see in her diary, all the people from the slum. Rather, she speaks as a specific kind of individual whose voice, because so idiosyncratic, so problematic, can function as a way for those of us, outsiders, to begin to understand the complexities both of the subject Carolina Maria de Jesus and of those other women who live at the margins of the capitalist society. *Child of the Dark* thus resists facile totalizing understandings of the real conditions in which marginal people live.

Unlike Domitila de Chungara and Rigoberta Menchú, Carolina Maria de Jesus did not have a formal occasion like the International Women's Year Tribunal in Mexico City, nor a sympathetic academic like

Elisabeth Burgos-Debray, to inspire her to tell her history. Even before Audálio Dantas "discovered" her, Carolina de Jesus wrote her diary in solitude, without a solidarity worker or somebody who bonded with her. According to the way the *testimonio* has been configured in the North American academy, a testimonial being exists *to be written about,* and this writing can only come into existence in accordance with strict ideological criteria.[26] Because of her literacy, however, Carolina is a testimonial person who *does not exist simply to be written about;* moreover, her writing does not conform to a prescribed format. *Child of the Dark* cannot, therefore, fit into an idealized North American academic imaginary of Latin America, which deems that the only accounts worthy of being considered *testimonios* are *necessarily* community-based, collectively-driven, racially homogeneous, transparently-gendered, and illiterate.

What the study of *testimonios* in the United States loses by excluding books such as Carolina Maria de Jesus's *Child of the Dark* from the canon is the possibility of incorporating a clearly gendered, and insistently feminine, account of an oppressed woman's life. As a subject, Carolina can never be considered transparently-gendered: her female body, much more than a mouthpiece for a community, has its own demands, its own desires, and she attends to these desires in the same way she attends to her children's basic needs for food and clothes. To ignore the human value, as well as the literary and historical value, of so many testimonials other than *I . . . Rigoberta Menchú* is to be indifferent to the oppression—or the annihilation—of so many people in Latin America, and to give in to a view of the Other that serves principally for North American academics to recreate themselves, every now and then, according to new ideological fashions.

NOTES

[1]In a recent issue of *Latin American Research Review,* Kathleen Logan discusses ten testimonial books by or on Latin American women. Logan states that for many of the recorder-editors of these books, their goal "is to open a channel to Latin American women that allows them to speak directly to a wider audience" (200).

[2]I prefer to use the word *Indian* instead of *Native American* because the latter has been mostly used to refer to Indigenous peoples of the territory of the United States.

[3]Here I do not mean that either woman has become a representative of her country: after all, neither holds any official title or represents Guatemala or

Bolivia in foreign affairs. They have, however, become symbols of Guatemala and Bolivia through the general teaching of *testimonio* in the United States. There are other texts produced by people of the same region Menchú comes from, but they have not acquired the same status as *I . . . Rigoberta Menchú.* John Beverley and Marc Zimmerman give a list of "quasi-testimonial" texts that appeared in the wake of Menchú's book: Valentín Solórzano's *El relato de Juan Tayín* (1985); Albertina Saravia's *El ladino me jodió: vida de un indígena* (1983), and Elvia Alvarado's *Don't Be Afraid, Gringo: A Honduran Woman Speaks from the Heart* (1987). As Beverley and Zimmerman write, there are differing accounts of the situations described by Rigoberta Menchú, especially the testimonials by Ignacio Bizarro Ujpán's *Son of Tecún Umán: A Mayan Indian Tells His Story* (1981), and *Campesino: The Diary of a Guatemalan Indian* (1985). Beverley and Zimmerman summarize their opinion of the two sets of texts: ". . . where Menchú's testimonio is conceived as a particular instance and instrumentality of a collective experience, Bizarro Ujpán's two books, for all the efforts of his interlocutor to see him as representative of the contemporary Maya in Guatemala, seem rather to represent that fraction of *ladinized* Indians broken away (often by service in the army) from their communities and integrated in relatively privileged ways into the dominant system" (*Literature and Politics in the Central American Revolutions,* 210–11).

⁴This is not to say that her book did not have consequences for the community where she lived when she wrote her diaries. Carlos Vogt writes that *Quarto de despejo*—[*Child of the Dark*]—"unleashed passions and (was responsible for) movements towards the elimination of *favelas* in São Paulo. There are people who say that the *favela* of Canindé disappeared in consequence of (Carolina's) denunciations" ["*Trabalho, pobreza e trabalho intelectual,*" 212, my translation]. What is extremely unfortunate, here, is that Carolina's book was understood not as a critique against the system that made the existence of *favelas* possible, but against the *favelas* themselves. So, the Canindé *favela* was destroyed either because of her writing, or because it was on the way of the construction of the Tietê highway (an important road in São Paulo). Nothing is said about the destiny of people who lived in Canindé. Like so many other poor in Brazil, they just disappeared, vanished, to make way for "progress."

⁵These two pieces appear on the back cover of the paperback edition of *Child of the Dark,* which I quote from throughout this essay.

⁶Both reviews appear on the back cover of the edition of *Let Me Speak!* I use for this essay.

⁷D'Souza's passage reads: "To celebrate the works of the oppressed, apart from the standard of merit by which any art and history and literature is judged, is to romanticize their suffering, to pretend that it is naturally creative, and to give

it an esthetic status that is not shared or appreciated by those who actually endure the oppression" (*Illiberal Education: The Politics of Race and Sex on Campus*, 87).

[8]Carlos Vogt argues that, contrary to general belief, Carolina did not die in poverty. Rather, she "died sad, abandoned and misunderstood." In the sixteen years between the publication of *Quarto de despejo* in 1961 and her death in 1977, Carolina was seen back on the streets, picking paper as she used to before her book was published. In 1966, she was interviewed by newspapers and complained that after her book was published it was more difficult for her to sell the paper she picked on the streets, because the buyers refused to do business with a "star" (*Trabalho, pobreza e trabalho intelectual*, 206). However, considering that the other books that Carolina de Jesus wrote (*Casa de alvenaria*, *Provérbios e Pedaços de fome*, *Um Brasil para brasileiros*, and the novels *Felizarda* and *Os escravos*) did not obtain any success, and that her attempt to open a little roadside store failed, it is not clear how Carolina would have avoided poverty. Disenfranchised and seen mostly as a "curiosity," once the novelty of *Quarto de despejo* wore off, Carolina was discarded.

[9]It is, of course, interesting to observe that the translation of the title of Rigoberta's testimony does exactly the contrary of what the title of Domitila's testimony does. Where one is tentative in the Spanish version—"if you let me speak . . ."—the other is assertive; in English, Domitila's title becomes assertive, whereas Rigoberta's becomes "neutral," as if the text was merely a description of the life of an Indian woman in Guatemala.

[10]Besides these two conference sessions in these prestigious professional occasions, a cursory list of publications on *I . . . Rigoberta Menchú* includes Doris Sommer's "Rigoberta's Secrets"; Britten and Dworkin's "Rigoberta Menchú: *Los indígenas no nos quedamos como bichos aislados*," qtd. in John Beverley's "The Real Thing (Our Rigoberta)"; Georg M. Gugelberger's *The "Real" Thing: Testimonial Discourse and Latin America*, in which Rigoberta Menchú's book appears in a prominent position; and Carey-Webb and Benz's book, *Teaching and Testimony: Rigoberta Menchú and the North American Classroom*. Informal research in a computer database gave me twenty-eight titles of articles in which Rigoberta Menchú is either mentioned or featured as the main subject.

[11]Perhaps one should add to the political also the moral (or moralistic) convictions. See, for instance, Doris Sommer's choice of words in the following statement, which is part of her presentation of the essays in *Modern Language Quarterly*. She writes: "Debra Castillo further complicates the assumptions [about *testimonios*] by considering *testimonios* written by professional con artists, *Mexican prostitutes who sell their lives to greedy readers*" (12, my emphasis).

Here the writer positions herself above both the phony ("con artists," "prosti-tutes") Mexican writers of *testimonios* and the ("greedy") readers who consume their products. A word that particularly strikes me here is "prostitute," especially because Sommer does not clarify if she is using it in a sense of sexual or of intel-lectual commerce; of course, it seems clear that she condemns both. It is also im-possible not to wonder whether the readers, at least, would receive a less harsh judgment if they were reading mainstream *testimonios.*

[12]By the same token, any study of *testimonios,* including this one, has to pass through Menchú's narrative in order to purchase its authority to speak about any other testimonials.

[13]Darcy Ribeiro is a widely known Brazilian anthropologist whose work concentrates on studies of primitive life. He was also rector of the University of Brasilia and counsellor to former president João Goulart. When the military junta seized power in 1964, Ribeiro was thrown in jail. The first edition of *As Américas e a Civilização* was suspended, and all copies of the book were destroyed. Ribeiro then lived and worked in exile for some years. *The Americas and Civi-lization* was first published in 1971. When Ribeiro finally returned to Brazil, he was Secretary of Education in the State of Rio de Janeiro in the early 1980s. To this day, he still continues working with education and anthropology in Brazilian universities.

[14]Ribeiro characterizes the "Transplanted People" as those "recruited from among the dissident European groups," the "maladjusted persons condemned to exile by the colonizing nations," and the migrants uprooted from Europe by the Industrial Revolution (85).

[15]For more detailed comments on Columbus's letters, see *Journal and Other Documents on the Life and Voyages of Christopher Columbus,* translated and edited by Samuel Eliot Morison, and E. Fitz's *Rediscovering the New World.* The utopian narratives about the Americas and its inhabitants include, for in-stance, Voltaire's novella *Candide,* James Fenimore Cooper's *The Last of the Mohicans,* and José de Alencar's *O Guarani.* In all these narratives, the primitive inhabitant of the Americas can hardly be distinguished from an ideal European noble.

[16]It is remarkable that even Bartolomé de Las Casas, ferocious defender of the Indians, did not extend his sympathy to Blacks. Todorov says that Las Casas "did not have the same attitude towards Indians and Blacks: he consents that the latter, not the former, be reduced to slavery" (*The Conquest of America,* 170). According to Todorov, although Las Casas writes in his *History of the Indies* that he considered the slavery of both groups unjust and tyrannical, as late as 1544 "he still possessed a black slave" (170). In Brazil, the seventeenth-century Jesuit priest Antonio Vieira spoke vehemently against the slavery of Indians, but, al-

though he later compared the Africans' suffering to the suffering of Jesus Christ, he never advocated their freedom. For more details on African slavery in Brazil, see Robert Edgar Conrad, Manuel Correia de Andrade, and Eliane Moury Fernandes, eds.

[17]The importance of language cannot be overemphasized. In "The Order of Discourse," for instance, Foucault remarks that in appearance speech may be of little account; however, he says, "the prohibitions that surround it very soon reveal its links with desire and with power" (110). Although the Africans brought to the Americas were completely displaced, and their language seemingly destroyed, this language continued to be present in the several languages of the Americas. Carolina Maria de Jesus, who certainly did not read Foucault, expresses the same understanding of the power of language when she says: "I don't have any physical force but my words hurt more than a sword. And the wounds don't heal" (*Child of the Dark,* 49)

[18]The novelist Lima Barreto, a mulatto, who (unlike the master Machado de Assis) opted for a closer relationship with the poor and ended up being disdained by the academicized literate elites, is another example of Brazilian Blacks who "hope to recover, through their intellectual prestige, the social prestige that they could never have" (Vogt, 213). For a very incisive study of Lima Barreto's marginalization and on how paradigmatic it is of the position of Black Brazilian intellectuals, see Beatriz Resende's "Lima Barreto: *A opção pela Marginália.*"

[19]One of the most poignant episodes in *Child of the Dark* occurs when Carolina is ill, and yet goes out in the morning to collect scrap mental. She cannot sell anything because the junkyard is closed, so she goes back to her shack and lies down. She writes: " I was cold and upset inside. The people of the favela know that I'm ill. But nobody shows up here to help me out" (83). On this occasion, using the rare opportunity she has to spend time with her children, Carolina speaks with her son João: "He talks to me and I tell him of the unfortunate things that exist in the world. My son now knows what the world is; between us the language of children has ended" (83). It is, of course, impossible not to associate this episode with many of those Rigoberta Menchú and Domitila de Chungara describe, when the elders speak to the young people and educate them on the history of their people and on the hardships that await them in life. The difference, once again, is that Carolina is alone, and, except on rare occasions, she feels completely surrounded by a hostile community.

[20]It is not that Carolina de Jesus is promiscuous; rather, she decided early on that she did not want to get married because she sees the horrible way husbands treat their wives. Indeed, she compares the lives of the married women of the *favela* to the lives of "Indian slaves" (21). Moreover, as the diary makes clear, a husband does not necessarily mean protection and economic support either for

the wife or for the children. On the contrary, many men in the *favela* not only do not work, but, in addition, continuously terrorize their families with beatings and threats against their lives.

[21]Adrianne Aron writes that the term *bond of commitment* was coined by two Chilean therapists, Elizabeth Lira and Eugenia Weinstein, who published anonymously the result of their work with victims of psychological trauma suffered under state-sponsored terrorism. Aron writes: "[t]he bond of commitment is one in which the therapist takes an ethically non-neutral attitude toward the client's suffering" (181).

[22]There is one episode in *Child of the Dark* which dramatizes, perhaps better than all the others that de Jesus narrates, the abyss between the poor and the rich in Brazil. On this occasion, Carolina is riding an elevator for the first time. She has gone to the building to collect some used newspaper a resident promised her. On the way down, "a man got into the elevator and looked at me with disgust. . . . He wanted to know what I was doing in the elevator. I explained to him that the mother of those two boys had given me some newspapers. And that was the reason for my presence in his elevator. I asked him if he was a doctor or a Congressman. He told me he was a Senator" (98). In this episode, Carolina goes through the same humiliation Rigoberta Menchú's father suffers when he goes into town to deal with bureaucrats and politicians. In both cases, the oppressed is looked upon as sub-human, not deserving of stepping on the same path as the rich Whites in de Jesus's text, or as the *ladinos* of the big city in Menchú's text.

[23]A similar thing can be said about de Chungara's and Menchú's testimonies: both also reach out to another, in their case an international community whose members can understand their plight and the seriousness of the histories they have to tell.

[24]Of course, the diary makes clear that Carolina is also aware of the existence of a larger, international society beyond Brazil. In January 19, 1959, she receives the rejected manuscripts of the novels she sent to *Reader's Digest* in the United States. Since she does not possess a typewriter, one can well imagine that the *Reader's Digest* people did not even read her handwritten work. Strangely, she does not seem aware that in the United States people speak a language other than Portuguese. But, like any other writer, she registers the universal pain of rejection: "The worst slap for those who write is the return of their books" (131).

[25]I do not mean that Blacks, as an ethnic group, have not struggled to keep their identity in Brazilian history. On the contrary, as early as the sixteenth century, slaves who escaped their owners formed communities called "Quilombos." Palmares was the most famous of these *quilombos,* and the leader Zumbi has become a symbol of Black resistance in Brazil. In the cities, Black brotherhoods flourished under the auspices of the Catholic Church. In other occasions, even

before the official freedom of the slaves, Black and Mulatto movements, some of which had their own newspapers, appeared in Brazil. Thomas Skidmore remarks, however, that "the study and preservation of Afro-Brazilian contributions to Brazilian culture and national character . . . has been politically safe[:] it fits perfectly with the elite view that Brazil's links to Africa are now essentially quaint" ("Race and Class in Brazil: Historical Perspectives," 110). For more details on the Black movements in Brazil, see also Skidmore's *Black into White; Race and Nationality in Brazilian Thought,* and A. J. R. Russel-Wood's "Black and Mulatto Brotherhoods in Colonial Brazil."

[26]The format of the witness who indefinitely agrees to be talked about is falling apart, to judge from one of Rigoberta Menchú's last published interviews in 1993. In this interview, Menchú insists on not being addressed familiarly as "Rigoberta," but as "Rigoberta Menchú." At the same time, she reclaims her rights as an author, as *the* author of *I . . . Rigoberta Menchú.* For the whole interview, see Britten and Dworkin.

WORKS CITED

Anderson, Benedict. *Imagined Communities; Reflections on the Origin and Spread of Nationalism.* New York: Verso, 1989.

Andrade, Manuel Correia de, and Eliane Moury Fernandes, eds. *Atualidade e Abolição.* Recife: Editora Massangana, 1991.

Aron, Adrianne. "*Testimonio,* a Bridge Between Psychotherapy and Sociotherapy." *Women and Therapy; A Feminist Quarterly,* Vol. 13, No 2, part II: 173–89.

Beverley, John. "The Margin at the Center: On *Testimonio* (Testimonial Narrative)." *Modern Fiction Studies* 35.1 (Spring 1989): 11–28.

———. "The Real Thing (Our Rigoberta)". *Modern Language Quarterly* 57, 2 (June 1996): 129–39.

Beverley, John, and Marc Zimmerman. *Literature and Politics in the Central American Revolutions.* Austin: U of Texas Press, 1990.

Britten, Alice and Kenya Dworkin. "Rigoberta Menchú: Los indígenas no nos quedamos como bischos aislados." *Nuevo Testo Crítico* (1993): 214.

Carey-Webb, Allen and Stephen Benz, eds. *Teaching and Testimony: Rigoberta Menchú and the North American Classroom.* New York: SUNY UP, 1996.

Carr, Roberto. "*Re-presentando el testimonio.*" *Revista de crítica literaria latinoamericana* 36, 2nd semester (1992): 73–94.

Chungara, Domitila Barrios de, and Moema Viezzer. *Let Me Speak!* Trans. Victoria Ortiz. New York: Monthly Review Press, 1978.

Conrad, Robert Edgar. *Children of God's Fire; A Documentary History of Black Slavery in Brazil.* Princeton: Princeton UP, 1983.

D'Souza, Dinesh. *Illiberal Education: The Politics of Race and Sex on Campus.* New York: Free Press, 1991.

Fitz, Earl E. *Rediscovering the New World; Inter-American Literature in a Comparative Context.* Iowa City: U of Iowa P, 1991.

Foucault, Michel. "The Order of Discourse." *Language and Politics.* Michael Shapiro, ed. New York: New York UP, 1984. 108–38.

Grogan, David, and Meg Grant. "Sister Courage." *People,* 21 December 1992, 87–8.

Gugelberger, Georg M., ed. *The "Real" Thing: Testimonial Discourse and Latin America.* Durham: Duke UP, 1996.

Jesus, Carolina Maria de. *Child of the Dark; The Diary of Carolina Maria de Jesus.* Trans. David St. Clair. London: Penguin Books, 1963.

———. *Diario de Bitita.* Rio de Janiero: Editora Nova Fronteira, 1986.

———. *Antologia pessoal.* Jose Carlos Sebe Bom Meihy, ed. Rio de Janeiro: Editora UFRJ, 1996.

———. *Casa de alvenaria. I'm Going to Have a Little House.* Trans. Melvin S. Arrington and Robert M. Levine. Lincoln: U of Nebraska P, 1997.

———. *Bitita's Diary: The Childhood Memoirs of Carolina Maria de Jesus.* Trans. Emanuelle Oliveira and Beth Joan Vinkler. Armonk, NY: M. E. Sharpe, 1998.

Logan, Kathleen. "Personal Testimony: Latin American Women Telling Their Lives." *Latin American Research Review* 32, 1 (1977): 199–211.

Marín, Lynda. "Speaking Out Together: Testimonials of Latin American Women." *Latin American Perspectives,* Issue 70, Vol. 18, No. 3 (Summer 1991): 51–68.

Menchú, Rigoberta, and Elisabeth Burgos-Debray. *I . . . Rigoberta Menchú; An Indian Woman in Guatemala.* Trans. Ann Wright. London, New York: Verso, 1984.

Morison, Samuel Eliot, ed. *Journal and Other Documents on the Life and Voyages of Christopher Columbus.* Trans. Samuel Eliot Morison. New York: Heritage, 1963.

Randall, Margareth. " Qué es, y cómo se hace un testimonio?" *Revista de crítica literaria latinoamericana* 36, 2nd semester (1992): 21–48.

Rangel, Carlos. *The Latin Americans: Their Love-Hate Relationship with the United States.* Trans. Ivan Kats. New York: Harcourt Brace Jovanovich, 1976.

Resende, Beatriz. "Lima Barreto: A opção pela Marginália." *Os Pobres na Literatura Brasileira.* Roberto Schwarz, ed. São Paulo: Brasiliense, 1983. 73–8.

Ribeiro, Darcy. *The Americas and Civilization.* Trans. Linton Lomas Barrett and Marie Mc David Barrett. New York: E. P. Dutton, 1972.

Russell-Wood, A. J. R. "Black and Mulatto Brotherhoods in Colonial Brazil: A Study in Collective Behavior." In *The Hispanic American Historical Review* 54, 4 (November 1974): 567–602.

Skidmore, Thomas E. *Black into White; Race and Nationality in Brazilian Thought.* New York: Oxford UP, 1974.

———. "Race and Class in Brazil: Historical Perspectives." *Luso-Brazilian Review* 20, 1 (Summer 1983): 104–18.

Spivak, Gayatri Chakravorti. "Can the Subaltern Speak?" *Marxism and the Interpretation of Culture.* In Cary Nelson and Lawrence Crossberg, eds. Urbana and Chicago: University of Illinois Press, 1988. 271–313.

Sommer, Doris. "Rigoberta's Secrets." *Latin American Perspectives* Issue 70, Vol 18.3 (Summer 1991): 32–50.

———. "The Places of History: Regionalism Revisited in Latin America." *Modern Language Quarterly* 57, 2 (June 1996): 119–25.

Todorov, Tzvetan. *Conquest of America.* Trans. Richard Howard. London: Harper & Row, 1984.

Vieira, Antonio. *Sermões e Cartas.* Rio de Janeiro: Livraria Agir Editora, 1968.

Vogt, Carlos. "Trabalho, pobreza e trabalho intelectual (*O Quarto de Despejo de Carolina Maria de Jesus*)." *Os pobres na literatura brasileira.* Roberto Schwarz, ed. São Paulo: Brasiliense, 1983. 204–13.

Yúdice, George. "*Testimonio* and Postmodernism." *Latin American Perspectives* 70, vol. 18, No. 3 (Summer 1991): 15–31.

Packaging "Huda": Sha'rawi's Memoirs in the United States Reception Environment

MOHJA KAHF

The memoirs of Huda Sha'rawi (*Mudhakkirati,* Cairo: Dar al-Hilal, 1981) have been abridged, translated, and transformed into a text widely available to the English-reading public and frequently taught in U.S. college courses in disciplines such as history and literature, and in interdisciplinary programs such as women's studies and Middle Eastern Studies. The translation endeavor that produced Margot Badran's *Harem Years: The Memoirs of an Egyptian Feminist* (New York: The Feminist Press, 1986) is a valuable one and alerts Anglophonic readers worldwide to the work of this woman of achievement and influence. *Harem Years* was what led me to deeper study of Huda Sha'rawi's life and work and to the research for this article. However, the translation and publication of *Harem Years* occurs within a specific reception environment—the "First World" Anglophonic market, which is shaped by a "horizon of expectations"[1] for writing by and about Arab and Muslim women. The process of this reception restricts the range of meaning made possible in the Arabic text. Knowing these distortions will help educators use the English translation more effectively, not only in teaching about Egyptian feminism but also in explaining how the politics of reception can constrain our reading of a text from an Arab woman.[2]

Hans Robert Jauss's work provides the insight that a reading public's "horizon of expectations" is formed by "what the public already understands about a genre and its conventions" (Guerin, 338) and by "a reader's knowledge and assumptions about the text and literature in general" (Childers and Hentzi, 258). The United States reading public, despite promising resistances here and there, takes in data about women from the Arab world mainly by using conventions emergent from a long history of Western stereotypes about the Arab peoples and the Islamic religion. I find that these conventions take shape today in three stereotypes about the Arab woman: One is that she is a victim of gender oppression; the second portrays her as an escapee of her intrinsically oppressive culture; and the third represents her as the pawn of Arab male power. To describe the process by which the Arabic text of the memoirs is transformed by being cast toward this of expectations is to shift from blaming the translator toward seeing the translation of a text as part of a process larger than one individual will.

The pressures of the United States reception environment work in four ways in the transformation of the Arabic text, *Mudhakkirati,* into the English text, *Harem Years.* Sha'rawi's engagement with Arab men in relationships that she saw as satisfying and enriching is minimized; her orientation toward Europe is exaggerated; and her command of class privilege is camouflaged. Finally, her story, which, in *Mudhakkirati,* is the story of a public figure, is recentered in *Harem Years* around private life and the "harem." In these ways, Sha'rawi can be accommodated within the United States reading environment as a victim and an escapee and shielded from the negative category of pawn.

PACKAGINGS: VICTIM, ESCAPEE, OR PAWN

Western literature has not always represented women from the Arabo-Islamic world in this threefold typology that I outline here. My study of the earliest representations of the Muslim woman in European literature suggests that medieval and Renaissance representations differed considerably from those of later periods and do not construct her as victim. Rather, the opposite—in these early texts, the Muslim woman is a virago.[3] Over the course of the past four hundred years, however, against the changing material and ideological grounds of the relationship between Western Europe and the Islamic world, a very different discourse emerged. The new discourse, Orientalism, expanded most during the nineteenth century and depended on a "*positional* superiority, which puts the Westerner in a whole series of possible relationships with the Orient without ever losing him the relative upper hand" (Said, 7). One of its constants has been the representation of Islam as innately oppressive to women. Drawing on the late nineteenth-century relations between Britain and Egypt, Leila Ahmed shows that "the thesis of the new colonial discourse of Islam centered on women—was that Islam was innately

and immutably oppressive to women, that the veil and segregation epito-
mized that oppression" (1994, 151–152). The twentieth-century U.S. reception environment is heir to this discourse. Decolonization, the Cold
War, the post-1967 emergence of independent Palestinian movements,
the 1979 Iranian Revolution, and the current climate of preoccupation
with an "Islamic threat," have shifted the material conditions and the
ideological climate for "the Western narrative of women in Islam"
(Ahmed's phrase, 1994, 149). For example, the image of Palestinian
women as fighters and Iranian women as supporters of the Islamic Revolution complicated the picture of Arab and Muslim women as having to
be either victims or escapees. The idea of a fanatic Arab or Muslim
woman who is a pawn of her culture is related to these developments.

Second-wave United States feminism of the 1960s and 1970s and
the ensuing critique of its limitations by women of color have opened
spaces where these stereotypes are reiterated on one hand and subjected
to new challenges on the other hand. Chandra Talpade Mohanty points
out that Arab women are specifically included in the process by which
Western feminist discourse "colonizes" an entity called "Third World
woman," casting her as silent victim in need of discursive succour from
her more liberated "Western" sisters. This process creates an irreducible
"Third World women's difference." With this useful term, Mohanty gives
a name to the assumption that the women of the "Third World" are somehow inherently oppressed and that this always already oppressed state is
defined by their gender and their being "Third World." Therese Saliba,
Marsha J. Hamilton, and others detail the ways this "third worlding"
continues to happen with regard to Arab women in United States academic and popular settings, feminist and otherwise.[4]

The concept of the Arab woman as "escapee" was given to me by
Barbara Nimri Aziz, a journalist with a disciplinary grounding in anthropology whose work intersects with academic discourse but occurs primarily in radio and print mass media.[5] Aziz, from her years of work
between the East Coast of the United States and the Arab east or *mashreq*
(Syria, Iraq, Palestine, Lebanon, and Jordan) interviewing people and
documenting lives, garnered the insight that United States audiences,
when faced with an Arab woman who did not fit the victim mold, tried to
understand the woman as an "escapee" from her culture. "How brave,"
they seemed to be saying, "she has been able to escape from that terribly
oppressive world" of Islam and Arab-ness.[6]

Marnia Lazreg's "Feminism and Difference: The Perils of Writing
as a Woman on Women in Algeria" suggested to me the third concept in

this typology describing the range of contemporary United States representations of "the Arab woman." Lazreg, in the course of a larger argument, says that one of the implications of United States feminist discourse "is that an Arab woman cannot be a feminist (whatever the term means) prior to disassociating herself from Arab men and the culture that supports them!" (332). Citing Elly Bulkin's work, she notes that if Arab women do not separate from common causes with Arab men, they "are accused of being 'pawns of Arab men.' " An Arab woman who seems to wield some degree of power in her society and/or does not divest herself of Arab culture and attachments to Arab men must be operating under a false consciousness and is a "pawn." The concept of the Arab woman as "pawn" is a useful refuge when a system of representation whose range for Arab women extends from "victim" to "escapee" is confronted with data that does not fit either of those categories. Like the other two concepts, it is an evasion of an alternative, if difficult, path: the deconstruction or demystifying of the irreducible difference attached (in Western discourse) to women in the Arabo-Islamic world and the approach to them and their texts with as much nuance, rigor, and openness of paradigm as is applied to the study of European and American women's literature and literary history.

Here, despite all my recourse to depersonalized processes, I wish to find succour in Lazreg's appeal to some late humanism and assert that none of this is inexorable. A "First World" feminist exercise of discursive power over "Third World" subjects is not an inescapable given determined by the identity or physical location or education of the writer or reader. In other words, all Western writers are not *a priori* guilty of colonizing Arab women, nor are all women and men of Arab origin automatically innocent of this distorting representational practice. The "victim, escapee, or pawn" triad is a frame of reference ready to bog anyone. I agree with Lazreg that "the misrepresentation of 'different' women is a form of self-misrepresentation" (338). Uncritical acceptance of these three stale categories for Arab women is a quagmire of unoriginal thinking that readers, as well as publishers and translators, can understand and resist. Responsible scholarship is still possible in the age of the postmodern.

COMPARING *MUDHAKKIRATI* TO *HAREM YEARS*

Sha'rawi (1879–1947) was a pioneer in the women's rights movement in the twentieth century and was as much in the vanguard of the Egyptian nationalist movement as a woman of her era could be. She was among those public figures who left us a written record of their lives as makers of modern Egypt, in such company as Sa'd Zaghloul and Muhammad Hassanein Haykal. After a coming-of-age section, which takes up thirteen of the forty-five chapters comprising the Arabic text, *Mudhakkirati,* her memoirs leave aside her personal life to tell mainly of her life as a public figure in Egypt's coming-of-age as a nation. This story includes the public debates taking place in Egypt in the early decades of the twentieth century, not only debates over women's roles, but debates over the type of government Egypt would have, its relationship with Sudan, the role of the king, relations with Turkey and Britain, and so forth. Her sweep of experience includes observations of nationalist leader and occasional Sha'rawi nemesis Sa'd Zaghloul, glimpses of Taha Hussain and other intellectuals, milestone events in Egypt's educational institutions, the emergence of international feminism, the emergence of inter-Arab feminism, the growth of Egyptian newspapers, and more.

The Arabic version tells the story by interspersing her narrative with reports, letters, and documents; approximately one hundred in all. About a fourth are penned by Sha'rawi; most of the other articles were written to or about her during the course of her life. The Arabic book consists of a one-page publisher's preface, a short introduction by Dr. Amina Sa'id, and 450-some pages of text, which end abruptly *in medias res* since Sha'rawi did not live to complete the task. *Harem Years* contains eighty pages of translation proper, preceded by a chronology, preface, and introduction and followed by an epilogue, appendix, and notes. It is a translation, with some rearrangement and abridgement, of the first thirteen chapters that are present in *Mudhakkirati.* The epilogue in *Harem Years* summarizes material corresponding approximately to the next dozen chapters of *Mudhakkirati.*

It is important to note that the person finally responsible for editing the manuscript resulting in *Mudhakkirati* was her secretary, Abd al-Hamid Fahmy Mursi. Amina Sa'id describes Mursi's role in her introduction to the memoirs: "He gave it to us without any compensation. He absolutely refused to allow us to recompense him even for a little of what he was burdened with in putting these memoirs in order and preparing them for printing and publication. He did this in fulfillment of his duty to execute the testament which his spiritual mother Huda Sha'rawi left for him. She chose him out of all her disciples, male and female, to order them and publish them at an appropriate time" (Sha'rawi, 9).[7] This appears to be an effort to confirm the legitimacy of Mursi's editorial work and establishes *Mudhakkirati's* line of descent, so to speak, from Sha'rawi. We see a parallel effort in *Harem Years* when the translator recounts that Sha'rawi's niece Hawa Idris granted Badran access to a copy or portion of the manuscript and gave her permission to translate and publish it. The manuscript Badran worked with and the manuscript Mursi worked with may not have been the same; apparently Mursi's manuscript was more complete. In any case, the Arabic version, in its arrangement and selection of documents, enacts the voice of a public figure, who, like all public figures, utilized the services of a committed, expert staff in producing her public voice. Thus, there is no need to continue the debate that occurred between Badran and Mervat Hatem on the pages of the Association for Middle East Women's Studies newsletter over whether or not there was one "pure," originary Arabic document embodying the intent of its author without mediation of any sort (see Badran, 1988a & 1988b, Hatem 1988). My purpose here is simply to compare the two published books to see what we can learn from the transfiguration of Sha'rawi's memoirs from one readerly context to another.

BANISHING BELOVED BASHAS

Sha'rawi's memoirs begin with her memory of the death of her father. Much has already been said about the importance of Sha'rawi's vindication of her father, Sultan Basha, in the second chapter of her memoirs and the inclusion of documents authored by his contemporaries to substantiate Sha'rawi's defense. Badran has been duly criticized for relegating it to an appendix and overriding the primacy of Sha'rawi's concern with this issue. Badran's response points out that much of the chapter is composed of documents authored by others, inserted into Sha'rawi's text by her secretary-editor. This rendering of the apologia for the father as an appendix has been criticized by Mervat Hatem (1988) and Leila Ahmed (1987), and responded to by the translator (Badran, 1988a & 1988b). My interest in the shift in the placement of the father between the Arabic and the English versions of the memoirs is that it is part of a pattern in which the English version minimizes the presence of male figures whom Sha'rawi describes with affection and pride. Huda Hanim's paternal grandfather, al-Haj Sultan, does not appear in the English version. The narrative about the father, aside from the apologia section, has been modified in specific ways. The brother, who is at least retained in the English translation, is nevertheless affected by the pressures of the reception process.

Sha'rawi's concern to establish her ancestral roots, very understandable in the Arabic context given the importance of genealogy in Arabic tradition, does not appear in the English version. She writes in *Mudhakkirati:*

> I have heard from some of our relatives who have heard from their fathers and grandfathers that my father was of Arab [i.e., Arab bedouin] origin. His ancestors settled in the land of Hijaz and a group of them migrated to Egypt before the era of Ali Basha and took it as their land and married Egyptian women. Based on what I have been told, my grandfather al-Haj Sultan was the head of the fifth generation of his family in Egypt . . . He was famous for generosity and kindheartedness and goodnaturedness. So involved was he in benevolent and charitable deeds and so overflowing was his piety that his contemporaries used to say: He is a saint who embodies all the blessings of his family and all those around him. (14)

Sha'rawi goes on to relate, with dramatic panache, several anecdotes illuminating her grandfather's generosity, charity, and kindliness. He was, she says, a man who even allowed his tenant farmers to cheat him out of money rather than embarrass them by calling their bluffs.

Aside from the issue of the apologia for her father, there are some other differences between the English and Arabic versions in the way Sha'rawi describes her father. In *Harem Years* we do not find Sha'rawi's praise of her father's virtues (e.g. "generosity, loyalty, elevation, attachment to the symbols of religion," 12). Adjectives such as "beloved" that Sha'rawi frequently uses when speaking about her father do not make it through the translation process (32). The translator says in her preface that she has made "some minor deletions to remove repetitions or the occasional over-elaboration" (3). It is true that Sha'rawi's praises of family and friends are repetitious and indulge in Arabic conventions that might be tiresome for the Anglophonic reader. Still Sha'rawi's gracious curtsies to these conventions of generous praise are part of her narrative persona.

While the tedious historical detail of Sha'rawi's apologia for her father might raise budgetary and marketing worries for a publisher, the omission of the charming stories about her grandfather and the adjective "beloved" modifying the father is puzzling. It can only be explained by the pressures of the reception environment that I have described. The excision of the paternal grandfather encourages the tendency of the Anglophonic reader to see Sha'rawi as a woman severed from her roots, a victim-turned-escapee. A kindly Arab paterfamilias does not fit the expectations of United States readership. A story of an Arab woman's escape from the gender oppression of the "harem" requires rather less glowing portraits of the Arab men who lived in those "harem years." If Badran were to translate Sha'rawi's warmth of tone toward her father and grandfather, the reception apparatus would veer toward labeling Sha'rawi a pawn of Arab men. The pawn stereotype is something Badran, as a sincere advocate for Sha'rawi before the United States readership, swerves to avoid. Whether this protective instinct is articulated and conscious or not, it is an observable example of the reception environment shaping the way the material emerges in English.

Sha'rawi's beginning her account with a recital of her lineage and the virtues of her fathers is a rhetorical move embedded in the traditions of Arabic literature. In Arabic poetry, for example, *fakhr* (the boast) and *nasab* (genealogy) are important initiatory elements. Sha'rawi's opening words in the Arabic version are: "When I stand before the memories of my childhood . . ." In this metaphor, memory is a site. She does not simply remember; she stands before the memory site. She goes on to remember and lament the way that knowledge of her father's death was kept from his children by "the kindred" and "the servants," and the sheltering customs of the upperclass in those days. The whole passage, then, is a circumspect way to lead into her father's death.

Where does Sha'rawi's language come from in this opening passage of her memoirs? Sha'rawi's opening alludes to a conceit that permeates all of Arabic culture from high poetry to folksong, the *waqf 'ala al-atlal* (standing at the deserted site). The classical Arab poet always stands figuratively before the old campsite in order to begin speaking. A renowned example is "Let us stand, you two, and weep, at the remembrance of loved one and home," the opening line of the best-known ode of pre-Islamic poet Imra'ul Qais.[8] In this conceit, remembering is a "standing before" and a calling up of the presences who used to inhabit the now-abandoned ruins. Sha'rawi activates this conceit at several points in a narrative that is also about the structure of memory and knowledge ("And today I close my eyes and I retrieve memories of those empty rooms one by one. I see my mother . . ." Sha'rawi, 57). Thus, not only the priority of place granted the father and grandfather in the memoirs, but the language of the narrative itself invests Sha'rawi in her Arabo-Islamic heritage. These enriching relationships of an Arab feminist with her own culture are difficult to portray given the poverty of a reception environment that wants to imagine Arab women only as victims, escapees, or pawns. *Mudhakkirati* evinces a woman who, far from desiring escape from her people, saw women's liberation as something nourished by love for her family and rooted in her own culture. In the Arabic version, Sha'rawi describes her close and loving relationship with her brother as a mainstay in her life, so much so that when he died suddenly, as a young man, she wanted to kill herself, reconsidering only when she remembered that she had two small children counting on her as a mother. Let us see how the relationship with the brother is transformed by the reception process. Here is a key passage about the brother from the Arabic version: "I loved my brother with an endless love, despite my jealousy of him. And my affection for him was increased by his delicate health. Knowing that he would keep alive the name of my beloved father also increased my love for him, love buoyed by the praiseworthy qualities with which he was graced. My attachment to my brother multiplied after a certain incident . . ." (Sha'rawi, 65). Sha'rawi goes on to describe a story Badran also includes, in which her brother refuses to snitch on her to their mother. Here is the translator's treatment of this passage: "Despite my jealousy I loved my brother very much. My attachment to him was strengthened still more by an incident that occurred one day . . ." (37). The translator changes the order, skips the praise, and leaves out the name of the father binding the siblings together, but does keep the general sense of the relationship and does include the incident narrated as evidence of her brother's loyalty to her. We may regard this as a good faith rendering of the Arabic version despite the reordering and excisions. From here, however, let us go to a blurb on the back cover of the English paperback edition, where reviewer Hanna Papanek characterizes Sha'rawi as expressing "bitter jealousy of the brother whom all favored over her." How far this is from what the Arabophonic reader is given to understand about the brother-sister relationship. This is an excellent example of how the process of reception is larger than the will of the individual translator. The translator has included the passages related to the brother Umar, passages that place young Huda's moments of jealousy in context as part of a relationship of mutual trust, intense loyalty, and tender, protective love. It is true that the translator has subtly shifted Sha'rawi's emphasis. However, it is quite a leap from there to Papanek's complete mis-characterization of the brother-sister relationship. I believe we must turn to the victim part of my threefold typology to understand this leap. The workings of a larger grid of reception, which insists on Sha'rawi as unidimensional victim of gender oppression, overcome, in this case, even the efforts of the translator to relay the textual evidence to the contrary. The Papanek blurb, in turn, becomes a frame of expectation influencing any reader who picks up the paperback edition.

EXAGGERATING EUROPE

Albert Hourani's blurb on the back cover of the English book reads, "*Harem Years* shows how a gifted and sensitive woman, brought up in seclusion but with a knowledge of French that opened a window onto European culture, gradually became aware of her own predicament and that of her sex and society." There is no doubt that Sha'rawi, as a member of the sophisticated Egyptian upper class under the Turkish *khedive* (ruler), was exposed to a wide variety of cultures, European cultures being significant among them. It is also clear that Europe was slowly replacing Turkey as a preferred focus for her class during the early decades of the century. However, the English version exaggerates the European element in Sha'rawi's memoirs.[9]

On the first page of her preface to the translation, Badran reverses the order in which Sha'rawi learned languages, emphasizing first the chronologically last of the three: "As an upper-class woman, Huda Shaarawi's social language was French. She also knew Turkish, the language of her mother and the Turco-Circassian élites and royal family. But Huda [sic] had a special fondness for Arabic', her father's tongue and the national language" (1). By contrast, we learn from Sha'rawi's narrative that French lessons did not begin until after she had finished her courses in Arabic, religion, and the *Qur'an* at age nine, and that she was eagerly buying cheap Arabic tales from the peddlers as well as reciting Turkish and Persian poetry, long before she could read a word of French (47). The Arabophonic reader would understand that Sha'rawi suffered from the common problem of diglossia resulting from the large gap between formal standard Arabic and the vernacular, a problem more pronounced for those with restricted access to education, and therefore, very much connected to gender. The Anglophonic reader may not, however, understand that Sha'rawi's primary language of daily interaction was Egyptian Arabic, even with the multilingualism common to her class. Sha'rawi's style of narration (inasmuch as it can be assumed to be basically hers, after editing by her secretary) shows the imprint of her early education in the occasional echo of *Qur'anic* diction (for example, the phrase "when war had put away its garments," 38, comes straight from the *Qur'an's* Sura Muhammad, verse 5).

Many of the Arab, Turkish, and African characters who people the Arabic narrative are eliminated or reduced in the English version. For example, Sha'rawi describes how her mother always observed the Night of Mid-Sha'ban by inviting a *sheikha* (religious female elder) to assemble everyone in the heart of the house and lead the family in a prayer recital: "After we finished feeding the poor, we would gather in a large room. Sheikha Jalsan would then come and sit in the middle of the room and recite for us the prayer of mid-Sha'ban and we would repeat after her in upraised voices. This prayer had an affect upon us of great awe and reverence" (54). The story of Fatanat, a feisty lower-class woman who leaves her husband and seeks refuge with Huda Hanim's mother, is left out of the English version. The intrigues of the lively lower-class peddler women—Sha'rawi goes on indignantly for pages about them—are given only a few lines. The Circassian cousin Huriya gets a whole page in *Mudhakkirati,* where Sha'rawi describes Cousin Huriya's adventures as a soldier and includes an interpolated story narrated by the warrior woman herself (37–38). This cousin only gets an aside in a subordinate clause in *Harem Years* (25). These omissions reduce the number of indigenous women who do not fit the victim mold and who provide the reader with non-European models that may have excited the imagination of young Huda Hanim. At the same time, almost every single mention of Mme Richard and Mme Rushdi, European friends of the family, is retained in the English version, which abridges so much else.

The way in which some European characters are cited is also relevant. The *Harem Years* text frequently uses the given name of Rushdi Basha's wife, Eugenie Le Brun, which has the effect of highlighting her Europeanness rather than the fact that she was the wife of a prominent Egyptian. In *Mudhakkirati,* Sha'rawi never calls her friend anything but "Haram Rushdi Basha." This is a reflection of Sha'rawi's respect for propriety, titles, and seniority, but it also draws the reader's attention to Mrs. Rushdi's investiture in her Egyptian context. Sha'rawi's memoirs certainly draw a picture of a close friendship with Mme Rushdi, and Badran transmits Sha'rawi's sense that her friend had a deep and lasting effect on her: ". . . even after [Mme Rushdi's] death I felt her spirit light the way before me" (Badran, 82). The significance of this passage, with its emphasis on Sha'rawi's friendship with the European woman, is granted more weight in the English version than in the Arabic by its positioning. The passage closes Part Three of the English text, whereas in the Arabic text it is embedded within a chapter. In contrast, the English text omits a similar sensation that Sha'rawi recounts after the death of another friend,

Egyptian feminist Malak Nasef: "After that, I used to search for her during the critical days that we traversed during the Revolution and after it, and I used to call to her in my soul, but her voice did not reverberate except within my conscience" (Sha'rawi, 160).[10] In *Mudhakkirati*, Sha'rawi mentions her love and admiration for the Princess Amina, wife of the Khedive Tawfiq, before her mention of Mme Richard, a European friend of her mother; the translated text reverses the order in which they are mentioned. The English text also leaves out an incident in which Mme Richard seeks refuge in the Egyptian customs of gender segregation to evade sexual harassment from a European man, her husband's boss (Sha'rawi, 68). In the Arabic memoir, European culture appears to be one influence among several present in Sha'rawi's world, without overshadowing the others. European friends and mentors are important in Sha'rawi's social circle, but there are Egyptian and Turkish friends and mentors who have comparable places in her life.

The Arabic narrative does not allow the impression that the European women are all liberated while Arab women are all oppressed. Sha'rawi in Arabic does tell the story of Eastern women who suffer from oppressive conditions, such as Atiyya Hanim, but also describes the case of a Frenchwoman condemned for murdering a man who slandered her sexual honor in the newspaper (Sha'rawi, 139–140). Sha'rawi is shocked that no one in Paris seems to sympathize with the woman, who is, in her view, a victim of male exploitation of women's vulnerability when sexual purity is the issue. This story does not make it into the English text. Atiyya Hanim's story of Eastern women's oppression, however, is translated in full as "Portrait of the Hard Life of a Woman."

The reader of Sha'rawi's memoirs in Arabic will be struck by the energy with which she decries Western stereotypes of Egyptian women and by Sha'rawi's refreshing assumption that women in Europe and the United States are as much in need of Arab feminists' succour as the reverse. When she is wrapping up the Rome conference in 1923, she and the other attendees are granted an audience with Mussolini. Sha'rawi does not miss the opportunity to put in a good word for the Italian woman: "I repeated my personal appeal that the Italian woman be granted political rights" (Sha'rawi, 260). The reader never gets the sense that Sha'rawi thought of herself on inferior ground with European women. A similar confident tone informs Sha'rawi's United States tour and her lectures to Americans in various venues, reminding the reader that American women were not that much further along in their struggle than Egyptian women at that time. Moreover, Sha'rawi narrates several incidents that highlight her insistence on Egypt's place among nations, as when the Egyptian delegation at the Rome conference notices the absence of an Egyptian flag among the other flags and quickly produces a large flag to be given pride of place next to the Italian flag. The Anglophonic reader would naturally have an interest in knowing about the European people in Sharawi's life. But the overall effect of this pattern of excisions and inclusions is to exaggerate the European element in the English text. This effect is shaped by the readerly expectation of Arab woman as escapee. The back cover blurb from the prominent Middle East Studies scholar Hourani reinforces the idea that Sha'rawi could only have been rescued from her narrow straits as an Eastern woman through a European "window" of rescue.

CAMOUFLAGING CLASS

The English version of *Mudhakkirati* softens Sha'rawi's class biases, very evident in the Arabic publication, in keeping with the pressures of the United States reception environment to see Sha'rawi as an idealized victim and a heroic rebel against her society. *Harem Years* does give the reader information about class in the front and end matter of the book, but does not reveal or analyze Sha'rawi's elegant dodging of class issues in her narrative.

Sha'rawi's nostalgia for the days when families such as hers were served by a small army of slaves, employees, and peasant farmers might temper the sympathy a United States readership would have toward the ostensible victim of harem life. She looks back on those years with happiness, she says, "especially when I am confronted with some of the modern customs, which make me long to return the past, and all it contains of custom and memories" (Sha'rawi, 56). What are these customs that she longs to revive? She continues:

> I recall, for example, our grand house with its spacious apartments and vast parlor, and how it used to teem with slavegirls and bondsmen. They were well-trained to work, sincere in performing their duties, sensitive to the responsibilities placed on their shoulders, respectful of their employers, careful with the things in their hands, and loving toward the children of their employers who were born under their hands. Each one would rise to his task in the best manner and would accompany us for better or for worse, and would never reach his hand toward anything, no matter how costly, and would not covet a single thing but

the good pleasure of those who had authority over him. And we recip-
rocated this love with them, and appreciated in them this loyalty.
(56–57)

Sha'rawi never baldly calls the eunuchs "eunuchs"; the translation does
(39). Nor does Sha'rawi nakedly term her husband's first consort a
"slave-concubine," as Badran does; rather she uses the decorous term
"um awladuhu" (mother of his children), which underlines the legal
rights and improved status (she could no longer be sold) the woman had
gained by virtue of bearing the children of a free man (Sha'rawi, 82).
This evasion on Sha'rawi's part might be clarified by a translator's note.
To eliminate Sha'rawi's evasion in the translation of the text itself, however, disables the reader from learning something from the narrator's delicate circumlocutions.

When the Revolution of 1919 excites the masses to do more than
just support the transfer of power from elite Britons to elite Egyptians,
but to revolt against the landowning system itself, Sha'rawi is quick to
censure the "excesses" of the crowds. These excesses are attacks on the
houses of English gentry in Sha'rawi's village, whose privileges strikingly resemble the privileges of Sha'rawi's own family. She reports that
her nephew risked his life to prevent this destruction of English residen-
tial property (Sha'rawi, 171). This passage is not in *Harem Years'* section
summarizing the Revolution.

Details in the Arabic text that allow the reader to see Sha'rawi's
class bias in play are more often than not absent from the English
version. One example is the story of Sha'rawi's first shopping trip. In
Mudhakkirati, Sha'rawi goes on for pages about the intrigues of the
door-to-door peddlers, lower-class women who, she says, ruined "great
families" with their intrigues, even attempting to fall between herself and
her husband. These entrepreneurs were also loansharks (Sha'rawi, 61).
Her fierce "I hated those women (*niswa*)" (Sha'rawi, 61) is translated as
"I didn't like most of these peddlers" in *Harem Years* (48). In *Mudhakkirati,* when Sha'rawi recounts how she gained her mother's approval for
her novel first shopping trip to a department store in the city, she says that
what finally persuaded her mother is the prospect of cutting out the profits of these meddlesome peddler middlewomen with "their evils and ma-
lignities" (89). In *Harem Years,* the class antagonism of this passage is
blunted. The desire to eliminate the peddlerwomen is not mentioned; that
part of the passage seems to have been abridged into the phrase "wise
spending": "I finally persuaded my mother to accompany me. She was

then quick to see the advantages of shopping in person. Not only was there a wide range of goods to choose from but there was money to be saved through wise spending." (Badran, 69). *Mudhakkirati* allows us to see, perhaps in spite of Sha'rawi, that feminist consciousness conceived in privileged terms of personal autonomy was played out against a colonial economy in which modernization profited Western business and certain affluent sectors of Egyptian society at the expense of vast numbers of local distributors and small producers (Ahmed, 1994, 146).

The English text changes Sha'rawi's use of the word "ladies" *(sayyidat)*, which, though it may be an unconscious reflex on Sha'rawi's part, is accurate, to "women" *(nisa')*. The title of the Wafd Central *Ladies* Committee is rendered "Wafd Central *Women's* Committee" in English. It was really composed of ladies, women of high status and great privilege in their society. (The high point of Sha'rawi's naiveté about class is when she—still very young—and Mme Rushdi decide that women's struggle in Egypt would best be furthered by building a tennis court [Sha'rawi, 99].) Softening the elitism of the committee's title in English translation makes invisible to the Anglophonic reader the most salient drawback of early feminism in Egypt. This is the will of elite women to "appear on the feminist stage as representatives of the millions of women in their own societies. To what extent they do violence to the women they claim authority to write and speak about is a question that is seldom raised" (Lazreg, 332). Leila Ahmed's reading of Sha'rawi is a critique of this violence, a markedly different reading from the naiveté about class that *Harem Years* asks its readers to have (Ahmed, 1994, 176–179). Badran's second book shows that she does understand the complex of class issues in which the nationalist and feminist activities began. It is the vulnerability of *Harem Years* to the pressures of reception reserved for Arab women's writing that obscures the issue of class.

To her immense credit, of course, Sha'rawi went on to found institutions that addressed women's health, education, and poverty. She generously opened her house and her patrimony to enable future generations of Egyptian women to reach the highest levels of a formal education denied to Sha'rawi, and generally to gain more access to the resources of their society. Her work netted a minimum marriage age for both sexes, pushed for limits on polygamy, and strove for women's inclusion in political rights. As Amina Sa'id puts it in her introduction to the Dar al-Hilal publication, Sha'rawi may have been "born in a golden cradle, but she rejected amusement and chose to spend her life in struggle and strife for the sake of the most noble and lofty of goals" (Sha'rawi, 7). It is that record of accomplishment, even with its flaws intact, which will serve Sha'rawi; there is no need to render her politically correct in our terms today. However, showing Sha'rawi's aristocratic bent would go against the grain of United States readerly expectations that an Arab feminist be an idealized victim rather than a grand and regal lady.

HAREMIZING THE NARRATIVE

Mudhakkirati means "My Memoirs." Amal Amireh points out that "Shaarawi's title puts her at the center of her own narrative, emphasizes her subjectivity and agency, and identifies her as the source of enunciation" (23). The Feminist Press book *Harem Years,* on the other hand, "identifies Shaarawi with an institution and locates the narrative in a harem" (23). *Harem Years* targets for translation, with rearrangement and abridgement, only the early chapters, which are about Sha'rawi's girlhood and coming-of-age. The translator's division of the material is structured around the notion of "harem": "The Family," "Childhood in the Harem 1884–92," "A Separate Life 1892–1900," and "A Wife in the Harem 1900–18." An epilogue summarizes the events of several more chapters, which cover the beginning of Sha'rawi's work as a nationalist and feminist public figure. Badran explains, "After Part Four, Huda's [sic] account changes in tone and content. She begins to speak about how she and other women became nationalist activists and started the feminist movement. This portion of her memoirs becomes fragmentary" (3). It is this portion that represents the bulk of the Arabic version. Its "fragmentary" nature consists of the back-and-forth between direct narration and interpolated documents. The meaning of Sha'rawi's story in the Arabic version lies, I believe, in the weaving between her narration and the documents, and in the relationship between the personal story and the much more expansive political story. The transformation of Sha'rawi's account into a harem memoir makes the English version a radically different reading experience from the Arabic version. The English version permits the reader to relegate Sha'rawi's writings to a harem of "First World" creation, a ghetto where Arab women's writing is put by the United States reception process, there to languish behind the mystique of "Third World woman's difference." Perhaps a full translation of the portion summarized in the epilogue would have counterbalanced this haremizing effect.

Every text creates its ideal reader by implying the body of knowledge and the expectations the reader is presumed to possess.[11] The readers toward whom the book *Harem Years* gestures in its title, prefatory and end matter, covers, and the texture of the text itself, are expected to approach the book with the harem genre in mind. The translator says that the text "will appeal to anyone eager to know about life in the harem—a word highly charged in the Western popular imagination. . . . First-hand accounts by women who lived in harems are rare." Here is the translator's explanation of the memoirs' importance: "The *Memoirs* of Huda Shaarawi have dual significance. They give insight into harem experience in Egypt in its final decades. At the same time they reveal how the roots of upper-class women's feminism in Egypt are found in the nexus of their harem experience and growing change around the turn of the century" (20). The Egyptian publisher's preface asserts the significance of the memoirs on very different grounds: "This book is considered among the most important and most valuable to appear in the Kitab al-Hilal series from its inception, because it treats the most monumental political events of the first half of our modern history. The immortal leader recounts these events within her memoirs, which she wrote herself, aiming at the utmost probity in every word which her pen inscribed" (Sha'rawi, 2). The Arabic version of Sha'rawi's memoirs calls for a reader with knowledge of certain conventions, too; the knowledge demanded is of the topography and society of pre-WWII Cairo, its old buildings, bridges, and streets, its customs, protocols, and niceties.

The translator seems to offer a critique of the Western harem genre, saying that it mystifies what was "simply the portion of the house where women and children conducted their daily lives" (7). Amal Amireh argues that "this critique of 'harem writing' turns out to be an empty gesture" (23), because so many other elements of the English text are cast toward the conventions of the harem literature genre. The diction and syntax of the English book's front matter, for example, calls into play the rhetorical affects of the Western harem literature genre: "The harem or household where Huda [sic] grew up in Cairo was in the then new and fashionable area of Ismailiya . . . Here the mature Sultan Pasha kept his Cairo harem—Huda's [sic] mother and his wife, (who figures in the memoirs) and their children." Sultan Basha's wives were not "kept" any more than Lady Cromer or Mme Rushdi or women of the upper classes in the United States were "kept" anywhere by anyone. Rather, they negotiate places for themselves among the choices made available to them in ways tempered by their degree of access to resources and privileges. The grammatical subordination of the Eastern women in this clause is a rhetorical trigger alluding to the Western heritage of harem stories about subordinated Eastern women and makes little sense if separated from this reception environment.

The placement and captioning of photographs in *Harem Years* refer the reader to knowledge gained elsewhere about "the harem." One photo placed in the section on holidays is captioned, "Huda [sic] and friend pose in Egyptian peasant dresses. Dressing up was a favourite pastime in the harem" (47). The second sentence reminds the reader of the framing notion "harem," although the word is not in the accompanying text at all. What the caption alludes to is the convention that *ennui* was a defining characteristic of "harem life" and required especial effort at amusement to relieve. This notion of "the harem" as a site of trivial amusements in-fantilized the women who were the objects of observation.[12]

The translator explains that she uses the English word *harem* because the "standard transliteration 'harim' would be unfamiliar to the general reader" (3). Perhaps the use of something unfamiliar to the general reader, with an explanation, might have jolted the reader out of the comfortable pattern of expectations and created a more challenging and transformative reading experience. In any case, there is barely any use of the word *harim* in the entire Arabic text to worry about. Sha'rawi only uses the word once in 457 pages.[13] The English version uses the word *harem* twenty-five times in the Introduction alone and numerous more times in endnotes and captions. By contrast, the only time Sha'rawi uses a special term to refer to a household location is when she mentions the *salamlik*, a room to which men were restricted when they came to visit (Sha'rawi, 33). In Ara-bic, Sha'rawi does use *"haram"* for "missus," so that, just as Lady Cromer is the woman whose name is subordinated to Cromer's by marriage, "Haram Rushdi Basha" is Rushdi's wife. *Harem* is not an operative term in the Arabic memoirs because it does not delineate a meaningful cate-gory for Sha'rawi. *Harem* is the word of the outside looking in. Sha'rawi's terms represent the narrative perspective of the writerly self looking out and moving about the world in ways that seem natural to her (and which are hardly more restrictive than the orbits of the average Victorian or Ed-wardian woman of the same class). When Sha'rawi does write specifically about the household site, her description does not have that oppressed vic-tim tone. Rather, she writes in glowing terms that "Our house was guided by regularity and was the epitome of calm. Tranquility was settled upon it, as a result of accord between the servants and concord and cooperation between all who were in it" (Sha'rawi, 58).

Not only is the word *harim* missing, but the issue of seclusion as a problem is not an organizing principle in *Mudhakkirati*. If Huda Hanim and her contemporaries seem to live in seclusion to Western observers, there is nothing secluded about her life as she describes it. Her mother's house is awhirl with guests, visitors, sojourners, petitioners, to the extent that young Huda Hanim finds the openness of the household taxing (33). The poor teem at the door for alms; the relatives come and go summer and winter; the upper-class men and women make the rounds of social calls; Mother plays cards with friends, does charitable affairs, keeps up with court life; Huda Hanim enjoys visiting friends, neighbors, kin, the palace, Jabaliya, and vacationing in Helwan, Ramleh, Alexandria, and Minya. A young woman of quality in turn-of-the-century London or Paris could not have led a less "secluded" life, except that she would have been permitted to sit, under close supervision, with gentlemen callers. By contrast, the problem of seclusion seems to the English reader a central issue defining Sha'rawi's lifestyle.[14]

Even the editorial mistakes in the text suggest that the editing process is not free from the pressures of the reception environment. One phrase in the Arabic version refers to Mme Sha'rawi and Mme Rushdi conversing about "offspring and *immortality*." This slips past the editors of the English version as "offspring and *immorality*," a strange association that caused me to do a double take. It could, of course, be a simple typographical error. On the other hand, the harem, in the conventions of Western discourse about the harem, was, in fact, considered a place of both excessive offspring and excessive immorality. Could this have contributed to this error getting past an editorial eye embedded in the United States horizon of expectations that I have described?

A final issue, albeit minor, that reinforces the packaging of Sha'rawi as a victim in the English version is the treatment of Sha'rawi's mother. *Harem Years* introduces Sha'rawi's mother by explaining that mother, though Circassian, was not a slave (16). Separated from a reception environment built for Muslim-women-as-victim stories, such an observation adds strangely little. Migration from the Caucasus to the Arab world was not unusual during this period of Czarist conquest, and free Circassians did live in Egypt. Introducing the mother as not-a-slave, then rearranging the material so that the memoir begins with the mother instead of the father, heightens the perception of the reader that this is the story of a victim, the subjugated daughter of supine "harem women" (a Badran term, 19). Shaw'rawi's narrative preserves enough indeterminacy and complexity in drawing the mother figure to allow the reader to wonder if she might have had more influence on her famous daughter than is assumed, as Leila Ahmed's invaluable work on Sha'rawi points out. It is the mother's angry stance against Sha'rawi's husband, for example, that enabled Sha'rawi to defy him and live apart because his polygamy was unacceptable to her. Here is a woman who could not read or write, and yet extracted from her daughter's suitor a pre-nuptial agreement preserving her rights—and insisted on enforcing it. The daughter later will lead a campaign that works within Islamic legal traditions to limit polygamy. Perhaps Iqbal Hanim had an unacknowledged influence on the work of her daughter.

REOPENING SHA'RAWI'S MEMOIRS

Let me say here, as I have maintained throughout, that this is not a criticism of particular translating individuals or editing individuals for anything so nebulous and B-movie conspiratorial as harboring neoimperialist sentiments or practicing neocolonial feminism. "The most I can say," to draw upon Spivak, "is that it is possible to read these texts . . . in a politically useful way. Such an approach presupposes that a 'disinterested' reading attempts to render transparent the interests of the hegemonic readership" (1989, 191). Amireh adds a moral motivation for examining this issue: "The emphasis on difference, unfortunately, undermines the book's ability to build bridges of solidarity and understanding among women from different cultures" (22).[15] There are also aesthetic reasons to call for the challenging of reader expectations in translating texts across culture. Wolfgang Iser says,

> . . . expectations are scarcely ever fulfilled in truly literary texts. If they
> were, then such texts would be confined to the individualization of a
> given expectation, and one would inevitably ask what such an intention
> was supposed to achieve . . . For the more a text individualizes or con-
> firms an expectation it has initially aroused, the more aware we be-
> come of its didactic purpose, so that at best we can only accept or reject
> the thesis forced upon us. More often than not, the very clarity of such
> texts will make us want to free ourselves from their clutches. (53)

This calls for texts that make reading less smooth. It calls for publishers, translators, authors, and readers to become conscious of comfortable patterns of reception of the sort that restrict Arab women's writings to the ghetto of victims, escapees, and pawns. If we are to continue discussing Huda Sha'rawi in English through the medium of *Harem Years,* it is important to be aware of the limitations put on the text by its Anglophonic reception environment. It may be desirable, in addition, to let multiple translations abound so that one English version does not become the only funnel through which the Anglophonic reader knows Sha'rawi.[16]

Looking forward, more study of the Sha'rawi phenomenon using reception theory may be able to make sense of the stridently conflicting views held about Huda Sha'rawi in Arab countries. In that contest, some on the Left who are in blithe ignorance of the woman and her work invoke her name willy-nilly. In one instance, she is invoked in support of change in the superstructure and the relations of production,[17] which might have perturbed her as much as did the attacks on propertied classes during the Revolution of 1919. Sha'rawi's moderate, reformist approach, which justified improving the education and position of women mainly in terms of women's roles as mothers in the new nation and which opposed a change in Islamic inheritance laws, was hardly radical feminism. Meanwhile, some people on the right consider her name anathema and her work a blasphemy against God, country, and family.[18] Sha'rawi's personal decorum and concern to observe propriety in all her actions can hardly have been studied by these opponents, with whom she actually may have more in common than some of her modern-day supporters. Happily, there are also more measured voices in the Arab reception of Sha'rawi. But a survey of *that* reading environment requires another politics of reception study.

Sha'rawi is a figure who merits careful rereading. What is the meaning of Sha'rawi's life and work—for Egypt in her own period, first of all? How has Sha'rawi's meaning changed since she became an icon for women's liberation and how is she read by contesting ideological groups? What local and regional meanings does her example hold for women's movements in Egypt, the Arab world, and the world? How can our "global" age benefit from the discursive record of her work in the international feminist arena? These are questions that take Sha'rawi's significance out of the harem of Third World women's difference and into relevance for women and men everywhere.

ACKNOWLEDGMENT

I thank the staff of the National Library in Abu Dhabi, United Arab Emirates, for their assistance, and Fulbright College at the University of Arkansas for the 1996 Research Assignment that allowed me to write this essay.

NOTES

[1]The term is from the work of Hans Robert Jauss. See *Toward an Aesthetic of Reception,* trans. Timothy Bahti (Minneapolis: University of Minnesota Press, 1982).

[2]I thank Lisa Suhair Majaj, Deborah Najor, and Amal Amireh for inviting me to be a discussant on their 1995 MESA panel on Arab Women's Writing and Politics of Reception. Exposure to their ideas, and encouragement from Leila Ahmed at the same MESA, invigorate the argument I develop here.

[3]*Western Representations of the Muslim Woman: From Termagent to Odalisque.* (Austin, TX: University of Texas Press, 1999).

[4]See their articles and also those by Azizah al-Hibri and Mona Fayad in *Food for Our Grandmothers: Writings by Arab-American and Arab-Canadian Feminists,* Joanna Kadi, ed. (Boston: South End Press, 1994).

[5]Places where her work can be found in this intersection are her essay "Unpicked Fruits" in *Food for Our Grandmothers: Writings by Arab-American and Arab-Canadian Feminists,* Joanna Kadi, ed. (Boston: South End Press, 1994), 56–61, and an essay on the tomboy in Arab culture, "Al-Dawwara," in *Jo's Girls; Tomboy Tales of High Adventure, True Grit, & Real Life,* Christian McEwen, ed. (Boston: Beacon Press, 1997), 250–256.

[6]Personal communication from Barbara Nimri Aziz, May 1993.

[7]All translations from the Sha'rawi text are my own.

[8]The first hemistich of Imra ul-Qais's famous "hanging ode" or *mu'allaqa,* a pre-Islamic poem whose opening lines are almost universally memorized in the Arab world (translation mine).

[9]Even a short account of Sha'rawi's earliest political and organizational experience, her membership in a ladies' committee supporting the Turks in their war against the Greeks in 1895, which in the Arabic account occurs in her early married life before separation, does not appear in *Harem Years.*

[10]Badran includes this passage in her book, *Feminists, Islam, and Nation: Gender and the Making of Modern Egypt* (Princeton, NJ: Princeton University Press, 1995).

[11]Walker Gibson calls this "the mock reader"; Gerald Prince, "the narratee"; others, "the implied reader."

[12]Some of the earliest examples of this convention occur in Samuel Johnson's *Rasselas* and Mary Wollstonecraft's *A Vindication of the Rights of Women.*

[13]Sha'rawi uses the word *harim* once, when she explains that she chose a man to tutor her in Arabic who was elderly enough to enter the *harim* of their house without offending the conservative sensibilities of her family (Sha'rawi, 83).

[14]See Leila Ahmed's review of *Harem Years,* "Women of Egypt," *The Women's Review of Books,* Nov. 1987, 7–8, and Amal Amireh, "Writing the Difference: Feminists' Invention of the 'Arab Woman,' " in *Interventions: Feminist Dialogues on Third World Women's Literature and Film,* Bishnupriya Ghosh and Brinda Bose, eds. (New York: Garland, 1996), 185–211.

[15]She is speaking here of Nayra Atiya's *Khul-khal: Five Egyptian Women Tell Their Stories* but in an essay that also analyzes *Harem Years,* beginning with her next sentence.

[16]I thank Heidi Liddle for the following references toward pursuing the translation angle: Susan Bassnett and André Lefevore, eds., *Translation, History, and Culture* (London: Printer Publishers, 1990); Lori Chamberlain, "Gender and the Metaphorics of Translation," in *Rethinking Translation: Discourse, Subjectivity, Ideology,* Lawrence Venuti, ed. (London: Routledge, 1992), 57–74.

[17]Abd al-Azim Ramadan does this in his introduction to Nabil Raghib, *Huda Sha'rawi wa 'Asr al Tanwir,* Tarikh al Masriyun (Cairo: al-Hay'a al-Masriya al-'Amma lil Kutub, 1988). Raghib himself shows he has read the memoirs only hastily by making obvious reading mistakes, such as when he assumes Sha'rawi is referring to her own mother instead of her father's other wife when she says, "I loved this woman with a great love" (in fact, she very pointedly does *not* say this about her mother) and goes on to explain how that "great love" was so formative an influence on the psychological preparation of the leader (55).

[18]One such attack is carried out by Muhammad Fahmy Abd al-Wahhab in a booklet entitled, "Women's movements in the east and their links to imperialism and international Zionism"—*Al-Harakat al-Nisa'iya fi al-Sharq wa Silataha bi al-Isti'mar wa,* al-Suhyuniya al-Alamiya (n.p.: Dar al-I'tisam, n.d.). Another example of this is Wahby Sulaiman Ghawaji, *Al Mar'a al-Muslima,* (Beirut: Mu'assassat al-Risala, 1982), 148–153.

WORKS CITED

Abd al-Wahhab, Muhammad Fahmy. N.d. *Al-harakat al-nisa'iyya fi al-sharq wa silatiha bi al-isti'mar wa al-suhyuniyya al-'alamiyya.* N.p.: Dar al-I'tisam.

Ahmed, Leila. 1987. "Women of Egypt." *The Women's Review of Books,* Nov. (1987): 7–8.

———. "Between Two Worlds: The Formation of a Turn-of-the-Century Egyptian Feminist." *Life/Lines: Theorizing Women's Autobiography.* Bella Brodzki and Celeste Schenck, eds. Ithaca, New York: Cornell UP, (1988). 154–174.

———. *Women and Gender in Islam: Historical Roots of a Modern Debate.* New Haven, Connecticut: Yale UP, 1994.

Amireh, Amal. "Writing the Difference: Feminists' Invention of the Arab Woman." In *Interventions: Feminist Dialogues on Third World Women's Literature and Film*. Bishnupriya Ghosh and Brinda Bose, eds. New York: Garland, 1996. 185–211.

Atiya, Nayra. *Khul-Khaal: Five Egyptian Women Tell Their Stories*. Syracuse: Syracuse UP, 1982.

Aziz, Barbara Nimri. "Al-Dawwara." In *Jo's Girls; Tomboy Tales of High Adventure, True Grit, & Real Life*. Christian McEwan, ed. Boston: Beacon Press, 1997. 250–256.

Badran, Margo, trans. *Harem Years: The Memoirs of an Egyptian Feminist*. New York: Feminist Press, 1986.

———. "Badran's Response [to Mervat Hatem's Review of *Harem Years*.]" *AMEWS NEWS* (Association of Middle Eastern Women's Studies), 2, 7 May (1988a).

———. "Critical Forum." *AMEWS NEWS* 2, 8 Oct. (1988b): 17–20.

———. *Feminists, Islam, and Nation: Gender and the Making of Modern Egypt*. Princeton, New Jersey: Princeton UP, 1995.

Bassnett, Susan and André Lefevere, ed. *Translation, History and Culture*. London: Printer Publishers, 1990.

Chamberlain, Lori. "Gender and the Metaphorics of Translation." In *Rethinking Translation: Discourse, Subjectivity, Ideology*. Lawrence Venuti, ed. London: Routledge, 1992. 57–74.

Childers, Joseph and Gary Hentzi. *The Columbia Dictionary of Modern Literary and Cultural Criticism*. New York: Columbia UP, 1995.

Hatem, Mervat. "Feminist Analysis and the Subjection World of Women." *AMEWS NEWS* (Association of Middle East Women's Studies) 2, 6 Feb. (1988): 7–9.

Ghawaji, Wahby Sulaiman. Al-mar'a al-muslima. Beirut: Mu'assassat al-Risala, 1982.

Guerin, Wilfred. *A Handbook of Critical Approaches to Literature*. New York: Oxford UP, 1992.

Iser, Wolfgang. "The Reading Process: A Phenomenological Approach." In *Reader Response Criticism: From Formalism to Post-Structuralism*, Jane Tompkins, ed. Baltimore: John Hopkins UP, 1980. 50–69.

Jauss, Hans Robert. Trans. Timothy Bahti. *Toward an Aesthetic of Reception*. Minneapolis, Minnesota: U of Minnesota P, 1982.

Johnson, Samuel [1709–1784]. *History of Rasselas, Prince of Abyssinia*. Oxford: Clarendon Press, 1927.

Kadi, Joanna. *Food for Our Grandmothers: Writings by Arab-American and Arab-Canadian Feminists*. Boston: South End Press, 1994.

Kahf, Mohja. *Western Representations of the Muslim Woman: From Termagant to Odalisque.* Austin: U of Texas P, 1999.

Lazreg, Marnia. "Feminism and Difference: The Perils of Writing as a Woman on Women in Algeria." In *Conflicts in Feminism.* Evelyn Fox Keller and Marianne Hirsch, eds. New York: Routledge, 1990. 326–248.

Mohanty, Chandra Talpade. "Under Western Eyes: Feminist Scholarship and Colonial Discourse." In *Third World Women and the Politics of Feminism.* Talpade, Ann Russo, and Lourdes Torres, eds. Bloomington: Indiana UP, 1991. 51–80.

ul-Qais, Imra. "Mu'allaqa," *Sharh al Mu'allaqat al'Ashr wa Akhbar Shu'ara'i-him.* Ahmad bin Amin al-Shanqiti and Fayez Tarhini, eds. Beirut: Dar al-Kitab al-'Arabi, 1994. 25–33.

Raghib, Nabil. *Huda Sha'rawi wa 'Asr al Tanwir.* Cairo: al-Hay'a al-Masriyya al-'Amma li al-Kutub, 1988.

Said, Edward. *Orientalism.* New York: Vintage Books, 1979.

Sha'rawi, Huda. *Mudhakkirati.* Cairo: Dar al-Hilal, 1981.

Wollstonecraft, Mary [1759–1797]. *A Vindication of the Rights of Woman.* London and New York: Penguin Books, 1992.

Identity and Community in Autobiographies of Algerian Women in France

PATRICIA GEESEY

*It is in France that I learned to be an Arab, it is
in Algeria that I learned to be an immigrant.* [1]

—SAKINNA BOUKHEDENNA

As Julia Kristeva notes in *Etrangers à nous-mêmes* (1988), being a foreigner in France has its distinct advantages and disadvantages:

> Nowhere else is one a foreigner *better* than in France. Since you remain incurably different and unacceptable, you are the object of fascination: you are noticed, talked about, you are hated or admired or both at the same time. [. . .] You are a problem, a desire: positive or negative, never neutral. (58–9)

In French society today, this description of a tension between positive and negative desire is particularly valid for the approximately four million Muslim Arabs and Berbers who have immigrated to France from North Africa. Since the 1980s, there has been a proliferation of mainstream and academic discourse concerning the possibility of "assimilating" Arab and Berber Muslim immigrants into France's secular and humanist republic. However, it is not only specialists who have fueled the discourse on and about North African women in France. Since the mid-1980s, Algerian women themselves have "come to the word," to paraphrase Hélène Cixous, to present their life stories and to describe their experiences as immigrants. [2] This paper examines three recent examples of Algerian women's life-writing published in France. My analysis focuses on the framing and marketing of Algerian women's narratives in France. The reception of Algerian women's autobiographies influences whether or not these works are read as challenging or as insidiously reaffirming the dominant discourse about North African women in France.

Autobiographical discourse might at first appear to be a privileged genre for the presentation and definition of one's identity as an Algerian woman in France. However, a series of ambivalent issues related to both the role of "Third World" or minority discourse in any "First World" society, and the politics of location concerning who is speaking about Algerian women, are implicit in the development of a subgenre of Algerian women's autobiographies in France. These narratives may be read on several levels as texts that seek to reformulate the debates on assimilation, integration, and cultural and identity politics within a new discursive territory. In general, it would be accurate to note that "testimonial" characterizes the three autobiographies discussed in this essay. Two of the publications have been transcribed and framed by another voice and authorial presence. The underlying concern of the three Algerian women autobiographers presented here is that of naming themselves and situating themselves within their original communities, while at the same time laying claim to their participation in French society.

However, in spite of the authors' expressed intended goal of "speaking for themselves" as Algerian women in France, their texts are at risk of being appropriated by the dominant discourses on/about North African women in France and in the Maghreb. The Algerian, female autobiographical subjects—who may or may not be mediated in their texts by the assistance of a transcriber—inevitably partake of and participate in the proliferation of the production of knowledge on postcolonial and migrant subjectivities. The reception of these autobiographies as cultural or literary artifacts produced by "Third World" voices for consumption by a largely "First World" readership becomes a crucial element in the analysis of these works. The extent to which Algerian women's autobiographies in France can resist becoming "a commodity" in the global publishing industry is a highly ambivalent issue. As Françoise Lionnet points out, all too often, when a Third World woman claims her right to subjectivity and her right to "name herself," forces effectively beyond her control influence the reception of her work. According to Lionnet, a significant question should be raised when dealing with autobiographical texts from Third World women: "How is she constructed by the paratextual apparatus that accompanies the marketing of her book and that may well contradict this self-naming?" (3). In the case of Algerian women's autobiographies in France, the marketing strategies of publishers are inextricably linked to attempts to capitalize on the public's interest in the lives of North African women and on those cultural practices that are perceived to affirm their "exoticism" and their alterity.

Therefore, any informed reading of Algerian women's autobiographies in France must analyze those narrative strategies that might resist appropriation and (re)inscription into the dominant discourse on North African Muslim women. In this essay, three such autobiographical narratives will be discussed: Nedjima Plantade's *L'Honneur et l'amertume: le destin ordinaire d'une femme kabyle* (1993); Djura's *Le Voile du silence* (1990); and Mimouna's *Ni le voile, ni l'oubli* (1995)[3]. Each of these texts epitomizes the problem of reception and framing of Algerian women's autobiographical texts. My analysis will be informed by several vital questions: Do these narratives merely offer a transparent critique of the women's own patriarchal cultures? While recounting their victimization at the hands of Arab-Muslim cultural traditions, how do these works destabilize the very notions of identity and community in the *transnational* and *translational* framework of the North African immigrant experience in France?

The underlying concern of most writing on and about North African women in France, and this is true of even those narratives penned by North African women themselves, is the notion of cultural assimilation and difference. Juxtaposed to what North African women in France write about themselves and their sense of identity and their relationship with both their own and the French community, is the French academic and media discourse that attempts to describe them as potential agents of cultural assimilation. In sociological analyses of North African women in France, their role in French society is perceived to be that of cultural chameleons—since women are believed to be more likely and more able to slide from one cultural and community context to another. François Dubet and Dominique Schnapper, two leading authorities on immigration in France, have proposed that for the North African community, acculturation will come about due to the efforts of women in the Arab-Berber community. In Dubet's and Schnapper's views, women from the Arab-Muslim world have much to gain by substituting European secular values for what French society tends to perceive as alien and retrograde cultural practices that victimize women. It is important to note that Dubet's and Schnapper's views describe a principal aspect of the dominant discourse in French society regarding Arab-Muslim women in

France and in North Africa, since Algerian women's autobiographies will most often be read as either supporting or challenging this dominant discourse.[4]

ALGERIAN WOMEN IN FRANCE

The presence of Arab and Berber immigrants living in France has produced a flurry of interest in the lives of Arab and/or Berber women.[5] Rabia Abdelkrim-Chikh has referred to the status of the immigrant Maghrebian woman in France as a "double alterity"; "doubly dominated because she is a woman *and* foreign," she is seen by an obsessively secular society as the epitome of women oppressed by religious tradition (236). Abdelkrim-Chikh suggests that since the "difference" of North African women can often be determined from such external markers as clothing, culinary habits, and higher fertility rates, their alleged alterity within French society comes to be viewed as a series of immutable traits.

Recent events in France and in Algeria that have been widely publicized and even sensationalized in the French media have also stimulated the production of discourses on/about North African women in France. These events include women participating in demonstrations in the late 1980s against the publication of the French translation of Salman Rushdie's *Satanic Verses;* and beginning in 1989, the "Scarf Affair," in which young, Muslim female students were expelled from school for wearing head coverings in class in violation of the school's policy of total secularism.[6] After 1992, frequent discussions in the French press regarding sectarian violence in Algeria, particularly those occurrences of aggression, intimidation, and outright murder of Algerian women, came to be seen as another marker of women's status as victims. Linked to the Algerian civil crisis is the fact that several prominent Algerian feminist activists (notably Khalida Messaoudi and Salima Gezhali) have made regular visits to France during which they have appeared on French television programs. In 1994, the Bangladeshi writer Taslima Nasreen, threatened by Muslim extremists, quickly became the subject of numerous magazine and television news stories. The French press, as well as made-for-television films, regularly detail incidents of honor killings, forced marriages, and spirit exorcisms among the North African community residing in France.

Autobiographies written in French by Algerian women immigrants and their daughters might, at first, seem to reinforce the dominant dis-

course on Algerian women in France. Popular images and academic research compete for the attention of the French public, which is already
convinced, according to surveys reprinted in *Francosopie,* that: "Islam
does not respect the rights of women," "Islam is incompatible with democracy," and Islam "represents a threat to French cultural identity" (Mermet, 210–11). When an autobiography of an Algerian woman in France
—whether it is framed as a novel or whether it is a transcribed testimonial—emphasizes her victimization at the hands of her male relatives, it
might be tempting to believe that these texts actually support the dominant discourse in French society that Maghrebian culture is retrograde
and denies women their most fundamental rights. On the other hand, if
Algerian women wish to publicly expose their sufferings to a French and
Maghrebian reading public, is it inevitable that their texts will fall into a
trap of sensationalizing the very cultural differences the women are trying to negotiate from the perspective of the cross-cultural, migrant experience?[7] How can Algerian women in France "speak for" themselves
without having their narratives appropriated by a voyeuristic tendency
that partakes of colonialist tropes of identity and difference? The question one must raise regarding Algerian women's autobiographies in
France is: can reading strategies be developed that resist Algerian women's
re-inscription into the dominant discourse?

ALGERIAN WOMEN IN FRANCE
AND THE COLONIAL PAST

The dominant ideology and the production of knowledge in French society concerning North African women are inextricably linked to France's
attitudes towards Arab-Muslim societies during the period of colonial
conquest and administration. Rabia Abdelkrim-Chikh notes that the belief in the willingness among Arab women in France to actively initiate
an acculturation process clearly echoes an ideology that is a vestige from
the colonial era. In a comment comparable to Gayatri Spivak's ironic reference to the colonialists' collective fantasy of "White men saving brown
women from brown men" ("Subaltern," 296), Abdelkrim-Chikh points
out that the paternalistic concern for the status of North African Muslim
women living in France is a manifestation of a kind of *"philogynie"*—a
curious opposition to "misogynie"—that reveals French society's "nar-
cissistic satisfaction which evokes a symbolic abduction, or better yet, a
confirmation of self-admiration of its own values, in which the abducted
woman is an accomplice and consenting" (241). It is entirely possible

that the present-day concern for Arab and Berber women (manifested by a reading public avid for Algerian women's self-portraits) indeed harkens back to France's colonial domination of the Maghreb. In today's multiracial and multicultural French society, in which now, more than ever, many individuals appear to be informed of cultural practices that the North African immigrant community has brought to France, is it possible to escape the ramifications of France's colonial ties with Algeria? When French readers read autobiographies of Algerian women, to what extent does France's colonial past affect the reception of Algerian women's texts in France in the 1990s? Marnia Lazreg points out that, in addition to the numerous military, political, judicial, and racial injustices carried out against the Algerian people by the French during the more than 130 years of colonial rule, one of the most insidious (and thereby even more difficult to eradicate) was the "discursive injustice of fictionalizing women's lives" (*Eloquence,* 3). The colonial tendency to view women as victims because it reinforced the colonizer's belief that Arab-Muslim culture was backward is a practice that might still affect the reception of Algerian women's autobiographies. Lazreg notes that, from the early days of the French colonial venture, when the wives and daughters of Algerian opponents to French rule were labeled "prostitutes," and Algerian women of lower socioeconomic strata became "*Fatmas,*" right up to the independence movement in the 1950s-1960s when female militants became "terrorists," the French colonial regime attempted to define and categorize Algerian women in order to suit the needs of imperialist designs.

In response to the French colonial practice of essentializing Algerian women into "*natives*" and "*Fatmas,*" the early history of Algerian French-language literary production is, not surprisingly, dominated by autobiographical and semiautobiographical narratives. Quite simply, it might be suggested that autobiographical writing provides a deceptively simple *locus* from which an individual could assert her subjectivity, especially in response to the destructive and essentializing discursive practices that characterize colonialist depictions of indigenous subjects. Representative autobiographical works by Algerian women from an earlier period include Zoubida Bittari's *O mes soeurs musulmanes, pleurez!* (1964) and Fadhama Amrouche's *Histoire de ma vie* (1968). These works have raised questions both about the alleged transparency of autobiographical writing and the reception of these works in the former colonial power. In an essay published in 1990, Jean Déjeux develops one of the most commonly held readings of Algerian women's autobiographies written in French. Generally stated, this belief holds that Algerian women write in French because it is more "liberating" for them, and their objectives are usually to bring criticism against Arab-Berber culture for its treatment of women. Déjeux points out that women's self-portraits from Algeria assert the female protagonists' right to exist as individuals. His analysis of Algerian women's autobiographies praises yet simultaneously undermines the possible reception of these works by suggesting that their main interest lies in the fact that these texts should be read as sociological documents. He notes that "even if these works do not possess a great literary value" (42), they are useful for learning more about the forceful character and personalities of their authors. Déjeux ends his essay with the observation that, even after Algeria's independence from France in 1962, the fact that Algerian women's narratives are written in French and not Arabic leads to one inescapable conclusion: "It would seem that French gives these writers the possibility to tell of themselves as they wish to be and to dream of a world where they would be fully liberated" (43). Obviously, Déjeux believes Arabic and Arab-Muslim cultural paradigms to be stifling to women's sense of self, hence their decision to write in French and to proclaim their subjectivity in the language of the former colonizer to a readership that would largely be made up of a French, metropolitan public.

If Déjeux suggests that Algerian women's autobiographies are solely influenced by the writer's own concerns, Charles Bonn has more recently alluded to the politics of the French publishing industry as being a decisive factor in the proliferation of Algerian women's autobiographical discourse. Commenting both on novels that purport to be autobiographical and on texts that present themselves as "pure" testimonials from women in France's North African community, Bonn notes that North African women's writing—as an emergent literature—has been effectively "ghetto-ized" by the French publishing industry (99). Bonn also points out that when it comes to narratives dealing with immigration, whether from male or women authors, the French reading public has been conditioned to expect "testimonials" and "documentary style" accounts. As Bonn observes: "The installation of these ghettos corresponds to an editor's commercial recipe: they sell texts whose literary quality is simply not an issue, by soliciting a sympathetic yet unconsciously voyeuristic reading by a public that is favorable toward immigration. This same public demands "testimonials," all the more "true" since they are awkward in literary terms" (99). Bonn is entirely correct to allude to the voyeuristic tendencies of the French reading public for Algerian immigration narratives, particularly those of women. Again, the framing of these texts and their reception inevitably evokes a reading practice that is inherited from the colonial era; it is a reading practice that revives the ambivalent paradigm of foreign (French) readers and/or onlookers examining Algerian (pre/postcolonial) society.

In her study, "La Femme Arabe: Women and Sexuality in France's North African Empire," Julia Clancy-Smith exposes the underlying ideological assumptions of the "official" (military) and the "unofficial" (civilian/suffragist) discourses on colonial Algeria. Not surprisingly, "reading" Algerian women's lives—their sexuality and their role in religion and society—became the European standard of measure for the entire culture. Clancy-Smith observes that Algerian women, in the colonialist discourses that flourished regarding their lives and identities, "demonstrated the immutable otherness of the indigenous population, especially when it came to matters of sexuality" (63). According to Clancy-Smith, women's sexuality was a central concern to colonialist policy because the "strange" and "foreign" sexual mores of the "natives" were seen to be the major obstacle to their potential assimilation (58). Women in colonial Algeria came to represent all that was concealed yet so curiously on display, a trope that influences the reading and reception of present-day autobiographies by Algerian women immigrants who live in France. In the colonial era, French men and women wrote about Algerian women. After independence in 1962, Algerian women wrote *about themselves,* but in the language of the former colonizer. By "exposing" Algerian women's private existence in France through autobiography, have Algerian women autobiographers successfully reappropriated colonialist ethnographic discourse? The issue is whether or not autobiographies of Algerian women in France are able to rewrite the dilemma of "assimilation" and cross-cultural reception. Colonial officials examined the lives of women to determine whether or not Arab and Berber Algerians could be assimilated into French society. Do Algerian women autobiographers phrase the question differently so that it asks: Can French society make a space for postcolonial women to define an in-between identity? In spite of the potential for reappropriation of colonialist tropes, do Algerian women's texts continue to be read in France from the voyeur's position?

Perhaps the most problematic aspect for the reception of Algerian women's autobiographical narratives in France and how these works deal with the issues of identity and community is the fact that the immigrant discourse is invariably situated as minority discourse in relationship to the host, or dominant, society. In order to read and interpret minority discourse without falling into essentializing traps, the subject-position of the autobiographer must always be defined in terms of the politics of location.[8] For Algerian women's texts in France, interpreting the subject-position would entail an awareness of the implications of past and present identity politics as they have been played out between France and Algeria both within the context of colonialism and in today's context of emigration/immigration. In *The Location of Culture* (1994), Homi K. Bhabha explains that the Third World migrant in a European context is situated within a "borderline" position. Bhabha asks whether crossing cultural and national borders allows for the "freedom from the essence of the self," or whether immigration only produces surface-level changes, thereby enabling the subject's identity or the "self" to remain fundamentally unchanged (224).[9] Indeed, immigrant autobiographies problematize notions of community and identity at their most basic level. This problematization, in turn, affects the reception that immigrant autobiographies receive in the host country. Bhabha observes that the cultural difference of immigrants, since it exists within the "interstices" of the host country's culture, destabilizes the concept of "trans" [Latin: "across" or "over"] as it figures in such key notions as "transnational," "translatability," and "transitional" (224). Existing then as an "interstice" within the French literary scene, North African women's autobiographies clearly demonstrate a desire to dramatize, as well as acquaint French readers with, the very real and often painful processes of splitting, "hybridity," and cultural mediation and negotiation.

Yet inscribed onto the margins of Algerian women's autobiographies lies the implicit ambiguity of the role these works play in possibly participating in the dominant discourse about North African women in France or subverting that same dominant discourse. Leigh Gilmore's recent work on women's autobiographies considered in the light of postmodernism (I would also add: "postcolonialism") focuses needed critical attention on "the 'self,' as it has been constructed in and by autobiography, by questioning the methodologies that produce and reproduce its cultural identity" (5). According to Gilmore, self-writing for women textualizes the female subject ideally through autobiographical narrations that "both resist and produce cultural identities" (*Autobiography*, 4). Yet, as shall be seen upon closer analysis, Algerian women's self-portraits produced for the publishing market in France demand different reading strategies, as they are not cultural and/or literary productions in *exactly* the same way as autobiographies from "First World" authors. In her essay

"Resisting Autobiography: Outlaw Genres and Transnational Feminist Subjects," Caren Kaplan points out that different methods of reading and "receiving" Third World women's autobiographical texts are required. In Kaplan's view, the central issue concerning the "politics of location" in First World criticism and reception of Third World women's texts is to avoid the danger of "exoticism." Kaplan also points out that the use of testimonial in Third World women's texts "requires new strategies of reading cultural production *as* transnational activity. Treating the 'author' of the 'testimonial' as an authentic, singular voice without acknowledging the mediation of the editors and market demands of publishing can result in new forms of exoticism and racism" (122). Kaplan insists upon the political relationship between the woman whose "voice" is transcribed in the testimonial, the person who edits or transcribes it, and the publisher who brings forth the volume. It is precisely within the parameters of this relationship that the political questions of identity, community, the "Othering" of Third World women, and the reception of their texts are played out, both overtly and implicitly. Given the fact that notions of the (neo?)colonial and postcolonial also come into play for Algerian women's texts in France, it is useful to cite Gayatri Spivak's concern for the location from which subjects speak—particularly immigrant women, who are "still caught in some way within structures of 'colonial' subject-production; and especially, . . . the historical problem of ethnic oppression on First World soil" ("Political," 226).

PLANTADE'S *L'HONNEUR ET L'AMERTUME*: CROSSING OVER AND MEDIATION

Nedjima Plantade is a professor of anthropology whose previous research involved the study of magic and women's relationships within the Kabyle-Berber community of Algeria. Plantade is herself a member of the Kabyle-Algerian[10] community of France, having immigrated as a child with her family in 1960; this information is provided to the reader of *L'Honneur et l'amertume* in Plantade's preface.[11] Plantade is at once the translator, transcriber, and transmitter of the autobiography of Louisa Azzizen, a Kabyle woman who immigrated to France in 1960 at the age of thirty-three in the company of her children and her husband, already an immigrant worker in France for several years. Louisa's story is unique in the collection of North African women's autobiographies because it is the story of a *primo-arrivante,* a woman who has come to France for the first time as an adult immigrant. Louisa Azzizen's narrative describes her childhood, adolescence, marriage, and young adulthood in Kabylia, followed by her emigration to France and the first ten years of her new life in France.

Plantade's preface both frames the life story of Louisa Azzizen and attempts to entice the reader to perform a particular reading that she, and perhaps Louisa herself, hope the work will produce. Plantade's preface makes it clear that she is not expecting an exclusively French readership. Her ideal readers are clearly identified in the preface; they are the children of North African immigrants whom she hopes will read *L'Honneur et l'amertume* in order to recover a part of their own history.[12]

Like many autobiographies of Third World women, Louisa Azzizen's story is "told to" an interested party—not precisely a "First World feminist" interlocutor, but rather another Algerian woman who has herself immigrated to France from Algeria. Plantade begins the preface to the work by noting this bond of a shared experience of migration between herself and her informant-subject. In a gesture whose purpose is to legitimize the transcription from oral Kabyle Berber dialect into French and the subsequent publication for a French or Franco-Maghrebian reading public, Plantade assures the reader that the exchange between herself (as an anthropologist) and Louisa (as informant) unfolded "with the sincerity and freshness that a mother would have towards her daughter" (11). Plantade consciously seeks to subvert the traditional power/knowledge relationship between the anthropologist and her "native informant." Plantade also insists that it is Louisa Azzizen who holds sought after knowledge on cultural difference and identity. Plantade observes that during the interviewing process, Louisa was "convinced that she was teaching me a great deal about myself, and I had no doubts about this" (11). In an attempt to obscure the obvious "differences" that exist between Louisa, an illiterate woman who has mainly remained at home to tend to her family's needs, and Plantade herself, a professor of anthropology, Plantade evokes their shared experience of emigration as wiping out all but a virtually insignificant difference, that is, their age: "therefore, the entire difference between Louisa and myself is summed up by the space of one generation" (11). Why does Plantade feel a need to occlude the obvious differences between her life experiences and current social position and Louisa Azzizen's? I believe Plantade is attempting to reassure readers that she has no wish to usurp Louisa's speech and life-story. Plantade's framing of Louisa Azzizen's narrative reveals that she is aware of the ambivalence of a mediated autobiography of a Third World, postcolonial subject, particularly for a text that is destined for a First World or, ideally, a Franco-Algerian cross-cultural readership.

Carol Boyce Davies has addressed the problem of oral autobiographies and their transcription into print within the context of minority and/or Third World women's life-histories, and she notes that the fundamental and often inescapable dilemma is how to assign "control and authority over the text" (3). Due to the collaborative process undertaken in the production of such works and due to "the displacement" of the oral text by the written text, Boyce Davies points out that a certain amount of "manipulation" and "ordering" of the chronology and of the "telling" of the life story are bound to occur (4). Furthermore, Boyce Davies notes that in translated and transcribed autobiographies, there is an inherent danger that a woman who orally narrates her story will be "effectively erased" from her own autobiography (10).

Plantade would appear to be aware of this potential for the erasure of the individual for whom she is hoping to facilitate a "coming to the word." In the preface to Louisa Azzizen's narrative, Plantade not only insists upon the intimacy, the sincerity, and the solidarity established between herself and Louisa during the interview process, but she also asserts Louisa's own role as a mediator—hence herself an agent—in a legitimate quest for identity for Franco-Algerians. According to Plantade, Louisa's narrative establishes her subject-position as an archetypal Algerian woman who has "crossed over" to France from Algeria, and whose autobiographical account now crosses the barrier of silence regarding the origins of the Franco-Maghrebian community in France:

> In her [Louisa], young French people who are the products of Algerian immigration in France in a legitimate quest for memory, will discover or will find again the face of their mother or grandmother, silent women with worn-out husbands who have never disturbed France, but have given birth to a sometimes noisy youth. These young people will learn that the generations that preceded them have something to say to them about themselves, if only they will lend these women their ear and free themselves from the amnesia that has made them beings without History, mutants only incarnated in statistical data, if not in phantasms. (13)

No doubt to downplay Plantade's own ambivalent role as translator, transcriber, and arranger of Louisa Azzizen's story, her preface attempts to frame Louisa's narrative itself as a mediating text, a mediation between generations—the one that came over and the one born in France as a result of the "crossing over." Plantade's arrangement of Louisa's memories and anecdotes allows for the creation of a text that may be read as a mediation between cultural identities. It is not possible, however, for the reader to completely ignore Plantade's own presence in the orchestration of Louisa's memoir. The text is narrated entirely in the first person *as if* Louisa herself were relating all of the events. There are, however, markers of Plantade's presence in the narrative in the form of footnotes explaining numerous aspects of Kabyle customs, beliefs, vocabulary, and culinary references. If the ideal reader Plantade alludes to in the preface is a second-generation Algerian immigrant, is it really necessary to explain so many terms? Here again, it is evident that the readers of Algerian women's autobiographies are mainly French readers who would certainly expect (and require) explanations concerning many of Louisa's references.

Furthermore, it must be noted that in spite of Plantade's expressed desire to engender equality and transparency between herself and Louisa, and, thereby, simply play the role of "midwife" bringing Louisa's narrative into the world, the finished work—in literary, published form—immediately circulates in a marketplace that "reads" and "receives" Third World women's texts as re-presentations of alterity and exoticism. The fact that Louisa's story develops into an indictment of Kabyle culture—through Louisa's own insistence (or Plantade's ordering?) on her victimization at the hands of her husband and his family—raises the issue of how Algerian women's texts may ideally wish to *resist* appropriation by the dominant discourse of negative depictions of Algerian and North African cultural traditions where women are concerned, but by the very fact that the women's texts in question delve into their abuse and the sufferings, make this ideal and transparent reception highly unlikely.

Once told, Louisa's story highlights the fundamentally ambiguous notions of "community" and "identity" that are developed in North African women's autobiographies. Identifying on a basic level *with* her original community, Louisa, in her autobiographical account, as told in seamless first person narration by Plantade, nevertheless paints an entirely negative portrait of the feminine condition within the Kabyle cultural context. In a review of *L'Honneur et l'amertume,* the French critic Jean Déjeux also "reads" the work as offering not just a portrait of Louisa's despicable in-laws, but by extension, Kabyle culture in general. Déjeux concludes his review by observing: "Let us thank Nedjima Plantade for delivering in French this account that allows us to discover "an ordinary" fate that one would take to be extraordinary, but which is however, the lot of numerous other women in Kabylia . . ." (50). Déjeux has perhaps unwittingly raised a central issue for a work like *L'Honneur et l'amertume*. Although presenting the life story of a single woman, this text circulates and is received as the portrait of an entire group. Plantade's attempt to direct the text's reception toward younger members of Louisa's own community is indicative of her own awareness of the potential for an overdetermined and overly representational reception by the French public at large. In addition, Louisa's narrative text will be seen as offering French readers "privileged" access to, and information on, Kabyle culture, because autobiography and testimonial are always perceived to be more "real" and closer to "the truth."

Louisa's account demonstrates that her own bonds to the Kabyle community, both at home and in France, are extremely problematic. Louisa presents her husband's family as lacking the expected Kabyle ethics of hospitality and dedication to other family members. It is, therefore, not surprising that, after several years in France, Louisa openly expresses her ambivalent feelings toward her fellow Kabyles. She observes that: "For a long time now I have been indifferent to many members of my family and of my family-in-law, or they even seem detestable to me, while the French are becoming closer in spite of this darn language block" (240). Such a statement may be read as noting Louisa's slipping into a different subject-position, one in which she is becoming aware of shifting alliances concerning her ties with her own ethnic community, and her growing sense that life in France is becoming less like exile and more like a mediated space in which she might establish new links among other women, regardless of their nationalities.

Louisa's narrative insists upon the new cultural choices made by her daughters. Implicit in their rejection of certain values from the Kabyle community is Louisa's own uncertainty about the negotiations made with French practices. Her daughters do well in school and decide to pursue their studies into the secondary level. Tensions mount and Louisa feels herself eclipsed as her older daughter refuses to consider any marriage proposals. When faced with her daughter's obstinate refusal and her threat to run away if forced to marry, Louisa has the opportunity to evaluate her own youth. The reader, at this point, must surely be aware of the unresolved conflict between Louisa's expressed unhappiness at her own marriage and the subsequent decades of abuse and bitterness, and her alleged "confusion" about her daughter's refusal to be pushed into an arranged marriage with an older Kabyle immigrant in France. Louisa is left with many questions: "I felt as if I did not recognize my daughter. Why this stupid obstinacy? I suddenly felt that something had changed without really knowing what or understanding how that could have come to be" (256). The cultural negotiations made necessary by the migrant experience also include the painful realization that one's children have made an even deeper transference of cultural identity. At the same time, this blurring of cultural identities is reflective of and implicitly linked to Louisa's own ambivalence toward the cultural practices she has distanced herself from through emigration and through her own narrative reconstruction that problematizes her sense of identity and community.

Louisa comes to terms with her daughter's choices as she begins to understand more fully the aspects and changes in her own sense of self and sense of community. In what can only be the result of Plantade's transcription and ordering of Louisa's autobiography, suspense builds at the end of the book as the reader approaches the ultimate moment of self-realization for Louisa. After several years in France, Louisa becomes more mobile outside her home, winning her husband's permission to accompany her youngest children to school. There, she meets other North African women, some who are from her own region. The Kabyle immigrant community slowly becomes Louisa's point of attachment in France. Louisa's solution to an untenable intermediary position between French and Kabyle society is to form an attachment to those most like her—other immigrant women from Kabylia and other regions of Algeria. Visits back to Algeria are infrequent, and are fraught with tensions and bitterness as the "difference" of the émigré(e)s is openly juxtaposed to the lives of family and countrymen and women who have remained in Algeria. Louisa recounts that arguments frequently occur during return visits when the émigrés are accused of having become "too French." In the final analysis of the situation of Kabyle immigrants that Louisa offers to her interlocutor, she employs a metaphor for change, mediation, and cultural translation that evokes the essence of the immigrant experience: "How can we get a grip on this world? You go to bed clean, you wake up soiled! Exile makes you take on seven different languages, each one contradictory; God does not know anymore what to do with us, where to put us . . ." (264).

The issue of "cultural contamination,"[13] and the adoption of different and contradictory "languages," behaviors, or even cultural viewpoints, is felt most keenly in relation to the children born to immigrants in France. Children and the lives they choose to lead in France are most often the cause of the cultural negotiations that must be made by North

African women in France. Louisa's story ends with her awareness of
how she herself has made a kind of contract with French society—taking
on and assimilating its positive aspects while attempting to hold on to
certain beliefs that have come with her from Kabylia. In this sense,
Louisa's narrative demonstrates that she resists the French dominant assumption that assimilation to French society is simply a matter of choice,
one that Algerian women will be eager to make *because* of the suffering
and difficulties they have experienced within the parameters of Berber-
Arab culture. Louisa consciously rejects the notion that first-generation
immigrant women from Algeria have welcomed and actively participated in an acculturation process:

> In truth, France, this country that Algerians continue to dream about, is
> only good for those who know it well, those who can come here and
> feel like a fish in the water. But for the poor folk like us, it will always
> remain inaccessible. Only our children, and that's for the best, will be
> able to live full lives here, the ones who have grown up here, who have
> become caught up in material things, education, comfort, and above all
> liberty—this strange idea that, for so many years, seemed so shocking
> to me and that today I have somehow managed to accept without even
> knowing how . . . (265)

Louisa's avowal of still feeling like "a foreigner," a nonassimilated immigrant, should be read as her refusal of the dominant discourse on Algerian women. In noting that she still feels that integration is
inaccessible for women like her, Louisa's story underscores the ambigui-
ties inherent in the entire juxtaposition of Algerian women's first-person
discourse *as* immigrants in France with the dominant discourse that
holds that assimilation is simply a matter of personal choice. By concluding her life story with a reference to her gradual acceptance of the
notion of "liberty"—implying that she lacked this liberty before coming
to France—Louisa posits a subject-position that emphasizes choice
above all else. This, above all, is Louisa's recognition of one positive element that she has appropriated for herself from French society.

LE VOILE DU SILENCE: TRANSLATION
OR DISPLACEMENT?

In Gayatri Spivak's groundbreaking and provocative article "Can the
Subaltern Speak?" she raises an ideological issue that scholars of post-

colonial and especially feminist studies continue to grapple with, namely: what is at stake when First World feminists and/or researchers "talk about" women's lives from the Third World? Women from the Third World, more so than their male counterparts, are, in Spivak's words, more likely to find themselves "doubly effaced" (287), due first to colonial hegemony and more recently, due to academic politics of the First World. The reception of Algerian women's autobiographies in France, especially of Djura's *Le Voile du silence,*[14] raises the issue that Spivak has described as "This benevolent first-world appropriation and re-inscription of the Third World as an Other [which] is the founding characteristic of much third-worldism in the U.S. human sciences today" (289). Djura's autobiography may be read as a text that insists upon the *negative* differences of Kabyle culture. Djura's account of her life reads like a tribute to the liberating possibilities of acculturation with French society. Her text does not problematize total assimilation; instead, it is presented as the only means of salvation for an Algerian woman who hopes to escape her family's (and by extension her culture's) misogynist persecution.

Djura, the stage name used by the Kabyle pop singer who created the successful musical group Djurdjura in France in 1977, published an account of her life in 1990. Unlike in the other two autobiographies discussed in this essay, Djura is the single author of her narrative. It might be suggested, however, that although another individual has not framed her text, Djura's status as a popular singer before she published *Le Voile du silence* acts as a mediating element between herself, her text, and her readers. In *Le Voile du silence,* she states that the writing of her work was therapeutic since she was still trying to recover from a vicious attack in 1987 on her and her French partner/manager (who has since become her husband) while she was seven months pregnant with his child. She and her partner were victims of a vendetta carried out to wash the family honor clean of Djura's endogamous (and, thereby, unacceptable in the eyes of her family) relationship. The attack was carried out by her brother and her adolescent niece. Djura was beaten and her partner was shot. In her autobiography, Djura describes how they both survive this violent incident, and a lengthy round of ensuing court battles, in which Djura is sued by family members for slander and for theft of creative property, and in which she attempts to instate restraining orders against them.

Quite simply, *Le Voile du silence* is the horrifying tale of Djura's upbringing, first in Kabylia, then in France, and of her rise to stardom, first as a documentary filmmaker, then as a pop singer. Her autobiography is replete with incidents of aggression and violence against her and other women in the family, her family's rejection of her lifestyle as an entertainer, and their imprisonment of her to attempt to force her to agree to an arranged marriage and to prevent her involvement with French men. Djura's publication fits smoothly into the dominant discourse on women's status in Algerian society. In Djura's tale, Kabyle (and by extension Algerian) men—particularly her father, brothers, and uncles—are all portrayed as violent, misogynistic, excessively concerned with honor and vendettas, alcoholic, criminal, and jealous of their successful sister. Djura maintains in her preface that she is writing the account of her life to "exorcise the past" (9). According to Djura's presentation of the incidents in her life and the interpretation she makes of them, it gradually becomes clear to Djura that her story is not unique. She sees her life story as replicating and representing the story of so many other women from Algeria, so much so that Djura feels she is writing a collective autobiography (9).

Djura includes a preface to *Le Voile du silence*. In framing her own autobiography, she explains the choice of the title's "veil" image and metaphor. According to Djura's preface, she felt it necessary to publish an account of her life so that fans of her music would learn of how she has had to struggle to make her own choices in life against her family's violent oppression. In Djura's narrative, she attributes her family's rejection of her choices and of her independence to their Kabyle and Islamic cultural values and practices that attempt to limit women's access to public life. As a successful Franco-Algerian entertainer, she may have been thought by observers to represent the ideal "cultural cross-over" figure: blending French and Kabyle influences in her music, Djura represented the ultimate "évoluée," the Maghrebian woman who has become "the same" (i.e. "assimilated"), while maintaining the appropriate degree of exotic "Otherness."[15] Djura tells the reader that, due to her family's violent persecution, she has decided her story must be told; the truth must be known and "the veil of silence" must be raised from her story, as from those of the many other Maghrebian women in France who have told Djura similar tales of oppression. In the dominant discourse about Algerian women, they, of course, cannot speak for themselves since the patriarchal traditions impede their free speech. Djura frames her narrative clearly within the parameters of the dominant discourse by evoking this rather worn-out paradigm concerning the "silence" of Algerian women.

The implication, of course, is that the veil is a metaphor for the weight of cultural and religious traditions that gag women's expression. The preface makes it clear that the autobiography to follow is the story of Djura as well as of the women who have confided their own tales of horror about their treatment by the men of their family and community. Djura states that "The drama that follows, as much as the confidences entrusted to me at the end of my concerts,[16] made me aware that my fate—as exceptional as it might seem—was also, in part, that of thousands of other daughters, sisters, or wives mute with fear, in search of well-being and yet forbidden to exist" (9). The fact that Djura believes these women to be without a voice inspires her to link their stories to her own. On the surface, this appears to be a worthy project. However, the reader is presented with a text that purports to be an ethnographic résumé of women's lives in all of Kabylia. No negative image (negative, that is, in the eyes of the French popular reading public) is left out. Women and children are beaten on the slightest pretext, young women believed to have "sinned" are murdered by male family members, sterile women are repudiated, obstinate women are made compliant by the addition of a co-wife, parents arrange marriages for their daughters to further their own interests, and women, above all, are held responsible for educating their daughters to be submissive and patient in the face of abuse and misery. Djura's framing of her text as a document that can bear witness for the entirety of the Kabyle feminine community posits her text as effectively situating all Kabyle (and by extension all Algerian) women within the static role of eternal victims.

In *Le Voile du silence,* the reader is introduced to almost no positive, meaningful aspect of Kabyle and Algerian culture and society. Through Djura's reconstruction of her past, her life takes on the appearance of a never-ending nightmare. How might the reader react to this litany of dismal conditions under which women live? Third World and First World feminists agree on the need to realistically examine the injustices women face in other cultures without essentializing their lives and experiences. One must not deny Djura the right to construct her autobiography in the manner she sees fit. At the same time, however, it is vitally important to consider the possible effects on a Western readership of even the most sincerely narrated life story from North Africa. Chandra Talpede Mohanty has observed, in her insightful essay "Under Western Eyes: Feminist Scholarship and Colonial Discourse," that it is normal and perfectly acceptable that First World feminists should be interested in exposing and hopefully changing the poor conditions under which many of the world's women are living. However, Mohanty warns that scholars must also be aware of the danger of creating a monolithic, discursive "*Third World Woman*" who is only defined in terms of her victimization and oppression (58).

The concern for the representation of Third World women is an issue in postcolonial studies as well, as is evidenced by the growing concern paid to the notion of "displacement" or "speaking for" the very individuals whose subjectivity and whose voices are frequently silenced. While Louisa Azzizen's narrative is "told to" Nedjima Plantade, and then presented to the reading public with Plantade herself listed as the author, *L'Honneur et l'amertume* is actually *less* likely to be read as creating a monolithic portrait of "Algerian women as Victims." Plantade facilitates and frames Louisa Azzizen's life story, but she does not situate the narrative as a universal portrait of Kabyle women. Furthermore, in Plantade's arrangement, she has created the illusion of direct first-person narration. For Djura, given her expressed desire to "raise the veil of silence" for all those Algerian women whose speech is silenced by the weight of patriarchal oppression, it is clear that she believes the account of her own life to have wider implications in representing the lives of other women. The fact that even before Djura published *Le Voile du silence* she was a recognized celebrity in France makes the danger of Djura's "representing" others through her *own* discourse more apparent.

Marnia Lazreg, writing in "Feminism and Difference: The Perils of Writing as a Woman on Women in Algeria," reminds First and Third World scholars alike that a desire to bring women's oppression to the attention of the world may also produce the unwanted effect of essentializing and objectifying the same women, freezing them into that role of "eternal victims." Lazreg's point is particularly well taken for research and writing on women in the Muslim-Arab world:

> This search for the disreputable, which reinforces the notion of difference as objectified otherness, is often carried out with the help of Middle Eastern and North African women themselves. Feminism has provided a forum for these women to express themselves and on occasion for them to vent their anger at their societies. The exercise of freedom of expression often has a dizzying effect and sometimes leads to personal confession in the guise of social criticism. Individual women from the Middle East and North Africa appear on the feminist stage as representatives of the millions of women in their own societies. To

what extent they do violence to the women they claim to write and
speak about is a question that is seldom raised. (89)

Indeed, one would not wish to detract from the violent opposition or the
serious hardships that Djura has overcome in order to achieve her success
and present status in French society. But keeping Lazreg's warnings in
mind, *Le Voile du silence* may very well have an opposite effect from the
author's intention, because, once published in France, her text circulates
in and contributes to a discursive exchange whose insistence—however
righteous—on the violence done to women by men acting in the name of
custom and religion reifies women in a unidimensional cultural identity.
Djura's autobiography, by following the model of auto-cultural denigra-
tion, risks imprisoning her own textual quest for a new negotiation with
her Kabyle heritage and the values she has assimilated through her upbringing in France within a static, negative stereotype of cultural alterity.

However, *Le Voile du silence,* on some levels, does explore the potential for a richer expression of cultural and communal identity that is
the hallmark of the translational and transnational experience of the
North African immigrant in France. The positive value of Djura's text, in
spite of its indulgence in negative cultural themes, lies in the solution of
cultural *métissage,* a "mixing" that is both real and symbolic, which she
finds to be the answer to her quest for fulfillment in her career and her
life. At the conclusion of her memoir, Djura places the nightmares of the
past behind her, believing that she has found her personal salvation
through her acculturation in French society. Content in her married life
with a Frenchman, Djura sees the future destiny of their children as a
hopeful sign for Franco-Algerian relations. Addressing herself to her
son: "I hope that this testimony [. . .] will help the children born in
France or elsewhere, mono- or pluricultural, not to cultivate the dangerous hatred of the Other. Because that is what engenders hatred: the fear
of difference, this source of richness that still terrifies so many human
beings that they are prevented from trying to understand each other and
to love each other, or at the very least, to live together without conflict"
(189). In spite of her own insistence on the negative *difference* of Kabyle
traditions for women when compared to the "freedom" guaranteed by
French society, Djura's autobiography ends with her stated conviction
that eventually the heritage of mistrust and fear between the French and
Algerian people will disappear. She thereby assumes her text will be read
and understood as assisting in the development of that future cultural
harmony.

NI LE VOILE, NI L'OUBLI: TRANSGRESSION AND RE-INSERTION

Published in Paris in 1995, *Ni le voile, ni l'oubli* is an account of the life of Mimouna, the daughter of an Algerian immigrant worker who brought his family to France during the years of the Algerian war.[17] Mimouna's account (told in French), is transcribed by the Franco-Algerian novelist Mohand Mounsi, who has also provided an afterword for the book. However, the narrative, whose style reflects actual speech, is related through direct first-person narration. Mounsi's collaborative presence is not overtly felt in *Ni le voile, ni l'oubli;* his afterword (like Plantade's preface) directs the reader to an appropriate understanding of Mimouna's testimony.

Ni le voile, ni l'oubli is published as part of a series entitled "Témoignages," [testimonials]. The stated goal of this series is explained on the last page of the book. This objective is: "To give voice to all those who live day to day with the problems of our society. Through these accounts of authentic experiences, the only ambition of these books is to provide a means of understanding and a reason to hope." The "problems" that this text intends to address are the experiences of Algerian women raised in France and the rise of Islamic activism in French society.[18] The language in which Mimouna relates her story is simple and, at times, even colloquial. The intended reader for this work could be a person from any social or educational background. The directness and simplicity of the narrative style enhances the text's status as a *témoignage,* or "testimonial," thereby also enhancing the sense of a "true-to-life" account. As Charles Bonn has suggested, the French reading public, sympathetic to immigrant narratives, expects a simple narrative style because it enhances the supposed "veracity" of the immigrant's life story (99).

Mimouna's story begins with her discovery that the office of the community cultural and social association she directs in a Paris suburb has been vandalized by—she suspects—Islamic fundamentalist sympathizers who condemn her work with young Franco-Algerian women who are in difficulty. The title chosen for her story (the veil or oblivion) contrasts what her narrative will develop as the two opposing identity poles offered to Algerian women in France by the dominant discourse about them: assimilation or acculturation, which would entail the erasure ("the forgetting") of cultural origins, or assumption of the "veil," meaning acceptance of a totalizing monolithic identity as an Algerian Muslim woman.[19] Mimouna comes to reject this binary opposition between silence and tradition (in other words, the veil) and assimilation and moder-nity (in other words, forgetting one's cultural origins). Instead, Mimouna consciously seeks another option; she neither forgets her own culture (which assimilation and acculturation would entail) nor is willing to as-sume an essentialized identity as a Muslim Arab woman. Discovering the ransacked offices causes her to reflect on the trajectory her life has taken, from dropping out of school in her early teens, to becoming mili-tant in the workers movement of the late 1960s, and subsequently be-coming active in the Beur cause and the antiracism movement of the mid-1980s.[20] Mimouna's narrative insists upon the fact that she has re-peatedly made her own choices concerning her actions. Her account demonstrates that she has consistently struggled to find her own place in both the Algerian immigrant community and French society at large.

Mimouna's story speaks of the difficulties of being the first in her family to hope to pursue a different fate as an Algerian woman living in France. Refusing an early marriage, Mimouna runs away for the first time and then returns. She soon takes a job in a factory to help support her siblings after her father's illness. Her interest in community and cul-tural associations begins early and, after joining a group that helps immi-grants and their children maintain ties to Algeria, Mimouna meets an Algerian student in France. She falls in love with him and becomes preg-nant. She decides to have the baby even though there is little hope that the two lovers will be able to marry in the near future. Djamel must finish his studies and he then returns to Algeria to find a job as a journalist. Mi-mouna feels unable to reveal her pregnancy to her family. She relates that she feared violent retribution from her brothers for the scandal and stain to family honor caused by her pregnancy. Mimouna turns to the French Bureau of Social Services for help in carrying out her plan to leave her family and bear her child in secrecy. Mimouna is placed in a residence for unwed mothers and she successfully hides from her family for nearly two years.

Mimouna's tale, while often melodramatic in tone, does not fall into the trap of making "tradition" or "modernity" the only two choices avail-able to North African women in the immigrant context. She is very pre-cise about her sense of self-identity; her autobiographical text is not a quest for that identity, instead it may be read as an account of how other family members were obliged to accept her life on her own terms: "I am the daughter of an Algerian immigrant worker confronted with the con-flict between the culture that comes to me from my father and that of the country where I became a woman. My own story" (81).

Mimouna's pregnancy and delivery alone in a Parisian clinic, far away from her family in the north of France, causes her to assert her difference and her rupture with what the text establishes as Algerian Arab-Muslim tradition. Her inner strength and determination to survive on her own terms help her endure this struggle: "I am the woman who hides because she is pregnant, alone, and Arab. I am the woman alone who is going to give her name to the child. I am the woman alone, throat constricted with anger against the man who has left her alone to face this ordeal" (91). Her affirmation of her Arab identity at the very moment she recognizes the transgression of her life and her choices in the eyes of her father's community highlights the main theme of *Ni le voile, ni l'oubli:* a cultural transgression that brings with it the potential for reinsertion into and redefinition of a new cultural and communal space.

In the final chapter, "I Have Found My Place," Mimouna reintegrates life with her family, again on her own terms. Thanks to the support of one of her brothers (married to a French woman), and with the help of a sister-in-law from Algeria who herself was a freedom fighter during the Algerian War and who fell in love with and bore two children to Mimouna's brother before he died in that same war, Mimouna makes her peace with her family. Yet, she still finds on both sides of the Mediterranean many who "absolutely did not understand what it meant to be an Algerian woman immigrant in France" (136). She finally refuses to marry the father of her child, knowing that to do so and to move back to Algeria would mean living "defensively" or "changing her behavior" (137), something Mimouna rejects. Mimouna relates that after this decisive decision her true calling in life is established: community work among the immigrant population of a poor and violence-ridden Parisian suburb. Reintegrating all aspects of her identity—female, Algerian, and French—Mimouna recognizes that, in French society, the worst exclusion is that due to economic and not necessarily cultural or religious factors. Along with three other immigrant women and an indigenous French woman, she forms a feminist and activist community organization called A.F.R.I.C.A. (Association, Formation, Racisme, Identité, Culture, Algérienne). Their goal is to fight exclusion and racism for all ethnic groups in their community. Mimouna's autobiographical narrative presents the portrait of a successful negotiation between the culture of her parents and that of the host country. Her sometimes difficult itinerary provides her with the courage and self-assurance to work in the Franco-Maghrebian community of the Paris outskirts where drugs, violence, and despair are taking a high toll on many young men and women. Mimouna's example is, according to Mohand Mounsi's afterword, the best antidote to the ills of the Arab ghettos and the illusory attraction of Islamic radicalism:

> Refusing to be veiled phantoms under veils, they [second-generation Maghrebian women] advance with their faces uncovered and project to the world the undeniable modernity of their presence. All of them, like Mimouna, have the awareness of belonging to their origins, as well as belonging to the *community*[21] in the classical sense of the word. (142)

Mimouna's text, as framed by Mounsi's afterword, makes the Algerian woman's own definition of modernity and her own unique cultural and communal space within French society the major issue for her interpretation of the choices she has made in her life. Clearly, for Mounsi as well as for many other sociologists working in the field of Maghrebian immigration in France, the future integration of the second generation, and of the other generations to follow, will pass through the women—perhaps not because they seek personal advantage, as has been suggested by Dubet and Schnapper, but because they, more then men, seek to "translate the silences and the cries that protest" (143). Mimouna's insistence on making her own choices and defining her own identity—without reinscribing her text upon the dominant discourse on and about Algerian women in France—frames her autobiography within the parameters of a new "politics of location." Living and working as a social worker in the North African immigrant ghettos on the outskirts of Paris, Mimouna's narrative reflects her outsider/insider status within both French and Algerian society.

CULTURAL NEGOTIATION WITHOUT ABSORPTION

Maghrebian women's autobiographies in France clearly posit the exploration of cultural difference, translation, and negotiation as operating in the "in-between" space of the minority position (Bhabha, 224). In the context of minority or migrant culture, the space of the "interstice" reveals what Bhabha terms (borrowing from Walter Benjamin) "the element of resistance in the process of transformation" (224). The cultural negotiations and mediation of communal identity that occur within North African women's experiences in France demonstrate that they refuse "assimilation" as it is defined *by* and *for* them by French sociologists and social programming. A woman's autobiographical narrative in any cultural context, as Bella Brodski and Celeste Schenck have noted, "replaces singularity with alterity" (11). "Otherness," a discursive and political category once applied to North African women in France, is then appropriated through autobiographical writing to make the site of the migrant's cultural "in-between" a position from which that alleged "alterity" is assumed and "translated" for the French reader.

Assuming "Otherness" through a process of cultural mediation, and establishing new definitions for the concept of "community"—both that of the host society and that of the country of origin—Maghrebian women in France become figures that Abdelkrim-Chikh refers to as "*femmes-frontières*" [border-women] (246). Assimilation into French culture, meaning absorption into the mold of identity that is established by a cultural *Other,* is rejected out-of-hand. In Abdelkrim-Chikh's inquiry among Maghrebian women in France who have made the ultimate "crossing over" as Muslim Arab/Berber women by marrying outside the Muslim community, the desire to remain "different" on one's own terms characterizes their sense of identity. Autobiographical narrative, with its capacity to "resist and produce cultural identities" (Gilmore, 4), also defies the closure and absorption of identity that is rejected by North African women in France. Akin to the life stories related in these texts is one of Abdelkrim-Chikh's informant's descriptions of the "in-between" space of identity she has struggled to create for herself living in France: "For years I have fought not to occupy *their* territory, but to make one *on the side,* to make a *bridge,* I have often told myself that I am on a bridge, going back and forth: I respect their territory and they must respect mine. [. . .] I am the one who built the bridge all alone; what I am asking for is to be along side it, at the foot of the bridge saying Yoo hoo! Yoo hoo! I am here, that's all" (247). Algerian women's autobiographies in France, in spite of, or perhaps because of, the politics of readership and reception, clearly tell us that their authors *are* and that they have made a space for themselves "in-between" French and Algerian societies.

NOTES

[1] All translations from the French are my own.

[2] In the 1980s, the *Beur* literary movement brought forth several women authors whose first (sometimes their only) novels were autobiographical. *Beur,* or *Beurette* for women, refers to second-generation, Franco–North Africans, mainly from Paris and its surrounding areas. Some of the most important women writers of this group include Tassadit Imache, Soraya Nini, Farida Belghoul, and Leïla

Houari. In addition to fictionalized autobiographies, there are several notable "true" autobiographies and collections of "life stories" that are not discussed in this essay. They do, of course, merit interest as these works often present "mediated" and "transcribed" life histories from North African women to a French readership. Works in this category include: Aicha Lemsine's (a novelist in her own right) *Ordalies des voix* (1983), Fettouma Touati's *Le Printemps désespéré: vies d'Algériennes* (1984), more recently Yamina Benguigui's *Femmes d'Islam* (1996) and Djura's second publication, a collection of personal anecdotes and socio-cultural commentary garnered from her meetings with other Algerian and North African women in France, entitled *La Saison des narcisses* (1993).

[3]To date, none of these works have been translated into English. Literal English translations of the titles would be: Plantade's *Honor and Bitterness: The Ordinary Fate of a Kabyle Woman;* Djura's *The Veil of Silence;* and Mimouna's *Neither the Veil nor Forgetting.*

[4]For more information on this topic see Dubet, 58–66 and Schnapper, 139–181. See also the publication authored by the French Haut Conseil à l'intégration, *Liens culturels et intégration,* 55–67.

[5]For further information on the history of North African immigration in France see Gérard Noiriel, *Le Creuset français* (1988) and Mohand Khellil, *L'Intégration des Maghrébins en France* (1991). After World War I, French authorities actively encouraged indigenous Algerians to come and work in France. At first, only men emigrated to become "foreign workers." In the 1970s, French immigration laws allowed men to bring their wives and children to France as part of "family regroupment" plans. As more and more families arrived in France, the existence of a North African community within French society became a reality.

[6]For more information regarding the specific causes and the ensuing national debates involving the "Scarf Affair," see David Beriss's article "Scarves, Schools, and Segregation: The *Foulard* Affair."

[7]One of Abdelkrim-Chikh's informants raises the issue of how difficult it is for North African women in France to express their legitimate concerns about family, social, and religious pressures within the Maghrebian community that curtail their freedom, without appearing to "side with" the French and the dominant discourse about Arab-Muslim culture. Speaking of the French media and sociologists, Y. Y., an Algerian woman and naturalized citizen of France, states: "At the start of your revolt, you are angry and you speak out and they (the sociologists and the media) are only too happy to fixate on the negative, and they don't need to know any more than that since *we* are the ones who are telling them everything they want to hear. They are only too satisfied and then they don't listen. [. . .] They only hear that our parents are retrograde bastards and they don't even try to find out if it's really true" (Abdelkrim-Chikh, 245).

[8]For further discussion on the situation and reception of minority discourse see *Cultural Critique* 6 (Spring 1987), a special issue devoted to "Minority Discourse," edited by Abdul JanMohammed and David Lloyd.

[9]For an in-depth, earlier study on the concept of "change" for Arab women immigrants' self-perception see Isabel Taboada-Leonetti and Florence Lévy's study *Femmes et immigrés: l'insertion des femmes immigrées en France*.

[10]The Kabyles (from the region of Kabylia in the mountainous regions of northern Algeria), consider themselves to be Berbers, not Arabs. They are Muslim, and their maternal languages may be any one of numerous Berber languages, including Kabyle. According to most studies, Kabyles make up more than half of all Algerian immigrants in France. The singer Djura is a Kabyle. Mimouna's *Ni le voile ni l'oubli* does not specify if she is from a Kabyle- or Arab-Algerian family.

[11]It must be noted that even the title of Plantade's work is highly evocative in the context of previous studies of North African women. The reference to "honor," or *nîf,* in the Kabyle tradition is a loaded term that evokes the often-described Kabyle code of honor in which women play the role of guardians of men's honor by remaining chaste before marriage and submissive and retiring after marriage. "Bitterness" describes the tone in which Louisa recounts 90 percent of her life. Recollections of hard work, malnutrition, war with France, successive pregnancies, an abusive husband, and the ordeal of emigration to a foreign land basically constitute the content of her memoirs. See, for example, Khellil's *L'Intégration des Maghrébins en France*.

[12]In a letter dated June 13, 1994, Nedjima Plantade responded to my inquiry concerning the reception her work has had among the second-generation Franco-Maghrebian community in France. She notes that, in general, she is aware of only a few reactions, and these, for the most part, are limited to younger people remarking that Louisa Azzizen's story has reminded them of "some things" their own mothers have told them about their lives before and after immigration to France.

[13]In Louisa Azzizen's account of her life, she stresses the fact that Kabyle cultural values tended to discourage men from taking their wives to France. It was feared that Kabyle women would become "corrupted" and "contaminated" by living in close proximity to French women who lived according to a completely different behavior code. She points out that once in France, Kabyle women were actually "less free" to go out in public because if they would be seen by another Kabyle, that individual would most likely spread gossip back in the village about how "Mrs. So and So" had become tainted by living in France since she was now going out and about in public. See *L'Honneur et l'Amertume,* 188–90 and 234.

[14]*Le Voile du silence,* originally published by the Parisian editor Michel Lafon, has been made available in the inexpensive and popular "Livre de Poche" collection. The book jacket notice on Djura's second work announces that 500,000 copies of *Le Voile du silence* have been sold. In the dedication of *Voile,* Djura acknowledges the assistance of Huguette Maure, who, "with a talented sensitivity, was able to polish my text while still respecting it." It is, however, not possible to know the exact extent to which Djura's text was edited or modified.

[15]The glamourous cover photograph of Djura enhances her public image as an "exotic" figure. The photo shows her in close-up, wearing elaborate eye makeup and Berber jewelry. In contrast, Plantade's work has a cover photograph of a Kabyle woman seated on the ground in front of a doorway that can be easily identified as belonging to a rural, Kabyle home. Moreover, the seated woman is shown in profile, but her head is turned away from the camera. For Mimouna's text, again the image of a veil is evoked, as the close-up photo of a woman's face has been cropped. Only the eyes and nose of a woman (who may or may not be the subject Mimouna herself), are portrayed. Cover art for publications about women in the Muslim-Arab world have frequently made use of the veil metaphor as both a symbol of the Arab-Muslim woman's "exoticism"—sexual attraction—and oppression. See, for example, the cover photographs on such works as Fatna Aït Sabbah's *La Femme dans l'inconscient musulman,* Yamina Benguigui's *Les Femmes d'Islam,* and Nina Bouraoui's *La Voyeuse interdite.*

[16]Djura's second publication, *La Saison des narcisses* (1993), continues her project of making the stories of Maghrebian women's lives in France more widely known to the French public. This second work contains a discussion of women's rights in Islam and their status in contemporary societies of North Africa, as well as the narratives of women in France who have been brutalized by male family members in the name of "tradition."

[17]The lives and experiences of children born to North African immigrants in France have received a great deal of attention and have been the subject of some noteworthy sociological research. Two of the most insightful works on what is often called *"la deuxième génération issue d'immigration maghrébine"* (as if immigration, instead of the parents, gave birth to the next generation!) include: Abdelmalek Sayad's *L'Immigration ou les paradoxes de l'altérité* (see especially the chapter *"Les enfants illégitimes")* and Camille Lacoste-Dujardin's *Yasmina et les autres de Nanterre et d'ailleurs.*

[18]French society's concern with the increase of Islamic militancy in the Arab neighborhoods of Paris and other large French cities has become a national phantasm, fueled by media coverage of the Paris bombings of the summer of

1995 that culminated in late September 1995 with the televised police shooting of Khaled Kelkal, a young Franco-Algerian suspect in some of the attacks. See Gilles Kepel's *A l'ouest d'Allah* and *Le Nouvel Observateur* numéro 1613, du 5 au 11 octobre, 1995.

[19]It is useful here to recall Marnia Lazreg's warning on the overuse and essentialism of the "veil" image when discussing Arab-Muslim women. Lazreg notes that, often, this trend is not so much part of an international plot to equate Arab women with the veil, but the ruse of the publishing industry who recognize the sensational impact of the image of the veil for the book-buying public in the West ("Writing . . . ," 84–5). In Mimouna's account, the veil does largely "stand for" the traditionally historic fate of women within the Arab-Muslim community: early marriage and then seclusion.

[20]*Beur* is the slang term (although now accepted by most dictionaries) for young Parisians of Algerian origin. The feminine equivalent is *Beurette* and the term's origins are the reverse pronunciation (called *verlan* slang) of "Arabe." The 1980s was the decade of the *Beur* movement, beginning in 1983 with the "*Marche des Beurs*" to bring attention to the second-generation members of the Franco-North African community and culminating in the widespread antiracism campaign of 1986–87. The group S.O.S. Racisme, whose slogan was "*Touche pas à mon pote*" [Hands off my buddy], has been credited with organizing millions of young French citizens to protest incidents of racist violence that targeted members of the North Africa community in France. In spite of this and other social movements, such incidents still occur; for example, the drowning of a Moroccan immigrant in France who was thrown into the Seine by several neonazi sympathizers in the spring of 1995, following a large right-wing political demonstration.

[21]The word Mounsi employs is that of *la cité*. In the French urban context of migration, *cité* is a word with multiple connotations that are difficult to render exactly into English. For many immigrants in France, "la cité" refers to the planned, subsidized housing projects located in the suburbs of most major French cities. For most *Beur* fiction, the *cité* is the site of cultural exclusion. The other word for "city" is *la ville,* which implies the city-proper or the affluent urban environment of the French "downtown." Mounsi's choice of the phrase "*l'appartenance à la cité au sens grec*" therefore suggests the richer meaning of *cité* as a physical location, urban yet on the margins, but also a state of mind, a sense of belonging that derives from a solidarity among "*résidents de la cité,*" born of the shared bond of exclusion from the "*ville*" experienced by France's cultural and socioeconomic "Others." Consult Azzouz Begag, *L'Immigré et sa ville.*

WORKS CITED

Abdelkrim-Chikh, Rabia. "Les femmes exogames: entre la loi de dieu et les droits de l'homme." In *L'Islam en France*. Bruno Etienne, ed. Paris: Editions du CNRS, 1991. 235–54.

Aït Sabbah, Fatna. *La Femme dans l'inconscient musulman*. Paris: Albin Michel, 1981.

Amrouche, Fadhma Aït Mansour. *Histoire de ma vie*. Paris: Maspéro, 1968.

Begag, Azzouz and Abdellatif Chaouite. *L'Immigré et sa ville*. Lyon: Presses Universitaires de Lyon, 1984.

———. *Ecarts d'identité*. Paris: Seuil, 1990.

Belghoul, Farida. *Georgette!* Paris: Editions Barrault, 1986.

Benguigui, Yamina. *Femmes d'Islam*. Paris: Albin Michel, 1996.

Beriss, David. "Scarves, Schools, and Segregation: the 'Foulard Affair.'" *French Politics and Society* 8, 1 (Winter 1990): 1–13.

Bernard, Philippe. *L'Immigration*. Paris: Editions Le Monde, 1993.

Bhabha, Homi K. *The Location of Culture*. London, New York: Routledge, 1994.

Bittari, Zoubida. *O mes soeurs musulmanes, pleurez!* Paris: Gallimard, 1964.

Bonn, Charles. "Romans féminins de l'immigration d'origine maghrébine." *Notre Librairie* No. 118 (July–Sept. 1994): 98–107.

Boukhedenna, Sakinna. *Journal: Nationalité: Innigré(e)*. Paris: Harmattan, 1987.

Bouraoui, Nina. *La Voyeuse interdite*. (Folio Coll. #2479.) Paris: Gallimard, 1991.

Boyce Davies, Carole. "Collaboration and the Ordering Imperative in Life Story Production." In *De/Colonizing the Subject: The Politics of Gender in Women's Autobiography*. Sidonie Smith and Julia Watson, eds. Minneapolis: U of Minnesota P, 1992. 3–19.

Brodski, Bella and Celeste Schenck, eds. "Introduction." In *Life/Lines: Theorizing Women's Autobiography*. Ithaca, NY: Cornell UP, 1988. 1–15.

Cixous, Hélène. *Coming to Writing and Other Essays*. Cambridge: Harvard UP, 1991.

Clancy-Smith, Julia. "La Femme Arabe: Women and Sexuality in France's North African Empire." In *Women, The Family, and Divorce Laws in Islamic History*. Amira El Azary Sonbol, ed. Syracuse: Syracuse UP, 1996. 52–63.

Déjeux, Jean. "Récits de vie et témoignages d'Algériennes." *Présence Francophone* Vol. 36 (1990): 35–44.

———. Review of *L'Honneur et l'amertume: le destin ordinaire d'une femme kabyle* by Nedjima Plantade. *Hommes et Migrations* No. 1164 (April 1993): 49–50.

Djura. *La Saison des narcisses*. Paris: Editions Michel Lafon, 1993.

———. *Le voile du silence*. Paris: Michel Lafon, 1990. Rpt. Collection "Livre de Poche," 1993.

Dubet, François. *Immigrations: qu'en savons-nous?* Paris: La Documentation Française, 1989.

Gilmore, Leigh. *Pour un modèle français d'intégration*. Paris: La Documentation Française, 1991.

———. "The Mark of Autobiography: Postmodernism, Autobiography, and Genre." In *Autobiography and Postmodernism*. Gilmore, Kathleen Ashley and Gerald Peters, eds. Amherst: U of Massachusetts P, 1994. 3–18.

Haut Conseil à l'intégration. *Liens culturels et intégration*. Juin (1995). Paris: La Documentation Française, 1995.

Hifi, Belkacem. *L'Immigration algérienne en France: origines et perspectives de non-retour*. Paris: Harmattan, 1985.

Houari, Leïla. *Zeida de nulle part*. Paris: Harmattan, 1985.

Imache, Tassadit. *Une Fille sans histoire*. Paris: Calmann-Lévy, 1989.

JanMohammed, Abdul and David Lloyd. "Introduction: Toward a Theory of Minority Discourse." *Cultural Critique* 6 (Spring 1987): 5–10.

Kaplan, Caren. "Resisting Autobiography: Outlaw Genres and Transnational Feminist Subjects." In *De/Colonizing the Subject: The Politics of Gender in Women's Autobiography*. Sidonie Smith and Julia Watson, eds. Minneapolis: U of Minnesota P, 1992. 115–138.

Kepel, Gilles. *A l'ouest d'Allah*. Paris: Editions du seuil, 1994.

Khellil, Mohand. *L'Intégration des Maghrébins en France*. Paris: PUF, 1991.

Kristeva, Julia. *Etrangers à nous-mêmes*. Paris: Gallimard, 1988.

Lacoste-Dujardin, Camille. *Yasmina et les autres de Nanterre et d'ailleurs: filles de parents maghrébins*. Paris: Ed. de la Découverte, 1992.

Lazreg, Marnia. *The Eloquence of Silence: Algerian Women in Question*. New York: Routledge, 1994.

———. "Feminism and Difference: Writing as a Woman on Women in Algeria." *Feminist Studies* 14.1 (Spring 1988): 81–107.

Lemsine, Aïcha. *Ordalie des voix*. Paris: Encre Edition, 1983.

Lionnet, Françoise. *Postcolonial Representations: Women, Literature, and Identity*. Ithaca: Cornell UP, 1995.

McKesson, John A. "Concepts and Realities in a Multiethnic France." *French Politics and Society* 12, 1 (Winter 1994): 16–38.

Mermet, Gérard. *Francoscopie 1993*. Paris: Larousse, 1992.

Mimouna. *Ni le voile, ni l'oubli*. "Témoignage sur l'immigration." Mohand Mounsi, ed. Paris: Editions Numéro 1, 1995.

Mohanty, Chandra Talpade. "Under Western Eyes: Feminist Scholarship and Colonial Discourse." In *Third World Women and the Politics of Feminism*.

Mohanty, Ann Russo, and Lourdes Torres, eds. Bloomington: Indiana UP, 1991. 51–80.

Nini, Soraya. *Ils disent que je suis une beurette*. Paris: Fixot, 1993.

Noiriel, Gérard. *Le Creuset français: histoire de l'immigration XIXe-XXe siècles.* Paris: Seuil, 1988.

Le Nouvel Observateur. Numéro 1613 (du 5 au 11 octobre, 1995).

Plantade, Nedjima. *La Guerre des femmes: magie et amour en Algérie*. Paris: LaBoîte a Documents, 1988.

———. *L'Honneur et l'Amertume: le destin ordinaire d'une femme kabyle.* Paris: Balland Document, 1993.

Sayad, Abdelmalek. *L'Immigration ou les paradoxes de l'altérité*. Bruxelles: Editions De Boeck, 1991.

Schnapper, Dominique. *La France de l'intégration: sociologie de la nation en 1990*. "Bibliothèque des Sciences Humaines." Paris: Gallimard, 1991.

Spivak, Gayatri. "Can the Subaltern Speak?" In *Marxism and the Interpretation of Culture*. Cary Nelson and Lawrence Grossberg, eds. Chicago: U of Chicago P, 1988. 271–313.

———. "The Political Economy of Women as Seen by a Literary Critic." In *Coming to Terms: Feminism, Theory, and Politics*. Elizabeth Weed, ed. New York: Routledge, 1989. 218–239.

———. "Poststructuralism, Marginality, Postcoloniality, and Value." In *Literary Theory Today*. Peter Collins and Helga Geyer-Ryan eds. Ithaca, NY: Cornell UP, 1990. 219–244.

Taboada-Leonetti, Isabel and Florence Lévy. *Femmes et immigrées: l'insertion des femmes immigrées en France*. Coll. "Migrants et Société," No. 4. Paris: La Documentation Française, 1978.

Touati, Fettouma. *Le Printemps désespéré: Vies d'Algériennes*. Paris: Harmattan, 1984.

SECTION III
Resistant Readings

"Sharp contrasts of all colours": The Legacy of Toru Dutt

ALPANA SHARMA KNIPPLING

In her memoir, *Fault Lines,* the New York–based Indian diasporic writer and professor Meena Alexander relates an incident in which the chair of her department calls her in to his office to complain that her publications do not fall in the area in which she was hired.[1] When she points to a book on his desk and asks him to look up its table of contents, he seems taken aback and then unwilling to give her literary output any credence whatsoever; to him, she is a sari-clad nonentity because she does not fall within his cultural frame of reference. As the text puts it:

> I was sitting there, quite proper in my Kashmir silk sari, erect at the edge of the chair. His eyes shifted to the titles of chapters listed in the table of contents. There was a gap there, a split second. I shivered . . . because I suddenly saw something. There was no way the man who sat in front of me could put together my body with any sense of the life of the mind. I had fallen under the Cartesian blade. . . . The trouble was what I was, quite literally: female, Indian. Not that I had not published in my designated area, but that I had also published outside that docket.
> (1993, 114)

Alexander's anecdote should drive home the grim point that Third World women's literary production is ridden with risks and difficulties. It is a sober reminder that despite the caché apparently given to writing by Third World women in the American academe today, the term "Third World women" itself is—and should be understood as—problematic. Much like another homogenizing term, "women of color," it stands to maintain unequal race and gender relations even as it gives the illusion of benign inclusion and participation in the mainstream of American literary production. Hence, we need to maintain a healthy scepticism as to the publication, circulation, and imagined popularity of Third World women's writing, much of which, in fact, takes place against the greatest possible odds in an arena that is at worst hostile and at best unreceptive to its feminist articulations and aspirations. For "minority women" to write, publish, and be read is itself a "minority" enterprise, a risky proposition, bound on the one side by its ambivalent mode of reception by "majority" readers and on the other by its own internalized pressure to surpass all conventional standards of writing in order simply to be admitted as a viable literature or cultural production.[2] This points to a central, but I hope not ultimately debilitating, contradiction: Third World women's writing in the transnational era seeks to distinguish its own set of aims from those of the mainstream (including those of mainstream White feminism), yet its own material production and dissemination paradoxically are, to a large extent, sustained by the institutional mechanisms of that mainstream culture (publishing companies, book or poetry tours and readings, and academic conferences, most of which are located in the West).

In the face of such an imminent co-optation, Third World women writers should insist on a productive in-between stance, one that steadfastly refuses both the imagined sanctity of a pure position on the outside and the imagined comfort of standing in for a familiar and domesticated Other. For example, Meena Alexander's own fine introduction to the anthology of Indian women's short stories, *Truth Tales: Contemporary Stories by Women Writers of India,* walks the tightrope between the articulation of a radically different feminist agenda and the kind of reportage of oppressive sexist practices in India that Euro-American readers have grown accustomed to hearing. But even at the risk of assuming that the gendered subaltern speaks for herself, Alexander's introduction productively insists on the power and fluidity of women's writing, and on the possibility of a space for some measure of self-determination in women's everyday life and labor. She writes of the female characters in the short stories anthologized in *Truth Tales:*

> Whether these women live in solitude, in extended families, or in nuclear families, we see clearly how female labor stitches the world together. And in choosing to speak from within woman's condition, these female voices have already decolonized themselves. Nor are they

haunted by a gaze that makes them Other, in the Western use of the term. Whatever the actual and often desperate marginality of their lot, there is a fierce attachment to the material conditions of life, and the women in these fictive worlds speak for themselves. (1990, 12)

While it sounds idealistic and wildly optimistic, Alexander's bold assertion that "the women in these fictive worlds speak for themselves" may be read as a necessary, even irreducible, strategy by which to combat Western stereotypes of passive, victimized South Asian women; for ultimately, posing the possibility of these women's agency even in the most abject and oppressive circumstances is preferable to stereotyping them as mindless victims.[3]

A brief clarification: I do not mean to conflate the author's subject position with that of the actual human subjects who inspire her writing. The distinction is an ontological, ideological, and geopolitical one. It is public knowledge that many Third World women writers constitute the elite in their society and that some of these have also made the West their domicile, even as they retain an imaginative and social interest in subjects quite different from themselves. Meena Alexander's own *Nampally Road* is a case in point. In the novel, the narrator, Mira, returns from England to a city in the midst of political strife and corruption—it is the period of Emergency in post-Independence India—and finds herself haunted by the specter of an orange seller who was abducted and raped by the police; she is able (willing?) only to make geometric sketches, which the narrator must decipher. While one may argue that the author merely advances a suspect politics of victimization (women and the poor against the dominant regime of power), what, in fact, is readily evident is that Alexander exhibits a critically engaged social conscience that at once acknowledges the agency of oppressed peoples and the function of writing to provide the space for a meaningful intervention in the socioeconomic structures of oppression. This is writing refigured as social commitment, with gender and class lines intersecting and interrogating one another in necessary and productive ways.

True to Alexander's assertion ("the women in these fictive worlds speak for themselves"), the stories anthologized in *Truth Tales* thoroughly and convincingly attest to women's power in the space of their labor and in their "fierce attachment to the material conditions of life." In one of the most powerful stories in the collection—"Midnight's Soldiers" by Vishwapriya Iyengar—a poor fisherwoman who was talked into a birth control operation by a middle-class social worker and who

makes her grim livelihood by walking ten miles to sell fish withstands
the death of one child while knowing that the remaining child, already
sick with a terminal disease, will die too. As the story draws to a close,
what readers take away is a searing image of long rows of fisherwomen
standing in twos behind Matilda and weeping with her. They are "midnight's soldiers," these women who fight tooth and nail with one another
for the best fish but who provide community and support for one of their
own in times of crisis.[4] Through the depiction of women struggling and
surviving against all odds on the fringes of society, and through commentary on stories such as "Midnight's Soldiers," Iyengar and Alexander, respectively, evade co-optation of their feminist discourse by
focusing on the materiality of women's existence: women's strength,
women's labor, and women's ability to speak for themselves. Alexander
puts it eloquently in her memoir: "In America the barbed wire is taken
into the heart, and the art of an Asian American grapples with a disorder
in society, a violence. *In our writing we need to evoke a chaos, a power
equal to the injustices that surround us. A new baptism. Else even without knowing that we are buying in, we are bought in, brought in, our images magnified, bartered in the high places of capitalist chic*" (1993,
195; my emphasis).

Similarly, Chandra Mohanty and Satya Mohanty's introduction to
the recently published short story collection, *The Slate of Life: More
Contemporary Stories by Women Writers of India,* productively stresses
that these women's writings do not constitute an "inarticulate [cry] in the
dark":

> While the authors of these stories describe various kinds of violence
> and dispossession that define women's lives, we have argued that a
> feminist reading of these stories would be partial and inaccurate with-
> out an appreciation of the extent to which these women are moral and
> indeed historical agents, the subjects of their own lives. . . . These sto-
> ries are not about inarticulate cries in the dark. They mark complexly
> determined spaces in which a critical awareness is developed, choices
> are made, meanings are analyzed and reformulated—in short, where
> lives are lived. (21)

Like Alexander, Chandra Mohanty and Satya Mohanty are arguing for
Indian women's material subjectivity, making this subjectivity a strategic
means by which Third World feminism may foreground subaltern

agency. In one of the stories in this collection, "The Subordinate," by K. Saraswathi Amma, the main character, Parukutty, who is a temple sweeper, takes the life of her own illegitimate daughter to avoid the daughter's rape by her own father. The story unravels an impossibly possible ethics of infanticide, ending with Parukutty claiming her real name, Paru Amma, and aligning her newly formed identity with a higher moral order or *dharma* that transcends both caste and patriarchy. As with Matilda, here, too, readers come up against a bold assertion of self-determination and autonomy that demands recognition and acknowledgment on its own terms.

LATE NINETEENTH-CENTURY INDIAN WOMEN'S WRITING: A HISTORICAL BACKGROUND

Having begun with a consideration of how Third World women writers may resist the co-optation always imminent in the production and reception of their work, I turn to the subject of this essay: the curious reception of the late nineteenth-century writing of Indian poet and translator Toru Dutt (1856–77). With the aid of this example, I intend to show that late nineteenth-century Indian women's writing in English traversed a risk-ridden, in-between, yet productive space in the international arena of textual production and reception. First, however, I offer a historical account of the political, social, and cultural pressures operating upon Indian women writers from the late nineteenth to the early twentieth century. This was a period of volatile changes brought about by the interface of nascent nationalist awareness and imperialist policy. Significantly, it is in this period that women's concerns and ameliorative campaigns to redress women's wrongs—sati, purdah, child marriage, women's literacy and education, and widow remarriage—gained importance. Yet the route that these campaigns for social reforms took was a peculiarly circuitous one. Postcolonial historian Partha Chatterjee has argued that in nineteenth-century India, even as the outer or material sphere of Indian culture conceded to the modernizing impulse, the inner or spiritual sphere insisted on its inviolability and resistance to British influence.[5] The custodians of this essential inner core of the nation were women, whose potential Westernization and formal education thus entailed a complicated maneuver: women's progress had to be charted in such a way that women's traditional identity would not be sacrificed for the superficiality of Western "trends." Ultimately, however, by the early twentieth century, campaigns for social reform lost their urgency and the "women's question," according to Chatterjee, was resolved by its disappearance from the public sphere of nationalist debate.

The editors of the two-volume anthology, *Women Writing in India: 600 B.C. to the Present,* Susie Tharu and K. Lalita, concur with Chatterjee's argument, but they usefully shift attention from Chatterjee's emphasis on resolution to, instead, women's *creation* of a "new resilient self, one that is not easily understood or explained, but is, all the same, a power to be reckoned with" (vol. 1, 185).[6] In the nineteenth-century texts excerpted by Tharu and Lalita, we see strikingly subversive and overtly feminist articulations which, while they contrast visibly with the muted tones of the early twentieth-century texts, still share with this later material a common goal to locate "dignity and personhood outside the double-edged promises of the Enlightenment and the social reform movement" (186).

Tharu and Lalita include some wonderfully aggressive and articulate female authors in their first volume. For instance, one writer, Mokshodayani Mukhopadhyay (ca. 1848–?), an advocate of women's education and independence, when provoked by a leading male poet's depiction of Bengali women as vain and frivolous, responded with a satirical poem of her own, "The Bengali Babu" (1882). The poem portrays men as puffed up, self-important hypocrites who drink pegs of whiskey, spit tobacco, and espouse nationalist views at night but who, in the sober light of the morning, all hatted, booted, suited, with cheroot and cane in hand, go tremblingly to work for the same English they had trashed the night before. For her deflating depiction of cultured and educated Bengali men, this writer received much censure from her male reviewers. Another writer, Tarabai Shinde (ca. 1850–ca. 1910), wrote a bitter feminist essay in response to a weekly magazine article, which attacked the apparent loose morals of a woman who aborted her baby and received a death sentence from the court as a result. In her 1882 essay, "A Comparison of Men and Women," Shinde isolates each of the charges leveled against women—suspicion, impudence, adultery, transgression, deceit, and so on—and redirects them towards men. It is worthwhile to quote this inimitable and direct voice at some length:

> I'm sure there are very few men who are ruined by women. But it would be difficult even to guess at the number of women ruined by men. You are far too clever for women. You are, in fact, nothing but scoundrels of the first order! You are so cunning that you will pass

through a sugarcane field without letting those sharp leaves touch you, let alone scratch you. You organize big meetings every day, deliver impressive speeches, offer unwanted advice to all and sundry, and do a hundred other such stupid things. You are nothing but learned asses! Yes, that's what you are, really. . . . If only you realized how much evil you contain, it would break your heart! (235, trans. from Marathi)

In her down-to-earth, idiomatic language, which constitutes a deliberate departure from the "standard" diction of normative patriarchy, Shinde reveals a withering contempt for men, including her husband, for whom she had lost regard very early in their marriage. For her lively riposte, she was attacked by men who did not even read her essay carefully. Finally, there were writers who, like the novelist Indira Sahasrabuddhe (ca. 1890–?), tackled the key reformist issues of the day—child marriage and widow remarriage—head-on, risking the charge of Westernized feminism as they did so. That Sahasrabuddhe's feminism cannot simply be dismissed on the grounds of Westernization is tellingly asserted by one of her prefaces, in which Sahasrabuddhe states: "Significantly even the Western-educated characters in the novel cannot appreciate that women may want more than home, marriage, and motherhood" (385).

TORU DUTT: A LIFE OF SHARP CONTRASTS

Bold articulations such as Mukhopadhyay's, Shinde's, and Sahasrabuddhe's are the more valuable for their explicit willingness to explode the constricted social and religious walls that sought to imprison these women. In contrast to their lives of public protest stands the sheltered life of young Toru Dutt.[7] Toru was one of three children born to an upper-class Bengali couple (the oldest, a son by the name of Abju, died in 1865 at the age of fourteen). Her father, Govin Chunder Dutt, worked for the colonial government but soon resigned due to the lack of promotion opportunity for Indians in government jobs; later, in his autumn years, he was to become honorary magistrate, justice of the peace, and a fellow of the University in Calcutta. Govin Chunder Dutt was a convert to Christianity along with his brothers, following the oldest brother's mystical vision of the other world while on his deathbed; the remaining brothers and their families were all baptized in 1862. Toru doted on her father, who whiled away his time writing poetry fashioned after his favorite poet William Wordsworth. At age twelve, she went with her family to Europe; she learned French in Nice, music in London, and, in 1871, attended the

Higher Lectures for Women in Cambridge. The family returned to Calcutta in 1873, and within a year the older sister, Aru, died of tuberculosis.

Toru, who was to outlive her sister by only three years, began to publish her writing at this time: essays on Leconte de Lisle and Henry Derozio for the *Bengal Magazine* and translations of French verse into English, compiled in *A Sheaf Gleaned in French Fields* (1876). She took up the study of Sanskrit in 1875 and was preparing a collection of translated verse from Sanskrit to English at the time of her death in 1877; the collection appeared posthumously in 1882 under the title *Ancient Ballads and Legends of Hindustan,* with an introduction by Edmund Gosse. Two novels were also published posthumously: *Bianca, or the Young Spanish Maiden* (1878) and *Le Journal de Mlle. d'Arvers* (1879). She died a painful death at the age of twenty-one, leaving behind a prodigious amount of writing feverishly produced in a mere three years.

Given the different trajectory of her life and her prolific literary output, it is remarkable that there is very little written on Toru Dutt. What little there is tends either to glorify her as one of India's "true daughters" or to dismiss her as imitative of Western poetic trends (noteworthy exceptions are Alexander and Tharu, each of whom has written a useful, albeit brief, feminist analysis of her work). Certainly no critic has credited Toru with a full-blown ability to address the big issues of her day and to nuance her poetry accordingly. For many Indian critics in particular, Toru's work merely represents a precedent—and a rather isolated one at that—to Indian literature in English, which they perceive as coming into its own only in the early to mid-twentieth century with the novels of R. K. Narayan, Mulk Raj Anand, and Raja Rao. Her own biographer, Harihar Das, often resorts to an apologetic tone when analyzing perceived weaknesses in her writing. Nor is Toru's work read by Western feminists or anthologized in Western publications; it is even absent in Tharu and Lalita's anthology of women's writing in India.

However, I would argue that what makes Toru's case distinctive and worthy of critical attention is that, despite her extensive nontraditional education and middle-class Christian identity, both of which spared her the tricky maneuverings Chatterjee describes as the common denominator of educated Indian women in the nineteenth century, Dutt achieved neither literary success in England nor freedom and mobility in India. Excluded by orthodox Hindu society on account of her family's conversion, yet not wholly included in the British social order on account of her Indian/"native" origin, Toru traversed the improvisational space in-

between these two positions. European reviewers of her French translations were more astounded at her polished literary skills than accepting of
them; they neutralized their astonishment with a patronizing stance
toward the imagined oddity of the exotic colonial creature they were dealing with. Indian readers, on the other hand, felt that Toru's Sanskrit translations redeemed and corrected her prior Westernization, making her a
genuine "daughter of India"; still others regarded her Sanskrit translations as naive and amateurish forays into a world about which she knew
very little. Thus, Toru's life and work constitute an overdetermined site
upon which both colonial and anticolonial imperatives competed to
weave a complicated pattern indeed. When read against the grain of these
overdeterminations, her poetry demonstrates that it is produced, not from
the site of a monolithic "truth" and "native" authenticity, but from the
infinitely more fascinating site (in Homi Bhabha's language, an "interstitial passage between fixed identifications"[8]) of reinvention and improvisation. Such a reading, in turn, may make possible a subversive reading
of both the European colonial and Indian patriarchal systems prevalent in
Toru's time.

The critical reception of Toru Dutt's Indian publication of *A Sheaf
Gleaned in French Fields,* a translation project she undertook with her
sister Aru (who was to die of tuberculosis two years before it appeared in
print), occurred accidentally and abroad. Edmund Gosse happened to
visit the office of the *Examiner,* stumbled upon *A Sheaf,* and subsequently reviewed it for the newspaper in August 1876. Very put off by the
book's appearance ("a most unattractive orange pamphlet of verse . . .
destined by its particular providence to find its way hastily into the
waste-paper basket"; a "shabby little book . . . without preface or introduction"; a "hopeless volume . . . with its queer type"[9]), Gosse nevertheless steels himself to read the verse, only to be shocked out of his
complacency by a great surprise, "almost rapture," for he reads:

> *Still barred thy doors! the far East glows*
> *The morning wind blows fresh and free.*
> *Should not the hour that wakes the rose*
> *Awaken also thee?*

> *All look for thee, Love, Light, and Song,*
> *Light, in the sky deep red above,*
> *Song, in the lark of pinions strong,*
> *And in my heart true love. (Das, 291)*

Gosse appears to resolve his unexpected surprise at this lyrical verse by assuming a benevolent and paternalistic attitude towards the Dutt sisters. According to him, Toru achieved brilliance not because of, but *in spite of,* her Indian identity; it is as if she had to surmount the greatest odds to produce such accomplished verse in English. In his introductory memoir to *Ancient Ballads and Legends of Hindustan,* he says: "[*A Sheaf*] is a wonderful mixture of strength and weakness, of genius overriding great obstacles and of talent succumbing to ignorance and brilliance. That it should have been performed at all is so extraordinary that we forget to be surprised at its inequality" (Das, 300). And again: "Toru's command of English is wonderful, and it is difficult to realize that the book is not the work of an English writer" (301). Gosse's fluctuating between praise and criticism reveals a measure of baffled colonialist outrage that an Indian, a "native," could write sophisticated English verse (translations, no less, from French to English). How interesting, then, that he refers to her as "Hindu," orientalizing her even though she wrote as a Christian. "The English verse is sometimes exquisite," writes Goss; "at other times the rules of our prosody are absolutely ignored, and it is obvious that *the Hindu poetess was chanting to herself a music that is discord in an English ear*" (300, my emphasis). Toru's reception demonstrates that an Indian writing fluently in English was still, in imperialist eyes, only second-best, a shadow, a mere copy whose chief merit was to accentuate the power and authority of the original "English book."

But herein also lie the theoretical conditions for a subversive reading of Toru's verse. Although her poetry takes the power and authority of the original—the great Western male tradition—for granted, it is not located at the source of that "original truth" and "authenticity" but finds its articulation elsewhere, in another place where textual play and improvisation replace cultural pieties and fixed literary standards. The rules of Toru's poetic translation are best described as arbitrary. If a word or idea sounded good and looked good, it went in. This is not to say that her verse was sloppy or haphazard. But, cloistered at home and accessing European literature through her father's library, English newspapers, and articles of random interest to her in the *Revue des Deux Mondes,* she subjected her verse to her own rigorous standards and the influence of her own personal favorites in the canon. Gosse points out some of her subsequent (mis)readings : "She eschewed the Classicist writers as though they had never existed. . . . She was ready to pronounce an opinion on Napol le Pyrénéen or to detect a plagiarism in Baudelaire. But she thought that Alexander Smith was still alive, and she was curiously vague about the career of Sainte-Beuve" (Das, 300). But what constitutes an "inequality of equipment" (ibid.) for Gosse is for others, perhaps less intimate with the hallowed literary tradition Toru was translating and revising, a pleasure. For instance, she rendered Victor Hugo's antiroyalist, republican dislike of Louis Napoleon Bonaparte: *"Toi, tu te noyeras dans la fange,/Petit, petit!"* thus: "Thou too shalt drown, but drown in slime,/Tom Thumb, Tom Thumb!"[10] Worth noting here is the free translation of "petit" as "Tom Thumb," which rather irreverently and delightfully transfers Bonaparte from Hugo's literary France to the annals of British nursery rhyme.

Toru's translations from French to English did not, of course, make her an "Indian poet" in the eyes of Indians. It took her translations from the Sankritic texts of the *Mahabharata, Ramayana, Vishnu Puranas,* and *Bhagavata Gita,* compiled in *Ancient Ballads and Legends and Ballads of Hindustan,* to make this poet "the genuine daughter of Hinduism."[11] These translations were inspired by the Hindu hymns young Toru's mother often sang at dusk, which moved the daughter almost always to tears; she discusses this deep emotional response to her mother's songs both in her letters and in her poetry. This has led critics to read her translations from the Sanskrit as evidence of her great need to connect with her quintessentially Indian past. Symptomatically, the mother-figure (in nationalist thought always standing for the nation) constitutes the locus for a feminized nationalism. Says Indian critic K. R. Srinivasa Iyengar,

> She was an Indian poet writing in English—she was "autochthonous", [sic] she was one with India's women singers. . . . No room now for artificiality or stimulated hot-house efflorescence: now Toru has roots in her own land, and she agreeably responds to the heart-beats of the antique racial tradition. As children, she and her brother and sister had heard stories of the Hindu epics and Puranas, stories of mystery, miracle and local tradition from the lips of her own mother. . . . They really seemed to answer to a profound inner need for links with the living past of India, and she cared not if Christian or sceptic cavilled at her.[12]

The mother's oral narration of religious Hindu stories to the Dutt children, the young Toru's "profound inner need" to connect with an ancient racial memory: these combine, according to Iyengar, to create an "Indian poet" who has cast out all jarring, foreign, artificially induced tones. In short, the "real," the "Indian" Toru Dutt has emerged with *Ancient Ballads.* Similarly, according to Amaranatha Jha, who wrote the introduction to the 1941 and 1969 editions of *Ancient Ballads and Legends of Hindustan,* the translations show that "[f]or all her Western training and the faith under the influence of which she had been brought up, she never ceased to be Indian" (33).

The impulse to reclaim Toru on these nationalist grounds is hardly reprehensible. But, as with her Western readers like Edmund Gosse and Clarisse Bader (a French author whose interest in women of ancient India sparked a correspondence with Toru in the last year of Toru's life), it is her ambivalence that opens the door to the other side and accommodates nationalist interpretations such as Iyengar's and Jha's. Here too, "foreign" notes are struck, for Toru was not very conversant with Sanskrit in the short time that she devoted to its study (one year). If Toru's French-to-English poetry did not find altogether safe harbor on English soil (deemed not English enough), her Sanskrit-to-English verses did not meet with unanimous success in India either (they were not Indian enough). Thus, some felt that the "plaintive cadence" and "natural charm" of the original Sanskrit was lost in English.[13]

A reading of what is perhaps the most well-known poem in *Ancient Ballads,* "Savitri," will show that Toru's poetry traversed the risky in-between position that was neither purely English nor solely Indian. Viewed in connection with her letters to a friend in England, her poetry may offer us an alternative, interstitial locus from which to articulate Third World feminist politics. A "free" translation of a legend from the *Mahabharata* that produced the myth of the archetypal self-sacrificing wife so central to Hindu thought, the poem details the heroic and ultimately successful efforts a wife, Savitri, makes to bring her husband, Satyavan, back from the realm of the dead. The salient points of the original story are as follows. Savitri was the beautiful daughter of Asvapati, king of Mudra, born to him after many years of praying for a son to the goddess Savitri. When his daughter reached a marriageable age, Asvapati was unable to find her a good suitor because she was considered too perfect by eligible bachelors in the neighboring provinces. So Savitri undertook to find her own husband, selecting a young man who lived in a hermitage in the forest and tended to his blind father. Satyavan, however, had a grim forecast: he was destined to die within a year. Savitri, who soon proved an exceptional wife and daughter-in-law, determined to avert her husband's destiny through fasting, dedication, and perseverance. On the appointed day and time, when the figure of death, Yama, appeared to carry Satyavan's body to his kingdom, Savitri's persistent pleading broke Yama down to the point of granting her the ultimate boon: the restoration of her dead husband's life. While Hindu tradition emphasizes the wifely qualities of self-sacrifice and devotion in this legend—and this emphasis is greatly complicated by the fact that the texts of Hinduism were themselves largely shaped by the colonial encounter in the nineteenth century—it is interesting to note that Toru emphasizes other neglected aspects of the myth: Savitri's freedom, mobility, individuality, and right to self-determination. Toru's Savitri comes and goes as she pleases; she chooses her own husband; and even when she obeys the rigors of tradition, she does so of her own volition.

> *In those far-off primeval days*
>   *Fair India's daughters were not pent*
> *In closed zenanas. On her ways*
>   *Savitri at her pleasure went*
> *Whither she chose . . .*
> *. . .*
> *Her father let her have her way*
>   *In all things, whether high or low;*
> *He feared no harm . . .*
> *. . .*
> *And so she wandered where she pleased*
>   *In boyish freedom . . . (Dutt, 38–9)*

The authorial insertion ("In those far-off primeval days/Fair India's daughters were not pent/In closed zenanas") constructs an idyllic mythic past by which the poet offsets the harsh glare of an undesirable present. This temporal strategy worked ultimately to forestall direct criticism of imperialism, so that orthodox Hinduism, and not its strategic manipulation by the British to foreground their own assumed emancipated ideology, is to blame for the loss of women's freedom, mobility, and self-determination in "Savitri." In this, Toru had internalized the British notion of Hinduism's treatment of women. In a letter to her English friend, Mary Martin, dated 3 May 1876, she writes:

> Marriage, you must know, is a great thing with the Hindus. An unmarried girl of fifteen is never heard of in our country. If any friend of my grandmother happens to see me, the first question is, if I am married; and considerable astonishment, and perhaps a little scandal, follows

the reply, for it is considered scandalous if a girl is not "wooed and married and [all]" before she is eight years old! The other day one of my grandmother's cousins was not a little taken aback on my replying to his question if I were not married, that I was now going to, since I had his permission, for it was only his permission that I had waited for!
(Das, 152)

The excerpt delineates a rather perky and audacious approach towards the sacred topic of Hindu marriage. However, the tone of an acutely felt cultural difference from her Hindu relatives that one may evince from this excerpt is greatly complicated by Toru's nascent awareness of India, not England, as her "homeland." An earlier letter to Mary, written when the Dutt family had newly arrived back in Calcutta, made mention of Indians as "natives." Upon Mary's surprise and chastisement at Toru's use of this alienating word, Toru expresses shame and begins to practice a rather moving and rigorous self-censorship: "Thank you very much for what you say about calling my countrymen 'natives'; the reproof is just, and I stand corrected. I shall take care and not call them natives again. It is indeed a term only used by prejudiced Anglo-Indians, and I am really ashamed to have used it" (Das, 131–32).

Later letters show her growing political consciousness about imperialism in India; many of these angrily describe the one-sided workings of colonial law in events involving injustice, brutality, and wanton murders of Indians at the hands of British judges and officers. In a letter dated 26 June 1876, Toru writes: "You are indignant at the way some Anglo-Indians speak of India and her inhabitants. What would you think if you read some of the Police reports which appear in the Indian daily papers?" She proceeds to tell of some British soldiers who began shooting at peacocks on the property of a farmer. The farmer protested, was cursed, and soon, a fight broke out in which the farmer's neighbors participated:

> [O]ne soldier was severely beaten; the others decamped, leaving *nine* Bengalis *dead* and some seven Bengalis wounded. The case was brought before the magistrate; and what do you think his judgement was? The villagers were fined each and all; the soldiers acquitted: "natives should know how precious is the life of one British soldier in the Eyes of the British Government—". (Das, 169; emphases in the original)

Toru returns to the subject of brutal and random violence exerted against Indians by the British in yet another letter, proving its tenacious hold over her. This case involves a "Mr. F" who, upon setting out to church with his family, found the carriage groom absent. The groom appeared when called for, but was then punished by being struck in the face and head with "open hand" and having his hair pulled so as to cause him to fall to the ground. The beating resulted in death just moments later. But the death was ruled euphemistically as accidental:

> The medical officer . . . states that the man had died from rupture of the spleen, which very slight violence, either from a blow or a fall, would be sufficient to cause, in consequence of the morbid enlargement of that organ. The Joint-Magistrate, Mr. L., found Mr. F guilty of "voluntarily causing what distinctly amounts to hurt" and fined Mr. F. *thirty rupees* (L2), and let him off scot free! The High Court of the North-West Provinces did not find that the sentence was open to any objection. You see how cheap the life of an Indian is, in the eyes of an English Judge—L2! (Das, 191; emphasis in the original)

These and other controversial legal cases stemming from British brutality constituted an intense area of interest for Toru in her letters to Mary.[14] Verging on an anticolonial attitude towards the country in which she had spent some of her most formative years, her letters to Mary radically complicate any simple attribution of "Westernness" or "Westernization" to her body of writing. Indeed, according to Alexander, some of her translations from the Sanskrit (the poem "Prahlad," for instance) show Toru using Hindu mythology to *confront* British imperialism (Alexander 1989, 14).

Alexander does not elaborate on this key idea. For her, Toru's life is rendered "unreal" ("Outcaste Power," 15) by virtue of the contortions produced by Toru's adoption of a foreign language. But perhaps reality is not always susceptible to full and adequate description, and who is to say that only writers writing in non-English languages have access to it? In fact, the colonial period throws up countless examples of Indian writers creatively rewriting English and putting it to very non-English uses such as Indianization and the articulation of a nationalist sensibility. Tharu comes closer to the stakes involved in women's writing in the colonial period in her essay, "Tracing Savitri's Pedigree: Victorian Racism and the Image of Women in Indo-Anglian Literature." In this essay, Tharu discusses the psychosocial anxieties underpinning Indo-Anglian women's literature at a time when educated Indians confronted their image in British eyes.[15] Anxious, overwrought, and defensive, their reaction to

British stereotyping was to try to prove that they were not inferior but equal to the British in intellect and character. Toru's competence in English *and* French proves, according to Tharu, that "[b]eing both Indian and female, she has not just to match, but to *outdo,* the British who found French notoriously difficult" (258, italics in the original). This sense of having to exceed expectations because she was writing against enormous odds and the psychosocial contortions produced as a result are throughout prevalent in Toru's writing, about which she herself was very modest and diffident. Hence, it is likely that Toru's Savitri, who goes wherever she wishes in "boyish freedom," whose mate will be chosen not by her parents in an arranged marriage but by her, has an individuality that has less to do with "those far-off primeval days" than with the defensiveness with which many elite Indians countered negative British stereotypes of Indians.

My own analysis adds two elements missing in Tharu and Alexander's. First, Toru's writings dislodge fixed binaries of sedimented thought and force us into a place where we may consider the productive politics of an in-between position. Not quite Indian yet not English either; well-versed in European literature, yet not writing from the "original" place of that literature's imagined "truth" and "value"; female and cloistered, yet (relatively) liberated; young, yet mature beyond her years: it is seeming conflicts such as these that make Toru's phrase, "[s]harp contrasts of all colours," in "Sonnet—Baugmaree," so descriptive of her own life and work. The poem lovingly dwells upon the visual contrasts in the landscape of her family home Baugmaree and recalls the vicissitudes within Toru herself. It is these "sharp contrasts of all colours" that impart to her work a degree of latitude that allows her to seriously play with and unsettle aspects of the social and imperialist patriarchy of her time. The implications of such a nonbinary, serious playing bring me to the second aspect perhaps missing in Tharu and Alexander's analyses, namely, the way in which Toru's case establishes a useful precedent for Third World women's writing in the transnational arena. To make this point means articulating those interventionist aspects that appear to be only partially thought out by Toru Dutt herself. I conclude the essay by elaborating upon one of these.

CONCLUSION: THE LEGACY OF TORU DUTT

Granted, the disjunctive character of our current transnational era does not allow us to draw a direct continuum from the past to the present. Still, the discourses of modernity and imperialism continue to shape and inform the current moment. The line running from Toru to Alexander is jagged yet capable of yielding certain truths about what it means to be a "woman poet, a woman poet of color, [an Indian] woman poet who makes up lines in English, a postcolonial language . . ." (1993, 193). In the writing of both poets, what emerges is the violence of a reclamation that stitches together not only disparate fragments of being (those "[s]harp contrasts of all colours"), but also a material practice rooted in the struggle for social justice. What, taking Toru's case as exemplary, may be the productive aspects of what it means to be an Indian woman poet? One that I have attempted to outline is the power of an interstitial position, which enabled her to seriously play with the patriarchal norms of her time. In particular, I would emphasize her inability and, to some extent, refusal to settle neatly into only one side of any number of binary relations: female/male, colonized/colonizer, Indian/Western, original/imitative, young/old, sheltered/"free," and so on. Fixed binaries such as these would arrest the dynamic nature of her resistance to both the colonial and Indian patriarchy. Translated into current discourse, this is a way of saying that Third World feminists should not find it necessary to consolidate their politics in binary terms. In the postcolonial context, this means that it is entirely possible to contest the patriarchal neocolonial nation-state without subscribing to an essentialized notion of national identity on one hand or falling prey to the charge of Westernization on the other. At the same time, it is not—and nor should it ever be understood as—a situation where "anything goes." Our "racial uniform"[16] will always remind us of the line that cannot be crossed ("I can make myself up and this is the enticement, the exhilaration, the compulsive energy of America. But only up to a point. *And the point, the sticking point, is my dark female body*" [Alexander 1993, 202; my emphasis]). Then let it constitute the ground for a new politics of reception.

NOTES

[1]This essay is part of an early chapter of a book-length project, currently in progress, which examines the history and development of Indian women's literature in English from its inception in the nineteenth century to its current diasporic articulations. The essay's title, "Sharp contrasts of all colours," is borrowed from Toru's poem, "Sonnet—Baugmaree," found in *Ancient Ballads and Legends of Hindustan,* 171.

[2]I do not mean to imply that all Third World women's work is bound in this way. Notable exceptions include the powerful avant garde films and writings of Trinh T. Minha. At the same time, I do not wish to suggest that responding to

mainstream pressures and using mainstream avenues is in itself a bad thing. The British films of Indian diasporic filmmaker Pratibha Parmar make frank and full use of state funds to expose the sexism, racism, and homophobia simmering below the surface of dominant English culture.

[3]I am implicitly referring in this section on women "speaking for themselves" to the debate unleashed by Gayatri Chakravorty Spivak's essay, "Can the Subaltern Speak?" in which Spivak uses the case of *sati* or widow immolation in India to argue that elite intellectuals need to examine the ideological interests that lead them to assume either that the underclasses speak for themselves or that they can be heard or be spoken for. Spivak's persuasive argument has decisively changed the way in which scholars broach the whole troubling question of the (self) representation of Third World underclasses, although it should be noted that some Indian feminists have attempted qualifications of Spivak's argument. See, for instance, Lata Mani's "Cultural Theory, Colonial Texts: Reading Eyewitness Accounts of Widow Burning," in *Cultural Studies,* Grossberg, Nelson, and Treichler, eds. (New York: Routledge, 1992), 392–408. At this early point in my essay, I argue that Third World feminist writers *have* to imagine and foreground the whole question of gendered subaltern agency in order to maintain a critical vigilance about their own co-optation by First World circuits of production and reception.

[4]See *Truth Tales,* 160–72.

[5]See Partha Chatterjee, "The Nationalist Resolution of the Women's Question," in *Recasting Women: Essays in Colonial History,* 233–53.

[6]A recent review of *Women Writing in India* argues that the anthology was compiled for Western consumption, judging from, among other things, the (hidden) politics of inclusion and exclusion of texts. (See Harveen Sachdeva Mann, "*Bharat Mein Mahila Lekhana,* or, Women's Writing in India: Regional Literatures, Translation, and Global Feminism," *Socialist Review* 24, 4 [1995]: 151–71.) According to Mann, Tharu and Lalita's focus on "the contested margins of patriarchy, empire, and nation" (*Women Writing in India,* vol. 1, xvii) limits the scope of the anthology to a "feminism-nationalism thesis" (as if this were a narrow topic!), excluding key texts by Assamese, Punjabi, and Kashmiri writers and the oral literature of peasant, Dalit, and tribal women. The exclusion of this material is indeed unfortunate, but the material that Tharu and Lalita do include *is* capable of achieving their goal, which is to "create a context in which women's writing can be read . . . as documents that display what is at stake in the embattled practices of self and agency, and . . . at the margins of patriarchies reconstituted by the emerging bourgeoisies of empire and nation" (*Women Writing in India,* vol. 1, 36). I base this view on a difficult semester's worth of teaching Volume 2 in an upper-level women's studies course in which many of the White, self-professed feminist students resisted Tharu and Lalita's challenge to mainstream White feminism and the anthology's selection of texts.

[7]I write mindful of the limitations resulting from my choice of Toru Dutt as a subject for the essay and not a less privileged figure. In large part, my choice is dictated by my fascination with the ways Toru defies easy classification. For this reason, I should clarify that my intent is not to make her representative of *all* Indian women's writing; instead, I wish to discuss the productivity enabled by such a lack of classification and make that productivity an exemplary one for Third World women writers.

[8]See Homi Bhabha, "Introduction: Locations of Culture," in *The Location of Culture* (New York: Routledge, 1994), 4.

[9]Quoted in Harihar Das, *The Life and Letters of Toru Dutt*, 291.

[10]Das quotes both the original stanza and its translation in full on 307.

[11]Padmini Sen Gupta, *Toru Dutt,* 83.

[12]K. R. Srinivasa Iyengar, "Toru Dutt," in *Indian Writing in English,* 63–4.

[13]Admittedly, this is an English reviewer quoted in Sen Gupta, 83. Sen Gupta, however, tends to corroborate the reviewer's judgement when she says, "there is a flowery phraseology, an excess of praise of the hero and heroine . . . which Toru has not been able accurately to reproduce, for she has modernised and shortened her translations to suit a foreign audience" (84). And Iyengar says that some Indian readers will "remember the nectarean Sanskrit originals, and feel disappointed at the inadequacy of the English versions" (65).

[14]In another instance, Toru related the controversial case of a young Indian boy who was given three weeks of imprisonment with hard labor when he rescued a laborer's goat from some attacking dogs that belonged to an English Magistrate: "The papers are speaking against this crying scandalous shame; the magistrate and the sessions judge ought to be dismissed for so monstrous a perversion of the law. Imagine the row that would have been made in England at a Magistrate sending a boy to a treadmill under such circumstances" (Das, 184).

[15]In *Recasting Women: Essays in Colonial History,* eds. Kumkum Sangari and Sudesh Vaid, 254–268; 258.

[16]Robert E. Park's wonderful coinage, quoted by Ronald Takaki in *Strangers from a Different Shore: A History of Asian Americans* (New York: Penguin Books, 1990), 13.

WORKS CITED

Alexander, Meena. "Outcaste Power: Ritual Displacement and Virile Maternity in Indian Women Writers." *Journal of Commonwealth Literature* 24, 1 (August 1989): 12–29.

———. Introduction. *Truth Tales: Contemporary Stories by Women Writers of India.* Kali for Women, ed. New York: Feminist Press, 1990.

———. *Fault Lines.* New York: Feminist Press, 1993.

Bhaba, Homi. "Introduction: Locations of Culture." In *The Location of Culture*. New York: Routledge, 1994. 1–18.

Chatterjee, Partha. "The Nationalist Resolution of the Women's Question." In *Recasting Women: Essays in Colonial History*. Kumkum Sangari and Sudesh Vaid, eds. New Delhi: Kali for Women, 1989. 233–53.

Das, Harihar. *The Life and Letters of Toru Dutt*. London: Oxford UP, 1921.

Dutt, Toru. *Ancient Ballads and Legends of Hindustan*. With an introductory memoir by Amaranatha Jha. Allahabad: Kitabistan, 1941; 1969.

Dutt, Toru. *A Sheaf Gleaned in French Fields*. Bhowanipore: Saptahik Sambad Press, 1876; London: Kegan Paul and Co., 1880.

———. *Le Journal de Mademoiselle d'Arvers*. Paris: Didier, 1879.

———. "Bianca, or The Young Spanish Maiden." *The Bengal Magazine* (January–April 1878): np.

Iyengar, K. R. Srinivasa. 1962. "Toru Dutt." In *Indian Writing in English*. New York: Asia Publishing House, 1973. 55–73.

Iyengar, Vishwapriya. "Midnight's Children." *Truth Tales*. Kali for Women, ed. New York: Feminist Press, 1990. 160–72.

Mani, Lata. "Cultural Theory, Colonial Texts: Reading Eyewitness Accounts of Widow Burning." In *Cultural Studies*. Lawrence Grossberg, Cary Nelson, and Paula Treichler, eds. New York: Routledge, 1992. 392–408.

Mann, Harveen Sachdeva. "*Bharat Mein Mahila Lekhana,* or, Women's Writing in India: Regional Literatures, Translation, and Global Feminism." *Socialist Review* 24, 4 (1995): 151–71.

Mohanty, Chandra Talpade and Satya P. Mohanty. "Introduction—Lives of Their Own." In *The Slate of Life: More Contemporary Stories by Women Writers of India*. 1990. Kali for Women, ed. New York: Feminist Press, 1994. 1–25.

Sen Gupta, Padmini. *Toru Dutt*. New Delhi: Sahitya Academi, 1968.

Spivak, Gayatri Chakravorty. "Can the Subaltern Speak?" In *Colonial Discourse and Postcolonial Theory: A Reader*. Patrick Williams and Laura Chrisman, eds. New York: Columbia University Press, 1994. 66–111.

Takaki, Ronald. *Strangers from a Different Shore: A History of Asian Americans*. New York: Penguin Books, 1990.

Tharu, Susie. "Tracing Savitri's Pedigree: Victorian Racism and the Image of Women in Indo-Anglian Literature." In *Recasting Women: Essays in Colonial History*. Kumkum Sangari and Sudesh Vaid, eds. New Delhi: Kali for Women, 1989. 254–268.

Tharu, Susie and K. Lalita, eds. *Women Writing in India: 600 B.C. to the Early Twentieth Century*. Vol. 1. New York: Feminist Press, 1991.

Grim Fairy Tales:
Taking a Risk, Reading
Imaginary Maps

JENNIFER WENZEL

*A many-leveled problem. It is improper to pass
quick judgment from a safe distance. . . . To say
something too quickly is wrong.*

—MAHASWETA DEVI, *IMAGINARY MAPS*[1]

*In one way you take a risk to criticize, of criti-
cizing something which is* Other—*something
which you used to dominate. I say that you have
to take a certain risk: to say "I won't criticize"
is salving your conscience, and allowing you
not to do any homework. On the other hand, if
you criticize having earned the right to do so,
then you are indeed taking a risk and you will
probably be made welcome, and can hope to be
judged with respect.*

—GAYATRI CHAKRAVORTY SPIVAK,
"QUESTIONS OF MULTI-CULTURALISM" [2]

Like many in the Anglo-American academy, I first read Mahasweta Devi's
fiction in Gayatri Chakravorty Spivak's translation, from Bengali, of
"Draupadi."[3] Mahasweta's story of Dopdi Mehjen, a tribal female Nax-
alite activist, still defiant after having been captured, "countered," raped,
and tortured in rural West Bengal, haunted me long after I had finished
the story and put Spivak's *In Other Worlds* back on the shelf. Like most
graduate students, I had volumes to read, courses to take, and papers to

write. Mahasweta and Spivak,[4] too, had work to do: while Mahasweta has continued her organizing, journalistic, and literary work with and for India's rural poor, Spivak and others have since published several translations and readings of Mahasweta's fiction.[5] The growing body of Mahasweta's writing available in English merits sustained critical attention, but the event around which this essay will focus is the publication in 1995 of *Imaginary Maps: Three Stories by Mahasweta Devi,* translated and framed by Gayatri Chakravorty Spivak.

Reading *Imaginary Maps* from what might seem to be a "safe distance" is no easy task; indeed, the book is in some ways a critique of the process of reading, talking, and writing on demand that constitutes graduate education and the scholarly profession beyond, or more broadly speaking, any profession that revolves around investigation, reportage, and action, whether textual or material. I have not, literally nor figuratively, tucked *Imaginary Maps* away comfortably on the shelf since I began reading it well over a year ago. But is sustained reading and rereading, punctuated by research, presentations, and deadlines, the kind of "homework" Spivak posits as a prerequisite for taking the "risk to criticize"? Reading Mahasweta in English is, to some degree, reading Spivak, and thus, I must listen to Spivak's answers while considering my own when she asks, "What is it to learn? What does it mean to learn?"[6] In examining Spivak's explorations of what it means to learn from Mahasweta, my purpose is decidedly not to trace her "progress," but rather to illustrate the very difficulty, and necessity, of teaching oneself and allowing oneself to be taught to read *Imaginary Maps.* Though my own "homework" on Mahasweta has attended both to her writing and to its regional, Indian, and international contexts, I will not here "show my work" by reviewing that contextual reading in detail; rather, I will speculate, by way of allusion to those contexts, on the consequences of *not* doing such reading, especially when one reads and writes from a space on the map far removed from the lives of Mahasweta's subjects.

Thus, I must open this essay by claiming that I have earned the right to write. Such a rhetorical move, I suspect, is unusual not for its invocation, but instead for its explicitness. Public writing on a text implies what may have once been called *mastery,* not far removed from what Spivak calls in my epigraph "what [we] used to dominate"; we might now choose *engagement* as a more palatable term. Spivak reformulates her question "What is it to learn?" and provides a kind of answer in her afterword to *Imaginary Maps:* "I am learning to write on Mahasweta as if an attentive reading of her texts permits us to imagine an impossible undivided world. . . . This is a learning because such permission can be earned only by attention to the specificity of these writings."[7] Because of the anxiety now often assumed to be inherent in the distance between First World[8] critics and Third World texts, it is easy to misread this process of earning the right to criticize. "Permission" is "earned" by attention to "specificity," but only attention to the specificity of Spivak's words will reveal that the careful reader earns "permission to imagine an impossible undivided world," not permission to "write on Mahasweta." Such permission would be granted by the text and not by Mahasweta or Spivak: this distinction is important to remember when considering Spivak's seemingly proprietary comments about Mahasweta's work. Spivak's consideration here of what it means to learn is perhaps emblematic of the profound attention required of a reader to begin to understand the "many-leveled problem" that is *Imaginary Maps*.

Judging the book by its cover, one gets subtle indication of the interpretive challenges of *Imaginary Maps*. The nearly unrecognizable, sixteenth-century map of India that spans the book's jacket suggests that the India represented inside bears little resemblance either to Rushdie fiction or to *Lonely Planet* guides. Enclosed within this archaic cartography is a series of documents that aims to render legible the complex, contemporary connections between the abject lives of India's sixty million *adivasis* (literally, original inhabitants, or indigenous peoples), the nation-state of India, international development, financial, and political organizations like the World Bank and the United Nations, and the First World academy.[9]

The structure of the book also indicates the multilayered exchanges that constitute Mahasweta and Spivak's collaboration. A conversation between them at the beginning of the book provides an account of Mahasweta's literary and material work on behalf of India's Fourth World proto-nation. In introductory and concluding essays, Spivak attempts to guide the reception of Mahasweta's fiction in terms of her own evolving "feminist Marxist deconstructionist" ecological critical practice.[10] At the heart of the book, Mahasweta narrates (in Spivak's English) three fictional encounters between *adivasis* and those who seek, alternately and simultaneously, benevolently and malevolently, to help and to exploit them.

Mahasweta's transcribed conversation with Spivak does much to provide the beginnings of an immediate context for the stories, as well as a glimpse of what Spivak has called the "textile" of theory and practice, or fiction and action:[11] Here, Mahasweta describes in her own words the

relationship between literature, activist journalism, and grass-roots organizing in her decades of work on behalf of the tribal peoples and rural
poor in the Indian states of West Bengal, Bihar, and Orissa. The stories
themselves—"The Hunt," "Douloti the Bountiful," and the novella
"Pterodactyl, Puran Sahay, and Pirtha"—are difficult, compelling, alienating, and visceral. Most pressing to my concerns in this essay are the
ways in which Mahasweta embeds within the fiction a dramatization of
the difficulties of reading and writing about O/others. Spivak's question,
What is it to learn? can productively guide a reading of *Imaginary Maps,*
where Mahasweta seems to be asking, What is it to write?—a question
posed most explicitly in "Pterodactyl, Puran Sahay, and Pirtha." In the
internal voice of her journalist character Puran, Mahasweta disavows
"quick judgment" and insists upon acknowledging positionality in representation and reception, an admonition I have placed at the head of this
essay.
     While the stories, to varying degrees of explicitness, are fraught
with warnings about the perils of reading and writing, Spivak's framing
essays function at times as preemptive (presumptive?) scoldings for
readings gone wrong. As mediating documents between the First World
literary academy and Mahasweta's fiction,[12] Spivak's essays warn that
the fiction not be misread, read as a "romanticization of the tribal," or
"commodified as a 'national cultural artefact.' "[13] In a 1991 interview,
Spivak admitted that "I'm somewhat dismayed by the currency she [Ma-
hasweta] has received as a result of my translations and the quick fixes
that are being organized now on her."[14] Such a concern, that Mahasweta
has fallen prey to a kind of sinister "pitstop" criticism, helps to explain
the cautionary tone of Spivak's essays in *Imaginary Maps,* which occasionally veer towards viciousness. Alluding to archival materials she decided not to discuss in the essays, Spivak explains: "The misguided and
uninvolved benevolence that sometimes stands for political pedagogy in
the United States might find in this particular documentation as interesting a research novelty as Madonna" (xxvii).
     While it is true that Routledge published both *Imaginary Maps* and a
collection of takes on the Nancy Kerrigan/Tonya Harding episode in the
same year,[15] Spivak, perhaps, overstates the equal transparency of all
"texts" to critical/pedagogical scrutiny, at least when her immediate audience is a reader already twenty-some pages into *Imaginary Maps.* In
my own experience as a critic interested in/dedicated to human rights, I
have found the moments most full of gut-wrenching affect in my work to
be those when in conference presentations I read aloud from the texts I

have written about. Frequent glances around the audience are transformed for me, when reading Mahasweta's lyric prose, from a method of monitoring attention into a re-recognition of the power of her words. At the risk of pressing Spivak's point too far, or in the wrong direction, I do hope (and here I recognize that perhaps I am misguided, too well-meaning) that an audience recognizes a difference[16] between Madonna writhing on a bed and Mahasweta's character Douloti Nagesia collapsed on a chalk map of India, a difference between a lead pipe striking an Olympian's knee and an oxcart crushing Crook Nagesia's back. At the very least, Crook Nagesia doesn't have to ask "Why?"

The bonded laborers Douloti Nagesia and her father, Crook Nagesia, née Ganori Nagesia, are characters in "Douloti the Bountiful," the middle story in *Imaginary Maps*. Crook "earns" his new name after a steer disappears under his supervision and his bondmaster orders him to pull a cart in its place: "The scene is delightful. The big *officer's* Dad, the big landowner of the area, Munabar Singh Chandela has put the axle of the carriage on the shoulders of a human being and is screaming his abuse, shaking his whip in the air" (34).[17] Since Crook has borrowed three hundred rupees from Munabar and cannot work fast enough, even when healthy, to keep up with the usurious interest, he has no choice but to exchange Douloti, under pretext of marriage, to a brahman, for a remission of his loan. Douloti becomes a *kamiya*-whore, a bonded prostitute, and her earnings pay her loan hundreds of times over. She remains bonded until her bounty runs out, her body wracked by venereal disease and tuberculosis, and on the morning of August 15th, she collapses on a liquid chalk map of India prepared for that day's Independence celebration.

Mahasweta's unrelenting account of Douloti's patient suffering invites the reader into a world far removed from American pop culture icons and, indeed, Indian ones as well. Spivak rightly suggests that one of the most valuable aspects of Mahasweta's fiction, for readers on both sides of the black water, is the lie it gives both to the achievement of Indian Independence and to the conception of hyphenated Americanism as paradigmatic of the postcolonial condition:

. . . there is always a space in the new nation that cannot share in the energy of [the colonization–decolonization] reversal. This space had no established agency of traffic within the culture of imperialism. . . . If contemporary neocolonialism is seen only from the undoubtedly complex and important, but restrictive, perspective or explanatory context of metropolitan internal colonization of the postcolonial migrant or neocolonial immigrant, this particular scenario of displacement is cut out, becomes invisible, drops out of sight.[18]

Mahasweta targets this displaced, easily forgotten space in her fiction; in "Douloti," she points to a chain of moneylenders, bondmasters, lumber contractors, "development" and "relief" workers, industrialists, religious authorities, and government officials, who collude in the continuing oppression of *adivasis*. These figures are the personnel of economic development and national integration; it is they who carry out, at the economic, cultural, and human expense of the *adivasis,* what Spivak identifies in her afterword as "internal colonization in the name of decolonization" (205).

Mahasweta tells Spivak in conversation, "Each tribe is like a continent. But we never tried to know them. Never tried to respect them. . . . And we destroyed them" (xxi). Working against the silence and malign neglect imposed upon the tribals, Mahasweta herself dramatizes the dynamics and the implications of making the story of the *adivasis* heard. The brahman's offer to marry Douloti and free her family from bondslavery is "a strange fairy tale," and when benevolent-seeming outsiders come, wanting to provide relief and to hear the bonded tribals tell their stories, these events are also labeled "fairy tales" (49). Such fairy tales punctuate the narrative of "Douloti"; more grim(m) than Disney, they are not without a dark side. The informants are suspicious of the outsiders' capacity to understand or to help meaningfully; what relief they do provide ends when they leave; pimps sometimes appear in brahmans' saffron clothing. As the narrator of "Douloti" insists, "Everything would have remained a fairy tale, but the conclusion of the fairy tale is life, bloody, pain-filled life" (50).

While the characters in "Douloti the Bountiful" warily welcome those who would listen to and document their stories, "Pterodactyl, Puran Sahay, and Pirtha," the novella that follows "Douloti," measures, at length, the relative value and harm done by representations of *adivasi* life from the outside. This ongoing discussion in "Pterodactyl" provides another angle from which to examine Spivak's anxiety about "quick fixes" on Mahasweta's own work.

The *adivasi* inhabitants of Mahasweta's Pirtha face permanent famine exacerbated by drought; countless generations ago the Nagesia tribals found, on a barren hilltop, refuge from successive waves of encroachment on their land. The death knell of their existence seems to be the appearance of a creature, a prehistoric shadow, a pterodactyl posited by Mahasweta as the soul of their ancestors. When Puran, a mainstream Bihari journalist,[19] arrives in Nagesia village to get the scoop, he finds himself drawn into a debate about what story, if any, can and should be told about Pirtha. We get here an internal monologue, thought but not delivered aloud to Bikhia, a Nagesia with whom Puran shares the responsibility of caring for the pterodactyl:

> Bikhia, I don't want anyone to know of our dreadful discovery, because if we let them know there will be an invasion of the *media* of the inquisitive world. You will be shown on television, and the soul's warning message, the terrifying news of the tribal being of Pirtha, will all lose their perspective, by many analyses the rodent and the rhododendron will be proven the same. And who can tell, all the countries of the world will conduct investigations out of Pirtha everywhere, into the last forest, the last cave, to see where the prehistoric time and creature are still hidden. That invasion will be inevitable. (162)

While Puran fears the "inevitable" material encroachment of investigators moving in on Pirtha to get the story, his concern about an absence of perspective in their accounts is perhaps more relevant to Spivak's own anxiety about readings of Mahasweta's work. Rodent, rhododendron; Madonna, Mahasweta—in some ways, the undiscriminating hunger of the itinerant journalist and the peripatetic academic is the same. Both are creatures of the "inquisitive world."

Shankar, the most educated of the tribals in Pirtha, speaks for the community about the inadequacy of outsiders' representations of their plight. Kausalji, an NGO representative who wants to film Pirtha and his relief efforts there, encounters resistance to the filming that he cannot fathom, since increased visibility can only, to his mind, bring more aid. Shankar tells Puran in private: "Take *relief*, let 'em make *fillims*. We are hungry, naked poor. That will be known on the *fillims*. But the *fillims* won't say who made us hungry, naked, and poor. We don't beg, don't want to beg, will people understand this from those pictures?" (177). Shankar is worried both about Kausalji's representation of the cause of Pirtha's plight and about the audience's (in)ability to distinguish the rhetorical claims of the filmmaker from those of his subjects. While Kausalji would, in some sense, be pleading for aid from a potential audience, the people of Pirtha (at least in Shankar's mind) are not. Such a distinction is the crux of the complexity of reading "Pterodactyl." Bikhia manages the significance of the creature within his community, but his

self-imposed silence and the structure of the fictional narrative allow
Puran to be the interpreter of the event to a literate readership, including
both that of his newspaper and that of "Pterodactyl." That is to say, Puran
(as well as Mahasweta, in an authorial note),[20] and not the people of
Pirtha, identifies the pterodactyl as the vessel of a tribal ancestral soul
with a message that modern mainstream society cannot understand. The
unlikely medium is the unfathomable message. While the immediate result of the pterodactyl's appearance is an end to their death watch, their
period of mourning for countless calamities, "Pterodactyl" allows no access to what the pterodactyl actually said, or meant, to the people of
Pirtha.

Ironically, Spivak herself admits that she has fallen into the kind of
trap Shankar fearfully anticipates for Kausalji's film: she mistakes
Puran's representation of the pterodactyl, constructed by Mahasweta, for
the *adivasis*'s own take on it. Reproducing in her afterword an excerpt
from an address delivered in Cape Town, Spivak writes: "For the modern
Indian the pterodactyl is an empirical impossibility. For the modern
tribal Indian the pterodactyl is the soul of the ancestors" (204). For the
reader of *Imaginary Maps* who turns to the endnote after this statement,
the pterodactyl is no such thing: referring to Mahasweta's explanation of
the pterodactyl, Spivak comments, "This is counter-factual. 'The idea of
the ancestral soul is . . . my own,' Mahasweta writes in an authorial note
included with the story. She does not provide material for an anthropolo-
gistic romanticization" (213). I would add that Mahasweta not only dramatizes her experience with the tribals through the narrative of the
pterodactyl, but she also uses the mainstream character of Puran to illustrate the profound engagement, without absolute identification or transparency of representation, that constitutes her "estimation, born of
experience, of Indian tribal society." Within the realm of "Pterodactyl,"
the idea of the ancestral soul (as distinct from the material fact of the
creature) is accessible only as Puran's, not as Pirtha's.

The difficulty of distinguishing between the mediated layers of
Puran's experience of the pterodactyl, Mahasweta's explanation of it,
and Spivak's evolving interpretations of each indicates precisely the kind
of "many-leveled problem" that a reader of *Imaginary Maps* faces. Spivak's corrective footnote, which is literally the last word in *Imaginary
Maps,* only strengthens her argument that profound attention to specificity is imperative to do justice to Mahasweta's texts, which themselves
insist upon complicating the issue of representation. Spivak's own
process of learning to write on Mahasweta confirms Shankar's concerns

about misreadings and misrepresentations in Kausalji's film. Mahasweta is careful to problematize equally the notion of author (journalist, film-maker, fiction writer) and audience, including the nonliterate audience within Pirtha that finds itself the object of competing representations.

Messages from the government periodically reach the remote community at Pirtha in the form of posters aimed at educating the masses about family planning, health, and other social issues. Each of the posters is received differently by the audience in Pirtha, in terms that the government could not have anticipated. Reception is cool for a poster reading "End separatism, keep communal harmony intact, and renounce the path of violence," not for any communal sentiments in the audience, but rather because the "paper is not good, too thin" (153). For a leprosy treatment awareness poster, however, there is much demand: "The paper is good, the posters large-sized. The crowd has opined that it is a help that the government is giving such paper. Pasted on grass frames, such paper will keep out the wind. The women say they can lay their babies down on it. You can sift the relief food grains on it. It is useful in many ways" (174). Literacy and government-identified issue awareness are not exactly beyond the grasp of the audience in these exchanges; they are, more precisely, irrelevant, in the immediate sense, when the medium (with a "good" poster) makes itself available to so many necessary appropriations. My point here is not that literacy and practical education are useless or inappropriate for the people of Pirtha, but rather that these "readers" identify and grasp what they "need" in these government proclamations: their judgment of a message as successful would be seen by the government as failed reception.

This contest between pragmatic and failed reception helps to explain further the Nagesias's anxieties about Kausalji's film. The same woman who rejects the quality of the anti-communalism poster (too thin) pleads with Kausalji not to make his film. Identified only as "Dimag's wife" and "Motia's Ma," the woman rejects the second relational appellation, since her desperation forced her, in a cruel twist of irony, to sell her son immediately before relief arrived. She identifies an intellectually suspect yet experientially plausible cycle of relief, documentation, and exploitation, dependent upon her assumptions about the film's audience: "Why are you calling me Motia's Ma? Where is Motia? Take a *fillim* again, people will come again, they'll know famine is going on, again *tur-rucks* will come. They'll take all the children away" (168).

Kausalji cannot begin to take this subaltern logic seriously, as he assumes an absolute gulf between a benevolent (international) audience and a self-interested local one. The narrator summarizes Kausalji's response: ". . . all this should be captured in a documentary. Public opinion will be shaped, and relief help will come, in fact there are people and organizations in other countries of the world who think of the hungry humans of the Third World. . . . No child buyer will see this, but only those who need to see it" (168). Kausalji's argument, reliant on a conviction that his film is export quality, not intended for domestic consumption, has a certain appeal. Yet "Motia's Ma" has already demonstrated her ability to fill her own "needs" with a text directed at her only in the abstract: her "readings" of the posters are the best ones available without a concomitant governmental commitment to literacy and basic living conditions. With Kausalji's film, then, international and domestic audiences may very well see what they "need" to see, and these "needs" will not necessarily parallel the Nagesia's needs, nor Kausalji's stated intentions.

Even without the model of "Motia's Ma" as reader, however, Kausalji's ostensibly reasonable perspective must be considered alongside the big picture of his plan for Pirtha. The Nagesias' "irrational" attachments to the land notwithstanding, Kausalji offers to move the community down into the fertile valley below: economically sensible, culturally questionable. But that's not all; here Kausalji opposes Harisharan, the Block Development Officer, and his plan to dig wells on the hillside for the Nagesias: "If you help them that much they will get entrenched here. But this place has been *condemned*. If you can move them, and plant some more trees, this spot with the river, the hills, and the trees will make an excellent *picnic* area. In Madhopura my brother-in-law is the Managing Director of State Tourism. . . ." (151). While Kausalji's brother-in-law may not be among those who "need" to see his film, the Managing Director of State Tourism will certainly benefit from an international "reading" of the film that responds with funding for moving the community off the hillside. Kausalji considers "Motia's Ma's" fears of an opportunistic (or pragmatic) reading of the film to be an instance of failed reception that cannot possibly happen, but his own intentions for the film and Pirtha are not very different from the consequences that "Motia's Ma" fears.

Though a bit removed from Spivak's critique of uninvolved academic benevolence, Kausalji's master plan points to what Spivak might call a "traffic line" between Oxfam events in the North and leisure activities for India's growing middle class. Mahasweta's own work organizing self-help projects for tribals has drawn upon the cachet of ethnic chic: she has successfully encouraged tribal groups to produce and market handicrafts, one might suppose even in the air-conditioned government emporia one finds in the modern commercial centers of India's major cities. Purchasers of such precious artifacts probably do not recognize that some of these communities "never did handicraft work before" a market was created for it (xiv). At least in the case of the handicrafts, the joke is on the consumer; Mahasweta's sustained critique of India's development policies and their implementation, however, suggests that the funds for the transformation of the "condemned" hilltop into Pirtha Picnic Palace would be those earmarked for tribal development.

These audiences—international and domestic, with direct financial stakes in what kinds of stories are told about oppressed and marginalized peoples such as the *adivasis*—provide a partial explanation for Spivak's wary choice to make her work on and with Mahasweta public, even though she insists always on the peril of (mis)reading. In her afterword, Spivak refers to a 1992 World Bank initiative to collect and apply " 'indigenous knowledge' " in the service of Work Bank-sponsored agricultural development (199). She identifies the value of cultural studies in providing an oppositional critique to such a project, in which

> 'technical papers' that will extract methods from so-called 'indigenous knowledge' will not be accompanied by any change of mind-set in the researchers. By contrast, we draw out from literary and social texts some impossible, yet necessary project of changing the minds that innocently support a vicious system. That is what 'learning from below' means here. (200)

Insisting upon the complicity between world organizations and worldly criticism, Spivak nonetheless retains the hope (and the imperative) for a critical practice that can do better, not least through acknowledgment of its complicity. A case in point: the dedication of *Imaginary Maps* reads, "FOR ALL THE INDIGENOUS PEOPLES OF THE WORLD." While the playful reader might be inclined to give the dedication a second glance and remark, "Why, we're *all* indigenous peoples of the *world*!" the recent trope of the global tribe in telecommunications advertising suggests the costs of such a reductive reading.[21] It may be a Madison Avenue small world, after all, but Mahasweta's fiction reminds us of the ever-widening gulfs within it and points towards the forces that benefit from obscuring those distances.

Thus in "Pterodactyl," Puran finds himself caught between the urgency of making a story heard and the contamination of available means of storytelling. After the pterodactyl arrives in the hut where he is staying, Puran weighs his responsibilities to Pirtha against the dangers of fulfilling them. Speaking with Harisharan, the BDO and his old friend, Puran admits, "I am realizing how barbaric it is to photograph skeletal men and women" (147). Harisharan's response is brutally pragmatic, suggesting the gulf between the truth-value and use-value of Puran's anxiety: "Please avoid that realization. Make an uproar about Pirtha. Otherwise for me to do anything will be very . . ." difficult, one assumes. Harisharan's perspective recalls Mahasweta's insistence to Spivak that "What we need is mass-based public opinion formation, pressure on the government, vigilance" (xx). Yet "Pterodactyl" itself dramatizes the ethical and practical difficulties of such an undertaking. Consequently, Puran's tentative agreement to publicize what he's seen in Pirtha, both to the press and the state government, emerges with a concurrent understanding of the importance of focus. He demands one condition of Harisharan in exchange for his support: "Don't let them see Bikhia's drawing [of the pterodactyl]. Don't let them hear that stuff about the ancestor's soul. Let them be concerned only about this permanent famine. Otherwise their enthusiasm will veer the other way. Bikhia will become the center of their discussion, surely you don't want that?" (147). Puran's emergent understanding of the politics of reception suggests that the spectacle of human suffering, whatever its own representational pitfalls, simply cannot compete with the discovery of something out of *Jurassic Park;* Puran sees the hyphen-thin line between info or edu and tainment.[22]

Even without Spivak's admonitions, then, and in spite of Mahasweta's explanation that "I have merely tried to express my estimation, born of experience, of Indian tribal society, through the myth of the pterodactyl" (196), the reader of "Pterodactyl" as the unabridged account of Puran's extraordinary experience feels herself to be in possession of a terrible secret, with some awareness of the awesome responsibility of that privilege. Puran, like the reader, returns to "normal life" at the end of the novella, aware, however, that having "discovered what love for Pirtha there is in his heart, perhaps he cannot remain a distant spectator anywhere in life" (196). Recognizing his implication in the appearance of the creature and whatever it signifies, and at the same time the impossibility of identification with Bikhia, with whom he shares the responsibility of caring for the pterodactyl, Puran can be neither "distant" nor "spectator," but he cannot exactly be a "close participant" either. Mahasweta thus exposes the peril inherent in what may seem to be the "safe distance" from which we read *Imaginary Maps*. This distance is crucial in reading "The Hunt," the first story in the collection, from something like the First World, the "inquisitive world," where the secret of the pterodactyl must compete with our expectations of Third World women's narratives.

While the characters in "Douloti" and "Pterodactyl" refer explicitly to the fairy tale as a figure of both promising fantasy and unattainable (and thus harmful) fiction, "The Hunt" makes itself available to be read as a fairy tale of the Disney PG-13 variety. With the ubiquitous "once upon a time" in the first two lines, the hero(ine) who can do the work of twelve men, the villain who metamorphoses between man and beast, and the triumph of good over evil, the story of Mary Oraon provides a brief glimpse at a happy ending, complete with an implied marriage, in a book full of tragedy and nightmare.

"The Hunt" is also the most anthology- and syllabus-friendly of the stories in *Imaginary Maps*. The story of a racially hybrid woman who overcomes the sexual threat of a vulgar out-of-town member of the dominant society, all narrated in seventeen pages, is, and I must agree with Spivak here, likely grist for the mill of a naïve political pedagogy, whether feminist, multicultural, postcolonial, or environmental. When Tehsildar Singh, a lumber contractor, comes to the remote village of Kuruda to acquire the sacred sal trees that provide food and cultural continuity to the Oraon community, Mary Oraon recognizes the threat that he poses. She also resents his sexual overtures towards her, and by luring him into the forest on the day of a traditional women's hunting festival, she seemingly eliminates both the threat to her body and the threat to her community's relationship to the land. But Mary Oraon must be "read" in at least two ways. "At a distance," the narrator tells us as Mary Oraon first comes into view, "she looks most seductive, but close up you see a strong message of rejection in her glance" (2). From a "safe distance," the story of "The Hunt" is itself seductive, but in context, easy readings of feminist resistance are thrown off by the narrative.

In many respects, Mary is seemingly a role model for a brand of Third World feminism defined from the distance of the First World.[23] Traveling regularly to the nearby market town of Tohri to sell the estate's produce—as well as her own fiercely defended reserve forest produce—allows Mary to approximate financial autonomy and unimpeded mobility. Sexually, too, Mary is her own woman. She chooses to marry Jalim, a Muslim trader in Tohri who once protected her from a fight, only when he has saved one hundred rupees; Mary has quietly stored away at least that much. When Tehsildar Singh's unwanted advances strain her patience, she invokes cultural constraints upon women to delay strategically Tehsildar's advances, claiming that she is "unclean" and must wait until the next day, the day of the hunt, to tryst with him (13).

But Mahasweta makes clear that Mary is not a ready-made role model for the Third (or Fourth) World Woman, if only by accident of her birth. The illegitimate child of an Oraon woman and the Australian male heir of the sal estate in Kuruda, Mary moves from and through Kuruda, spatially and culturally, in a way unavailable to even the high caste family, the Prasads, who currently own the estate. "Everyone," even the Prasads, "is afraid of Mary" (5). Mary's mixed blood is repeatedly identified as the source of her power: when Mary raises her machete in defense of her right to forest produce, or sets the terms of her relationship with Jalim, the narrator editorializes, "It figures. White blood," or "the power of Australian blood" (4, 3).

Mary understands the advantages of the singularity of her position; had she "resembled any Oraon girl," she would not be free to come and go to Tohri, nor to attach herself to Jalim (6). Yet the narrator indicates Mary's ambivalence about this position:

> Because she is the illegitimate daughter of a white father the Oraons don't think of her as their blood and do not place the harsh injunctions of their own society upon her. She would have rebelled if they had. She is unhappy that they don't. In her inmost heart there is somewhere a longing to be part of the Oraons. She would have been very glad, if, when she was thirteen or fourteen, some brave Oraon lad had pulled her into marriage. (6)

It is not Mary's desire for community, signified here by traditional marriage, that disqualifies her from being a feminist heroine, but rather the fact that she cannot, in the end, be "part of the Oraons," even when she revitalizes their own traditions.

Mahasweta describes the traditional Festival of Justice as an annual hunt, after which "the elders would bring offenders to justice" (xviii). Every twelfth year women take their turn at the hunt. Since years of encroachments have depleted the forests of game, Mary revitalizes both the hunt and its judiciary function when she arranges to meet the contractor Tehsildar Singh in the forest on the day of the hunt and subsequently "kill[s] the biggest beast" (17). The spectacular nature of the story's climax, which Mary experiences "with deep satisfaction. . . . [a]s if she has been infinitely satisfied in a sexual embrace," seems to advocate the sexual autonomy of a woman who can recognize Tehsildar for the beast that he is and deal with him as such. What is perhaps lost in the denouement, however, are the implications of Mary's action.

At the beginning of the story, the narrator traces the railway line near Kuruda and describes a billboard that reads " 'Kuruda *Outstation, Abandoned*' " (1). The village was probably cut off from rail service because it was not profitable. "The Hunt" suggests that Tehsildar Singh is only the first of many contractors interested not only in obtaining Kuruda's forest resources, but also in having the transportation infrastructure "developed" in order to make the extraction of lumber more cost-effective. Kuruda, in other words, is not likely to be "Abandoned" for long. When Mary is unable to persuade anyone in Kuruda (from the estate owner to the Oraons who will provide cheap labor for the felling) to resist Tehsildar's plan to take their trees, she takes action against him. But with Tehsildar dead, his money at her waist, she follows the railway line away from Kuruda, "abandoning" it on her way to Jalim, Tohri, and points beyond. By following Mary in her triumph as she abandons Kuruda, the reader may also be tempted to think of Kuruda as only the one-dimensional "setting" in which Mary's tale unfolds.

A reader looking single-mindedly for textual examples of gendered subaltern autonomy and resistance may experience a "deep satisfaction" with Mary's revenge—a satisfaction that obscures the causes of the plight of those who remain in places like Kuruda. The trajectory of Mary's wonderful tale in no way changes the lives of the Oraons in Kuruda, and her own singularity lessens the likelihood of her resistance becoming exemplary. Other contractors will come; Prasad will sell his trees again; future hunts (if there is any forest left) will find no more beasts to kill. If Mary's triumph allows the reader to abandon consideration of Kuruda, the secret of the pterodactyl is betrayed: the attraction of the fantastic overwhelms attention to more "mundane" suffering and exploitation. To reverse the emphasis of the narrator's reminder in "Douloti," "In the world of Seora village, Bono is just as true as Ganori" (31); the story of the *adivasi* whose back is broken under the burden of bondslavery is just as true as that of the one who throws off his (or her) bonds and escapes.

Read as fairy tales and as evaluations of the promise and betrayal of fairy tales, "The Hunt," "Douloti," and "Pterodactyl" seem to argue against Disneyesque, seductive celebrations of the fantastic and their reassuring resolutions, and in favor of the more ambivalent narratives associated with the Grimms. The secret of the pterodactyl obliges a reader to

244

Resistant Readings

look beneath the veneer of Mary Oraon's seemingly magical kingdom to the menacing social contradictions potentially obscured by her temperamental abandon and her geographic abandonment of Kuruda. In Mahasweta's fiction, there is much to marvel at and much to abhor.

Mahasweta would probably add that in her stories there is much to love. This love is no comfortable fondness for a favorite book, but rather a vision of a life-giving relationship between intellect and emotion, or between thinking and living. Puran's experience in "Pterodactyl" challenges his penchant for "book learning" and its invitation to uninvolved abstraction. But Mahasweta does not permit a romanticized disavowal of intellectualism; Puran cannot go native. "How can he have faith in their faith? Puran must keep unshaken his faith in paper, pen, and the printing machine. Puran has nothing else. . . . The forest is not Puran's nurse. For him the pen" (186). What transforms Puran's heretofore mercenary relationship to the pen, however, is his profound response to Pirtha: "Only love, a tremendous, excruciating, explosive love can still dedicate us to this work when the century's sun is in the western sky" (196). In her final comment to Spivak, Mahasweta underscores the idea that Puran's challenge is also the reader's: "Our double task is to resist 'development' actively and to learn to love" (xxii).

Spivak explains Mahasweta's imperative "to learn to love" in terms more sympathetic to deconstruction: "ethical responsibility-in-singularity . . . in view of the impossibility of communication" (200). Her elaboration of this idea recalls both the encounters within *Imaginary Maps* and her own encounters with Mahasweta's work:

> We all know that when we engage profoundly with one person, the responses come from both sides: this is responsibility and accountability. We also know that in such engagements we want to reveal and reveal, conceal nothing. Yet on both sides there is always a sense that something has not got across. This we call the "secret," not something that one wants to conceal, but something that one wants to reveal. . . . In this secret singularity, the object of ethical action is not an object of benevolence, for here responses flow from both sides. (translator's preface, xxv)

Mahasweta would have us resist the one-sided "development" of the Third and Fourth worlds that is touted as First World benevolence. Instead, this "two way road—with the compromised other as teacher" (202), seems to be the heart of the answer to Spivak's question, "What is it to learn?" Because there is always something that "has not got across," and because of "the impossibility of 'love' in the one-on-one way for each human being," this ethical singularity, Mahasweta's "learn[ing] to love," is both necessary and impossible (xxv).

Spivak describes her collaboration with Mahasweta as an "embrace," in which Mahasweta has pulled her "from the web of her fiction into the weaving of her work" (205). While this relationship certainly approximates a kind of ethical singularity, what is more significant here is whether a reader can enter this embrace and learn, in the sense of ethical singularity, from *Imaginary Maps*. Can the text itself be that "compromised other as teacher"? On the one hand, Spivak's choice to end *Imaginary Maps* with a revision of her misreading of "Pterodactyl" represents a process of repeated revealing, a process of learning, that demands listening to another and reconsidering one's responses and responsibilities. *Imaginary Maps* does indeed "reveal and reveal," and yet, if the difference between benevolence and ethical singularity is that "responses flow from both sides," it seems dangerous to assume that one can "learn to love" merely by (re)reading *Imaginary Maps*. The text's "responses" to a reader's responses to it come necessarily from the reader, and the compromised nature of this exchange seems much more than merely symptomatic of always imperfect human intersubjectivity. Ethical singularity as a model for learning to read Mahasweta, then, is a kind of fairy tale: enabling in its possibilities, but limited by the constraints of real life. As Mahasweta's stories so painstakingly demonstrate, readers and writers mistake fairy tales (and texts) for real life at their peril.

It seems imperative, then, to consider, if only briefly, "real life" as framed within and beyond the fairy tales of *Imaginary Maps*. Mahasweta's conversation with Spivak begins to document the history and contemporary conditions that shape *adivasi* lives in India. Even in the stories themselves, Mahasweta shifts between a mythic mode and a documentary one quite similar to that of her journalism. She claims for each of the stories a kind of truth; "I know that area like the palm of my hand. . . . Every event narrated within that story is true," she says of "The Hunt," and she claims to have "seen with my own eyes" the people who become Mary Oraon, Douloti Nagesia, and Crook Nagesia in the fiction (xviii). Yet the specificity of her empirical knowledge, earned by traversing entire regions on foot, is simultaneously extrapolated into "a mirror of tribal India" (xii). Unlike with "Pterodactyl," in which Mahasweta explicitly transforms one remote village into *adivasi* society, the other stories are situated with geographic specificity, at the same time that she claims of both that they are "true, and true for the rest of India" (xx). Learning to read Mahasweta is thus, in part, learning to distinguish between the registers of her truth claims.

This learning seems to me impossible without reading the stories in some kind of historical context. While I have focused in this essay on the ways in which *Imaginary Maps* problematizes the transformation of reading into writing and thus, in some way, teaches a reader to read it, this method of reading is woefully incomplete even outside of the model of ethical singularity. In her afterword, Spivak admits that her previous critical interventions accompanying her translations of Mahasweta's work have suffered from an "insufficient preparation in the specific political situation of the Indian tribal" (197). The conversation between Mahasweta and Spivak at the beginning of the book is aimed at correcting this inadequacy. But Mahasweta's account of her experience, though specific and profound, nearly elides a crucial aspect of *adivasi* engagement with Indian political life; a reader without an awareness of this aspect of *adivasi* "real life" may be misled by the historical claims that Mahasweta's fairy tales seem to make.

Spivak argues that ethical singularity is the necessary supplement of collective struggle, and thus one might look for the convergence between "learn[ing] to love" and learning to resist together in *Imaginary Maps* (Translator's preface, xxv). This proposition is based not merely on a desire for theoretical consistency, but more on the "specific political situation of the Indian tribal." For nearly a century, tribals in parts of West Bengal, Bihar, Orissa, and Madhya Pradesh—the region that Mahasweta knows so well and portrays in her fiction—have been engaged in a struggle to improve their lives, to have their interests recognized in the post-Independence process of national integration, to regain control over their land and its natural and economic resources, and to win political autonomy for the region they refer to as Jharkhand.

This movement has consistently suffered internal divisions, from its origins in the beginning of the century in Christian missionary outreach, to its development into a tribal autonomy movement at mid-century, and its current status as a regional movement encompassing both tribals and non-tribal agricultural laborers. Beyond the regional level, national movements for tribal autonomy have very recently won small victories; at the international level, indigenous peoples are attempting to define and protect their rights through the United Nations Working Group on Indigenous Peoples.[24]

Despite her claim that "Wherever there is someone fighting for the tribal cause, I am fortunate enough to be linked with it," Mahasweta makes almost no mention of Jharkhand. In *Imaginary Maps,* those fighting for the tribals are, for the most part, not tribals themselves. Her only explicit mention of Jharkhand in *Imaginary Maps* suggests a tension between abjection and agency in her estimation of the tribals: "They are the suffering spectators of the India that is traveling toward the twenty-first century. That is why they protest, that is why there is Jharkhand" (xi). In addition to Douloti's silent suffering and Mary Oraon's limited protest, there is Jharkhand. Mahasweta may have her own reasons for not incorporating a more thorough depiction of *adivasi* collective struggle in these stories, but the distant reader must understand that Mahasweta's representation of *adivasis* in *Imaginary Maps* is only one among many.[25] Without a consideration of the many ways in which indigenous peoples are striving to represent themselves in regional, national, and international arenas, we risk mistaking Mahasweta's rhetorical claims for those that *adivasis* might make, much as the Nagesias fear we might do with Kausalji's film. The paper of the Routledge *Imaginary Maps* is acid-free, of good quality; the book has many uses for a reader of the "inquisitive world." In reading *Imaginary Maps,* a reader takes the necessary risk of bringing her own needs and desires to those of Spivak, Mahasweta, the characters, and their "real-life" models, all already competing in the book. Thus, one potential lesson of *Imaginary Maps* is that the responses we construct are always fairy tales that we want and need to hear; these fairy tales are never innocent.

NOTES

[1]Mahasweta Devi, *Imaginary Maps: Three Stories by Mahasweta Devi,* trans. Gayatri Chakravorty Spivak (New York: Routledge, 1995), 116–119.

[2]With Sneja Gunew, in *The Post-colonial Critic: Interviews, Strategies, Dialogues,* Sarah Harasym, ed. (New York: Routledge, 1990), 62–63.

[3]See "'Draupadi' by Mahasweta Devi," in *Critical Inquiry* (Winter 1981), 381–402 (with translator's foreword); " 'Draupadi' by Mahasweta Devi," in *In Other Worlds: Essays in Cultural Politics* (New York: Routledge, 1988), 179–186 (with translator's foreword); and "Draupadi," in Mahasweta Devi, *Bashai Tudu,* trans. Samik Bandyopadhyay and Gayatri Spivak (Calcutta: Thema, 1990), 149–162.

[4]I will employ both the Bengali and American conventions of respectful reference to proper names, as appropriate.

[5]See especially six stories by Mahasweta in Kalpana Bardhan's *Of Women, Outcastes, Peasants, and Rebels* (Berkeley: U of California P, 1990).

[6]"Acting Bits/Identity Talk," *Critical Inquiry* 18 (Summer 1992), 773. As I am working toward a proficiency in Hindi but cannot read Bengali, I will not explore the myriad issues surrounding the production and reading of a translated text; my focus will be on what Spivak writes in English rather than her engagement with Mahasweta's Bengali. For a brief discussion of Spivak's translations of Mahasweta's work, see Sujit Mukherjee, "Mahasweta Devi's Writings—An Evaluation," *Book Review*, xv, 3 (May-June 1991), 30–31, to which Spivak responds in her "translator's preface."

[7]Afterword, *Imaginary Maps*, 197.

[8]I use the term "First World" advisedly, since "the West" and "the North" do not sufficiently connote the neo-imperialist tendencies of EuroAmerican political, economic, and intellectual projects. The disappearance of the Second World and the mobilization of the Fourth World—a global population of indigenous peoples—complicate, but do not make unmeaningful, the economic and geographic assumptions of Three Worlds theories. Indeed, one of the projects of *Imaginary Maps* is to show how both the First World and the Third World participate in the oppression, in the name of "development," of India's indigenous peoples.

[9]An excerpt from Spivak's afterword may help to delineate further this cartography, whereby Mahasweta suggests the "complicity, however apparently remote, of the power lines of local developers with the forces of global capital. . . . [A] strong connection, indeed a complicity, between the bourgeoisie of the Third World and migrants in the First cannot be ignored. We have to keep this particularly in mind because this is also the traffic line in Cultural Studies" (198–9).

[10]I borrow and add to Colin McCabe's 1987 description of Spivak, since her continuing work on Mahasweta suggests yet another set of "contradictions, traces, inscriptions" (foreword, *In Other Worlds,* ix).

[11]See, for example, translator's preface, xxiv; afterword, 201; and "Acting Bits/Identity Talk," 794–5.

[12]I refer here strictly to the Routledge edition published in New York and London. Spivak indicates that because of the book's simultaneous publication by Thema in Calcutta, "it faces two directions, encounters two readerships" (translator's preface, xxiii). Elsewhere she indicates that she planned to write a separate introduction for each edition (Sara Danius and Stefan Jonsson, "An Interview with Gayatri Chakravorty Spivak," *boundary* 2 20, 2 [1993]: 34). I have not yet had the opportunity to compare the two editions, and my focus here, for the most part, is not on the Indian readership.

[13]Afterword, 199; translator's preface, xxiii.

[14]"An Interview with Gayatri Chakravorty Spivak," 34.

[15]Cynthia Baughman, ed., *Women on Ice: Feminist Essays on the Tonya Harding/Nancy Kerrigan Spectacle* (New York: Routledge, 1995).

[16]I use *a difference* and not *the difference* because I believe that there are multiple differences available between the cases; I do not mean to construct an easy hierarchy of suffering within which to locate the suffering of Mahasweta's characters and Nancy Kerrigan (or Tonya Harding or even Madonna). What makes each case a "research novelty," in the sense of "new" or "different," not in Spivak's sense of a passing distraction, must be made clear, and the claims made from that case must be based within its own specific context.

[17]In all quotations from the stories in *Imaginary Maps,* italicized words indicate that Mahasweta used those words in English in the Bengali original.

[18]"Woman in Difference," in *Outside in the Teaching Machine* (New York: Routledge, 1993), 78.

[19]Mahasweta locates Pirtha in the state of Madhya Pradesh, literally and geographically India's "Middle State." Bihar, which, like Madhya Pradesh, has a substantial *adivasi* population, lies to the northeast of Madhya Pradesh and is India's poorest state. I provide this information with a proviso from Mahasweta's authorial note to the novella: "In this piece no name—such as Madhya Pradesh or Nagesia—has been used literally. Madhya Pradesh here is India, Nagesia village the entire tribal society" (196).

[20]"I have deliberately conflated the ways, rules, and customs of different Austric tribes and groups, and the idea of the ancestral soul is also my own. I have merely tried to express my estimation, born of experience, of Indian tribal society, through the myth of the pterodactyl" (196).

[21]Most egregious in this genre was an AT&T television ad in late 1995 that made an analogy between "traditional" communications by drum in New Guinea and satellite-facilitated global communications networks. "But our world is a little bigger," the commercial concluded, "and our tribe includes all mankind." My thanks to Joseph Slaughter for an ongoing shared discussion of this trope.

[22]Anecdotally speaking, friends in Varanasi, in the state of Uttar Pradesh in northern India, tell me that *Jurassic Park* was the must-see movie there in the summer of 1994. Puran himself would label my allusion both inaccurate and unmeaningful; he locates the pterodactyl in "the axial moment of the end of the third phase of the Mesozoic and the beginnings of the Cenozoic geological age. . . . The Mesozoic ended in a tremendous turbulence, with the inception of the ancestors of the human being, and the Cenozoic, which is still going on, got its start. That is when the continents drifted again and took their current shape. You [the pterodactyl] were supposed to have become extinct then" (156). Any maps that the pterodactyl could have imagined, in other words, would have been very different from the subsequent ones that Mahasweta interrogates.

[23]"The Hunt," "Douloti," and Mahasweta's extraliterary comments about the position of women in Indian and tribal society add a necessary, additional

laycr of complexity to the issue of Third World feminism(s) discussed in Chandra Talpade Mohanty's well-known essay, "Under Western Eyes: Feminist Scholarship and Colonial Discourse," in Mohanty, Ann Russo, and Lourdes Torres (eds.), *Third World Women and the Politics of Feminism* (Bloomington: Indiana UP, 1991), 51–88.

[24]For information on Jharkhand, see especially Susana B. C. Devalle, *Discourses of Ethnicity: Culture and Protest in Jharkhand* (New Delhi: Sage, 1992) and K. S. Singh, ed., *Tribal Movements in India,* vol. 2 (New Delhi: Manohar, 1982). The Fourth World Documentation Project Home Page (http://www.halcyon.com/FWDP/fwdp.html) is an excellent source of information on international movements of indigenous peoples.

[25]I refer specifically to the stories in *Imaginary Maps,* which are more widely available in English than others of Mahasweta's stories that narrate 19th and 20th century *adivasi* resistance. Mahasweta has previously stated an aversion to "narrow party politics," for "All parties to the Left as well as to the Right have failed to keep their commitment to the common people" (qtd. in Samik Bandhyopadhyay, Introduction, *Five Plays* by Mahasweta Devi, trans. Samik Bandhyopadhyay (Calcutta: Seagull, 1986), x). In "The Call Never Comes: Unemployment Among Tribals" (*Economic and Political Weekly,* July 9, 1983, 1216–17), Mahasweta expresses a similar concern about Jharkhand specifically: "It is very, very bad to be a Jharkhandi in this state," for Jharkhand's association with socialism and terrorism hampers individual tribals' attempts to improve their lot.

WORKS CITED

Bardhan, Kalpana. *Of Women, Outcastes, Peasants, and Rebels*. Berkeley: U of California P, 1990.

Baughman, Cynthia, ed. *Women on Ice: Feminist Essays on the Tonya Harding/Nancy Kerrigan Spectacle*. New York: Routledge, 1995.

Danius, Sara and Stefan Jonsson. "An Interview with Gayatri Chakravorty Spivak." *boundary 2* 20, 2 (1993): 24–50.

Devalle, Susana B. C. *Discourses of Ethnicity: Culture and Protest in Jharkhand*. New Delhi: Sage, 1992.

Devi, Mahasweta. "The Call Never Comes: Unemployment Among Tribals." *Economic and Political Weekly,* 9 July 1983. 1216–17.

———. *Five Plays*. Bandhyopadhyay, Samik, trans. Calcutta: Seagull, 1986.

———. "Draupadi." *Mahasweta Devi, Bashai Tudu,* trans. Samik Bandyopadhyay and Gayatri Spivak. Calcutta: Thema, 1990. 149–162.

—————. *Imaginary Maps: Three Stories by Mahasweta Devi.* Gayatri Chakravorty Spivak, trans. New York: Routledge, 1995.

Mohanty, Chandra Talpade, Ann Russo, and Lourdes Torres, eds. "Under Western Eyes: Feminist Scholarship and Colonial Discourse." In *Third World Women and the Politics of Feminism.* Bloomington: Indiana UP, 1991. 51–88.

Mukherjee, Sujit. "Mahasweta Devi's Writings—An Evaluation." *Book Review,* xv, 3 (May–June 1991): 30–31.

Singh, K. S., ed. *Tribal Movements in India,* Vol. 2. New Delhi: Manohar, 1982.

Spivak, Gayatri Chakravorty. "Acting Bits/Identity Talk." *Critical Inquiry* 18, 4 (Summer 1992): 770–803.

—————. *Outside in the Teaching Machine.* New York: Routledge, 1993.

—————, with Sneja Gunew. *The Post-colonial Critic: Interviews, Strategies, Dialogues.* Sarah Harasym, ed. New York: Routledge, 1990.

—————, trans. "'Draupadi' by Mahasveta Devi." *Critical Inquiry* 8, 2 (Winter 1981): 381–402.

—————, trans. "'Draupadi' by Mahasweta Devi." In *In Other Worlds: Essays in Cultural Politics.* New York: Routledge, 1988. 179–186.

—————, and Samik Bandyopadhyay, trans. "Draupadi." Mahasweta Devi, *Bashai Tudu,* trans. Calcutta: Thema, 1990. 149–162.

Trajectories of Change: The Politics of Reading Postcolonial Women's Texts in the Undergraduate Classroom

SALLY Mc WILLIAMS

In the United States undergraduate literature classroom, issues of identity politics complicate the study of international fiction and theory authored by women with connections to postcolonial societies.[1] How do we, both students and instructors, read texts from cultures other than the ones with which we are most familiar from daily experience? What literary and social criteria are we to use in analyzing the protagonists' actions and beliefs in texts from postcolonial societies, given the differences between their representations of experiences and our American context? Such questions hinge on the connecting line between identity politics and the politics of interpretation. Identity politics foregrounds the positionalities that readers construct and deploy in their analyses of literary and theoretical texts. To understand how the positionalities of readers function in relation to the production of knowledge through literary and theoretical interpretation, we must investigate how student-critics conceptualize the dialectical relationship between themselves and the voices presented in the international fiction and theory they read.

Unlike the study of American literature, for example, the study of international fiction presents students with the difficulty of seeing themselves as already implicated in the issues invoked by the assigned reading material. As in all literature classes, they attempt to delineate a critical space from which to generate meaning; the difference in an international fiction course is that no unproblematical interpretive stance readily presents itself. The student-critics with whom I've recently worked have opted to employ a hierarchical reading paradigm; they explain (however well-meaning and sincere) that they have signed up for a course on international fiction to "observe" the "authentic Other" through her "own" words. This ethnographic articulation may initially suggest that the object under scrutiny will form the focal point of the interpretation. But instead of letting the texts speak, the student-critics center themselves in the analytical process by defending their rights to interpret the texts as they see fit, which oftentimes means transforming complex cultural and historical situations and associations into United States-based analogies or oppositions. Their initial interpretive strategies function in one of two ways and offer complementary colonizing strategies. According to one method, they try to interpret the texts according to criteria they have used for everything they have ever read, thereby eradicating any differences that threaten their frameworks of interpretation (a strategy I call the "we are one" point of view).[2] Searching for similarities favors their Western values and standards; this way of reading can quickly move into a prejudicial approach, one in which thematic, stylistic, and narrative qualities that are not in the students' repertoire of literary and/or lived experiences are deemed as unintelligible and, thus, inferior. This need for commonalties or unity to the exclusion of differences is the basis for this type of colonizing reading strategy. The flip side of "we are one" is another colonizing approach, which takes the text as a representation of the "exotic Other." In this approach, the students see only differences and hold at arms' distance any influence the text might exert on their interpretive knowledges. Differences become defining examples of foreign otherness; the disorientation of such perceived otherness pushes some students into an isolationist stance.

The challenge I face, shared by many of my colleagues who teach world literature and United States multicultural literatures[3] in departments of English in the United States, is to assist students so that they may begin to see how their role as critical readers does not require them to position themselves and the texts within this either/or dyad for interpretation. By examining their reading strategies, the students reexamine their relationships to the assigned texts: What happens in the process of reading if students assume neither the position of master interpreter of the text nor that of a passive audience member hearing an authentic voice of truth? A closer look at how the politics of location impacts the politics of reception opens the way to a multifaceted discussion about interpretive approaches, hierarchies of authority surrounding types of texts (theoretical vs. literary, for example), and the role of authenticity ("who has the right to speak?") in the production of knowledge in the classroom.

The focus of my course "Women Prose Writers" offered at Montclair State University in the spring 1995 semester was to explore how women from various countries represent the complexities of women's experiences and the different spaces to which they have access in their lives. The course had four aims: (1) to explore how material and discursive circumstances affect the struggles women confront and challenge; (2) to analyze the concept of marginality in its various modalities and its relationship to questions of power and gender formation; (3) to deconstruct naturalized hierarchies among types of peoples, discourses, and texts; and (4) to examine the complicated processes of interpretation and identification that occur in the classroom. Some of the questions that formed the backdrop of our class discussions were: How do women writers of both literature and literary theory conceive of gender and its relationship to other aspects of women's identities? What geographical, personal, and imaginative spaces do women occupy, disrupt, create? In what ways do women move through the world, both literally and figuratively? How is the desire for access to language represented in the narratives? And what avenues to the powers of discourse are opened by the narrative and theoretical texts themselves and in conjunction with each other? We read an array of novelists and theorists from various countries so that we could explore the concept of marginality in some breadth. In each case, the text or essay displayed not only different avenues into the broad topic of marginality, but also a critical analysis of the topic. The meta-critical stances elaborated by both literary and theoretical narratives set the scene for our class discussions on the politics of location, interpretation, and authority. This combination of narratives and theoretical essays from across the globe posed the primary problem of how to approach the selected texts in ways that allow for productive readings to occur, without overshadowing the texts with United States-influenced and -bound interpretive strategies.[4]

In crafting the syllabus for the course, I confronted two sets of student anxieties, the first having to do with the literature and the second having to do with the theoretical materials assigned for the course. On the first day of class the students expressed their anxieties about the literature in one of two ways: (1) since they couldn't know everything about the author's country of origin and the text's setting prior to reading the novel, they felt they couldn't even begin to understand the narrative and might mistakenly misinterpret the texts; and (2) as experienced readers, they could read these texts by placing full responsibility with the author to make the story clear, but felt uncomfortable with their role as passive readers who demand that the writer explain the cultural and narrative contexts.[5] Underlying both sets of fears are the beliefs that the text and its author are one, and the text and author offer the only authentic voice of the culture under discussion. The first reaction implicitly sees the text as a cultural artifact unintelligible when removed from its cultural context, while the second reaction demands that the transparency of cultural understanding be shared between writer and reader. The notion of authenticity implicit in both approaches puts pressure on the writer to be the objective bearer of cultural knowledge and on the reader to relinquish an active role in the production of meaning. By adhering to a strict interpretation of the politics of location as built upon identity, these readers voiced the important concern that the act of reading international fiction should not be an invasive act of crossing over into other cultural and personal narratives if such a crossing-over enacts imperialistic reading strategies. The students were rightfully wary that if they spoke for someone other than themselves they might misrepresent the other person and her culture. But this wariness is based on the belief that interpretation is a form of imperialist speech, in other words, that a reader differentiates herself from the text by seeing the text as the foreign discourse of an "Other" woman that can be better explained by someone from a dominant vantage point or culture, or else as a text that can't be explained at all because it diverges so dramatically from dominant society's expression of experience. Critical analysis and discussion that speaks for someone else does, in certain circumstances, obscure, erase, and silence the voice within the text, but as Audre Lorde asserts, racism looms behind a view that suggests that people are so different from one another that there are no points of commonality.[6] I would argue that my students' initial anxieties about "speaking for" others and confronting unbridgeable differences are best described as verging on an ethnocentrism of alienation rather than racism. While the students desired a connection with the voices and stories in the novels, they lost their footing when texts such as El Saadawi's *Woman at Point Zero*, Aidoo's *Our Sister Killjoy* and Morgan's *My Place* challenged their knowledge of the cultural backgrounds, social contexts, languages, and narrative structures invoked by each text. The student-readers wanted the writers' worlds explained in such a way as to calm the sea of differences. They were uneasy with this dual need to hear different voices but not to be lost in the act of listening.

The second type of anxiety my students exhibited had to do with the fact that we were going to read theoretical articles. The split between theory and practice has chilled the atmosphere in many a literature course. Students bring with them a wariness about "theory"—a wariness that itself is founded on a hierarchical divide separating the theorists from the

student-readers who feel themselves unable to grasp the theory even before they have read any of it. This anxiety parallels, to a considerable
degree, the fear they feel about the literature by postcolonial female
writers. In both cases, the students see a divide between their ways of
knowing and speaking and those of the writers. The addition of such
theorists to the course discussion posed the problem of how to approach
these theoretical texts without reinstituting a hierarchy of authority in
which the theory explains the literary texts. I wanted my students to
experience the voices of literary and cultural studies critics who write
about the complexities of being marginalized due to race, ethnicity, sexuality, and socioeconomic class markers while also being recognized as
important voices of contemporary intellectual thought. By approaching
the theorists as women writers with personal concerns, rather than seeing
the theoretical articles as the intellectual presentations of disembodied
concepts, the students could peer over their walls of scepticism and uncertainty with higher levels of self-confidence. Our collective efforts to create a space of exploration in the classroom for questioning, confronting,
and expanding on the ideas of theorists, within the context of reading international fiction, became a much-valued activity by the students as they
began to construct connections between location and interpretation.

My design for the course paired fiction by women from across the
globe with theoretical essays by women marginalized by dominant
American society due to their gender, ethnic, and cultural positions. Pair-
ing novels with theoretical essays opened paths for students to reexamine
their views on gender, class, domination, resistance, and language.[7] I selected novels that foreground questions about the concept of marginality
and also theorize issues of identity politics through their respective narrative styles, plot, and language. The selected essays were not written in
response to specific novels; they were not textual commentaries or secondary sources on the narratives. I chose essays that enacted, by way of
their content and construction, questions about margins and centers and
the ensuing questions about power, discrimination, and resistance to naturalized authorities. The pairings put the essays into a framework for
analysis that evolved from the classroom discussions about the literary
texts. Constructing a trajectory of change from this new "imagined community" of novels, essays, and readers, the course set into motion a dialogue based on affinities.[8] The students learned to see themselves as
participants in an ongoing and multi-voiced conversation.

Course content and methodology focused on displacing an oppositional framework for interpretation and creating one based on affinities

between texts and readers. Critical analysis based on affinities looks different from both the "we are one" and the "exotic Other" perspectives mentioned earlier. These two perspectives see literary discourse as always dependent on a fixed dyad of insider/outsider. Premised on the need for unity, reading for evidence that "we are one" shunts aside differences, thereby favoring the center (that is, identification of sameness) over the margins (that is, differences). Premised on the anxiety of difference, reading for "the exotic Other" offers safe haven on the inside by acknowledging differences as "Other than ourselves" but keeping them outside the center of knowledge. In contrast, reading through affinities conceptualizes a new sense of discursive wholeness in which differences are not reduced to oppositions, but rather are accepted as viable locations of knowledge within the whole.

By reading the texts in a context that prized affinities rather than oppositions, and by engaging in explorative writing assignments, students began to experience transformations in their interpretive approaches. Over the course of the semester they produced numerous exploration papers.[9] Based on student-generated topics and peer-critique responses, these papers related thematic, stylistic, and meta-critical issues to questions of identity, authenticity, power, and resistance. Having other students engage with their written insights and points of discomfort dismantled the implicit hierarchy of the production of knowledge that typically conditions and constrains the learning environment of the classroom. Their explorative writings about and responses to the texts and each other's positions vis-à-vis the issues under discussion allowed a creative dialogue about the concepts of differences and the importance of locations to occur. Rather than seeing the texts as representing either a universal sameness or an unbridgeable otherness, the student-critics entered a new arena in which they saw themselves as speaking *nearby* these novelists, essayists, and their own peers. As eloquently expressed by Trinh Minh-ha, such an interpretive strategy proposes that difference is not reducible to otherness; rather "difference always implies [an] interdependency" of identification combined with difference while "unsettling every definition of otherness [difference] arrived at" ("Questions of Images and Politics," 152). Reading "nearby" initiates a reading sensitive to cultural context, social pressures, and opportunities for resistance plus narrative provisions of power through language.[10] It also brings the reader to a point in which s/he is able to recognize that her/his position as reader-critic is already anticipated by and implicated in the text's narrative, but never categorically defined. S/he interprets by reflecting on the text in the concomitant act of analyzing her/his own role and values as reader and critic, thereby slipping away from any role as distant observer. This dual act of interpretation and exploration never totally displaces the anxieties about "foreign" texts and "speaking for" another, but it moves students towards a space that is continually opening, in which they can productively investigate the literary and ethical risks raised by their location in relation to the act and power invested in producing interpretations.

WOMAN AT POINT ZERO AND THE FEARLESS VOICE

"The woman sitting on the ground in front of me was a real woman, and the voice filling my ears with its sounds echoing in a cell where the window and door were tightly shut, could only be her voice, the voice of Firdaus" (*Woman at Point Zero,* 7). The Egyptian novel from which this passage is taken, *Woman at Point Zero,* narrates the story of Firdaus and of her life leading up to her imprisonment in Qanatir Prison. The book consists of three chapters: the brief first and third chapters are narrated by a female psychiatrist; the second chapter, which makes up the bulk of the novel, is narrated by Firdaus.[11] Condemned to death for killing a male pimp, the female prisoner Firdaus controls not only the space within the room in which she is detained, but also, by means of her commanding narrative voice, the discursive spaces of the classroom. Moreover, Firdaus's voice disrupts the psychiatrist's presumed control over the situation. As the psychiatrist explains, "suddenly we were face to face. I stood rooted to the ground, silent, motionless . . . It was as though I died the moment her [Firdaus's] eyes looked into mine" (*Woman,* 6). The psychiatrist narrator of the framing chapters wishes to study the personalities of certain female prisoners with the aim of linking gender, criminality, and personality into a meta-narrative of psychiatric knowledge. This research framework subsumes the subject's tale into a larger tale to be retold from a position distanced from the speaker's experience and sustained by the class and education privileges of the researcher. Hoping to turn these women's personal stories into public research data, the psychiatrist enters the prison chained to her own methodological and epistemological ideologies of subjugation. Hers is a discourse of the "Other" which, in bell hooks's words, functions to annihilate the speaking woman because there is

> no need to hear your [the speaker's] voice. Only tell me [the psychiatrist/reader/critic] about your pain. I want to know your story. And then

I will tell it back to you in a new way. Tell it back to you in such a way
that it has become mine . . . I am still author, authority. I am still the
colonizer, the speaking subject, and you are now at the center of my
talk. (152)

The psychiatrist's desire to speak "for" the women prisoners provoked
my students to question their intentions in reading a novel like *Woman at
Point Zero*. When the psychiatrist is silenced by Firdaus, students recognized the interruption to the psychiatrist's discourse of domination. Firdaus' use of the autobiographical to defuse and ultimately refuse
domination presented the class with the opportunity to reevaluate the relationship between positions of power, insider vs. outsider, and center vs.
margin.

A small-group presentation focused on these questions through the
dual lens of Firdaus's narrative and bell hooks's essay, "Choosing the
Margin as a Space for Radical Openness." This essay foregrounds language as a site of struggle and resistance against prevailing modes of national, racial, class, and gender domination. The students considered
how cultural views about women, language, and socioeconomic class
can reify the center/margin paradigm of oppression. They were struck by
the similarity of both hooks's and Firdaus's desires to be heard against
the almost deafening backdrop of colonizing discourses. This resistance
involved, for hooks, asserting her position as a woman of working-class
African American descent, and for Firdaus, asserting her position as an
Egyptian woman from a lower class with a criminalized background.
Firdaus's first person narrative fractures the presumed totalitarian domination of patriarchal and psychological discourse while hooks's use of
the autobiographical displaces the assumed position of privilege taken by
dominant White United States culture and society.

Early in her essay, hooks poses two questions aimed at practitioners
of counter-hegemonic acts of resistance that spoke to students' concerns
about their roles as readers. hooks writes:

Within complex and evershifting realms of power relations, do we position ourselves on the side of colonizing mentality? Or do we continue
to stand in political resistance with the oppressed, ready to offer *our*
ways of seeing and theorizing, of making culture, towards that revolutionary effort which seeks to create space where there is unlimited access to the pleasure and power of knowing, where transformation is
possible? (145; my emphasis)

It was the "our" that posed the thin line of reflective scrutiny for the student-critics; as readers, like the psychiatrist in Saadawi's text, we must formulate relationships with the narratives without overwriting and silencing the diverging voices expressed in the texts. hooks writes, "This is an intervention. I am writing to you. I am speaking from a place in the margins where I am different, where I see things differently. I am talking about what I see" (152). As intervention into the neoimperialist realm of reading about "Others," her words highlighted for students their tenuous and tense interpretive relationship with the texts; as invitation to listen to differences spoken by women with stories to tell, her words aided students in reshaping their interpretive frameworks through the erasure of the "othering" process.

hooks's redefinition of the margins as a chosen space of resistance, paired with Firdaus's definition of liberatory resistance as an act of empowerment rather than victimization, provided the student-critics with an opening in which they experienced a newly energized form of listening through engagement, rather than feeling compelled to explain a narrative such as *Woman at Point Zero*.[12] Here I take the verb "to explain" in its imperialistic guise of rationality. To explain a text puts into play the idea that the texts present fixed representations of cultures, societies, and identities that are to be dissected by and translated into the readers' more exacting language. This view of the interpretive process forces students to assume positions of mastery over the texts, as does the psychiatrist in the opening of El Saadawi's novel. Shifting the emphasis away from explanation (a form of "speaking for") to exploration (a form of "speaking nearby"), the interpretive act invokes a feminist discourse that allows reflective movement and critique to occur between texts and student-critics.

My students struggled with this shift in their interpretive methods. For example, in an act of misquotation, one of my students wrote that "when we hear [Firdaus's] voice in the novel, she's speaking from the perspective of someone who, in the words of hooks, talks from the 'reality of what it means to be taught in a culture of damnation [sic] by those who dominate' (150)."[13] By unconsciously substituting "damnation" for "domination," the student actualizes the hellish overtones of Firdaus's storytelling and situation. The student's slip reveals how segments of dominant society can condemn those they see as inhabiting the margins. Yet the student's slippage also suggests that such a formulation (domination means damnation) is a cultural construct taught by those in power and subconsciously purveyed by society. Although the student didn't catch the misquotation, he recognized Firdaus's triumph over her captors and her equally powerful determination not to succumb to the imposed role of the damned (that is, the culturally denied and denigrated position of working-class prostitute) when she decrees that it is "our fears that enslave us" (95). The student-critic reflected that "in fact, she seems to pity those miserable wretches who [quoting Firdaus] 'want to live . . . so that they can commit more crime and plunder' (100). They seem to be the ones who are really enslaved by their fears [not Firdaus]."

Similarly, by following out Firdaus's own line of thought, the student sees the connection between gender and trespass as he points out that those who plunder are criminals and "to be a criminal one must be a man" (100). Firdaus's condemnation of men repeats, although with a difference, the student's earlier domination *qua* damnation. Whereas the student's misquotation implicates Firdaus as a victim to the ideology of damnation, Firdaus condemns not herself but the male-dominated society as those caught up in their own ideology of domination/damnation.[14]

Firdaus's pronouncement against the patriarchy and her self-conscious recognition that she "is speaking the truth. And truth is savage and dangerous" (*Woman,* 100) slips beyond the patriarchal controls of juridical, psychiatric, economic, moral, and educational discourses by revealing the patriarchy's ideology of fear.[15] Firdaus's voice disrupts the discourses and mechanisms of surveillance and punishment.[16] Her act of speaking frames hooks's assertion that "language is a place of struggle" (145). The fearless "I" of her first-person narration risks closure (death) for change (the power of her voice). By situating hooks's statement on how the listener might try to wrest authority from a speaker who inhabits the margins in conjunction with Firdaus's statements of resistance, the students saw that the autobiographical "I" refused to yield authority to the colonizer in whatever guise s/he may attempt to assume (psychiatrist, educator, reader-critic).[17]

Within the classroom space, both texts disturbed the readers' equanimity. The student-critics felt how powerfully Firdaus's life narrative disrupted their views about the submissiveness of Egyptian women and the reprehensibility of prostitution, just as hooks's delineation of power within a seemingly dominated space unsettled their views on the dialectic of insider/outsider as the equation of powerful/powerless. Firdaus tells us that through a patriarchal interpretive screen her death

> means their [the men of all professions and relationships] life. They want to live. And life for them means more crime, more plunder, unlimited booty. I have triumphed over both life and death because I no

longer desire to live, nor do I any longer fear to die. I want nothing. I
hope for nothing. I fear nothing. Therefore I am free. For during life it
is our wants, our hopes, our fears that enslave us. The freedom I enjoy
fills them with fear. (*Woman*, 100–101)

And hooks shares with us her views on escaping the fears that constrain
existence:

> I make a definite distinction between that marginality which is im-
> posed by oppressive structures and that marginality one chooses as a
> site of resistance—as location of radical openness and possibility. . . .
> We know struggle to be that which pleasures, delights, and fulfills de-
> sire. We are transformed, individually, collectively, as we make radical
> creative space which affirms and sustains our subjectivity, which gives
> us a new location from which to articulate our sense of the world.
> ("Choosing the Margins," 153)

Recognizing their own fears regarding how to read and interact with texts
previously marked as "alien" and "alienating," the students began to see
through the old frameworks of oppositions to new interpretive possibilities strengthened by an awareness of differences. Their fears about interpretive domination and responsibility came under scrutiny as they
enacted hooks's invitation to engage with voices previously silenced by
dominant cultures and Firdaus's exhortation to risk speaking with one's
own voice.

OUR SISTER KILLJOY AND READING LETTERS OF LOVE

Recognition of difference as empowering doesn't necessarily translate
into a space of comfort in the classroom. For when we began reading
Aidoo's *Our Sister Killjoy or Reflections from a Black-Eyed Squint*, the
students saw not productive difference but "otherness" in the text's content and even in its physical construction. They felt they had entered into
the "bad dream" forecast by the introductory chapter's title and could
only hope that the prediction, "Things are working out" (3), would come
to pass. *Our Sister Killjoy* is a prose poem in four sections: "Into a Bad
Dream," "The Plums," "From Our Sister Killjoy," and "A Love Letter."
The prose poem is a personal journey for the protagonist Sissie into the
politics of racism linked to imperialism, exile, gender relations, sexuality, and national identity, set against the locales of Germany, Britain, and

Ghana. The physical construction of Aidoo's text begins with just a few words per page; this gives way on page six to a strident outburst of prose against internalized colonialism. Throughout the next sections of the text, prose and poetry are commingled.

In an exploration paper, a student linked the graphic display with the thematic concerns of center/margins. Bringing hooks into the discussion, the student wrote, "it is the physical representation of the text upon the page that seems to play [with] bell hooks'[s] view of the uses of space, of the redefinition of boundaries and margins."[18] The student's connection of the graphic depiction of margins with the theoretical implications of margins prompted her to consider space as no longer a fixed commodity but as having taken on the properties of a fluid element that can be resculpted and thus reinterpreted. This fluidity represents the mutability in the relationship between margins and center; it sets the stage for Aidoo's combination of poetry and prose to reformulate the discourse of postcolonial subjectivity for readers.

This exploration of space, language, and subjectivity appears, for example, during Sissie's work stint in Bavaria, where she is befriended by Marija, a German housewife, and introduced to Marija's child, Little Adolf. Sissie declares the child beautiful as Marija explains that since Adolf is her only child she is very happy he is a boy. An external narrator interjects a poetic recitation at this point, disrupting any potential for a mundane interpretation of their conversation:

> *Any good woman*
> *In her senses*
> *With her choices*
> *Would say the*
> *Same*
> *In Asia*
> *Europe*
> *Anywhere:*
>
> *For*
> *Here under the sun,*
> *Being a woman*
> *Has not*
> *Is not*
> *Cannot*
> *Never will be a*
> *Child's game*

From knowledge gained since—

So why wish a curse on your child
Desiring her to be female
?
Beside, my sister,
The ranks of the wretched are
Full,
Are full. (51)

The narrator acknowledges Marija's point of view and then goes on to underscore the misogynist tendencies of contemporary cultures, implicating not only Europe (and the United States by extension of the Western gaze) but likewise Sissie's own country. Implicating her gender in this passage, the narrator questions her own role in the critique by allowing the question mark to stand on its own. Is it wrong to want female children? Is misogyny a fixed state of affairs? The narrator's observation that women fill up the ranks of the wretched is not dismissed in this interjection; by playing with the term "sister," extending her words to Sissie and to other women (including women readers), this narrator suggests that if the space of wretchedness is full then a new space not based on this demarcation and desolation may slip into view for women. This overture to a sense of global sisterhood is not naive; rather it is complicated by the politics of reproduction, the overtones of neo-Nazism given the child's name and physiognomy, the markings of exoticism assigned to Sissie, and the colonizing morality against lesbian sexuality. The narrative shift between plot and critical poetic commentary is echoed by the theoretical presentation of Trinh Minh-ha's moment of the "inappropriate/d-ness": this is a moment precipitating the interdependency of identification ("we are like each other, yet different") while drawing upon a difference that can't be easily solidified ("we are different in ways not yet defined").[19] Setting Trinh's ideas about difference next to Aidoo's critical narrative commentary and textual representations, we see how each text refuses to allow us to collapse those connections into any sort of universalizing reductionist definition of womanhood.

In reflecting on the narrative shifts that highlight the complexity of difference marked by gender, race, and imperialist history, one student from my course explained that

> At times, particularly initially, the shifts [between narrative voices] irritated me. I had felt [these shifts] interfered with my attention to the

story. But upon reflection, that may have been precisely what [they] were supposed to do. If one considers the position of [Sissie], she must constantly stop, and rethink; stop and try to interpret the messages society sends her regarding her place, and position in the spaces which she is forced to occupy.[20]

The student's response reveals her sensitivity to her position as critic of a text that forces her to occupy a space to which she is unaccustomed. She notices that what she had taken to be outside the story (that which "interfered with . . . the story") works integrally to the story's telling. This student-critic recognizes that linearity and monologism as narrative devices fail to encompass the polyvocal space of self-discovery Sissie has embarked upon when she enters "into a bad dream" and ends up in "a love letter" to herself, her country, and her readers. The student-critic insightfully suggests that

> the author was playing with us, the readers, challenging us to *see* differently. It is a purposeful interruption of our expectations of what we feel the text *should* be. The author had learned the oppressor's language. She had learned to use the master's tools. (Trinh "Differences," 79–80) And perhaps now this is her attempt to deconstruct, to use the master's tools differently and possibly create a new form, a form of her own, which would suit her needs. (emphasis in original)

Through Trinh's writing the student reconsiders Lorde's statement about the inefficacy of using the master's tools; she sees powerful resistance being enacted through Aidoo's reworking of the colonizer's language, narration, and ideas. So while the narrative presents moments of metacritical commentary, such a reworking and rewriting of colonial tools leads this student-critic to question her own interpretive habits and reading history. This double movement of reflection joins narrative and student in similar activities of interpretation, without erasing the differences that ensue from how the discourses of race, gender, sexuality, and domination play off their different contexts.

The final section of the text substantiates the student's assertion that seeing/reading with a difference produces new forms of knowledge production that veer off and away from previously ingrained patterns of interpretation. Sissie no longer inhabits a space of exile from Ghana in London. She is no longer an itinerant traveler in her country's "motherland"; instead she is in transit between countries on her way back to

Ghana. This site of relocation, a location of both/and, combines her questions, insights, and knowledge in a contemplative letter to her lover, herself, and us. The love letter forms a bridge connecting her early concerns about her society and its members-in-exile with her newfound determination to reintegrate with a difference into Ghanaian society:

> She was never going to post the letter. Once written, it was written. She had taken some of the pain away and she was glad. . . . She was going to let things lie where they had fallen. Besides, she was back in Africa. And that felt like fresh honey on the tongue: a mixture of complete sweetness and smoky roughage. Below was home with its unavoidable warmth and even after these thousands of years, its uncertainties. (133)

Sissie commits herself to her country and her people's history of uncertainties, all the while acknowledging that her views are "reflections from a black-eyed squint," as suggested by the text's subtitle. The term implies both struggle and determination to make sense of the material world within its working context. Sissie's "squint" isn't omniscient, universal, or ahistorical, nor by being "black-eyed" is it without the dual markings of its race and the metaphorical overtones of antagonism that race can engender (her eye color is black; her eyes have been blackened by racialism and its racist discourse). The subtitle and the subsequent passages of the final section emphasize her rejection of the role of authentic spokeswoman for all Africans while reasserting the legitimacy of her reflections because of their social, cultural, and political location. The "both/and" of a narrative that demonstrates both resistance and assertion allows students to relax their desire for a singularly authentic speaker. When the narrative prompts the protagonist to assume a critical perspective on such issues as gender and colonialism (117), language enslavement (112), and equality of oppressions (93), the experience of reading transmutes itself from the dissection of original subjects as objects under scrutiny into a dialogue with multiple speakers engaging in acts of interpretive connections. No absolute grounding is provided in such an engagement; students strive to use these moments of questioning in their interpretations of the text and in their relationship to the process of interpretation.

The collective of voices that includes hooks, Trinh, and the multiple narrators in *Our Sister Killjoy* moves students to see themselves implicated in this changing landscape of the production of knowledge. When they become aware of their expectations about narratives and "authentic subjects," when they see those expectations dislodged from an ideology of pure and static knowledge, student-critics move into a transitional space in which they begin to analyze how their locations impact their interpretations of postcolonial subjects and cultural contexts. This transition or displacement, in Trinh's words, "involves the invention of new forms of subjectivities, of pleasures, of intensities, of relationships, which also implies the continuous renewal of critical work that looks carefully and intensively at the very system of values to which one refers in fabricating the tools of resistance" ("Cotton and Iron," 19). In this space, the student-critics disengage themselves from the role of readers *qua* voyeurs to become recipients of and respondents to Sissie's letter and story. This dialectic of receipt and response stemming from Sissie's narrative brings the student-critics into a reciprocal reevaluation of their own roles as readers of global fiction, and as citizens in a global society.[21]

READING "NEARBY" THE "MY" IN *MY PLACE*

While Aidoo's prose poem *Our Sister Killjoy* destabilizes assumptions about subjectivity and authenticity through its interplay of narrative and genre techniques, Sally Morgan's autobiographical narrative *My Place* challenges the concepts of identity and history by writing her family's and her own story in contradistinction to the existing national history of Australia. *My Place* is the life story of a young woman who finds out about her Aboriginal past when she is a teenager. The first half of the autobiography is told from Sally's perspective. The next three sections are the first-person narratives (as told to Sally during personal interviews) of her uncle, Arthur; her mother, Gladys; and her grandmother, Daisy. The final section returns to Sally's narration. Her multi-vocal narrative, like Aidoo's, dismantles the reader's reliance on an all-knowing authentic subject, thus providing a space for the exploration of questions about the role of the experiential in the process of interpretation occurring between text and student-critic. Whereas Aidoo's text disturbs because of its narrative technologies as prose poem, the first person point of view of Morgan's story reassures students, leading them to expect a traditional, straightforward, autobiographical narrative. It is not the form that they find disturbing, but their lack of knowledge about the people named Aborigines in the text. They confront a radical fissure in their methods of interpreting the text when, like the principal narrator Sally Morgan, they realize they don't know what cultural markings the term carries. During an early discussion about ethnicity between the sisters, Jill and Sally, Jill breaks the silence surrounding racial heritage by berating Sally for not recognizing their socially unacceptable difference:

> 'You know what we are, don't you?' [Jill]
> 'No, what?' [Sally]
> 'Boongs, we're Boongs!' I could see Jill was unhappy with the idea.
> It took a few minutes before I summoned up enough courage to say,
> 'What's a Boong?'.
> 'A Boong. You know, Aboriginal. God, of all things, we're Aboriginal!'
> 'Oh.' I suddenly understood. There was a great deal of social stigma attached to being Aboriginal at our school. (*My Place,* 98)

While Jill is disgusted by their position and uses a racially derogatory epithet to emphasize her views, Sally begins to resist the language as it is presented to her. She remarks on the racism but it isn't until a little later in her life that she begins to suffer personally from the internalized racist sentiments of both White and Aboriginal Australians. Incidents such as losing a close friend due to parental intervention because of her race, recognizing her grandmother's fear of claiming her Aboriginal heritage, and sensing her mother's pain at not knowing her own birth father, propel Sally to search for her definition of self through her family's collective sense of identity and to reject and reverse dominant society's demarcation and erasure of their lives.

The composite construction of Morgan's narrative reveals the multi-layered structure of identity from within an Aboriginal cultural context. The narrative's attention to the process of building a personal subjectivity from diverse stories of experiences brought students an awareness of the significance of materialist discourse. The students were touched by the personal struggle Sally was undergoing in her search for a racial and familial history; from Morgan's narrative they began to understand the stultifying nature of the definitions of "Aborigine" presented by dominant Australian history. The oral histories of Sally's uncle, Arthur, her mother, Glad, and her grandmother, Daisy question the opacity and fixity of Australia's national history. Sally's library research reveals the story of colonialism and the one-sidedness of history; after Sally tells her uncle of her failure to uncover any empowering Aboriginal stories during her library research, Arthur agrees with Sally that his story and those of his relatives are "the other side of the story" (*My Place,* 164). Sally's family's narratives cannot be collapsed into a universalist or ahistoricist view of events, as their voices insist on their specificity in materialist discourse. At this point in Sally's autobiography, her individual voice has been reshaped by Arthur's story. The same is true for the reader's experience. We have moved from questioning the viability of Aboriginal culture to desiring to read more about its past and the potential for its future legacy.

This recognition of White society's predilection to ossify those deemed as "Other" resonated with similar insights invoked in the other texts we had read up to this point in the semester. But identification of such parallels wasn't an end point. Rather, the students turned these comparisons towards themselves as they read Chandra Talpade Mohanty's essay, "Cartographies of Struggle: Third World Women and the Politics of Feminism." Adding to the rich combination of voices addressing the power of language and its connection to subjectivities, Mohanty's article, paired with Morgan's autobiography, provided the students with the opportunity to examine the effect of location on the interpretation of narrative discourse. The essay begins with a previously unpublished poem by Audre Lorde. Through reading it, the students saw themselves marked as potentially "different" in ways they had never before imagined or named. Lorde's language dramatically repositioned them on a new map of cultures, languages, and geographies:

> *Most people in the world*
> *are Yellow, Black, Brown, Poor, Female*
> *Non-Christian*
> *and do not speak English.*
>
> *By the year 2000*
> *the 20 largest cities in the world*
> *will have one thing in common*
> *none of them will be in Europe*
> *none in the United States.*

This terrain of differences—ranging from religious, cultural, and social to linguistic—challenged my White American students to reconsider their naturalized positions of authority and encouraged my students of color to reassess their internalized sense of disempowerment. In both instances, when we shifted the context from one of division (United States vs. postcolonial cultures) to one invoking the interplay of differences in assessing the literary and experiential representations of women's lives, the students began to shed their reliance on the superiority of their

United States connection and their sympathetic interpretations couched in nationalist rhetoric.[22] Recognizing the ethnocentrism of her interpretive views as she read *My Place*, one student saw the importance of cultural and materialist politics in this way: "Mohanty elaborates on the necessity of writing, as well as the necessity of rethinking the existing state of society, as one attempts to establish the framework for [her] own personal identity."[23] The important dynamics of contextualization and materiality depicted through the act of writing came home to my students as they saw their own positions as interpreters reframed through the texts.

Morgan's autobiography involves the act of remembering a past that has been obscured and overwritten. Sally sees how her family and people have been frozen into the category of despised Other by dominant Australian legal and historical texts. Using Sally's quest for personal Aboriginal visibility as a backdrop for a discussion of Mohanty's dense article, three students provoked a conversation on the pertinent topic of gender and political struggle. In response to the student presentation, other students began to realize that gender alone isn't the only factor that affects how women build or express their lives and ideas. One student wrote,

> I really took notice when Susan [a student presenter] raised the subject of whether 'it was politically correct to say that everyone is the same,' i.e., all women are alike regardless of their background and culture. I strongly agree that it isn't fair to group various bands of people together because of their gender or race. It's obvious through the various novels [and essays] we've read so far this semester that women from different cultural backgrounds each [sic] have something important to say about their unique experiences.[24]

Here the student reflects on the limitations of the "we are one" interpretive technique while simultaneously recognizing the significance of hearing stories of difference. The response implicitly links experience and written expression as a way of breaking through the walls of ahistoricism. Studying Morgan's autobiography, along with Mohanty's critique of not only patriarchy but Western feminism's concept of "Third World Women," pushed students to explore the concept of self-identity and its relationship to writing. Mohanty states:

> Feminist analysis has always recognized the centrality of rewriting and remembering history. This is a process which is significant not merely

as a corrective to the gaps, erasures, and misunderstandings of hegemonic [and here we could say colonialist] masculinist history, but because the very practice of remembering and rewriting leads to the formation of politicized consciousness and self-identity.... If the everyday world is not transparent . . . it becomes imperative that we rethink, remember, and utilize our lived relations as a basis of knowledge. Writing (discursive production) is one site for the production of this knowledge and this consciousness. (34–5)

The discursive site of autobiography takes up the challenge to repeat life's experiences as it reaches out to be "life writing." Yet when the discourse is situated in an Aboriginal context, the concept of the self-identifying individual is recast and reconstructed—it repeats, but with a difference, the tales told and retold by their tellers. The Eurocentric tradition of autobiography is based on the concept of the individual self set in opposition to others.[25] When this binary is displaced, the self at the center of the autobiography is reformulated. Thus, when Sally's story becomes intertwined with that of her immediate elders and previously unknown extended Aboriginal family, the presumed transparency of the narrating self grows less masterful and more critically engaged with the process of collective identification.[26] Morgan's autobiographical occasion disrupts the mastery of the authorial "I" as she places the oral histories of her family elders within the site of her own writing.

Margery Fee in "Who Can Write as Other?" frames a larger issue confronting Morgan as autobiographer and us as readers of the genre of autobiography looking for authentic voices aligned with prescriptive identity politics: How do we determine authenticity when "the problem is complicated by the increasing number of writers who, like [Keri] Hulme [Maori writer], are of mixed ancestry; who, like Aboriginal writer Sally Morgan, have been raised in ignorance of their ancestry?" (242) She goes on to point out the bifurcating principles that can hamper our recognition of change:

> The demand for 'authenticity' denies Fourth World writers [e.g., Aborigines of Australia, the Maori of New Zealand, Native Peoples of Canada, Native Americans from the United States] a living, changing culture. Their culture is deemed to be Other and must avoid crossing those fictional but ideologically essential boundaries between Them and Us, the Exotic and the Familiar, the Past and the Future, the 'Dying' and the Living. (243)

It is within this dualistic landscape that Sally begins to explore for herself what it means to be Aboriginal. She, like the students reading her narrative, is naïve about its meaning and initially sets it up against the term "White," a marker that implies superior racial lines, cultural mores, and linguistic power. The personal anecdotes and tales told by Arthur and Daisy reveal how Aboriginal culture, language, and identity were suspect and constrained by legal, social, and individual regulations and views. Glad's oral history enables a greater understanding, not only of her life and the questions remaining about it, but also of how the relationship between Glad and Sally's father, a White Australian, developed. These stories combine to reframe Sally's understanding of her identity, not in terms of trying to reclaim a previously silenced Aboriginal heritage and eradicate her other parental history, but in terms of recontextualizing her previously white-washed heritage within its multicolored and multicultural complexity. Her "place," geographically, familially, socially, and personally, is mapped by these criss-crossing markers. Her authenticity rests on linkages of connection rather than on a nostalgic drive for purity.

Morgan's inclusion of the oral histories embodies this struggle for relocation through language. The voices of other people are incorporated into the autobiography to embody its collective resonance. However, a question arises. Students wonder if Morgan has reinstituted a new hierarchy of written over spoken words, one that allows her to occupy the oral histories in an accommodationist yet imperializing move.[27] Is she doing to her family's stories just what the students are struggling to resist doing: is she using someone else's words to expand her own knowledge in an imperialist move for power and control? Is she "speaking for" in an act of imperialist speech? In a discussion about the connections of power and language in life writing, Carol Boyce Davies explains how such a potentially imperialist move is refused formation given the context of the storytelling: "Writing another person's life can become an act of power and control," yet "in the oral literary tradition, the subject [the speaker] nevertheless resists complete framing, only telling as much as needs to be told for each particular production" (12–13). Juxtaposing Davies's point with Morgan's text, we can see how this slippage or refusal of totalization disallows the transcriber/editor, in this case Sally Morgan, final control. For example, the refusal to cede total control of the narrative is emphasized in Daisy's section when she won't confirm her granddaughter's suspicions of incest at the hands of the landowner towards his female Aboriginal indentured worker. This circumspect silence gives agency to the speaking subject. As the transcriber who respects the silences of her grandmother, Sally undermines the traditional role of objective knowledge-gatherer. Sally realizes the strength of character her grandmother's story epitomizes, set as it is against the dehumanizing tactics of past and contemporary Australian society. It is this powerful spirit that invigorates Sally's promise to never forget the significance of her family's struggles as they shape her current life through the writing of her narrative.

In *My Place,* the written word functions only as a temporary closure for the oral histories; the inclusion of the oral histories in the written narrative is a closure, but as Trinh suggests, "closures need not close off: they can be doors opening onto other closures and functioning as ongoing passages to an elsewhere(-within-here)" ("Cotton and Iron," 15). For Sally's family, the deaths of the older generation prefigure the closing off of certain oral histories; but it is only because of these gifts of the spoken word that Sally's autobiography can exist. Morgan's conclusion makes it clear that she sees her story as linked to other family narratives. But far from enclosing them in her narrative, she means their inclusions as an opening to alternative histories. Her story only gains body and meaning within the context of the other stories. The students recognize that Sally's story is a composite life writing that breaks certain silences but maintains others around Aboriginal lives of pain and struggle. The older generations' injunctions to be careful with their stories bind us as readers into a community built on mutual concern and trust. The student-critics don't read these voices of different events, histories, and lives as "other" than Sally's own voice; instead, they register the overlap of narration that creates her place within the spheres of family, community, and self-identity, while Sally concomitantly recognizes her own difference as not already defined through their stories. The seemingly authentic narrating voice reveals its own critical position and development, thereby problematizing and recasting the concepts of authenticity, individual identity, and authority.

TRAJECTORIES OF CHANGE IN THE CLASSROOM

Building upon these textual interruptions into and interrogations of the tightly patterned world of the literary production of meaning—when Firdaus in El Saadawi's text chooses the margins of prostitution and embattled individuality, when Aidoo's protagonist Sissie enacts a consciousness of marginality by reclaiming race and gender enroute to her African land, when Sally Morgan reframes national and individual iden-

tity through collectivity, when bell hooks and Trinh Minh-ha recognize
the power available to the marginalized through language—students' reliance on the formerly clean break between center/margin began to give
way. By the end of the course, the students' focus had shifted: they no
longer stood outside the theoretical and narrative texts in fear of misin-
terpretation; instead they were formulating questions about reception
and location that picked up the challenge Trinh proposes, namely, "how
can one re-create [in the act of interpretation] without re-circulating
domination" ("Cotton and Iron," 15). The content and structure of the
course enabled students to set aside their need for a master's voice (be it
from the author, text, theorist, or teacher); they welcomed the opportunities to engage with the complex issues of marginality and authority from
a variety of positions, none of which claimed overarching power in the
classroom.

    This is not to say, however, that the student-critics concluded that
pluralism was a primary good or even a desired outcome; rather they saw
how location plays a significant part in the production and reception of
divergent and overlapping knowledges. They generated this insight for
themselves in several ways. Through their written conversations in the
exploration paper assignments, they began to see how differing responses to issues could add to their own nascent interpretations; in the
give-and-take of the student presentations, they discussed the theoretical
articles through the lenses of the novels; in their reflection papers on the
presentations, they engaged in critical analysis not only of the power of
location represented in the texts but also of the effect of their own locations on their interpretive acts. Through these individual and collaborative activities, the student-critics heightened their abilities to evaluate the
contours and significance of differences in the interpretative process.
They became practitioners who, in the words of Cornel West, worked to
keep open "a skeptical eye to avoid dogmatic traps, premature closures,
formulaic formulations or rigid conclusions" (31).

    Critical analysis of the relationship between texts and interpreters
transforms the classroom from a space for observation into a space of engagement. Learning to read the texts and also one another differently
(not oppositionally), student-critics initiate a process that questions the
divisions established between sameness and otherness as they explore
the loci of power that enforce such divisions. Turning the light of critical
thinking on themselves as interpreters takes on the force of disturbance
that Trinh describes as

questioning over and over again what is taken for granted as self-evident, by reminding oneself and the others of the unchangeability of change itself. Disturbing thereby one's own thinking habits, dissipating what has become familiar and cliched, and participating in the changing of received values—the transformation (with/out master) of other selves through one's self. ("Cotton and Iron," 21)

Participants in international literature courses displace the drive for mastery or imperialistic "othering" in the reading process by assessing and addressing their own locations and shifting subjectivities as readers and critics. Reflective assessment of their trajectories of analysis creates a discursive classroom space in which differences (among texts, students, and interpretations) become avenues for exploration rather than fixed meanings. Such meta-critical commentaries via student-produced portfolios divulge how differences are put into play through the various textual alignments while likewise investigating moments of cohesion across texts and other readers' interpretations.[28] In such a space universalism yields to what Haraway has called "situated knowledges," and monolithic hierarchies of authority fracture into polyvocal sites of affinities. A classroom dynamic energized by investigations into the situatedness of literary, theoretical, and readerly voices moves away and, to my view, forward from the neocolonial reading strategies to which our students may have grown accustomed. Analysis into the spaces created through the overlap of location and interpretation opens the way for students to discover unexpected sites of knowledge.

NOTES

I want to express my appreciation to the students in my spring 1995 course, "Women Prose Writers: Bodies, Space and Motion." Their fine work in class discussions and written assignments provided the impetus for the writing of this paper. I want to thank my colleagues in the English Department at Montclair State University, especially those involved in the World Literature Concentration (Fawzia Afzal-Khan, Grover Furr, Deena Linett, and Sharon Spencer). I also am indebted to Beth Hutchison for once again taking the time to critically discuss my pedagogy and the explanations included in this article. And finally I want to thank the editors of this collection for their constructive comments as this article was taking shape.

[1]Problems of terminology abound in trying to use an inclusive phrase for a group of societies that possess a wealth of differences among them. I avoid terms that categorize and implicitly evaluate societies against a Western standard of importance, productivity, and dignity (for example "Third World," "Fourth World," and developing nations). I have chosen to use the term "postcolonial" because it invokes the common situation of societies (and subcultures within societies) that are struggling with the shadows of colonialism in its various guises while at the same time calling into question whether such societies will ever be totally severed from their colonial imprints. This formation is important to the discussion of the relationship between center and margins that ensues in my article.

[2]As they strive to evaluate narratives from other cultures and countries, students may feel so uncomfortable with the differences portrayed that they erase those moments of narrative unease by searching for sameness. This strategy also refuses to see the narratives in their own terms and instead homogenizes them into a comfortable, yet colonized, space.

[3]See Sharon Stockton's discussion of readers and Chicano texts in " 'Blacks vs. Browns': Questioning the White Ground" as an example of how identity politics enters into the English classroom during discussions of United States literature by writers of color.

[4]John Champagne addresses this concern when he explains that the call for greater cultural diversity in the college curriculum may open the way for world literature to be displayed like an ethnic food fair: benevolent multiculturalism "may treat the artifacts of 'foreign' cultures simply as commodities for Western consumption" (" 'A Feminist Just Like Us?' Teaching Mariama Ba's *So Long A Letter,*" 22). His article sets Ba's text within a history of imperialism as a theoretical example revealing the interestedness of historical and cultural contexts. He then discusses his pedagogical goal to "help [the students] to theorize their own practices of reading as necessarily structured by, among other things, the history of imperialism" (40). In my analysis of teaching "Women Prose Writers," I will explore how reading theoretical and literary texts side by side allows students to investigate their role as student-critics within a contemporary history of marginality. To that end, the following discussion will not be an explication of the texts we read, but rather an examination of the classroom dynamics engendered by the reading of such texts.

[5]During our first class meeting, I explained to the students that I didn't know everything about the cultures and issues we'd be reading about in the novels and theoretical essays. I also told them that I found the theoretical articles difficult to read but worthwhile. By admitting that there was a great deal I didn't know and that I had problems of interpretation myself, the students felt it was permissible to talk about what they didn't know and the reaction such admissions created for

them. By opening up the conversation early on in the course and accepting that we'd all be participating in explorative discussions, I established the classroom space as a forum for honest dialogue instead of teacherly monologue.

[6]Lorde's sentiments on difference verging on racism were voiced in a conversation between Lorde and Maureen Brady, cited in Bonnie Zimmerman's "afterword" to Brady's *Folly*. Lorde expresses similar ideas in her article "Age, Race, Class, and Sex: Women Redefining Difference" in *Out There: Marginalization and Contemporary Cultures*.

There are instances when "speaking for" has political efficacy. For example, Linda Alcoff points out how Rigoberta Menchú spoke for numerous Indian communities facing genocide and how Steven Biko spoke for the Black Consciousness movement in South Africa. Alcoff writes that "the point is not that for some speakers the danger of speaking for others does not arise, but that in some cases certain political effects can be garnered no other way" ("The Problem of Speaking for Others," 107). However, in contrast to the situation my students confront, the speakers in Alcoff's examples have direct ties to the groups they speak for.

[7]The syllabus included the following groupings of texts (the parenthetical notations indicate the author's country of origin):

a.) *The Journey* by Ida Fink (Poland); "Technologies of Gender" by Terese de Lauretis

b.) *Woman at Point Zero* by Nawal El Saadawi (Egypt); "Choosing the Margins" by bell hooks

c.) *The Passion* by Jeanette Winterson (Great Britain); "Cotton and Iron" by Trinh Minh-ha

d.) *Our Sister Killjoy* by Ama Ata Aidoo (Ghana); "Difference: 'A Special Third World Women Issue' " by Trinh Minh-ha

e.) *Folly* by Maureen Brady and *Stone Butch Blues* by Leslie Feinberg (U.S.); "afterword" to *Folly* by Bonnie Zimmerman

f.) *Paradise of the Blind* by Duong Thu Huong (Vietnam) and *My Place* by Sally Morgan (Australia); "Cartographies of Struggle" by Chandra Talpade Mohanty

[8]I derive this sense of an "imagined community" from Chandra Mohanty's elaboration of Benedict Anderson's terminology. Instead of focusing on the bridging of "Third World" women's oppositional struggles as Mohanty does in her essay "Cartographies of Struggle," I want to apply the term to the space of the classroom, in which students engage in examining how connections are (or are not) formed among texts, theorists, and readers.

[9]The exploration paper exchanges take place after students have read approximately one-half of a novel. In class, we brainstorm topics that the students are interested in pursuing; they choose one topic to write about overnight. In

class the next day, each student randomly exchanges his/her 1–2 page paper with another student. After thoroughly reading the peer's paper, the responder writes a critically engaged reflection discussing ideas s/he found intriguing, ambiguous, and/or challenging. This response should be directed to the writer, not toward the teacher (thus, the students are encouraged to participate in the written equivalent of a focused conversation not moderated by the instructor). The papers are graded on the basis of constructive analysis and creative insight; the students only receive a grade for their work if they have done both parts of the assignment, that is, written an exploration and a response to a peer's paper. I see these exploration papers as a way to help students collaboratively process some ideas and use these ideas as a staging ground for essay assignments. They also learn to be academically responsible in crediting other students' ideas in their written work. They are to think analytically about the material they've read/discussed and not simply summarize the plot or what we have already said in class. I encourage them to develop an idea as coherently as possible, which means that they should work through a tentative interpretation, but they don't need to append any concluding remarks. They may also use these papers and responses as sites for metacritical dialogue on the process of interpretive production.

[10]Nawal El Saadawi writes that Western feminists often ask her how they can help Arab women, without realizing the racist implications of their question: "It is always assumed that we women of color need assistance and that so-called First World women must help us. And so we often hear, 'How can we help you?' We usually respond by saying 'Well, you can help us by fighting here in your country against the same system that is oppressing us all' " ("Conference Presentation" in *Critical Fictions,* 155). As suggested by El Saadawi's comments, Western feminism can easily overshadow other feminisms instead of working "nearby."

[11]Some critics equate the psychiatrist with the author (see Harlow, for example). Since psychiatric discourse and practitioners come under scrutiny in the novel, I interpret the psychiatrist as a character, not a direct reflection of the author. [Please note that parenthetical citations for the novel will be abbreviated as *Woman.*]

[12]My language for the interpretive act invokes a feminist discourse that allows for reflective movement and critique to occur within the texts and likewise among student-critics. See Spivak's essay "Explanation and Culture: Marginalia" for a more exacting discussion of the masculinist overtones of the term *explanation* and the deconstructive work of feminism.

[13]The quotes are taken from J. Klossek's final essay for the course; the essay is entitled "Making Their Way Home."

[14]I am using the construction of "repetition with a difference" from Trinh's work, but the concept is also separately theorized in Homi Bhabha's essay, "Of

Mimicry and Man." According to Bhabha, mimicry is that discourse in which the colonized mimics the colonizer; when this mimicry takes place, what emerges is "the almost the same, but not quite" repetition of a partial presence that threatens to disrupt the colonial power. The colonizer's seemingly natural state of domination is questioned by the mimic's "almost but not quite" repetition. Thus, Firdaus's act of condemnation reveals her role as the damned as only a partial truth, the other part of the truth being the disruption of patriarchal power by her acts of physical and discursive resistance.

[15]Klossek voiced his feelings of being implicated in Firdaus's condemnation of all men as perpetrators of crimes. He could no longer take refuge in being an American reading an Egyptian text once gender became an issue for consideration. In a parallel development, when Firdaus equates all women as prisoners of heterosexual societal regulations and formulations, the women in my class entered into a heated discussion about the veracity of this equation. Gender became a contested site throughout the course, as all three narratives (*Woman at Point Zero, Our Sister Killjoy,* and *My Place,* in addition to the other assigned texts) are connected through gender to the larger political and social orders represented in their respective texts. The implications of gender within varying systems of control and change produced lively debates and explorations throughout the semester.

[16]Barbara Harlow writes that Firdaus's agreement to meet with Nawal El-Saadawi, to tell her story, "signals . . . the permission that will allow her individual act of challenge and defiance to become part of the public record of social opposition to the authoritarian political structure and patriarchal hierarchies of Egyptian society" ("From the Women's Prison: Third World Women's Narratives of Prison," 512). Although I don't agree that the psychiatrist narrator is the author as Harlow asserts, I do agree with Harlow when she sees Firdaus's narrative entering into the collection of texts shaping not only Egyptian society but also the face of resistance literature by and about women.

[17]In her chapter on *Woman at Point Zero,* Malti-Douglas explains that the female-to-female narrative dynamic brings the psychiatrist into a position of rebirth through the force of Firdaus's narrative; see page 55.

[18]This quote comes from M. Sauer's exploration paper on *Our Sister Killjoy.* Sauer was motivated to write about this subject because of a class discussion that caused her to become, as she describes it, "alternately disappointed and amused by [my] classmates' genuine annoyance" with Aidoo's conscious play with words, the page, and boundaries.

[19]Trinh imagines this movement as "inappropriate/d"—a movement of double displacement that unsettles the self vs. other dichotomy because the second movement disallows the binary to remain fixed. She names this figure the "inappropriate/d other," a figure of hybridity that reveals the responsibility of surviv-

ing through displacement by creating new networks of values, languages, and images. Aidoo's text is infused with Trinh's idea of "inappropriate/d-ness." For a fuller description of this figure, see Trinh's "introduction" to *Discourse* 8.

[20]This quote and the following one are from M. Sauer's exploration paper on *Our Sister Killjoy*.

[21]The students gain an awareness of themselves as readers who, in Linda Alcoff's words, are "collectively caught in an intricate, delicate web in which each action [they] take, discursive or otherwise, pulls on, breaks off, or maintains the tension in many strands of the web in which others also find themselves moving." Alcoff continues, "When I speak for myself, I am constructing a possible self, a way to be in the world, and am offering that, whether I intend to or not, to others, as one possible form of existence" ("The Problem of Speaking for Others," 109).

[22]For example, early in the semester, several students ventured to explain that Firdaus from *Woman at Point Zero* would never have had to make her murderous decision if she had lived in America. Their views moderated when we discussed how their beliefs in the United States as the land of opportunity were circumscribed by an ideology of democracy that kept veiled the restrictions that gender, socioeconomic class, race, and religion put upon individual options. We also discussed how restraints on women take on a different look in the United States, but are no less debilitating than those in Egypt.

[23]A. Arvary's comments are taken from her reflection paper to the panel presentation on Mohanty's article.

[24]This quote is from J. Klossek's reflection paper to the panel on Mohanty's article.

[25]Gusdorf in Olney's *Autobiography: Essays Theoretical and Critical* establishes the generic limitations of autobiography.

[26]Kateryna Olinyk Longley writes that "rules of authorship, ownership, and authority, for example, are so differently understood by Aboriginal people that the term autobiography is immediately problematized when it is used in an Aboriginal context" (371).

[27]Anne McClintock points out that oral history is not a simple technology to recover the pure past: "The production of oral history is a technology of power under contest, which cannot be seen in isolation from the contexts of power from which it emerges. . . . No oral history is innocent of selection, bias, evasion, and interpretation. . . . Frequently oral histories . . . perpetuate the hierarchy of mental and manual labor of the societies from which they emerge: the hierarchy of those who work and speak, and those who think and write" (226–227).

[28]In a future course, I plan to further this introspective vein of critical analysis by having student-critics produce portfolios with accompanying reflective essays from their exploration and reflection papers. Each student would select

those pieces of writing that s/he felt represented the trajectory of thought on important issues from the semester. The reflective essay would be an exposé of how the selected writings in the portfolio demonstrate his/her role as a thinker, a reader, and a critic of texts. The students would consider how their own differences are pointed to and reshaped by the texts. This assignment allows student-critics to inhabit a space "nearby" the texts and their own constructed positions as interpreters; this meta-critical stance provides them with a moment in which they don't have to fix either themselves or the texts into positions of authentic and static partners in the interactive production of knowledge.

WORKS CITED

Aidoo, Ama Ata. *Our Sister Killjoy or Reflections from a Black-eyed Squint*. New York: Longman, 1977.

Alcoff, Linda. "The Problem of Speaking for Others." In *Who Can Speak? Authority and Critical Identity*. Judith Roof and Robyn Wiegman, eds. Urbana: U of Illinois P, 1995. 97–119.

Bhabha, Homi K. "Of Mimicry and Man: The Ambivalence of Colonial Discourse." *October* 28 (1984): 125–133.

Brady, Maureen. *Folly*. New York: The Feminist Press at CUNY, 1994.

Champagne, John. "'A Feminist Just Like Us?' Teaching Mariama Ba's *So Long A Letter*." *College English* 58, 1 (Jan. 1996): 22–42.

Davies, Carol Boyce. "Conference Presentations." *Critical Fictions: The Politics of Imaginative Writing*. Philomena Mariani, ed. Seattle, WA: Bay Press, 1991. 155–156.

———. "Collaboration and the Ordering Imperative in Life Story Production." In *De/Colonizing the Subject: The Politics of Gender in Women's Autobiography*. Sidonie Smith and Julia Watson, eds. Minneapolis: U of Minnesota P, 1992. 3–19.

Duong, Thu Huong. *Paradise of the Blind*. Trans. Phan Huy Duong and Nina McPherson. New York: Penguin, 1993.

Fee, Margery. "Why C.K. Stead Didn't Like Keri Hulme's *The bone people*: Who Can Write as Other?" *Australian and NZ Studies in Canada* 1 (1989). Rpt. in *The Post-Colonial Studies Reader*. Bill Ashcroft, Gareth Griffins, and Helen Tiffen, eds. New York: Routledge, 1995. 242–245.

Feinberg, Leslie. *Stone Butch Blues*. Ithaca, New York: Firebrand Books, 1993.

Fink, Ida. *The Journey*. Trans. Joanna Weschler and Francine Prose. New York: Plume, 1993.

Gusdorf, Georges. "Conditions and Limits of Autobiography." Trans. James Olney. *Formen der Selbstdarstellung: Analekten zu einer Geschichte des literarischen Selbstportraits.* Gunther Reichenkron and Erich Haase, eds. 1956. Rpt. in *Autobiography: Essays Theoretical and Critical.* James Olney, ed. Princeton: Princeton UP, 1980.

Harlow, Barbara. "From the Women's Prison: Third World Women's Narratives of Prison." *Feminist Studies* 12, 3 (Fall 1986): 501–524.

hooks, bell. "Choosing the Margin as a Space for Radical Openness." In *Yearning: Race, Gender, and Cultural Politics.* Boston: South End Press, 1990. 145–153.

de Lauretis, Teresa. "Technologies of Gender." In *The Technologies of Gender.* Bloomington: Indiana UP, 1987. 1–30.

Longley, Kateryna Olinyk. "Autobiographical Storytelling by Australian Aboriginal Women." In *De/Colonizing the Subject: The Politics of Gender in Women's Autobiography.* Sidonie Smith and Julia Watson, eds. Minneapolis: U of Minnesota P, 1992. 370–384.

Lorde, Audre. "Age, Race, Class, and Sex: Women Redefining Difference." In *Out There: Marginalization and Contemporary Cultures.* Russell Ferguson, et. al., eds. New York: The New Museum of Contemporary Art, 1990. 281–287.

Malti-Douglas, Fedwa. *Men, Women and God(s): Nawal El Saadawi and Arab Feminist Poetics.* Berkeley: U of Calif. P, 1995. Ch. 1–3.

McClintock, Anne. "'The Very House of Difference': Race, Gender, and the Politics of South African Women's Narrative in *Poppie Nongena.*" In *The Bounds of Race: Perspectives on Hegemony and Resistance.* Dominick LaCapra, ed. Ithaca, NY: Cornell UP, 1991. 196–230.

Mohanty, Chandra Talpade. "Cartographies of Struggle: Third World Women and the Politics of Feminism." In *Third World Women and the Politics of Feminism.* Chandra Talpade Mohanty, Ann Russo, and Lourdes Torres, eds. Bloomington: Indiana UP, 1991. 1–47.

Morgan, Sally. *My Place.* Boston: Little, Brown and Co., 1987.

Olney, James, ed. *Autobiography: Essays Theoretical and Critical.* Princeton, NJ: Princeton UP, 1980.

El Saadawi, Nawal. *Woman at Point Zero.* Trans. Sherif Hetata. London: Zed Books, Ltd., 1983.

Spivak, Gayatri Chakravorty. "Explanation and Culture: Marginalia." In *Out There: Marginalization and Contemporary Cultures.* Russell Ferguson et al., ed. New York: The New Museum of Contemporary Art, 1990. 377–393.

Stockton, Sharon. "'Blacks vs. Browns': Questioning the White Ground." *College English* 57, 2 (February 1995): 166–181.

Trinh, T. Minh-ha. "Introduction." *Discourse* 8 (Fall-Winter 1986–87): 3–9.

———. "Difference: 'A Special Third World Women Issue.' " In *Woman, Native, Other: Writing Postcoloniality and Feminism*. Bloomington: Indiana UP, 1989. 79–116.

———. "Cotton and Iron." In *When the Moon Waxes Red: Representation, Gender and Cultural Politics*. New York: Routledge, 1991. 11–26.

———. "Questions of Images and Politics." In *When the Moon Waxes Red: Representation, Gender and Cultural Politics*. New York: Routledge, 1991. 147–152.

West, Cornel. "The New Cultural Politics of Difference." In *Out There: Marginalization and Contemporary Cultures*. Russell Ferguson et al., eds. New York: The New Museum of Contemporary Art and M.I.T. Press, 1990. 19–36.

Winterson, Jeanette. *The Passion*. New York: Vintage, 1987.

Zimmerman, Bonnie. Afterword. *Folly*. By Maureen Brady. New York: The Feminist Press of CUNY, 1994. 197–215.

Coming to America: Reflections on Hair and Memory Loss

ELLA SHOHAT

IN SEARCH OF FATIMA

In the century-old film *Fatima,* a dark-haired woman, dressed in "exotic" fashion, with navel exposed, performs a "strange" dance in which her belly wiggles conspicuously. Her appearance triggers a number of questions. Who is this Fatima? What kind of a name does she have? What genre of dance is she performing? And what is she doing in an American film? Anthologized in the Museum of Modern Art series of 1890s films, *Fatima* is mentioned in most scholarly books on film history. Yet the silently dancing Fatima has also elicited a curious century-old silence about her identity, the nature of her dance, and her baffling presence on the American screen. Is she a unique sensational dancer captured accidentally by a tantalized camera? Or does her screen appearance point to a larger cultural phenomenon? And what was the context for this exotic display?

Although I have not finished my research on Fatima's identity, I pose these questions here in the hope of raising more fundamental questions about the place of non-European women in the narrative of immigration to the United States and in the imagination of "America." To unveil the mysteries around Fatima is, for me, a way of unfolding the entangled relationship between immigration, identity, and contemporary cultural critique. Fatima, in this sense, serves as both metonym and metaphor for the imagination of the East in the West. Her documented presence on the screen only accentuates her elision—and that of Middle Easterners as a whole—from the grand narrative of coming to America.

Indeed, cinema invented a geographically incoherent Orient, prodding this Orient into coherence through the production of visual consistency, mechanically reproduced from film to film and from genre to genre, even as cinema itself evolved and changed over a century. Orientalism was also symptomatic of the relationship between popular culture and scientific exhibitions. Fatima, in this sense, was not conjured up like a genie from a bottle. A clear historical, cultural, and institutional context provided the ground for her appearance on the screen, which occurred as early as 1897. Writing about his encounter with the Egyptian belly dancer Kuchuk Hanem, Flaubert, for example, established an important paradigm for representing the Orient. His Oriental travels inspired his fictional description, in Herodias, of Salome's dance, a description that itself inspired a series of Orientalist visual representations of dangerously seductive dancers with exposed navels and draped snakes. Meanwhile, travel narratives about camel-riding, paintings of harems, photographs of narrow-laned bazaars, and postcards of veiled women with exposed breasts generated a greater appetite for flesh-and-blood Arab female dancers.

Belly-dancers were not invited to display their performative-choreographic talents in European and American theaters and music halls, however; rather, they were themselves displayed as freakish specimens in colonial exhibitions where the non-European "world" was reconstructed for local consumption. The "authentic" Algerian villages and Cairo streets fabricated in Paris, London or New York, with their detailed objects *(killims, nargilas, diwans),* offered a rich *mise-en-scene* for the rituals performed by their colorfully-dressed "dwellers," who were brought all the way from Egypt and Algeria and paraded before the West's bemused eyes. Drinking Turkish coffee, baking Berber bread, or dancing and singing were just a few of the "rituals" that went into the staging of the Orient. Following the popularity of the French-coined "dance du ventre," American entrepreneurs decided to bring the novelty to United States expositions: The Philadelphia Columbia Exposition of 1876 featured Tunisian dancers; the 1893 Chicago "Century of Progress" exposition imported a whole Algerian village from France, including a dancer called "Little Egypt." The latter inspired the hoochie-coochie craze (with many Little Egypt imitators from Brooklyn), blending the Orientalism of "exotic dancers" into the American burlesque as well as into diverse striptease shows.

This "freakish" history was rarely featured in the account of immigration to the Land of Freedom. Take the history of Middle East/North

Africa in the United States. Media portrayals typically assume this to be a short history of the past few decades, one that has little impact on mainstream culture. But while it is true that the liberal 1965 Immigration Act opened the gates, relatively, to Third World immigrants, the story of Middle Eastern immigrants as a group already dates back to the nineteenth century. The majority of these immigrants from what was then the Ottoman Empire came from Syria/Lebanon. Although standard Arab-American historiography focuses on success stories, particularly of immigrants who took up peddling as their route to the "American Dream," many of these immigrants were in fact factory laborers, recruited to work in the United States during a period of labor shortage.[1] Fatima was in a sense one of the early hyphenated Arab-American performers. Indeed, the question of the hyphen is in some ways central to the ways in which immigrant identity is represented. Not all countries and regions that precede the hyphen in the United States are equal, nor do they carry the same burden of association. Sometimes sheer ignorance guides the reception of hyphenated culture.

In preparation for a volume of essays and images I was working on several years ago, the artist Lynne Yamamoto sent me Xeroxed reviews of her work, including a 1995 *New York Times* article, where the reviewer wrote, "Yamamoto inscribes the biography of her Chinese grandmother, a laundress, on nails hammered into the wall." The Xerox sent to me included Yamamoto's handwritten correction with a red pencil: "Chinese" is crossed out to read "Japanese." How often, I wondered, had Lynne needed to correct that Asian-confusion syndrome of "they're all the same"? Of course, "we/they" are not all the same. At the same time, however, it is important to look at commonalities among the experiences of immigrant women of color, especially vis-à-vis institutionalized mapping of identities. Here I want to argue for a multi-cultural feminist reflection on the analogies that link these diverse experiences. Throughout this essay, I will come back to looking at these personal histories from East and West Asia: histories that culturally have apparently little to do with each other, but which, in the context of multiple displacements—in Lynne Yamamoto's case, Japan, Hawai'i, the continental United States, and in my case, Iraq, Israel/Palestine, the United States—strangely echo each other. In interweaving these disparate narratives, I want to illuminate, through associative juxtapositions, the role of memory in the making of hyphenated identities. In this sense my essay "travels" not only between different continents but also between different genres of writing. By placing my journey in relation to that of Yamamoto, I want to create a contrapuntal dialogue between usually separate geographies and histories.

I also want to call into question the binarist approach through which immigrant narratives in the United States are only told vis-à-vis a White dominant norm. "Writing back" and "talking back" have indeed been important for multicultural feminists. Yet often this has meant a rotating chain of women of color confronting a dominant White culture. In the process we have tended to neglect the complex relationships among communities of color in general, and more specifically among immigrants and non-immigrants. Looking into the lives of immigrants of diverse colors challenges the limitations of a Black/White framing of identities. Although the Black/White binarism is strongly inscribed in the material and ideological structures of the United States, it is crucial for multicultural feminists to examine the multi-lateral interplay of diverse communities, especially since the 1965 Immigration Act, which, by relatively democratizing access to the United States, added even more "dark" layers to an already multilayered amalgam. Yet these recent waves of immigration by people of color are a result, not only of the inclusiveness of the 1965 Immigration Act, but also of United States imperial interventions, and of a globalized economic structure in which the United States has played a central and oppressive role.

REDRAWING UNITED STATES CARTOGRAPHIES OF ASIA AND AFRICA

One of the central issues of crossing borders has to do with the classification and cataloging of identities. Although immigration from North Africa and the Middle East dates back to the end of the last century, and although this flow has increased since the 1960s, North Africans and Middle Easterners are seen as "forever foreign," only "from there." Chicano/as, to take another example, are also treated by the media as ontologically, quintessentially alien ("from there"), although many did not cross the border to the United States; it was the borders that moved around them. The first "illegal alien," Columbus, is celebrated as a discoverer, while indigenous Mexicans are seen as "infiltrating" a barbed border, one that in fact divides their former homeland. Native Americans, similarly, are "from here," but for many Native American communities, such as the Cherokees, Net Perce, and Modoc, their geographical dispersal across scattered swaths of United States territory "hides," as it were, their "trail of tears" as internal refugees. The implicit nationalism even of multicultural maps and grids disallows a narrative of refugees within the borders of the "Land of Freedom," nor does it account for displacements caused by devastating United States global politics.

Within the contemporary academic context, rigid classifications have affected the ways in which curricula are formed and institutional politics are shaped. What does it mean, for example, to be labeled as "Asian-American"? While until the 1990s the field of American Studies largely ignored the perspective of people of color, Ethnic Studies programs—the hard-won achievement of 1960s battles—were set up precisely to study the historical perspective of racialized minorities. The subject of Ethnic Studies has been often apportioned among communities that have been fundamental to the history of the United States: Native-American, African-American, Chicano/Latino American and Asian-American. Within this generally critical field of inquiry, however, the term "Asian" came to reflect a Euro-American labeling, often undermining at least a century-old history of other marginalized Third World immigrant communities largely from South and West Asia, just as the term "African" came to ignore North Africa.

As an immigrant from the continent of Asia I have often been quite bewildered to learn that, despite Iraq and Mesopotamia being my family's geography of origins, I am not an Asian. And as someone who grew up in Israel/Palestine, and who was called Black there, I soon learned that few understand this conjunctural definition of Blackness. The "shock of arrival," to borrow Meena Alexander's phrase,[2] begins when one runs into the border patrols of New World naming. The diverse cultures of Asia are condensed into a homogenizing label that erases their difference and complexity: hence the typical conflation of Japanese with Chinese.

My family, like most Jewish-Arab families after the colonial partition of Palestine, became refugees from Iraq in the 1950s and ended up in Israel due to what was styled a "population exchange," whereby Palestinians and Jewish-Arabs were massively swapped across borders. Once in Israel we became the *schwartzes* ("Blacks" in Yiddish) of Euro-Israelis. Our Asianness in Israel was bureaucratically defined. In the highly centralized Israeli state, every aspect of our lives, whether at school, work, or hospital, was determined by checking that fatal box on official documents: "Of Asiatic/African origins."

In the United States I quickly learned that my previous scars of partition and the traumatic memories of crossing the borders from Iraq to Israel/Palestine have little resonance, or else are simply censored. I also learned that not all hyphenated identities are permitted entry into America's official lexicon of ethnicities and races. I could see in people's faces how this corporeally inscribed hyphen, Iraq-Israel, produced a kind of classificatory vertigo, with the result that the hyphen immediately disappeared into an assimilable identity: "Ah, so you're Israeli!" Only one geography is allowed prior to embarking: this is the made-in-U.S.A. predicament of the single hyphen. Although in Israel we were not exactly "from here," in the United States we are only "from there." While "there" we are "immigrants from Asian and African countries," here, in the United States, we are not; in fact, our Asianness disappears, subsumed under the dominant Eurocentric definition of Jewishness (equated with Europe) and Arabness (equated with Islam) as antonyms. Millennia of existence in Iraq are erased in the name of a mere three decades in Israel. I remember, during the Gulf War, reading a *New York Times* book section article in which the Euro-American Jewish reviewer suggested that something was as "rare as a synagogue in Baghdad." He was obviously unaware that Baghdad, as late as the 1950s, was twenty five percent Jewish and that it was crowded with well-attended synagogues. (And where did he imagine the major Judaic text, "The Babylonian Talmud," was written?)

Some parts of Asia, namely West Asia (that is, the Middle East), are simply dropped out of the continent, just as Morocco, Algeria, Tunisia, Libya, and Egypt are dropped out of United States mental projections of Africa, leaving these immigrants to America standing on unstable ground with regards to the continents on either side of the hyphen. The predicament of the single hyphen in the United States reception of immigrants has to do with essentialist assumptions about identity as reducible to one country and one ethnicity or race. The master narrative of immigration is fixed within the rigid boundaries of the nation-state and its often-concomitant nationalist ideology. Thus, our historical intra-continental and watery routes within Asia come up against the *terra firma* of Eurocentric and nationalist chartings of regions and populations.

These master narratives of immigration have been fundamentally locked into the binarism of "East" and "West" as the twain that shall never meet. But the schism of East and West, so deeply ingrained in the Eurocentric accounts of American identity, is misleading in a number of ways. "East," "West," "North," and "South," after all, are relational terms, inseparable from the way we conceive history and geography. The "East" is divided into "Near," "Middle," and "Far," making Europe/United States the arbiter of spatial evaluation, just as the establishment of

Greenwich Mean Time produces England as the regulating center of temporal measurement. The neat divisions of East/West and North/South impose a double axis on a globe inhospitable to such conceptual rigidities. In a topographical sense, the terms are relative: what is East from one angle is West from another. The terminology to demarcate space implies a point-of-view: Near, Middle, Far East, but in relation to whom? The "Far" East is not far from China; nor is the "Near" East near to itself. The Near of Middle East, from a Chinese perspective, would refer to West Asia. The dominant terminology was generated by British colonial rule and shaped a whole field of scholarship, just as the formation of Area Studies in the United States began with the Department of Defense as part of the cold war re-mapping of spheres of influence. (In fact, during this period the British term "Near East" became "Middle East.") Each region, furthermore, has its own East/West, North/South: in Arabic, the word for West *(Maghreb)* refers to North Africa, the westernmost part of the Arab world, in contrast to the *Mashreq,* the eastern part. The South Seas, to the west of the United States, are often posited as cultural East. Israel is seen as part of the West, while Turkey (much of which lies to the west of Israel), Egypt, Tunisia and Morocco are all "Eastern." Thus, politics overdetermine cultural geography and cartographies of identity.

Since when did the vast continent of Asia shrink so incredibly that the face of the land is now superimposed onto a stereotypically "yellow" physiognomy? Even "Asian looks" can be deceiving in the American context, leading East Asians who have been here for generations to be perceived as "always foreign." And speaking accented English also marks the immigrant body as possessing a mysterious or menacing geography. Even as one's body crosses the Atlantic, the accent remains. The persistence of the accent is usually what distinguishes the Asian immigrant from the native born Asian-American in the public sphere. Being at once Inside and Outside places the immigrant in an ambivalent space. For people of my ancestry, being suddenly dropped off the Asian and African maps, after having these maps inscribed on us in a racist manner in Israel, perhaps brings, along with the frustration, a measure of relief at not being so easily boxed into one of the familiar corrals for "the Other." At times I am seduced by the possibility of a new, ethnically chaotic Babel here in the land that the Rastafarians also call Babylon.

The term "Asian-American," then, echoes for me with the voices, memories, and narratives associated with the very word "Asian." I oscillate between accepting United States racial discourses as they affect cartographies of memory and narratives of displacements, and feeling obliged to narrate them within their "Asian" contexts. I first have to pierce the veil of secrecy enveloping the racism toward Asian and African Jews in Israel, in hopes of invoking a multifaceted transnational dialogue among many racialized experiences. For what might seem "irrelevant" to American racialized identities, in fact, evokes deep historical affinities and structural analogies. If the Palestinians figure in official Euro-Israeli discourse as the Indians, associated in colonial discourse with nomadism and savagery, Asian and African Israelis are, on some levels, the Blacks. Not coincidentally, our major movement of resistance in the seventies was called "The Black Panthers," in homage to the American movement, while today we have adopted the name "Mizrahim" ("Orientals"). Despite its Orientalist lineage, this latter name carries an affirmation of our positive relation to the "East," within the context of a state that proudly proclaims its Westernness while choking off our "Eastern" cultural expression.

THE PREDICAMENT OF THE HYPHEN

The multi-layered history especially common to postcolonial displacements "exceeds" the misleadingly tidy five-part United States census categorization of "races." The census is in fact heterotopic, mingling issues of race (Blacks), language (Hispanics), and geography (Asians) as if they were commensurate categories. "Asian-American," for example, is often applied only to East Asians, excluding Iranians, Pakistanis, Lebanese, or others from South and West Asia (the Middle East). "African-American," similarly, does not usually denote immigrants from Africa, or Black immigrants from South America and the Caribbean. "Arab" is usually misconstrued as synonymous with Muslim, though some Arabs are Christian and others Jewish. Reductive categories like "Jew," "Arab," and "Latino/a," similarly, hide the racial variety of a chromatic spectrum that includes White, Black, Mestizo/a, and Brown. In the United States many communities and individuals fit only awkwardly into the single-hyphen boxes, yet bureaucratic pluralism does not allow for polysemy in the politics of color. The usual ways of talking about "minority" identities leave little room for the complexities of these categories, or for the porous borders between them.

The histories of Native Americans, African-Americans, Latino/as, and Asian-Americans may all have been shaped within United States colonialism, but the problematic nature of these categories becomes obvious when seen in relation to the parallel and inter-linked histories in the Americas. The "hyphenated American" is often assumed to sport only a single hyphen. But, in fact, the successive colonial and postcolonial displacements put considerable pressure on the already stressed and overdetermined single hyphen. Each chain of hyphens implies a complicated history of accreted identity and fragmented belonging, as multiple displacements generate distinct "distillations" of immigrant identity. But often the "host" country acknowledges only one link in the chain, and which link is stamped as "real" tells us less about the immigrant than about the geopolitical imaginary of the host. Even within a multicultural feminist space, identities can be misconstrued or misrecognized.

A desire for a chimerical "authenticity" and officially inscribed "coloredness" and "sexuality" can lead to misapprehensions. A female bisexual of Indian-African origin, for example, may be pressured to conform to sexual orientation as defined by United States norms, and may be accused of passing herself off as African, a charge carrying an implication of opportunism.[3] Yet the history of Indian-Tanzanian-Americans, which differs from that of both Africans and Indians who immigrated to the United States directly from their respective continents, should not be shorn of its Africanness. To take another example, Jewish Moroccans who came to the United States after living in Israel are often labeled simply "Israelis." Whereas in the Indian-Tanzanian-American case what precedes the first hyphen is "frozen" to capture the essence of a dispersed identity, in the Moroccan-Israeli American case it is the second term that is "frozen."

What is it about such multiple displacements on the way to the United States that make the first part of the hyphenated label (Indian) essential in one case and the second part (Israeli) essential in the other? In the Indian-Tanzanian-American case, the African link becomes taboo because, in the United States context, "African" can only be equated with "real" Black Africans. In the case of the Moroccan Israeli-American, Morocco is taboo because "Moroccan" is assumed to be only Arab (seen as an antonym to "Jewish") and Muslim, and because "Israeli" is associated with European Jews (when, in fact, the demographic majority of Israel is formed by relatively powerless Black Jews of Asian and African origin). Yet racial definitions, ethnic hierarchies, gender identities and sexual belongings are situated and conjunctural, shifting and transmuting across histories and geographies; they explode and implode a unified narrative of what constitutes "racial," "national," and "sexual" identifications and affiliations.

PROCESSED MEMORIES

In a kind of homage, Lynne Yamamoto narrates her grandmother's life through the very act of producing the material of her installation. Her installation *Ten in One Hour* reflexively alludes to the artist's own rate of production of the soap objects of the installation itself. Reenacting her grandmother's intensive labor, Yamamoto creates a parallel rhythm between her repetitive artistic work and her grandmother's repetitive movements of washing, wringing, hanging, folding. But this analogy also calls attention to class dissonance. While Lynne Yamamoto's images, like my texts, are currently produced and consumed within cultural institutions inseparable from late global capitalism, we, the granddaughters of diasporic domestic workers, have traveled a long road to join another class of cultural workers. Our art or cultural production places us now in a different category than that of our grandmothers and parents. In my writings, I have often felt a survivor's desire to tell again and again about the "hidden injuries" of translocated class, race, gender, and sexuality.

As I was looking into Yamamoto's work on the drudge labor of a laundress, I was wondering about our own work, hers and mine, as granddaughters of dislocated domestic laborers. A critic and an artist, in our new class spaces we continue rinsing, cleaning, and scrubbing, as it were, the misrepresentations that surround our hyphenated identities. Our grandmothers worked as domestic servants in new countries, unfamiliar with their new cultural and linguistic terrains: Hebrew-speaking Israel for my Arabic-speaking grandmother and English-speaking Hawai'i for Lynne's Japanese-speaking grandmother. In her installations *Night Waters* and *They All Fall Down,* Yamamoto uses archival photographs of Japanese women working as domestics for *haole* (Euro-American) families in Hawai'i. *They All Fall Down* uses a continuous video loop of Yamamoto's aunt's hands polishing a silver tea bell. "The installation," writes Yamamoto, "is based on stories my aunts told me about working as domestics for *haole* families, and particular memories of how they were called in to change dishes for the next course."

If Yamamoto's grandmother came as a "picture bride" to Hawai'i, my *seta* (Arabic for grandmother), Gurgeia, left Baghdad as a widower. My grandfather, Ya'aqub abu-Sasson, was buried in the 1930s in the Baghdadi Jewish cemetery on Sheikh Omar Street, which in the 1960s was itself apparently buried under the new national television station: our millennia traces were thus erased. I have often thought it ironic, in light

of this fact, that I became a professor of media studies, engaged in un-
earthing the deeper strata of the visual text.

I moved "Ila Amreeka," as my family would say in Arabic, in 1981. I
did not come to America as a picture bride, but pictures of America made
me come. I remember that as we were growing up, we loved watching
American television series. *Hawaii Five-O* was one of our favorites. The
Hula dancer in the opening credit sequence seemed by far more exotic
than our local belly dancers. Perhaps the hip movements of the Hula
dancer were familiar to us, but somehow we did not see this dance as part
of the "East," for we only learned to recognize it as "American" and
therefore as "Western." We were dreaming about a new world, even as
our old world of the Euphrates and Tigris was a forbidden memory in the
state of Israel.[4] Indeed, the global flow of American images and sounds
gave me the feeling of a *terra cognita* even prior to my voyage to the island of Manhattan. Here, in the Gramercy Park apartment I was cleaning,
I could repeat *seta's* rate of production, fighting so that my life, too,
wouldn't go down the drain.

Soap to wash the dirt off the shirt. To wash the dirt off your body.
Cleaning for others while being called dirty yourself. My dark friend
Na'eema used to frantically scrub her "dirty skin" in a violent cleansing
ritual that never reached the promised hidden layer of white skin she so
painfully desired, but that did leave her bleeding. In Israel we were called
"dirty Iraqis." I can still hear the Hebrew words "Erakit Masriha!"
("Stinky Iraqi") shouted at me by a blond boy whose relatives in Europe
were themselves turned into "sabonim"—soaps—by the Nazis.

My *seta,* who died last year in her mid-nineties, enjoyed cursing
back. She washed their dirty laundry as she joyfully rolled out her Arabic
obscenities. She never learned the language of *al beitheen* (Arabic for
"the Whites"). As she used several layers of *shaqsa* (Iraqi for female
head wear) to wrap her dwindling graying braids, she was amused by my
sister's efforts to bleach her hair, the stubborn roots refusing to fully
erase their black past. And like many women of her class, my grandmother did not wash out of her dictionary the dirty words reserved for
those whose houses emitted unpleasant smells in the absence of her ever-
bleaching hand.

Some of Lynne Yamamoto's work features old photos of Asian laborers in Hawai'i. I wondered how many of the photos actually belong to
Lynne's family album. Images of immigrant and refugee laborers are
often only distilled in the colonial visual archives. A few years ago,
around the Quincentenary for the Expulsion of Muslim and Jews from

Spain, I was desperately looking for images of Jews in the Islamic world to accompany an essay I wrote for *Middle East Report* on the subject. The editor and I approached the Yeshiva University Museum in New York (directed by Euro-American Jews), then sponsoring a photographic exhibition on the subject. Aware of my critical stance, the Museum refused to lend such images without first reviewing the political content of my essay, thereby barring access to my own community history. I have visited Jewish museums in the United States and in Israel, only to see nightmarish reincarnations on display. Precious objects that belonged to our community or to its individual members, ranging from religious artifacts to "Oriental" jewelry and dresses, are all exhibited in a way that fetishistically detaches them from their social context and cultural history within the worlds of Islam, of Asia, and of Africa. In places such as the Gothic building of the Jewish Museum in New York, "exotic Jews" are still silenced.

I flip through British collections of photos of Baghdad in an attempt to visualize my grandmother in the streets, houses, markets, carrying her *beqcha* (bundle) on her head. These processed images have become processed memories. Could it be that my endlessly deconstructed colonial images are now invading my own familial memories? I see the work of people like Lynne Yamamoto and myself as an effort to bring to life a frozen past captured in the colonial visual archive. We kidnap Orientalist images of "the exotic" and re-narrate them for our private/public memories. But that sense of the elusive homelands of Asia persists even after moving to a new continent.

In the aftermath of Pearl Harbor, many Japanese-Americans were forced to burn precious family possessions, eliminating any links to Japan. Similarly, Iraqi, Egyptian, and Yemeni Jews, after the establishment of Israel, were caught in the vice of two bloody nationalisms: Arab and Jewish. While Euro-Israel, in its need to secure bodies to perform "Black labor," had an interest in creating the terrorizing political climate that led to our mass exodus, Arab authorities added their own share of terror by suspecting us *a priori* of being traitors. At the same time, the two governments, under the orchestration of Britain, secretly collaborated in lifting us overnight from millennia in Mesopotamia. Although Arab-Jews were culturally closer to Muslim-Arabs than to the European Jews who founded the state of Israel, their identity was put on trial by both national projects. Even anti-Zionist Arab-Jews ended up in Israel, for in the bloody context of a nationalist conflict, they could no longer enjoy the luxury of their hyphenated identity. My parents had to burn our photos, leaving little photographic inheritance from Iraq. As refugees, we left everything behind. I cling to the handful of photos of my family in Baghdad, the city we still cannot go back to after four decades of traumatic separation.

I used to pore over the few photos in a half-filled family album in order to discern the contours of a history, a lineage. I remember inverting the traditional biblical verse (taken up again in the Jimmie Cliff Reggae song); instead of weeping by the waters of Babylon, it was by the waters of *Zion* that we lay down and wept when we remembered *Babylon*. Iraq, under Saddam Hussein, has featured its annual Babylonian Festival, even as devastating sanctions continue to "sanction" the death of many Iraqis. The staging of ancient "Babylon" boosts Iraqi national moral, but for displaced Iraqis, it is yesterday's Iraq that we cry over, as its images flicker across the television screen. In exile, Iraqi images, music, stories, and dishes are all digested in a kind of wake for what was lost. Wherever they go, London, New York, or Rio de Janeiro, my parents immediately reproduce the aromas of Baghdad, in their pots and in their tears, as they listen to the sounds of old Iraqi and Egyptian music frozen in time: Nathum Al-Ghazali, Salima Pasha, Um Kulthum, and Muhamad Abdul-Wahab. I got my parents a tape of a new Iraqi singer, Qathum Al-Sahir. They didn't enjoy it. Perhaps it was too painful to admit that, after their departure, life didn't stop "there." Perhaps that's why I have become obsessed with taking photos. It is as if I wanted to fill out the half-empty albums.

HAIRY VISIONS

In Lynne Yamamoto's *Wrung*, a long strand of artificial black hair hangs from a wringer, taken from an old-fashioned clothes washer. Displaced from their original context, seemingly unrelated objects are brought together, evoking a process, a narrative, and an action: something is being wrung. The clamp-like wringer and the disembodied hair highlight the potentially violent overtones of quotidian materials. But the very image of wringing long hair stands out with a nightmarish beauty. For one thing, the long black silky hair of Asian women has often stood as a metaphor for the fragile and docile "Orient." But here the image of the hair goes against the grain, intimating the pain and hardship of servitude, conjuring up the slow death of the female domestic laborer. The old wringer processes the hair like a meat grinder, as though devouring the woman whose body and face have been slowly consumed and worked over, as though the viewer is catching the last glimpses of her disappear-

ance. The washing cycle evoked by Yamamoto's work becomes a synec-
doche and a metaphor for the life cycle itself as experienced by a dislocated domestic laborer: Arrive, marry, cook, clean, boil, scrub, wash,
starch, bleach, iron, clean, hope, wash, starch, cook, boil, scrub, clean,
wring, starch, fear, iron, fold, bleach, cook, iron, hope, rinse, whisper,
boil . . . love, fear, weep, rinse, starch, fold, drown. (In Lynne Yamamoto's *Untitled,* from her installation *Wash Closet,* the narrative unfolds
through a sequence of these words inscribed on heads of 280 nails, ending with "drown," a reference to Lynne's grandmother, Chiyo, who committed suicide ten months after the bombing of Pearl Harbor by
drowning herself in an *ofuro,* a Japanese bathtub.) Playing the visible
hair off against the invisible body, *Wrung* chronicles the bitter disappearance of an alienated Japanese laborer on the "picturesque" island of
Kohala, Hawai'i.

The black and white photos taken on our roof in Baghdad gaze at me
in my New York living room. My mother wears my father's suit. ("Just
for the photos," she tells me smiling, blithely unaware of recent performance theories about cross-dressing). Elegantly she projects authority,
as she stands there, her long, thick and curly black hair flowing gently.
She lost much of that hair after they became refugees, in an epoch of
food rationing in the transient camps in Israel. She fell seriously ill, as
the cold wind and rainy winter in the tent inflicted her with crippling
rheumatoid arthritis. I often remember how I tried to reconcile these two
mothers, the one in the photos in Baghdad, and the other one that I knew,
the one courageously fighting economic and social degradation with a
weakened, broken body.

In *Wrung,* plentiful hair is attached to no-body. The pleasure and
pain of looking at this image has to do with the subliminal specter of disembodied hair. The visual archive is abundant with traumatic memories
of hair loss, yet somehow we find it easy to lose the memory of such
ghastly catastrophes. In recent years, interesting work has been done on
fashioning hair and diasporic identity,[5] but *Wrung*'s disembodied hair
has also to be placed within a different tradition. The aestheticized quality of the flowing silk hair, often appearing in the Orientalist erotic
dream—evoked in films from *The World of Suzie Wong* to Peter Green-
away's *Pillowbook*—in *Wrung* becomes nightmarish, set in the context
of a different kind of visual archive.

Disembodied hair, in this sense, evokes American frontier imagery
of scalping—whether in the popular Western genre depiction of "Indian
savagery," or in the critical Native American representation of European

settler cruelty. In 1744, for example, the Massachusetts General Court declared a general bounty on Indian scalps: 250 pounds; and in 1757 it was raised to 300, higher than the annual pay for many educated colonists.[6] A century later, the American West witnessed the horror of another wave of detached hair, in yet another twentieth-century scientific spirit of experimentation: civilian accounts of hair loss by unsuspecting onlookers of nuclear testing in Nevada, Arizona, or farther west in the "Oriental" Pacific Islands. How can we, to paraphrase Mitzy Gaynor in the 1950s musical *South Pacific,* wash that memory outta our hair?

I remember watching Alain Resnais's film *Hiroshima Mon Amour* for the first time: black and white images of the Hiroshima museum displaying piles of hair, remnants of the modern American annihilation of two cities in Japan. The film visually links two victims through the motif of hair: French women scapegoated for a more general collaboration with the Nazis have their hair cut at the end of the war, tonsured during the liberation in France. World War II also witnessed yet other mounted piles of hair in the concentration camps of Auschwitz, Dachau, Treblinka, and Bergen-Belzen, recycled for productive purposes. Nazi archival footage documents pyramids of watches, glasses, hair—visual evidence of the work of an "orderly regime."

Iraqi, Yemeni, and Moroccan refugees in the 1950s were welcomed to Israel with white DDT dust, to cleanse them, as the official Euro-Israeli discourse suggested, of their "tropical diseases." In the transient camps, their hair was shaved off, to rid them of lice. Children, some of them healthy, were suspected of ringworm, and were treated with massive doses of radiation. You could tell those who had been treated by the wraps covering their heads, covering the shame of hair loss. The Euro-Israeli authorities, wrapped in the aura of science, marched on us to eradicate our Asian and African underdevelopment. Decades later, as the children became adults, they had to wear wigs or hats to cover a second hair loss, this time due to radiation treatment for cancerous brain tumors, caused initially by their childhood early "treatment" for a simple skin disease that sometimes they did not actually have.

Can memory exist apart from the desire to memorialize? Perhaps our United States immigration narratives are no more than a monument to our parents' and grandparents' generations (some of whom performed "hairy" escapes across hostile borders); generations muted by the everyday burden of hyphenated realities, their dreams mutilated. And so we weave these narratives into our images and texts as a kind of a memorial, a portable shrine for those whom we fear have faded away. Perhaps the ethnicity of the silently dancing Fatima is erased from the pages of the American archive. But in the various Babylons of New York, Los Angeles and Detroit, new Fatimas vibrantly transform "Amreeka."

The canonical narrative of the birth of America—in the beginning was Columbus, in the middle the American Revolution and the Civil War, and in the end the "melting pot"—has been challenged by recent immigrants pouring in, "spoiling" the already overcooked stew. The desire for a tidy closure aims at disciplining this chaotic, open-ended notion of the "American Nation." Anti-immigrant hysteria can be seen as a phobic reaction to the disquieting perception that "the nation" might not be and never has been a fixed entity, a core of whiteness to which other "colors" were added later. The colors were there from the beginning. Indeed, over many millennia (Eurocentrically called "pre-Columbian," as if an entire hemisphere had been just waiting for Columbus to arrive) it was whiteness that was the absent color. All the waves of immigration to this country have stirred up national anxiety, not only because of their obvious social implications but also because of more subtle questions about what "Americanness" is and about who belongs to the "American family." Over the past centuries, the continually changing makeup of the United States has forced "us" always to rethink the "we." The idea of a unitary "American Nation" benevolently receiving new waves of immigrants suggests that only the immigrants, rather than the nation itself, are being transformed; the United States's openness is rarely conceived as multi-directional. "They," the new immigrants, are simply to be transformed into "us," when, in fact, the nation is transformed by each new wave washing up on its shores.[7] New immigrants stretch, with their bodies, the boundaries and definitions of Americanness.

NOTES

This article is based on a short piece entitled "Reflections on Hair and Memory Loss," forthcoming in *Fresh Talk*, ed. Elaine Kim and Margo Machida (University of California Press).

[1]See Alixa Naff, "The Early Arab Immigrant Experience," in *The Development of Arab-American Identity*, Ernest McCarus, ed. (Ann Arbor: U of Michigan P, 1994), 26.

[2]Meena Alexander, *The Shock of Arrival* (Boston: South End Press, 1996).

[3]See May Joseph, "Transatlantic Inscriptions," in *Talking Visions: Multicultural Feminism in a Transnational Age*, Ella Shohat, ed. (Cambridge: MIT Press and the New Museum, 1998), 357–390.

[4]See my article, "Taboo Memories, Diasporic Visions: Columbus, Palestine and Arab-Jews," in *Performing Hybridity,* May Joseph and Jennifer Fink, eds. (Minneapolis: U of Minnesota P, 1999), 131–158.

[5]I have in mind the works, for example, of Ayoka Chenzira, Kobena Mercer, Lisa Jones, and Lorna Simpson.

[6]See, for example, Raymond William Stedman, *The Shadows of the Indian* (Norman: U of Oklahoma P, 1971); James Axtell, *The European and the Indian* (Oxford: Oxford UP, 1981).

[7]The discussion here of the non-finalized American Nation is based in part on "Ethnicities in Relation" in *Unthinking Eurocentrism* (Chapter Six, 220–247). I thank Margo Machida and May Joseph for inviting me to serve as a final commentator on "New Hybridities: Immigration and Asian Arts" at New York University, June 1995, where I presented some of this material. I also thank Inderpal Grewal for sharing with me her work-in-progress, *Umrika,* which makes parallel arguments.

WORKS CITED

Alexander, Meena. *The Shock of Arrival*. Boston: South End Press, 1996.

Axtell, James. *The European and the Indian*. Oxford: Oxford UP, 1981.

Flaubert, Gustave. *Herodias*. New York: G. P. Putnam and Sons, 1903. *Trois Contes: Un Coeur Simple; La Légende de Saint-Julien l'Hospitalier; Herodias*. Paris: G. Charpentier, 1877.

Joseph, May. "Transatlantic Inscriptions." *Talking Visions: Multicultural Feminism in a Transnational Age*. Ella Shohat, ed. Cambridge: MIT Press and the New Museum, 1998. 357–390.

Naff, Alixa. "The Early Arab Immigrant Experience." *The Development of Arab-American Identity*. Ernest McCarus, ed. Ann Arbor: U of Michigan P, 1994. 23–35.

Shohat, Ella. "Taboo Memories, Diasporic Visions: Colombus, Palestine and Arab-Jews." *Performing Hybridity*. May Joseph and Jennifer Fink, eds. Minneapolis: U of Minnesota P, 1999. 131–158.

———, ed. *Talking Visions: Multicultural Feminism in a Transnational Age*. Cambridge: MIT Press and the New Museum, 1998.

——— and Robert Stam. *Unthinking Eurocentrism: Multiculturalism and the Media*. New York: Routledge, 1994.

Stedman, Raymond William. *The Shadows of the Indian*. Norman: U of Oklahoma P, 1971.

Index